Fodor's 2012

SOUTH
FLORIDA

Fodor's Travel Publications   New York, Toronto, London, Sydney, Auckland

www.fodors.com

Excerpted from *Fodor's Florida 2012*.

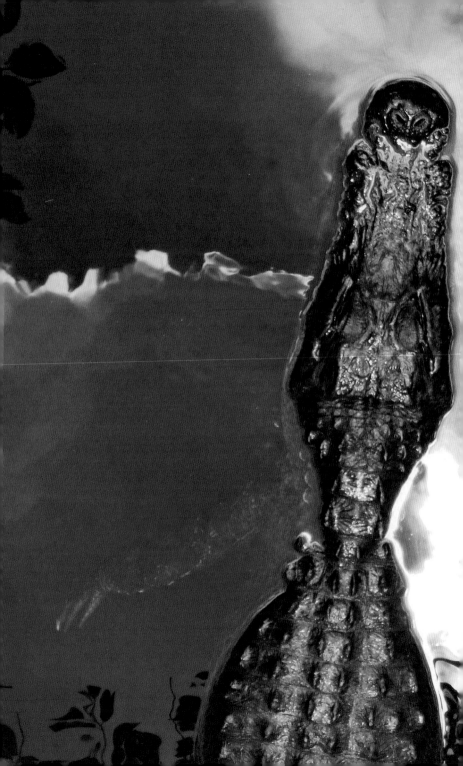

Eugene Fodor:
The Spy Who Loved Travel

As Fodor's celebrates our 75th anniversary, we are honoring the colorful and adventurous life of Eugene Fodor, who revolutionized guidebook publishing in 1936 with his first book, *On the Continent, The Entertaining Travel Annual.*

Eugene Fodor's life seemed to leap off the pages of a great spy novel. Born in Hungary, he spoke six languages and graduated from the Sorbonne and the London School of Economics. During World War II he joined the Office of Strategic Services, the budding spy agency for the United States. He commanded the team that went behind enemy lines to liberate Prague, and recommended to Generals Eisenhower, Bradley, and Patton that Allied troops move to the capital city. After the war, Fodor worked as a spy in Austria, posing as a U.S. diplomat.

In 1949 Eugene Fodor—with the help of the CIA—established Fodor's Modern Guides. He was passionate about travel and wanted to bring his insider's knowledge of Europe to a new generation of sophisticated Americans who wanted to explore and seek out experiences beyond their borders. Among his innovations were annual updates, consulting local experts, and including cultural and historical perspectives and an emphasis on people—not just sites. As Fodor described it, "The main interest and enjoyment of foreign travel lies not only in 'the sites,' . . . but in contact with people whose customs, habits, and general outlook are different from your own."

Eugene Fodor died in 1991, but his legacy, Fodor's Travel, continues. It is now one of the world's largest and most trusted brands in travel information, covering more than 600 destinations worldwide in guidebooks, on Fodors.com, and in ebooks and iPhone apps. Technology and the accessibility of travel may be changing, but Eugene Fodor's unique storytelling skills and reporting style are behind every word of today's Fodor's guides.

Our editors and writers continue to embrace Eugene Fodor's vision of building personal relationships through travel. We invite you to join the Fodor's community at fodors.com/community and share your experiences with like-minded travelers. Tell us when we're right. Tell us when we're wrong. And share fantastic travel secrets that aren't yet in Fodor's. Together, we will continue to deepen our understanding of our world.

Happy 75th Anniversary, Fodor's! Here's to many more.

FODOR'S SOUTH FLORIDA 2012

Editor: Stephanie E. Butler

Editorial Contributors: Laura Kidder (Travel Smart editor)
Writers: Lynne Helm, Dorthea Hunter Sönne, Chelle Koster Walton, Paul Rubio, Mary Thurwatcher

Production Editor: Carrie Parker
Maps & Illustrations: David Lindroth; Mark Stroud, *cartographers;* Bob Blake, Rebecca Baer, *map editors;* William Wu, *information graphics*
Design: Fabrizio La Rocca, *creative director;* Guido Caroti, *art director;* Tina Malaney, Nora Rosansky, Chie Ushio, Jessica Walsh, *designers;* Melanie Marin, *associate director of photography*
Cover Photo: (Florida Keys National Marine Sanctuary) Tom Stack
Production Manager: Angela McLean

ISBN 978-0-679-00946-7

ISSN 1526-2219

SPECIAL SALES

This book is available at special discounts for bulk purchases for sales promotions or premiums. Special editions, including personalized covers, excerpts of existing books, and corporate imprints, can be created in large quantities for special needs. For more information, write to Special Markets/Premium Sales, 1745 Broadway, MD 6-2, New York, NY 10019, or e-mail specialmarkets@randomhouse.com.

AN IMPORTANT TIP & AN INVITATION

Although all prices, opening times, and other details in this book are based on information supplied to us at press time, changes occur all the time in the travel world, and Fodor's cannot accept responsibility for facts that become outdated or for inadvertent errors or omissions. So **always confirm information when it matters,** especially if you're making a detour to visit a specific place. Your experiences—positive and negative—matter to us. If we have missed or misstated something, **please write to us.** Share your opinion instantly through our online feedback center at fodors.com/contact-us.

PRINTED IN COLOMBIA

10 9 8 7 6 5 4 3 2 1

CONTENTS

Fodor's Features

CONTENTS

The Middle Keys. 306
The Lower Keys 314
Key West 322
Everything's Fishy in the Keys . . . 344
TRAVEL SMART FLORIDA. . . . 355
INDEX. 362
ABOUT OUR WRITERS. 372

MAPS

Palm Beach and West Palm
Beach 40
Treasure Coast. 56
Fort Lauderdale 97
Broward County 117
Downtown Miami 141
Miami Beach and South Beach. . . 143
Coral Gables, Coconut
Grove, and Key Biscayne . . .160–161
Where to Eat in Miami Area. .200–201
Where to Stay in the
Miami Area 208–209
Key West 326

ABOUT
THIS BOOK

Our Ratings

At Fodor's, we spend considerable time choosing the best places in a destination so you don't have to. By default, anything we recommend in this book is worth visiting. But some sights, properties, and experiences are so great that we've recognized them with additional accolades. Orange **Fodor's Choice** stars indicate our top recommendations; black stars highlight places we deem **Highly Recommended**; and **Best Bets** call attention to top properties in various categories. Disagree with any of our choices? Care to nominate a new place? Visit our feedback center at www.fodors.com/feedback.

TripAdvisor ʘʘ

Fodor's partnership with TripAdvisor helps to ensure that our hotel selections are timely and relevant, taking into account the latest customer feedback about each property. Our team of expert writers selects what we believe will be the top choices for lodging in a destination. Then, those choices are reinforced by TripAdvisor reviews, so only the best properties make the cut.

For expanded hotel reviews, visit **Fodors.com**

Hotels

Hotels have private bath, phone, and TV, and do not offer meals unless we specify that in the review. We always list facilities but not whether you'll be charged an extra fee to use them.

Restaurants

Unless we state otherwise, restaurants are open for lunch and dinner daily. We mention dress only when there's a specific requirement and reservations only when they're essential or not accepted—it's always best to book ahead.

Credit Cards

We assume that restaurants and hotels accept credit cards. If not, we'll note it in the review.

Budget Well

Hotel and restaurant price categories from ¢ to $$$$ are defined in the opening pages of the respective chapters. For attractions, we always give standard adult admission fees; reductions are usually available for children, students, and senior citizens.

Listings
★ Fodor's Choice
★ Highly recommended
⊠ Physical address
✛ Directions or Map coordinates
⌑ Mailing address
☎ Telephone
🖷 Fax
⊕ On the Web
✉ E-mail
✇ Admission fee
☻ Open/closed times
Ⓜ Metro stations
▭ No credit cards

Hotels & Restaurants
☷ Hotel
⤷ Number of rooms
⟁ Facilities
†⊙† Meal plans
✗ Restaurant
⟰ Reservations
⋔ Dress code
✎ Smoking

Outdoors
🏌 Golf
⛺ Camping

Other
☕ Family-friendly
⇨ See also
⊠ Branch address
☞ Take note

1

Experience South Florida

WHAT'S WHERE

The following numbers refer to chapters.

2 Palm Beach and the Treasure Coast. This area scores points for diversity. Palm Beach and environs are famous for golden sand and glitzy residents, whereas the Treasure Coast has unspoiled natural delights.

3 Fort Lauderdale and Broward County. The town *Where the Boys Are* has grown up. The beaches that first attracted college kids are now complemented by luxe lodgings and upscale entertainment options.

4 Miami and Miami Beach. Art Deco buildings and balmy beaches set the scene. Vacations here are as much about lifestyle as locale, so prepare for power shopping, club-hopping, and decadent dining.

5 The Everglades. Covering more than 1.5 million acres, the fabled "River of Grass" is the state's greatest natural treasure. Biscayne National Park, the country's largest marine park, runs a close second. Also here is Big Cypress National Preserve.

6 Florida Keys. This slender string of landfalls, linked by a 113-mi highway, marks the southern edge of the continental United States. It's nirvana for anglers, divers, book lovers, and Jimmy Buffet wannabes.

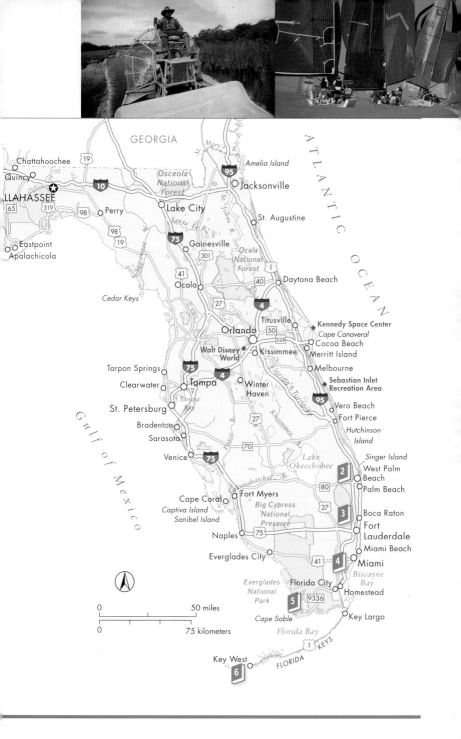

WHEN TO GO

South Florida is a year-round vacation venue, but it divides the calendar into regional tourism seasons. Holidays and school breaks are major factors. However, the clincher is weather, with the best months being designated as peak periods.

High season starts with the run-up to Christmas and continues through Easter. Snowbirds migrate down then to escape frosty weather back home, and festival-goers flock in because major events are held this time of year to avoid summer's searing heat and high humidity. Winter is also *the* time to visit the Everglades, as temperatures, mosquito activity, and water levels are all lower (making wildlife easier to spot).

Climate

Florida is rightly called the Sunshine State, but it could also be dubbed the Humid State. June through September, 90% humidity levels aren't uncommon. Nor are accompanying thunderstorms; in fact, more than half of the state's rain falls during these months. Florida's two-sided coastline also makes it a target for tropical storms. Hurricane season officially begins June 1 and ends November 30.

MIAMI EVENTS

HOMERUN HOMETOWN

Heading to South Florida in April 2012? You'll be just in time to catch the eagerly awaited first pitch at the new Marlins Ballpark. Their new digs, with a retractable roof and air conditioning, are making a big splash just in time for the hot stretch of regular season games. ⊕ *florida.marlins.mlb.com.*

LITTLE HAVANA

Each winter during Carnaval Miami, salsa tunes blare and the smell of spicy chorizo fills the air on Calle Ocho, the commercial thoroughfare and heart of Miami's Little Havana. The roaring street festival, which culminates in the world's longest conga line, is the last of 10 events comprising the Latin-spiked Carnaval. Ambience- and amenity-wise, it is as close as you'll get to Cuba without running afoul of the federal government. ⊕ *www.carnavalmiami.com.*

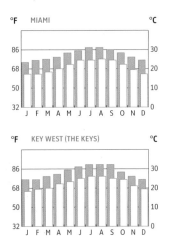

QUINTESSENTIAL SOUTH FLORIDA

Food, Glorious Food

Geography and gastronomy go hand in hand in Florida. Seafood is a staple almost everywhere, yet the way it is prepared changes considerably as you maneuver around the state. In South Florida, menus highlight Floribbean cuisine, which marries Floridian, Caribbean, and Latin flavors (think mahimahi with mango salsa), while inland, expect catfish, gator tails, and frogs' legs, all of which are best enjoyed at a Cracker-style fish camp with a side order of hush puppies. A trip to the Tampa area is not complete without a taste of Cuban food. The cuisine is heavy, with pork dishes like lechon asado, but the two most typical dishes are arroz con frijoles (the staple side dish of rice and black beans) and arroz con pollo (chicken in sticky yellow rice). Key West is a mecca for lovers of Key lime pie and conch fritters. Stone-crab claws can be savored from October through May.

The Arts

Floridians celebrate the arts year-round. Miami Beach's annual Art Basel festival draws 40,000 art lovers to town in the first week of December. Meanwhile, every April the Palm Beach International Film Festival, now in its 17th year, hosts world premieres, documentaries, shorts, and feature films. It's easy to catch a bit of bluegrass, country, classical, jazz, blues, or Americana with such festivals as the week-long SunFest in West Palm Beach, or hear some of the nation's best jazz performers at the annual Hollywood Jazz Fest. Miami's ArtCenter South Florida is dedicated to incubating Florida's cultural life with programs for emerging artists of all ages. The oral tradition remains vibrant with the South Florida Storytelling Project, where live readings, storytelling slams, and festivals are free and open to the public through Florida Atlantic University in Boca Raton.

Florida is synonymous with sunshine, and every year more than 80 million visitors come to revel in it. However, the people who live here—a diverse group that includes Mouseketeers, millionaires, and rocket scientists—know that the state's appeal rests on more than those reliable rays.

Water, Water Everywhere

Spanish explorer Ponce de León didn't find the Fountain of Youth when he swung through Florida in 1513. But if he'd lingered longer, he could have located 7,700 lakes, 1,700 rivers and creeks, and more than 700 springs. Over the centuries these have attracted American Indians, immigrants, opportunists, and, countless outdoor adventurers. Boaters come for inland waterways and a 1,200-mi coast, and anglers are lured by more than 700 species of fish. (Florida claims 4,780 past and present world-record catches, so concocting elaborate "fish tales" may not be necessary.) Snorkelers and divers eager to see what lies beneath can get face time with the marine life that thrives on the world's third-largest coral reef or bone up on maritime history in underwater archaeological preserves. Back on dry land, all those beaches are pretty impressive, too (⊕ *www.museumsinthesea.com*).

Superlative Sports

Panthers and Dolphins and Rays, oh my! South Florida is teeming with teams—and residents take the games they play *very* seriously. Baseball fans regularly work themselves into a fever pitch: after all, the state has a pair of Major League franchises (the Marlins in Miami are christening a brand-new stadium this year) and hosts another 13 in spring when the Grapefruit League goes to bat. Those with a preference for pigskin might cheer for NFL teams in Miami and Tampa. But the state is also home to top-rated college teams, like the Hurricanes. Basketball lovers meanwhile feel the "Heat" in Miami, especially now that Dream Team trio Dwayne Wade, Chris Bosh, and two-time MVP LeBron James are on the roster, and hockey fans stick around to watch the Florida Panthers and Tampa Bay Lightning. The Professional Golfers Association (PGA) is headquartered here as well.

SOUTH FLORIDA TOP ATTRACTIONS

The Florida Keys

(A) Little wonder these 800-plus islands are a prime destination for divers and snorkelers: they boast the world's third-largest reef and aquarium-clear waters that are brimming with sea life. Under the turquoise-blue waters lies a colorful world populated by 60-plus species of coral and more than 500 species of fish, which means you can spot purple sea fans, blue tangs, yellowtail snappers, stoplight parrotfish, and more. Locals debate the premiere place for viewing them, but John Pennekamp Coral Reef State Park is high on everyone's list. Underwater excursions organized by park concessionaires let you put your best flipper forward. (*See Chapter 6.*)

South Beach

(B) You can't miss the distinctive forms, vibrant colors, and extravagant flourishes of SoBe's architectural gems. The world's largest concentration of Art Deco

edifices is right here; and the Art Deco District, with more than 800 buildings, has earned a spot on the National Register of Historic Places (*see "A Stroll Down Deco Lane" in-focus feature in Chapter 4*). The 'hood also has enough "beautiful people" to qualify for the Register of Hippest Places. The glitterati, along with assorted vacationing hedonists, are drawn by über-trendy shops and a surfeit of celeb-studded clubs. Stellar eateries are the icing—umm, make that the ganache—on South Beach's proverbial cake. (*See Chapter 4.*)

The Everglades

(C) No trip to southern Florida is complete without seeing the Everglades. At its heart is a river—50 mi wide but only 6 inches deep—flowing from Lake Okeechobee into Florida Bay. For an up-close look, speed demons can board an airboat that careens through the marshy waters. Purists, alternately, may placidly

canoe or kayak within the boundaries of Everglades National Park. Just remember to keep your hands in the boat. The critters that call this unique ecosystem home (alligators, Florida panthers, and cottonmouth snakes for starters) can add real bite to your visit! (*See Chapter 5.*)

Palm Beach

(D) If money could talk, you'd hardly be able to hear above the din in Palm Beach. The upper crust started calling it home, during the winter months at least, back in the early 1900s. And today it remains a ritzy, glitzy enclave for both old money and the nouveau riche (a coterie led by "The Donald" himself, though he sold his house recently). Simply put, Palm Beach is the sort of place where shopping is a full-time pursuit and residents don't just wear Polo—they play it. Oooh and ahhh to your heart's content; then, for more conspicuous consumption, continue south

on the aptly named Gold Coast to Boca Raton. (*See Chapter 2.*)

Fort Lauderdale

(E) Mariners should set their compass for Fort Lauderdale (aka the Venice of America), where vessels from around the world moor along some two dozen finger isles between the beach and the mainland. Sailors can cruise Broward County's 300 mi of inland waterways by water taxi and tour boat, or bob around the Atlantic in a chartered yacht. If you're in a buying mood, come during October for the annual Fort Lauderdale International Boat Show. Billed as the world's largest, it has more than a billion dollars' worth of boats in every conceivable size, shape, and price range. (*See Chapter 3.*)

IF YOU LIKE

Animals

South Florida makes an ideal habitat for party animals, but there are other kinds of wildlife here, too. The state has more than 1,200 different kinds of critters.

■ **Alligators.** Florida has more than 1.3 million resident alligators. You can see them and even pet them at the Everglades Gator Park along Tamiami Trail, but "gator spotting" in swamps or roadside waterways is itself a favorite pastime. Eating the official state reptile in deep-fried nugget form is popular, too. Mmm . . . tastes like chicken.

■ **Birds.** Florida draws hundreds of species of birds, from bald eagles and burrowing owls to bubblegum-pink flamingos. The 2,000-mi Great Florida Birding Trail (⊕ *www.floridabirdingtrail.com*) helps you find them.

■ **Manatees.** They're nicknamed sea cows and resemble walruses. But Florida's official marine mammals are most closely related to elephants, which may account for their slow pace and hefty frames. In winter, scan the water for a telltale glassy patch (called a "footprint"), indicating a manatee swims below.

■ **Sea Turtles.** Ready for a late-night rendezvous with the loggerheads and the rare leatherbacks that lumber onto Floridian beaches to lay eggs between March and October? Sea turtle walks are organized at **Marinelife Center of Juno Beach** (⊠ *14200 U.S. 1, Juno Beach* ☎ *561/627–8280* ⊕ *www.marinelife.org*) near Jupiter, **John D. MacArthur Beach State Park** (⊠ *10900 Rte. 703, North Palm Beach* ☎ *561/624-6952* ⊕ *www.macarthurbeach.org*), and the **Museum of Discovery and Science** in Fort Lauderdale (⊠ *401 SW 2nd Street, Ft. Lauderdale* ☎ *954/467–6637*). It is best to call ahead and make a reservation for these.

They only happen in June and July, and there is usually a cost of less than $15.

Beaches

Each of us defines the "perfect" beach differently. But whether you want to swim, surf, lounge, or leer, Florida has one to suit your preference. Best of all, in this skinny state—bounded by the Atlantic *and* Gulf of Mexico—the coast is never more than 60 mi away.

■ **Miami Beach.** Over the past 20 years, no American beach has generated as much buzz as the one that hugs Ocean Drive, and it's easy to see why. Fringed with palms, backed by Art Deco architecture, and pulsating with urban energy, South Beach is the place to stretch out or strut.

■ **Crandon Park Beach, Key Biscayne.** You'll see why this beach is continually ranked among the nation's top ten. After two miles of lagoon-style beach, there's an amusement center and gardens to explore.

■ **Matheson Hammock Park Beach, Miami.** Pack a picnic and take the family to the safe, warm waters of this palm-tree fringed beach. Loll in the balmy breezes as you take in the amazing views or ditch your towel for the nature trails, full-service marina, and snacks at the restaurant built into a historic coral rock building.

■ **Dry Tortugas National Park, the Florida Keys.** Forget lazily reading a book under an umbrella on the sandy shores. Come here if you're looking for a beach where you can dive in—literally. Set among coral reefs and sparkling waters, this cluster of seven islands (accessible only by boat or seaplane) offers outstanding snorkeling and diving.

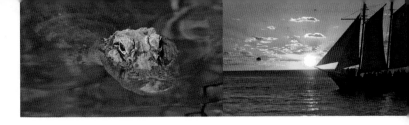

Golf

The Sunshine State is a golfer's dream come true. With more than 1,250 golf facilities (and counting), Florida has more green than any other state in the Union. Palm Beach County alone is home to more than 140 courses. The trend began in 1897, when Florida's first golf course opened in Palm Beach at the Breakers Resort. The turn-of-the-century guest book signatees included the Rockefellers, Vanderbilts, and Astors, and now the resort is listed on the National Register of Historic Places. In Southeast Florida there are enough golf courses to allow you to play a new course every week for two years. Even if you're new to the game, you can tee up with a PGA pro for a lesson and soak in the beauty of Florida's tropical flora among some of the country's most exquisitely designed courses. Floridians play golf twelve months out of the year, although the courses are never crowded between May and October.

■ **Boca Raton Resort & Club.** This scenic course has some of the most exotic terrain, water features, and floral landscapes outside of Hawaii.

■ **The Breakers, Palm Beach.** The 70-par Ocean Course offers spectacular views of the Atlantic and challenging shots on 140 acres.

■ **Doral Golf Resort & Spa.** Home of the "Blue Monster": Doral's famous 18th hole has been ranked the best in South Florida. The par-4 hole leaves little room for error with bunkers aplenty and a green that slopes toward water.

■ **The Club at Emerald Hills.** Test your skills on the course that has been the host site for the U.S. Amateur and U.S. Open Qualifiers since 2003.

Scenic Views

Florida is known for its sunsets, but there are other views worth scoping out, from aerial panoramic views to architectural wonders to nature's many surprises. Here are some we find delightful.

■ **Everglades National Park, from the tower on Shark Valley loop.** This 50-foot observation tower, about 35 mi from downtown Miami, yields a splendid panorama of the wide River of Grass as it sweeps southward toward the Gulf of Mexico. (And down below, on the ground, get views of otters, alligators, manatees, and more.) To get to the tower, you can hike or take the tram.

■ **Ocean Drive in the Art Deco district, Miami Beach.** Feast your eyes on brilliantly restored vintage Art Deco hotels at every turn. The palm-lined beachfront that the hotels are set along hops 24 hours a day. And when you're finished looking at the colorful hotels, you can catch the sea of colorful swimsuits parading by on nearby South Beach. (*For more details on this architecturally significant section of Miami Beach, see "A Stroll Down Deco Lane" in-focus feature in Chapter 4*).

■ **Sunset scene at Mallory Square, Key West.** Don't be surprised if someone claps for the sunset in Key West. It's that amazing, and those watching can't help but applaud. Along the waterfront the sunset draws street performers, vendors, and thousands of onlookers to the dock at Mallory Square (⊕ *www.mallorysquare. com* ⊕ *www.sunsetcelebration.org*). Fun attractions, like the Key West Aquarium, are nearby.

GREAT ITINERARIES

2 to 3 Days: Gold Coast and Treasure Coast

The opulent mansions of Palm Beach's Ocean Boulevard give you a glimpse of how the richer half lives. For exclusive boutique shopping, art gallery browsing, and glittery sightseeing, sybarites should wander down "The Avenue" (that's Worth Avenue to non–Palm Beachers). The sporty set will find dozens of places to tee up (hardly surprising given that the PGA is based here), along with tennis courts, polo clubs, even a croquet center. Those who'd like to see more of the Gold Coast can continue traveling south through Boca Raton to Fort Lauderdale (justifiably known as the "Yachting Capital of the World"). But to balance the highbrow with the low key, turn northward for a tour of the Treasure Coast. You can also look for the sea turtles that lay their own little treasures in the sands from March through October.

2 to 3 Days: Miami Area

Greater Miami lays claim to the country's most celebrated strand—South Beach—and lingering on it tops most tourist itineraries. (The Ocean Drive section, lined with edgy clubs, boutiques, and eateries, is where the see-and-be-seen crowd gathers.) Once you've checked out the candy-colored Art Deco architecture, park yourself to ogle the parade of stylish people, or join them by browsing Lincoln Road Mall, and check out its latest addition, the gleaming Frank Gehry–designed New World Symphony. Later, merengue over to Calle Ocho, the epicenter of Miami's Cuban community. Elsewhere in the area, Coconut Grove, Coral Gables, and the Miami Design District (an 18-block area crammed with showrooms and galleries) also warrant a visit. Miami is also a convenient base for eco-excursions. You can

TIPS

Now that one-way airfares are commonplace, vacationers visiting multiple destinations can fly into and out of different airports. Rent a car in between, picking it up at your point of arrival and leaving it at your point of departure. If you do this itinerary as an entire vacation, your best bet is to fly into and out of Orlando and rent a car from there.

take a day trip to the Everglades or get a spectacular view of the reefs from a glass-bottom boat in Biscayne National Park.

2 to 3 Days: Florida Keys

Some dream of "sailing away to Key Largo," others of "wasting away again in Margaritaville." In any case, almost everybody equates the Florida Keys with relaxation. And they live up to their reputation, thanks to offbeat attractions and that fabled come-as-you-are, do-as-you-please vibe. Key West, alternately known as the Conch Republic, is a good place to get initiated. The Old Town has a funky, laid-back feel. So take a leisurely walk; pay your regards to "Papa" (Hemingway, that is); then rent a moped to tour the rest of the island. Clear waters and abundant marine life make underwater activities another must. After scoping out the parrotfish, you can always head back into town and join local "Parrotheads" in a Jimmy Buffett sing-along. When retracing your route to the mainland, plan a last pit stop at Bahia Honda State Park (it has ranger-led activities plus the Keys' best beach) or John Pennekamp Coral Reef State Park, which offers unparalleled snorkeling and scuba-diving opportunities for beginners and veterans alike.

GONE FISHIN'

by Gary McKechnie

My favorite uncle has a passion for fishing.

It was one I didn't really understand—I'm more of a
motorcycle guy, not a fishing pole-toting one. But one day he piqued
my curiosity by telling me that fishing has many of the same enticements
as motorcycling. Come again? He beautifully described the peaceful pro-
cess of it all—how the serenity and solitude of the sport wash away concerns about work and tune him into the wonder of nature, just like being
on a bike (minus the helmet and curvy highways).

I took the bait, and early one morning a few weeks later, my Uncle Bud and I headed out in a boat to a secluded cove on the St. Johns River near DeLand. We'd brought our rods, line, bait, and tackle—plus hot chocolate and a few things to eat. We didn't need much else. We dropped in our lines and sat silently, watching the fog hover over the water.

There was a peaceful stillness as we waited (and waited) for the fish to bite. There were turtles sunning themselves on logs and herons perched in the trees. We waited for hours for just a little nibble. I can't even recall now if we caught any-thing, but it didn't matter. My uncle was right: it was a relaxing way to spend a Florida morning.

REEL TIME

Florida is recognized as the "Fishing Capital of the World" as well as the "Bass Capital of the World." It's also home to some of the nation's most popular crappie tournaments.

Florida and fishing have a bond that goes back to thousands of years before Christ, when Paleo-Indians living along Florida's rivers and coasts were harvesting the waters just as readily as they were harvesting the land. Jump ahead to the 20th century and along came amateur anglers like Babe Ruth, Clark Gable, and Gary Cooper vacationing at central Florida fishing camps in pursuit of bream, bluegill, and largemouth bass, while Ernest Hemingway was scouring the waters off Key West in hopes of snagging marlin, tarpon, and snapper. Florida was, and is, a sportsman's paradise.

When he wasn't writing, Ernest Hemingway loved to fish in the Florida Keys. He's shown here in Key West in 1928.

A variety of fish and plentiful waterways—7,800 lakes and 1,700 rivers and creeks, not to mention the gulf and the ocean—are just two reasons why Florida is the nation's favorite fishing spot. And let's not forget the frost-free attributes: unlike their northern counterparts, Florida anglers have yet to drill through several feet of ice just to go fishing in the wintertime. Plus, a well-established infrastructure for fishing—numerous bait and tackle shops, boat rentals, sporting goods stores, public piers, and charters—makes it easy for experts and first-time fishermen to get started. For Floridians and the visitors hooked on the sport here, fishing in the Sunshine State is a sport of sheer ease and simplicity.

An afternoon on the waters of Charlotte County in southwest Florida.

CASTING WIDE

The same way Florida is home to rocket scientists and beach bums, it's home to a diverse variety of fishing methods. What kind will work for you depends on where you want to go and what you want to catch.

From the Panhandle south to the Everglades, fishing is as easy as finding a quiet spot on the bank or heading out on freshwater lakes, tranquil ponds, spring-fed rivers, and placid inlets and lagoons.

Perhaps the biggest catches are found offshore—in the Atlantic Ocean, Florida Straits, or the Gulf of Mexico. For saltwater fishing, you can join a charter, be it a private one for small groups or a large party one; head out along the long jetties or public piers that jut into the ocean; or toss your line from the shore into the surf (known as surf casting). Some attempt a tricky, yet effective form of fishing called net casting: tossing a circular net weighted around its perimeter; the flattened net hits the surface and drives fish into the center of the circle.

Surf casting on Juno Beach, about 20 mi north of Palm Beach.

FRESHWATER FISHING VS. SALTWATER FISHING

FRESH WATER

With about 8,000 lakes to choose from, it's hard to pick the leading contenders, but a handful rise to the top: Lake George, Lake Tarpon, Lake Weohyakapka, Lake Istokpoga, Lake Okeechobee, Crescent Lake, Lake Kissimmee, Lake George, and Lake Talquin. Florida's most popular freshwater game fish is the largemouth bass. Freshwater fishermen are also checking rivers and streams for other popular catches, such as spotted bass, white bass, Suwannee bass, striped bass, black crappie, bluegill, redear sunfish, and channel catfish.

SALT WATER

The seas are filled with some of the most challenging (and tasty) gamefish in America. From piers, jetties, private boats, and charter excursions, fishermen search for bonefish, tarpon, snook, redfish, grouper, permit, spotted sea trout, sailfish, cobia, bluefish, snapper, sea bass, dolphin (the short, squat fish, not Flipper), and sheepshead.

Tarpon

DID YOU KNOW?

The Florida Keys is the Sportfishing Capital of the World. Among the bounty brought in are all kinds of tuna—blackfin, skipjack, blue, or yellowfin.

Florida Largemouth Bass	Striped Bass	Black Crappie
Channel Catfish	Bluegill	Redear Sunfish
Bonefish	Dolphin (Mahi-Mahi)	Red Snapper
Sheepshead	Snook	Sailfish

(top six) freshwater, (bottom six) saltwater

HERE'S THE CATCH

The type of fish you're after will depend on whether you fish in Florida's lake, streams, and rivers, or head out to sea. The Panhandle has an abundance of red snapper, while Lake Okeechobee is the place for bass fishing—although the largemouth bass is found throughout the state (they're easiest to catch in early spring, when they're in shallower waters). If you're looking for a good charter, Destin has the largest charter-boat fishing fleet in the nation. In the Florida Keys, you can fish by walking out in the very shallow water for hundreds of yards with the water only up to your knees; the fish you might reel in this way include bonefish, tarpon, and permit.

CHARTING THE WATERS

TYPE OF TRIP	COST	PROS	CONS
LARGE PARTY BOAT	$40/person for 4 hrs.	The captain's fishing license covers all passengers; you keep whatever you catch.	Not much privacy, assistance, or solitude: boats can hold as many as 35 passengers.
PRIVATE CHARTER	Roughly $1,200 for up to six people for 9 hrs.	More personal attention and more time on the water.	Higher cost ($200 per person instead of $40); tradition says you split the catch with the captain.
GUIDED TRIP FOR INLAND WATERS	Around $300–$400 for one or two people for 6 hrs.	Helpful if your time is limited and you want to make sure you go where the fish are biting.	Can be expensive and may not be as exciting as deep-sea fishing.
GOING SOLO	Cost for gear (rod, line, bait, and tackle) and license ($30-$100 depending on where you fish and if you need gear).	Privacy, flexibility, your time and destination are up to you; you can get fishing tips from your fellow anglers.	If you require a boat, you need to pay for and operate it yourself, plus pay for gear and a fishing license and find a fishing spot!

With a little hunting (by calling marinas, visiting bait and tackle stores, asking at town visitor centers), you can find a fishing guide who will lead you to some of the best spots on Florida's lakes and rivers. The guide provides the boat and gear, and his license should cover all passengers. A guide is not generally necessary for freshwater fishing, but if you're new to the sport, it might be a worthwhile investment.

On the other hand, if you're looking for fishing guides who can get you into the deep water for tarpon, redfish, snook, snapper, and dolphin, your best bet is to hang out at the marinas along the Florida coast and decide whether price or privacy is more important. If it's price, choose one of the larger party boats. If you'd prefer some privacy and the privilege of creating an exclusive passenger list, then sign up for a private charter. The average charter runs about nine hours, but some companies offer overnight and extended trips, too. Gear is provided in both charter-boat methods, and charters also offer the service of cleaning your catch. All guided trips encourage tipping the crew.

Most people new to the sport choose to do saltwater fishing via a charter party boat. The main reasons are expert guidance, convenience, and cost. Plus, fishing with others can be fun. Charter trips depart from marinas throughout Florida.

CREATING A FLOAT PLAN

If you're fishing in a boat on your own, let someone know where you're headed by providing a float plan, which should include where you're leaving from, a description of the boat you're on, how many are in the boat with you, what survival gear and radio equipment you have onboard, your cell phone number, and when you expect to return. If you don't return as expected, your friend can call the Coast Guard to search for you. Also be sure to have enough life jackets for everyone on board.

RULES AND REGULATIONS

To fish anywhere in (or off the coast of) Florida, you need a license, and there are separate licenses for freshwater fishing and saltwater fishing.

For non-residents, either type of fishing license cost $47 for the annual license, $30 for the 7-day one, or $17 for a 3-day license. Permits/tags are needed for catching snook ($2), crawfish/lobster ($2), and tarpon ($51.50). License and permit costs help generate funds for the Florida Fish and Wildlife Conservation Commission, which reinvests the fees into ensuring healthy habitats to sustain fish and wildlife populations, to improve access to fishing spots, and to help ensure public safety.

You can purchase your license and permits at county tax collectors' offices as well as wherever you buy your bait and tackle, such as Florida marinas, specialty stores, and sporting goods shops. You can also buy it online at ⊕ www.myfwc. com/license and have it mailed to you; a surcharge is added to online orders.

If you're on a charter, you don't need to get a license. The captain's fishing license covers all passengers. Also, some piers have their own saltwater fishing licenses that cover you when you're fishing off them for recreational purposes— if you're pier fishing, ask the personnel at the tackle shop if the pier is covered.

RESOURCES

For the latest regulations on gear, daily limits, minimum sizes and seasons for certain fish, and other fishing requirements, consult the extraordinary **Florida Fish and Wildlife Conservation Commission** (☎ 888/347–4356 ⊕ www.myfwc.com).

WEB RESOURCES
Download the excellent, and free, Florida Fishing PDF at www.visitflorida.com/planning/guide. Other good sites: www.floridafishinglakes.net www.fishingcapital.com www.floridasportsman.com

Palm Beach and the Treasure Coast

WORD OF MOUTH

"If you really want to be close to restaurants and shops in the Palm Beach area, check out the Marriott in Delray Beach or even the adjacent Residence Inn by Marriott . . . about 30 minutes south of Palm Beach."

—rattravlers

WELCOME TO PALM BEACH AND THE TREASURE COAST

TOP REASONS TO GO

★ **Beautiful Beaches:** From Jupiter's sandy shoreline, where leashed dogs are welcome, to the broad stretches of sand in Delray Beach and Boca Raton, swimmers, sunbathers, and surfers—and sea turtles looking for a place to hatch their eggs—all find happiness.

★ **Exquisite Resorts:** The Ritz-Carlton and the Four Seasons continue to sparkle with service fit for royalty. Two historic gems—the Breakers in Palm Beach and the Boca Raton Resort—perpetually draw the rich, the famous, and anyone else who can afford the luxury.

★ **Horse Around:** Wellington, with its jumping events and its popular polo season, is often called the winter equestrian capital of the world.

★ **Have a Reel Good Time:** From Lake Okeechobee, a great place to catch bass and perch, to the Atlantic Ocean, teeming with kingfish, sailfish, dolphinfish, and wahoos, anglers will find the waters here a treasure chest.

1 Palm Beach. With Gatsby-era architecture, stone-and-stucco estates, extravagant landscaping, and highbrow shops, Palm Beach is a must-see for travelers to the area. Plan to spend some time on Worth Avenue, also called the Mink Mile, a collection of more than 200 chic shops, and Whitehall, once the winter retreat for Henry Flagler, Palm Beach's founder.

2 West Palm Beach. Bustling with its own affluent identity, West Palm Beach has much to offer. Palm Beach–style homes line lovely Flagler Drive, and golf courses are abundant. Culture fans have plenty to cheer about, from the Kravis Center for the Performing Arts, to the Norton Museum of Art and the Armory Arts Center. Kids will love the Palm Beach Zoo.

3 South to Boca Raton. The territory from Palm Beach south to Boca Raton defines old-world glamour and new age sophistication. Delray Beach boasts a lively downtown, with galleries, shops, and restaurants. To the west are the Morikami Japanese Gardens and the headquarters of the American Orchid Society. Boca Raton's Mizner Park has tony boutiques, restaurants, and the Boca Raton Museum of Art.

4 Treasure Coast. Much of the shoreline north of Palm Beach remains blissfully undeveloped. Along the coast, the broad tidal lagoon separates barrier islands from the mainland.

ATLANTIC OCEAN

◆ Jupiter Island
◆ Hobe Sound
○ Tequesta
○ Jupiter
○ Juno Beach
  Singer Island
◆ Palm Beach Gardens
  Palm Beach Shores
○ Riviera Beach
  West Palm **1** Beach
○ Palm Beach **2**
○ Lake Worth
○ South Palm Beach
Lantana ○ Manalapan
● Boynton Beach **3**
◆ Gulf Stream
○ Delray Beach
○ Highland Beach
○ Boca Raton

GETTING ORIENTED

This South Florida region extends 120 mi from Sebastian to Boca Raton. The golden stretch of the Atlantic from Palm Beach southward defines old-world glamour and new age sophistication. North of Palm Beach, you'll uncover the comparatively undeveloped Treasure Coast, where towns and wide-open spaces along the road await your discovery. Altogether, there's a delightful disparity, from Palm Beach, pulsing fast with old-money wealth, to low-key Hutchinson Island and Manalapan. The burgeoning equestrian community of Wellington lies 10 mi west of Palm Beach. It is the site of much of the county's new development.

PALM BEACH AND TREASURE COAST BEACHES

While not as white and fine as the shores on Florida's west coast, the beaches here provide good stomping grounds for hikers, well-guarded waters for swimmers, decent waves for surfers, and plenty of opportunities for sand-castle building and shell collecting.

Miles of sandy shoreline can be found here beside gorgeous blue-green waters you won't find farther north. The average year-round water temperature is 74°F, much warmer than Southern California beaches that average a comparatively chilly 62°F.

Humans aren't alone in finding the shores inviting. Migratory birds flock to the beaches, too, as do sea turtles, who come between May and August to lay their eggs in the sand. Locally organized watches take small groups out at night to observe mother turtles as they waddle onto shore, dig holes with their flippers and deposit their golf-ball-size eggs into the sand. Hatchlings emerge about 45 days later.

WHEN TO GO

Palm Beach and Treasure Coast beaches are warm, clear, and sparkling all year long, but the best time to get in the water is between December and March. The shorelines are often more crowded then, but you don't have to worry about jellyfish or sea lice when you take a dip. Sea lice can cause welts, blisters, and rashes. The crowds thin out during summer and fall months, which is inviting, but jellyfish and sea lice can be a problem then.

BEST PALM BEACH AND TREASURE COAST BEACHES

DELRAY

If you're looking for a place to see and be seen, head for Delray's wide expanse of sand, which stretches 2 mi, half of it supervised by lifeguards. Reefs off the coast are popular with divers, as is a sunken Spanish galleon less than ½ mi offshore from the Seagate Club on the south end of the beach. **Pros:** good for swimmers and sunbathers; bars and restaurants across the street; cabanas and catamarans available for rent. **Cons:** often a long walk to the public restrooms. Best for families.

JOHN D. MACARTHUR STATE PARK

If getting far from the madding crowd is your goal, John D. MacArthur State Park on the north end of Singer Island is a good choice. You will find a great place for snorkeling, kayaking, birdwatching, and fishing. Part of the beach was once dedicated to topless bathers, but that is no longer the case. **Pros:** guides to local flora and fauna are available; a good place to spot sea turtles. **Cons:** beach is a long walk from the parking lot. Best for sand-castle builders and nature lovers.

JUNO BEACH

Juno Beach sports a 990-foot pier and a bait shop for those who like to spend their morning fishing. But the shoreline

itself is a favorite for families with kids who drag along sand toys, build castles, and hunt for shells. **Pros:** concession stand and a bait shop. **Cons:** beach isn't as wide as others. Best for anglers.

RED REEF PARK

Looking for a great place to snorkel? This Boca Raton beach is just the ticket, and it doesn't matter if you're a beginner or a pro. The reef is only about 50 feet offshore. Expect to see tropical fish and maybe even a manatee or two. **Pros:** the park's showers and bathrooms are kept clean and there's a playground for kids. **Cons:** if you go at low tide, you're not going to see as many tropical fish. Best for snorkelers.

STUART BEACH

When the waves robustly roll in at Stuart Beach, the surfers are rolling in, too. Beginning surfers are especially keen on Stuart Beach because of its ever-vigilant lifeguards, while pros to the sport like the challenges the choppy waters here bring. Beachgoers with kids like the snack bar known for its chicken fingers, and for those who like a side of museum musing with their day in the sun, there's an impressive collection of antique cars at a museum just steps from the beach. **Pros:** parking is easy to find, and there are three boardwalks for easy access to the beach. **Cons:** sand and surf can be rocky. Best for surfers.

Updated by Mary Thurwachter

This golden stretch of Atlantic coast resists categorization, and for good reason. The territory from Palm Beach south to Boca Raton defines old-world glamour and new age sophistication.

North of Palm Beach you'll uncover the comparatively undeveloped Treasure Coast—liberally sprinkled with coastal gems—where towns and wide-open spaces along the road await your discovery. Altogether, there's a delightful disparity, from Palm Beach, pulsing fast with plenty of old-money wealth, to low-key Hutchinson Island and Manalapan. Seductive as the beach scene interspersed with eclectic dining options can be, you should also take advantage of flourishing commitments to historic preservation and the arts, as town after town yields intriguing museums, galleries, theaters, and gardens.

Palm Beach, with Gatsby-era architecture, stone-and-stucco estates, extravagant landscaping, and highbrow shops, can reign as the focal point for your sojourn any time of year. From Palm Beach, head off in any of three directions: south via the Gold Coast toward Boca Raton along an especially scenic route known as A1A, back to the mainland and north to the barrier-island treasures of the Treasure Coast, or west for more rustic inland activities such as bass fishing and biking on the dikes around Lake Okeechobee.

WEST PALM BEACH PLANNER

WHEN TO GO

The weather is optimal from November through May, but the trade-off is that roadways and facilities are more crowded and prices higher. In summer it helps to have a tolerance for heat, humidity, and afternoon downpours. Hurricane season runs from June through November, not necessarily a bad time for a trip here as there's always plenty of warning before the big storms. For the best lodging rates consider summer months or the early weeks of December. Make sure to bring insect repellent for outdoor activities.

SPECIALTY TOURS

🕙 **DivaDuck Tours.** Amphibious tours, running 75 minutes, go in and out of the water around West Palm Beach/Palm Beach. Cruises run two or three times a day for $25. ⊠ *Rosemary Ave. and Hibiscus St.* ☎ *561/844–4186* ⊕ *www.divaduck.com.*

Old Northwood Historic District Tours. Two-hour walking tours include visits to historic home interiors in this West Palm Beach neighborhood. In season tours start Sunday at 2; a $5 donation is suggested. Tours for groups of six or more can be scheduled almost any day. (☎ *No phone* ⊕ *www.oldnorthwood.org*).

GETTING HERE

The best place to fly into is **Palm Beach International Airport** (*PBI ☎ 561/ 471–7420*).

For a cab, call **Palm Beach Transportation** (☎ *561/689–4222*), the hotline for the Yellow cab company.

Tri-Rail Commuter Bus Service (☎ *800/874–7245*), the commuter rail system, provides taxi and limousine service. For either, the lowest fares are $2.50 per mile, with the meter starting at $2.50. Tri-Rail has 18 stops altogether between West Palm Beach and Miami, where tickets can be purchased. The one-way fare is $5.50.

The city's bus service, **Palm Tran** (☎ *561/841–4200*), runs routes 44 and 40 from the airport to Tri-Rail's nearby Palm Beach airport station daily.

Amtrak (☎ *800/872–7245* ⊕ *www.amtrak.com*) connects West Palm Beach with cities along Florida's east coast and the northeast daily.

GETTING AROUND

Interstate 95 runs north–south, linking West Palm Beach with Fort Lauderdale and Miami to the south and with Daytona, Jacksonville, and the rest of the Atlantic Coast to the north. Florida's turnpike runs from Miami north through West Palm Beach before angling northwest to reach Orlando. U.S. 1 threads north–south along the coast, connecting most coastal communities, whereas the more scenic Route A1A ventures out onto the barrier islands. Interstate 95 runs parallel to U.S. 1 but a few miles inland.

ABOUT THE RESTAURANTS

Numerous elegant establishments offer upscale Continental and contemporary fare, but the area also teems with casual waterfront spots serving affordable burgers and fresh seafood feasts. Grouper, fried or blackened, is especially popular here, along with the ubiquitous shrimp. An hour's drive west of the coast, around Lake Okeechobee, dine on catfish panfried to perfection and so fresh it seems barely out of the water. Early-bird menus, a Florida hallmark, typically entice the budget-minded with several dinner entrées at reduced prices offered during certain hours, usually before 5 or 6.

ABOUT THE HOTELS

Palm Beach has a number of smaller hotels in addition to the famous Breakers. Lower-priced hotels and motels can be found in West Palm Beach and Lake Worth. To the south, the coastal town of Manalapan has the Ritz-Carlton, Palm Beach; and the posh Boca Raton Resort & Club is near the beach in Boca Raton. To the north in suburban Palm Beach Gardens is the PGA National Resort & Spa. To the west, small towns near Lake Okeechobee offer country-inn accommodations.

WHAT IT COSTS					
	¢	$	$$	$$$	$$$$
Restaurants	under $10	$10–$15	$15–$20	$20–$30	over $30
Hotels	under $80	$80–$100	$100–$140	$140–$220	over $220

Restaurant prices are per person for a main course at dinner. Hotel prices are for a standard double room, excluding 6½% sales tax (more in some counties) and 1%–4% tourist tax.

INLAND SIGHTS

Want to get away from the water? Head 40 mi west of West Palm Beach on to Lake Okeechobee for some wildlife viewing, bird-watching, and fishing.

You are likely to see alligators in the tall grass along the shore, as well as birds, including herons, ibises, and bald eagles, which have made a comeback in the area. A 110-mi trail encircles Lake Okeechobee atop the 34-foot Herbert Hoover Dike. On the lake you'll spot happy anglers hooked on some of the best bass fishing in North America. There are 40 species of fish in "Lake O," including largemouth bass, bluegill, Okeechobee catfish, and speckled perch.

Okee-Tantie Recreation Area. Direct lake access makes this a popular fishing outpost, with two public boat ramps, fish-cleaning stations, and a bait shop that stocks groceries. There are also picnic areas and a restaurant. ⊠ *10430 Rte. 78 W, Okeechobee* ☎ *863/763–2622.*

Getting Here: The best way to drive here from West Palm is to go west on Southern Boulevard from Interstate 95 past the cutoff road to Lion Country Safari. From there, the boulevard is designated U.S. 98/441.

PALM BEACH

78 mi north of Miami, off I–95.

Long reigning as the place where the crème de la crème go to shake off winter's chill, Palm Beach continues to be a seasonal hotbed of platinum-grade consumption. Other towns like Jupiter Island may rank higher on the per-capita-wealth meter, but there's no competing with the historic social supremacy of Palm Beach. It has been the winter address for heirs of the iconic Rockefeller, Vanderbilt, Colgate, Post, Kellogg, and Kennedy families. Even newer power brokers, with names like Kravis, Peltz, and Trump, are made to understand that strict laws govern everything from building to landscaping, and not so much as a pool awning gets added without a town council nod. If Palm Beach were to fly a flag, it's been observed, there might be three interlocking Cs, standing not only for Cartier, Chanel, and Christian Dior but also for clean, civil, and capricious. Only three bridges allow access to the island, and huge tour buses are a no-no.

To learn who's who in Palm Beach, it helps to pick up a copy of the *Palm Beach Daily News*—locals call it the Shiny Sheet because its high-quality paper avoids smudging society hands or Pratesi linens—for, as it is said, to be mentioned in the Shiny Sheet is to be Palm Beach. All this fabled ambience started with Henry Morrison Flagler, Florida's premier developer, and cofounder, along with John D. Rockefeller, of Standard Oil. No sooner did Flagler bring the railroad to Florida in the 1890s than he erected the famed Royal Poinciana and Breakers hotels. Rail access sent real estate prices soaring, and ever since, princely sums have been forked over for personal stationery engraved with 33480, the zip code of Palm Beach. To provide Palm Beach with servants and other workers, Flagler also developed an off-island community a mile or so west. West Palm Beach now bustles with its own affluent identity.

Setting the tone in this town of unparalleled Florida opulence is the ornate architectural work of Addison Mizner, who began designing homes and public buildings here in the 1920s and whose Moorish-Gothic style has influenced virtually all community landmarks. Thanks to Mizner and his lasting influence, Palm Beach remains a playground of the rich, famous, and discerning.

GETTING HERE AND AROUND

Palm Beach is 78 mi north of Miami. To access Palm Beach off Interstate 95, exit east at Southern Boulevard, Belvedere Road, or Okeechobee Boulevard. The city's Palm Tran buses run between Worth Avenue and Royal Palm Way in Palm Beach and major areas of West Palm Beach and require exact change. Regular fares are $1.50.

For a taste of what it's like to jockey for position in this status-conscious town, stake out a parking place on Worth Avenue or parallel residential streets, and squeeze in among the Mercedeses, Rolls-Royces, and Bentleys. Between admiring your excellent parking skills and feeling car-struck at the surrounding fine specimens of automobile, be sure to note the "Parking By Permit Only" and "Two-hour" parking signs, as a $25 parking ticket might take the shine off your spot. ■TIP➜ The best course for a half-day visit is to valet-park at the parking deck next to Saks 5th Avenue. Away from downtown, along County Road and Ocean Boulevard (the shore road, also designated as Route A1A), are Palm Beach's other defining landmarks: Mediterranean-style residences, some built of coral rock, that are nothing short of palatial, topped by barrel-tile roofs and often fronted by 10-foot ficus and sea-grape hedges. The low wall that separates the dune-top shore road from the sea hides shoreline that varies in many places from expansive to eroded. Here and there, where the strand deepens, homes are built directly on the beach.

A GOOD TOUR: PALM BEACH

Start at the **Henry Morrison Flagler Museum**—a 55-room villa Flagler built for his third wife—to get your first look at the eye-popping opulence of the Gilded Age, which defined Palm Beach. From here, turn left on Cocoanut Row, and right onto Royal Poinciana Way—outdoor cafés on the left and the Breakers golf course to your right—then right onto North County Road. Head south and look for the long stately driveway on the left that leads to the **Breakers**, built by Flagler in the style of an Italian Renaissance palace. Parking costs $20, and there are many valets under the porte cochere. Have your parking ticket validated while lunching at the Breakers and the parking fee is waived.

Continue south on South County Road to **Bethesda-by-the-Sea**, a Spanish Gothic Episcopal church. Keep driving south on South County Road until you reach Royal Palm Way; turn right, and drive a few blocks until you see the **Society of the Four Arts**. Turn left back onto Royal Palm Way and drive until it ends at the ocean, and turn right onto Ocean Boulevard until you reach famed **Worth Avenue** on the right, which is a one-way street running east to west. Park, stroll, and ogle designer goods. Then drive south back on Ocean Boulevard to peek at magnificent estates, including **El Solano**, designed by Addison Mizner, and the fabled **Mar-a-Lago**, a Mediterranean-revival palace with a distinctive 75-foot tower, now owned by Donald Trump and operating as a private club. At this point, if you want some sun and fresh air, continue south on South County Road until you reach **Phipps Ocean Park** and its stretch of beach, or head back toward town along South Ocean Boulevard to the popular Mid-Town Beach at the east end of Worth Avenue.

TIMING
You'll need half a day, minimum, for these sights. A few shops and attractions are closed Sunday and May through October. From November through April, often-heavy traffic gets worse as the day wears on, so plan to explore in the morning.

ESSENTIALS

Transportation Contact **Palm Tran** (☎ 561/841–4287).

Visitor Information **Town of Palm Beach Chamber of Commerce** (✉ 400 Royal Palm Way, Suite 106, Palm Beach ☎ 561/655–3282).

EXPLORING

TOP ATTRACTIONS

Bethesda-by-the-Sea. Donald Trump and his wife Melania were married here in 2005, but this Spanish Gothic Episcopal church had a claim to fame upon its creation in 1925: it was built by the first Protestant congregation in southeast Florida. Guided tours follow 11 am services on the second and fourth Sunday of the month. Adjacent are the formal, ornamental **Cluett Memorial Gardens.** ✉ 141 S. County Rd. ☎ 561/655–4554 ⊕ www.bbts.org 🎫 Free ☉ Church and gardens daily 8–5.

Draped in European elegance, the Breakers in Palm Beach sits on 140 acres along the oceanfront.

Fodor's Choice
★ **The Breakers.** Built by Henry Flagler in 1896 and rebuilt by his descendants after a 1925 fire, this magnificent Italian Renaissance–style resort helped launch Florida tourism with its Gilded Age opulence, attracting influential wealthy Northerners to the state. The hotel, still owned by Flagler's heirs, is a must-see even if you aren't staying here. Walk through the 200-foot-long lobby, which has soaring arched ceilings painted by 72 Italian artisans and hung with crystal chandeliers, and the ornate Florentine Dining Room is decorated with 15th-century Flemish tapestries. ⊠ *1 S. County Rd.* ☎ *561/655–6611* ⊕ *www.thebreakers.com.*

Fodor's Choice
★ **Henry Morrison Flagler Museum.** The opulence of Florida's Gilded Age lives on at Whitehall, the palatial 55-room "marble palace" Henry Flagler commissioned in 1901 for his third wife, Mary Lily Kenan. Architects John Carrère and Thomas Hastings were instructed to create the finest home imaginable—and they outdid themselves. Whitehall rivals the grandeur of European palaces and has an entrance hall with a baroque ceiling similar to Louis XIV's Versailles. Here you'll see original furnishings; a hidden staircase Flagler used to sneak from his bedroom to the billiards room; an art collection; a 1,200-pipe organ; and Florida East Coast Railway exhibits, along with Flagler's personal railcar, the *Rambler,* showcased in an 8,000-square-foot beaux arts–style pavilion behind the mansion. Tours take about an hour and are offered at frequent intervals. The café, open after Thanksgiving through mid-April, offers snacks and afternoon tea. ⊠ *1 Whitehall Way* ☎ *561/655–2833* ⊕ *www.flagler.org* ✉ *$18* ⊙ *Tues.–Sat. 10–5, Sun. noon–5.*

Palm Beach and
West Palm Beach

★ **Worth Avenue.** Called the Avenue by Palm Beachers, this ¼-mi-long street is synonymous with exclusive shopping. Nostalgia lovers recall an era when faces or names served as charge cards, purchases were delivered home before customers returned from lunch, and bills were sent directly to private accountants. Times have changed, but a stroll amid the Moorish architecture of its shops offers a tantalizing taste of the island's ongoing commitment to elegant consumerism. Explore the labyrinth of eight pedestrian vias, on both sides of Worth Avenue, that wind past boutiques, tiny plazas, bubbling fountains, and the bougainvillea-festooned wrought-iron balconies of second-floor apartments. The avenue underwent a $15 million makeover in 2010. Two hundred mature coconut palm trees were planted along the road, and a magnificent $600,000 clock tower was built on the beach to mark the entrance from A1A. ⊠ *Between Cocoanut Row and S. Ocean Blvd.*

WORTH NOTING

El Solano. No Palm Beach mansion better represents the town's luminous legacy than the Spanish-style home built by Addison Mizner as his own residence in 1925. Mizner later sold El Solano to Harold Vanderbilt, and the property was long a favorite among socialites for parties and photo shoots. Vanderbilt held many a gala fund-raiser here. Beatle John Lennon and his wife, Yoko Ono, bought it less than a year before Lennon's death. It's still privately owned and not open to the public. ⊠ *721 S. County Rd.*

Mar-a-Lago. Breakfast-food heiress Marjorie Merriweather Post commissioned a Hollywood set designer to create Ocean Boulevard's famed Mar-a-Lago, a 118-room, 110,000-square-foot Mediterranean-revival palace. Its 75-foot Italianate tower is visible from most areas of Palm Beach and from across the Intracoastal Waterway in West Palm Beach. Owner Donald Trump has turned it into a private membership club. ⊠ *1100 S. Ocean Blvd.* ☎ *561/832–2600* ⊕ *www.maralagoclub.com.*

Phipps Ocean Park. In addition to the shoreline, tennis courts, picnic tables, and grills, this park has a Palm Beach County landmark in the **Little Red Schoolhouse.** Dating from 1886, it served as the first schoolhouse in what was then Dade County. No alcoholic beverages are permitted in the park. ⊠ *2185 S. Ocean Blvd.* ☎ *561/838–5400* ⊠ *Free* ⊙ *Daily dawn–dusk.*

Society of the Four Arts. Despite widespread misconceptions of members-only exclusivity, this privately endowed institution—founded in 1936 to encourage appreciation of art, music, drama, and literature—is funded for public enjoyment. A gallery building—designed by Addison Mizner, of course—artfully melds an exhibition hall, library, and the Philip Hulitar Sculpture Garden, which underwent a major renovation in 2006. Open from about Thanksgiving to Easter, the museum's programs are extensive, and there's ample free parking. In addition to showcasing traveling art exhibitions, the museum offers films, lectures, workshops, and concerts. ⊠ *2 Four Arts Plaza* ☎ *561/655–7226* ⊕ *www.fourarts. org* ⊠ *Program admission varies* ⊙ *Galleries Dec.–mid-Apr., Mon.–Sat. 10–5, Sun. 2–5; library, weekdays 10–5, Sat. 10–1; gardens 10–5 daily.*

SPORTS AND THE OUTDOORS

BIKING

Bicycling is a great way to get a closer look at Palm Beach. Only 14 mi long, ½ mi wide, flat as the top of a billiard table, and just as green, it's a perfect biking place.

Lake Trail. This palm-fringed trail skirts the backyards of many palatial mansions and the edge of Lake Worth. ⊠ *Parallel to Lake Way.*

Palm Beach Bicycle Trail Shop. The Palm Beach Bicycle Trail starts at the Society of the Four Arts, heading north 8 mi to the end and back—just follow the signs. You can rent bikes by the hour or day at this shop, a block from the bike trail. It's open daily. ⊠ *223 Sunrise Ave.* ☎ *561/659–4583* ⊕ *www.palmbeachbicycle.com.*

GOLF

The Breakers Palm Beach. The historic Ocean Course, as well as its contemporary counterpart the Breakers Rees Jones Course and the John Webster Golf Academy by the Breakers, is open to members and hotel guests only. A $190 greens fee includes range balls, cart, and bag storage at The Breakers Rees Jones Course or at the Ocean Course. ⊠ *1 S. County Rd.* ☎ *561/655–6611.*

Town of Palm Beach Golf Club. The 18 holes include six on the Atlantic and three on the inland waterway; greens fee $45 riding, $32 to walk. The course was redesigned by Raymond Floyd and is a gem of a short-game course. ⊠ *2345 S. Ocean Blvd.* ☎ *561/547–0598.*

SHOPPING

★ **Worth Avenue.** One of the world's premier showcases for high-quality shopping runs ¼ mi east–west across Palm Beach, from the beach to Lake Worth. The street has more than 250 shops (more than 40 of them sell jewelry), and many upscale chain stores (Gucci, Hermès, Pucci, Saks Fifth Avenue, Neiman Marcus, Louis Vuitton, Emanuel Ungaro, Chanel, Dior, Cartier, Tiffany & Co., and Tourneau) are represented—their merchandise appealing to the discerning tastes of the Palm Beach clientele. ⊠ *Between Cocoanut Row and S. Ocean Blvd.*

South County Road. The six blocks of South Country Road north of Worth Avenue have interesting, and somewhat less expensive, stores.

Royal Poinciana Way. For specialty items like out-of-town newspapers, health foods, and books, try the shops along the north side of Royal Poinciana Way. Most stores are closed on Sunday, and many go on hiatus in summer.

Church Mouse. Many high-end resale boutique owners grab their merchandise at this thrift store. ⊠ *374 S. County Rd.* ☎ *561/659–2154.*

Déjà Vu. There are so many gently used, top-quality pieces from Chanel that this could be a resale house for the brand. There's no digging through piles here; clothes are in impeccable condition and are well organized. ⊠ *Via Testa, 219 Royal Poinciana Way* ☎ *561/833–6624.*

Worth Avenue is the place in Palm Beach for high-end shopping, from international boutiques to art galleries.

Giorgio's. Over-the-top indulgence comes in the form of 50 colors of silk and cashmere sweaters and 22 colors of ostrich and alligator adorning everything from bags to bicycles. ✉ *230 Worth Ave.* ☎ *561/655–2446.*

Greenleaf & Crosby. Jewelry is very important in Palm Beach, and for more than 100 years the divers selection here has included investment pieces. ✉ *236 Worth Ave.* ☎ *561/655–5850.*

Spring Flowers. Beautiful children's clothing starts with a newborn gown set by Kissy Kissy or Petit Bateau and grows into fashions by Cacharel and Lili Gaufrette. ✉ *337 Worth Ave.* ☎ *561/832–0131.*

Van Cleef & Arpels. Holding court for more than 60 years this shop is where legendary members of Palm Beach society shop for tiaras and formal jewels. ✉ *202 Worth Ave.* ☎ *561/655–6767.*

NIGHTLIFE AND THE ARTS

NIGHTLIFE

Palm Beach is teeming with restaurants that turn into late-night hot spots, plus hotel lobby bars perfect for tête-à-têtes.

Brazilian Court. Thursday night happy hours spiked by creatively named cocktails and live jazz draw a local crowd to the lobby lounge and outdoor patio. ✉ *301 Australian Ave.* ☎ *561/655–7740.*

Cucina Dell'Arte. Though popular for lunch and dinner, the younger trendier set comes late. ✉ *257 Royal Poinciana Way* ☎ *561/655–0770.*

Leopard Lounge. The old guard gathers for live music during cocktail hour and later to dance until the wee hours every night of the year. ⊠ *Chesterfield Hotel, 363 Cocoanut Row* ☎ *561/659–5800.*

THE ARTS

Society of the Four Arts. This venue hosts concerts, lectures, and films from November through March. ⊠ *2 Four Arts Plaza* ☎ *561/655–7226.*

WHERE TO EAT

$$$ ✕ **Amici.** The town's premier celebrity-magnet bistro is still a crowd
ITALIAN pleaser. When it moved across the street and down the block from its original location, the Palm Beach crowd followed. The northern Italian menu highlights house specialties such as rigatoni with spicy tomato sauce and roasted eggplant, potato gnocchi, grilled veal chops, risottos, and pizzas from a wood-burning oven. There are nightly pasta and fresh fish specials as well. To avoid the crowds, stop by for a late lunch or early dinner. ⊠ *375 S. County Rd.* ☎ *561/832–0201* ⊕ *www. amicipalmbeach.com* ⌢ *Reservations essential.*

$$$$ ✕ **Café Boulud.** Celebrated chef Daniel Boulud opened his outpost of
FRENCH New York's Café Boulud in the Brazilian Court hotel. The warm and
Fodor'sChoice welcoming French-American venue is casual yet elegant, with a pal-
★ ette of honey, gold, and citron. Plenty of natural light spills through arched glass doors opening to a lush courtyard. Lunch and dinner entrées on Boulud's signature four-muse menu include classic French, seasonal, vegetarian, and a rotating selection of international dishes. The lounge, with its illuminated amber glass bar, is the perfect perch to take in the jet-set crowd that comes for a hint of the south of France in South Florida. A DJ plays on Saturday nights. ⊠ *Brazilian Court, 301 Australian Ave.* ☎ *561/655–6060* ⊕ *www.cafeboulud.com* ⌢ *Reservations essential.*

$$$$ ✕ **Café L'Europe.** Even after 25 years, the favorite lunch spot of society's
ECLECTIC movers and shakers remains a regular stop on foodie itineraries. The management pays close attention to service and consistency, a big reason for its longevity. Best sellers include rack of lamb, Dover sole, and Wiener schnitzel, along with such inspired creations as crispy sweetbreads with poached pears and mustard sauce. Depending on your mood, the champagne-caviar bar can serve up appetizers or desserts. The place has an extensive wine list. A pianist plays nightly from 7 to 11 and a quartet plays dance music Friday and Saturday nights until 1 am. ⊠ *331 S. County Rd.* ☎ *561/655–4020* ⊕ *www.cafeleurope.com* ☺ *Lunch Wed.–Fri. Closed Mon. May–Dec.*

$$$$ ✕ **Chez Jean-Pierre.** With walls adorned with Dalí- and Picasso-like art,
FRENCH this is where the Palm Beach old guard likes to let down its guard, all
Fodor'sChoice the while partaking of sumptuous French cuisine and an impressive
★ wine list. Forget calorie or cholesterol concerns and indulge in scrambled eggs with caviar or homemade duck foie gras, along with desserts like hazelnut soufflé or profiteroles au chocolat. Waiters are friendly and very attentive. Jackets are not required, although many men wear them. ⊠ *132 N. County Rd.* ☎ *561/833–1171* ⌢ *Reservations essential* ☺ *Closed Sun. No lunch.*

2

$ | ✕ **Hamburger Heaven.** A favorite with locals since 1945, this quintessen-
AMERICAN tial diner with horseshoe-shape counter as well as booths and tables is loud and casual and has some of the best burgers on the island. Fresh salads, homemade pastries, and daily soup and hot-plate specials featuring comfort foods like meat loaf and chicken potpie are also available. During the week, it's a popular lunch stop for working stiffs. The staff is friendly and efficient. ✉ *314 S. County Rd.* ☎ *561/655–5277* ⊙ *Closed Sun.*

$$ | ✕ **Pizza Al Fresco.** The secret-garden setting is the secret to the success
PIZZA of this popular European-style pizzeria, where you can dine under a canopy of century-old banyans in a charming courtyard. Specialties are 12-inch hand-tossed brick-oven pizzas with such interesting toppings as prosciutto, arugula, and caviar. There's even a dessert pizza topped with Nutella. Piping-hot calzones, salads, and sandwiches round out the selection. Look for the grave markers of Addison Mizner's beloved pet monkey, Johnnie Brown, and Rose Sachs's dog Laddie (she and husband Morton bought Mizner's villa and lived there 47 years) next to the patio. Delivery is available. This bistro is dog-friendly. ✉ *14 Via Mizner, at Worth Ave.* ☎ *561/832–0032* ⊕ *www.pizzaalfresco.com.*

$$$ | ✕ **Ta-boó.** This 60-year-old landmark with peach stucco walls and green
AMERICAN shutters attracts Worth Avenue shoppers looking for a two-hour lunch
★ and a dinner crowd ranging from tuxed-and-sequined theatergoers to polo-shirted vacationers. Entrées include Black Angus dry-aged beef or roast duck. Don't miss Coconut Lust, a signature dessert. Drop in late night during the winter season when the nightly music is playing and you'll probably spot a celebrity or two. ✉ *221 Worth Ave.* ☎ *561/835–3500* ⊕ *www.taboorestaurant.com.*

WHERE TO STAY

For expanded hotel reviews, visit Fodors.com.

$$$$ | ⊤ **Brazilian Court.** A short stroll from Worth Avenue, the yellow-stucco
HOTEL Spanish-style facade and red-tile roof, and lobby with cypress ceilings
★ and stone floors, underscore this boutique hotel's Roaring '20s origins. **Pros:** one of the best restaurants in town; attracts a hip crowd; gorgeous courtyard; close to shopping and not far from the beach; free shuttle to the hotel's sister property on the beach, the Omphoy. **Cons:** fitness center is tiny; small pool. **TripAdvisor:** "far from world class," "business center had no computers," "without a personality." ✉ *301 Australian Ave.* ☎ *561/655–7740* ⊕ *www.thebraziliancourt.com* ↘ *80 rooms* ♧ *In-room: a/c, Internet, Wi-Fi. In-hotel: restaurant, bar, pool, gym, spa, laundry facilities, some pets allowed* ❚⃝| *No meals.*

$$$$ | ⊤ **The Breakers.** More than an opulent hotel, the Breakers is a mod-
HOTEL ern resort, built in an Italian Renaissance style, packed with ameni-
Fodor's Choice ties, from a 20,000-square-foot luxury spa and Medditerranean-style
★ beach club to clubhouses for the 10 tennis courts and two 18-hole golf courses. **Pros:** fine attention to detail throughout; beautiful room views; top-rate golf and tennis facilities. **Cons:** big price tag. **TripAdvisor:** "expensive but worth the money," "treated like royalty," "lovely little touches." ✉ *1 S. County Rd.* ☎ *561/655–6611 or 888/273–2537*

⊕ *www.thebreakers.com* 540 rooms, 68 suites In-room: a/c, Internet, Wi-Fi. In-hotel: restaurants, bars, golf courses, tennis courts, pools, gym, spa, beach, water sports, children's programs, business center, parking IOI No meals.

$$$$
HOTEL

The Chesterfield. Two blocks north of Worth Avenue, the distinctive white-stucco hotel with coral-color stucco walls and red-and-white-striped awnings offers 54 inviting rooms ranging from small to spacious. **Pros:** turndown service; complimentary beverages in king rooms and suites; elegant rooms; you can open guest-room windows, which is a treat for those who hate air-conditioning **Cons:** small elevator; narrow steps leading to presidential suite. **TripAdvisor:** "odd but in a very good way," "walking distance of the ocean shops restaurants," "good public spaces." ⊠ *363 Cocoanut Row* ☎ *561/659–5800 or 800/243–7871* ⊕ *www.chesterfieldpb.com* 44 rooms, 11 suites In-room: a/c, Internet. In-hotel: restaurant, bar, pool, business center, parking, some pets allowed IOI No meals.

$$$$
HOTEL

The Colony. What distinguishes this legendary British colonial–style hotel is that it's only one block from Worth Avenue and one block from a beautiful beach on the Atlantic Ocean. **Pros:** close to shopping; rich history; lots of luxury. **Cons:** elevators are small; price tag is high. **TripAdvisor:** "the villas are beautiful," "a piece of paradise," "rooms although on the smaller size are bright and sunny." ⊠ *155 Hammon Ave.* ☎ *561/655–5430 or 800/521–5525* ⊕ *www.thecolonypalmbeach. com* 64 rooms, 16 suites, 3 penthouse suites, 7 2-bedroom villas with Jacuzzis In-room: a/c, Wi-Fi. In-hotel: restaurant, bar, pools, spa, business center, parking, some pets allowed IOI No meals.

$$$$
RESORT
★

Four Seasons Resort Palm Beach. Relaxed elegance is the watchword at this four-story resort, which sits on 6 acres with a delightful beach at the south end of town. **Pros:** outstanding restaurants; all rooms have balconies and ocean views; kids eat free; top-notch spa. **Cons:** far from nightlife; pricey. **TripAdvisor:** "perfect for families," "lacked the elegance," "recently renovated." ⊠ *2800 S. Ocean Blvd.* ☎ *561/582–2800 or 800/432–2335* ⊕ *www.fourseasons.com* 210 rooms, 13 suites In-room: a/c, Internet. In-hotel: restaurants, bars, tennis courts, pool, gym, spa, beach, children's programs, parking, some pets allowed IOI No meals.

$$$$
RESORT

The Omphoy Ocean Resort. From exotic ebony pillars in the lobby to bronze-infused porcelain tile floors and a lounge area with a row of gongs guests are welcome to bang on, this Zen-like boutique hotel has a sexy sophisticated look. **Pros:** Michelle Bernstein restaurant; rooms have ocean views and most have balconies. **Cons:** the infinity pool is surrounded by a parking lot and you have to walk through or around the hotel to get to the beach from it. **TripAdvisor:** "staff was proactive," "absolutely beautiful modern decor," "pricing was very good." ⊠ *2842 S. Ocean Blvd.* ☎ *561/540–6440 or 888/344–4321* ⊕ *www. omphoy.com* 134 rooms, 10 suites In-room: a/c, Wi-Fi. In-hotel: restaurants, bars, pool, gym, spa, beach, business center, parking, some pets allowed IOI No meals.

WEST PALM BEACH

Across the Intracoastal Waterway from Palm Beach.

Long considered Palm Beach's less-privileged stepsister, sprawling West Palm has evolved into an economically vibrant destination of its own, ranking as the cultural, entertainment, and business center of the entire county and territory to the north. High-rise buildings like the mammoth Palm Beach County Judicial Center and Courthouse and the State Administrative Building underscore the breadth of the city's governmental and corporate activity. The glittering Kravis Center for the Performing Arts is Palm Beach County's principal entertainment venue.

GETTING HERE AND AROUND

West Palm Beach is across the Intracoastal Waterway from Palm Beach. The city's Palm Tran buses run between Worth Avenue and Royal Palm Way in Palm Beach and major areas of West Palm Beach and require exact change. Regular fares are $1.50. Alternatively, share space with local lawyers and shoppers on the free and frequent Molly's Trolleys, which makes continuous loops down Clematis Street, the city's main street, and through CityPlace, a shopping-restaurant-theater district. Hop on and off at any of the seven stops. The trolleys run Sunday to Wednesday 11–9 and Thursday to Saturday 11–11.

ESSENTIALS

Transportation Contacts **Molly's Trolleys** (☏ *561/838–9511*).**Palm Tran** (☏ *561/841–4200*).

Visitor Information **Chamber of Commerce of the Palm Beaches** (✉ *401 N. Flagler Dr.* ☏ *561/833–3711*).**Palm Beach County Convention & Visitors Bureau** (✉ *1555 Palm Beach Lakes Blvd., Suite 800* ☏ *561/233–3000*).

EXPLORING

With the $154 million City Center municipal and library complex and a $30 million waterfront complex with piers, a pavilion and a beach, downtown West Palm has an attractive, easy-to-walk downtown area. Along five blocks of beautifully landscaped Clematis Street, which ends at the Intracoastal Waterway and the new waterfront complex, are boutiques and outdoor cafés, plus the 400-seat Cuillo Centre for the Arts, which features shows and concerts; and Palm Beach Dramaworks, an intimate theater that often shows new plays. An exuberant nightlife has taken hold of the area. In fact, downtown rocks every Thursday from 6 pm on with Clematis by Night, a celebration of music, dance, art, and food at Centennial Square. Even on downtown's fringes there are sights of cultural interest.

West Palm Beach's outskirts, flat stretches lined with fast-food outlets and car dealerships, may not inspire, but are worth driving through to reach attractions scattered around the city's southern and western reaches. Several sites are especially rewarding for children and other animal and nature lovers.

The Armory Art Center in West Palm Beach helps students of all ages create works or art in various media.

DOWNTOWN

Ann Norton Sculpture Gardens. This monument to the late American sculptor Ann Weaver Norton, second wife of Norton Museum founder Ralph H. Norton, includes a complex of art galleries in the main house and studio, plus 2½ acres of gardens, where you'll find 300 varieties of palm trees, seven granite figures, and six brick megaliths. The plantings were designed to attract native birds. Call ahead—hours sometimes vary. ⊠ *253 Barcelona Rd.* ☎ *561/832–5328* ⊕ *www.ansg.org* ✉ *$5* ⊙ *Wed.–Sun. 10–4.*

Armory Art Center. Built by the WPA in 1939, the facility is now a non-profit art school hosting rotating exhibitions and art classes throughout the year. ⊠ *1700 Parker Ave.* ☎ *561/832–1776* ⊕ *www.armoryart.org* ✉ *Free* ⊙ *Weekdays 10–4, weekends 10–2.*

Currie Park. Frequent weekend festivals, including an annual celebration of seafood, take place at the scenic city park next to the Intracoastal Waterway. Sit on one of the piers and watch the yachts and fishing boats pass by. Put on your jogging shoes—the park is at the north end of a 6.3-mi biking-jogging-skating path. ⊠ *N. Flagler Dr. at 23rd St.*

Fodor's Choice
★

Norton Museum of Art. Constructed in 1941 by steel magnate Ralph H. and Elizabeth Norton, the museum has an extensive collection of 19th- and 20th-century American and European paintings—including works by Picasso, Monet, Matisse, Pollock, and O'Keeffe—and Chinese, contemporary, and photographic art. There are a sublime outdoor covered loggia, Chinese bronze and jade sculptures, and a library. Galleries, including the Great Hall, also showcase traveling exhibits. There's a good museum store, and lectures, programs, and concerts for children

A GOOD TOUR: WEST PALM BEACH

Head south from downtown and turn right on Southern Boulevard, left onto Parker Avenue, and right onto Summit Boulevard to reach the Palm Beach. In the same area (turn right onto Dreher Trail) and also appealing to kids, the South Florida Science Museum, with its Aldrin Planetarium and McGinty Aquarium, is full of hands-on exhibits. If a quick game of croquet intrigues you, head to the National Croquet Center, less than 2 mi from the museum, by turning onto Summit Boulevard from Dreher Trail north and proceeding to Florida Mango Road, where you will turn left. Backtrack to Summit Boulevard and go west to the 150-acre Pine Jog Environmental Education Center. For more natural adventures, head farther west on Summit until you reach Forest Hill Boulevard,

where you turn right to reach the Okeeheelee Nature Center and its miles of wooded trails. Now retrace your route to Summit Boulevard, drive east until you reach Military Trail, and take a left. Drive north to Southern Boulevard and turn west to reach Lion Country Safari, a 500-acre cageless zoo. For the last stop on this tour, backtrack to Military Trail and travel north to the Mounts Botanical Gardens.

TIMING
Tailor your time based on specific interests, because you could easily spend most of a day at any of these attractions. Prepare yourself for heavy rush-hour traffic, and remember that sightseeing in the morning (not *too* early, to avoid rush hour) will be less congested.

and adults. ■TIP➔ One of the city's best-kept secrets is this museum's Café 1451, with its artfully presented dishes that taste as good as they look. ✉ *1451 S. Olive Ave.* ☎ *561/832–5196* ⊕ *www.norton.org* 🎫 *$12* ⊙ *Tues.–Sat. 10–5, Sun. 1–5.*

Palm Beach Photographic Centre. Fatima NeJame, who started the center in Delray Beach in 1977, achieved her dream of a larger exhibition center by moving it to the City Hall complex in West Palm Beach in 2009. The bright spacious gallery is devoted to photography. The second floor is reserved for classes and has a large photo studio, but, with the digital age in mind, no darkroom. ✉ *415 Clematis St.* ☎ *561/253–2600* ⊕ *www.workshop.org* 🎫 *Free* ⊙ *Mon.–Thurs. 10–7, Fri. and Sat. 10–5, Sun. 1–5.*

AWAY FROM DOWNTOWN
TOP ATTRACTIONS

Lion Country Safari. Drive your own vehicle along 8 mi of paved roads through a 500-acre cageless zoo with a thousand free-roaming animals. Lions, elephants, white rhinos, giraffes, zebras, antelopes, chimpanzees, and ostriches are among the wild things in residence. Lions are fenced away from roads, but there's a good chance you'll have a giraffe or two nudging at your window. Exhibits include the Kalahari, designed after a South African bush plateau and containing water buffalo and nilgai (the largest type of Asian antelope), and the Gir Forest, modeled after a game forest in India and showcasing a pride of lions. (For obvious reasons, no convertibles or pets are allowed.) A walk-through area has bird feeding and a petting zoo. You can also take a pontoon-boat tour, go paddleboating, play miniature golf, or send the kids off to the play area with rides and sports fields. There's also a restaurant and a snack shop. ☒ *2003 Lion Country Safari Rd., at Southern Blvd. W, Loxa-hatchee* ☎ *561/793–1084* ⊕ *www.lioncountrysafari.com* ☒ *$26.50; $5 parking fee* ☉ *Daily 9:30–5:30; last entrance 4:30.*

★ **Mounts Botanical Gardens.** Take advantage of balmy weather by walk-ing among the tropical and subtropical plants here. Join a free tour or explore the 14 acres of exotic trees, rain-forest area, and butterfly and water gardens on your own. Many plants were significantly damaged during the 2004 and 2005 hurricanes, and new plantings will take years to reach maturity. There are lots of free brochures about tropical trees, flowers, and fruits in the main building. If you're feeling inspired, be sure to check out the gift shop's wide range of gardening books. ☒ *531 N. Military Trail* ☎ *561/233–1757* ⊕ *www.mounts.org* ☒ *Gardens: $5 suggested donation; tours $5* ☉ *Mon.–Sat. 8:30–4, Sun. noon–4.*

★ **National Croquet Center.** The world's largest croquet complex, the 10-acre center is also the headquarters for the U.S. Croquet Association. Vast expanses of manicured lawn are the stage for fierce competitions—in no way resembling the casual backyard games where kids play with wide wire wickets. There's also a clubhouse with a pro shop and Café Croquet, with verandas for dining and viewing, and a museum hall. You have to be a member, or a guest of a member, to reserve a lawn every day but Saturday, when lessons are free and lawns are open to all. ☒ *700 Florida Mango Rd., at Summit Blvd.* ☎ *561/478–2300* ⊕ *www. croquetnational.com* ☒ *Free admission; full day of play $25* ☉ *June–Sept., Tues.–Sat. 9–5; Oct.–May, daily 9–5.*

☺ **Palm Beach Zoo.** At this 23-acre wild kingdom there are more than 125 species of animals, from Florida panthers to the giant Aldabra tortoise. Here you'll find the country's first outdoor exhibit of Goeldi's mon-keys. The Tropics of America exhibit has 6 acres of rain forest plus an aviary, Maya ruins, and an Amazon River village. Also notable are a nature trail, the otter exhibit, a children's petting zoo, merry-go-round, interactive fountain and a restaurant overlooking the river. ☒ *1301 Summit Blvd.* ☎ *561/533–0887* ⊕ *www.palmbeachzoo.org* ☒ *$16.95* ☉ *Daily 9–5.*

WORTH NOTING

☺ **Okeeheelee Nature Center.** Explore 5 mi of trails through 90 acres of west-ern Palm Beach County's native pine flatwoods and wetlands. A visitor center gift shop has hands-on exhibits and offers guided walks by the center's volunteers. ☒ *7715 Forest Hill Blvd.* ☎ *561/233–1400* ☒ *Free* ☉ *Visitor center Tues.–Fri. 10–4:35, Sat. 8:15–4:30, Sun 10-4:30; trails daily dawn–dusk.*

☺ **Pine Jog Environmental Education Center.** The draw here is 135 acres of mostly undisturbed Florida pine flatwoods with 2½-mi of self-guided trails. Demonstration landscaping and interpretive signs around the Gold L.E.E.D. certified buildings teach kids about sustainable living. School groups use the trails during the week; special events include camping and campfires. The gift shop is closed on Saturday. Call for

2

an event schedule. ⊠ *6301 Summit Blvd.* ☎ *561/686–6600* ⊕ *www. pinejog.fau.edu* ⊠ *Free* ◷ *Weekdays 9–4, Sat. 9–2 (trails only).*

South Florida Science Museum. Here at the museum, which includes the Aldrin Planetarium and McGinty Aquarium, there are hands-on exhibits with touch tanks and laser shows with music by the likes of Dave Matthews. Galaxy Golf is a 9-hole science challenge. Weather permitting you can observe the heavens on Friday night through the most powerful telescope in South Florida. ⊠ *4801 Dreher Trail N* ☎ *561/832–1988* ⊕ *www.sfsm.org* ⊠ *$11.95, planetarium $4, laser show $10, galaxy golf $2* ◷ *Weekdays 10–5, Sat. 10–6, Sun. noon–6.*

OFF THE BEATEN PATH

Forty miles west of West Palm Beach, rimming the western edges of Palm Beach and Martin counties, **Lake Okeechobee,** the second-largest freshwater lake completely within the United States, is girdled by 120 mi of road yet remains shielded from sight for almost its entire circumference. Lake Okeechobee—the Seminole's Big Water and the gateway of the great Everglades watershed—measures 730 square mi, roughly 33 mi north–south, and 30 mi east–west, with an average natural depth of only 10 feet (flood control brings the figure up to 12 feet and deeper). Six major lock systems and 32 separate water-control structures manage the water. Encircling the lake is a 34-foot-high grassy levee—locals call it "the wall"—and the Lake Okeechobee Scenic Trail, a segment of the Florida National Scenic Trail, an easy flat ride for bikers. ■ TIP→ There's no shade, so wear a hat, sunscreen, and bug repellent. Be sure to bring lots of bottled water, too, because restaurants and stores are few and far between.

SPORTS AND THE OUTDOORS

GOLF

Palm Beach National Golf & Country Club. This classic course has 18 holes and a Joe Lee championship layout; greens fees $49/$75. The Joanne Carner Golf Academy is based here. ⊠ *7500 St. Andrews Rd., Lake Worth* ☎ *561/965–3381* ⊕ *www.palmbeachnational.com.*

SHOPPING

The free downtown trolley runs a continuous loop linking Clematis Street and CityPlace, so you won't miss a shop.

★ **Antique Row.** West Palm's "South Dixie Highway" is the destination for those who are interested in interesting home decor. From thrift shops to the most exclusive stores, it is all here—furniture, lighting, art, junk, fabric, frames, tile, and rugs. So if you're looking for an art deco, French-provincial, or Mizner pièce de résistance, big or small, schedule a few hours for an Antique Row stroll. You'll find bargains during the off-season (May to November). Antique Row runs north–south from Belvedere Road to Forest Hill Boulevard, although most stores are bunched between Belvedere Road and Southern Boulevard.

Clematis Street. If you're looking for a mix of food, art, performance, landscaping, and retailing, then head to renewed downtown West Palm around Clematis Street, which runs west-east from Dixie Highway to Flagler Drive and the new waterfront complex. Water-view parks with attractive gardens—and fountains where kids can cool off—add to the pleasure of browsing, window-shopping, and resting at an outdoor café. Hip national retailers such as Design Within Reach and the Jean Bar blend in with restaurants, pubs, and nightclubs.

CityPlace. The 55-acre, four-block-by-four-block commercial and residential complex centered on Rosemary Avenue attracts people of all ages to with restaurants, cafés, outdoor bars, a 20-screen Muvico, the Harriet Himmel Theater, and a 36,000-gallon dance, water, and light show. The dining, shopping, and entertainment are all family-friendly. Among CityPlace's stores are popular national retailers Macy's, Armani Exchange, Pottery Barn, Lucky Brand Jeans, Nine West, Sephora, BCBG Maxazria, Gap, Banana Republic, Anthropologie, and Restoration Hardware. There are also shops unique to Florida. Behind the punchy, brightly colored clothing in the front window of C. Orrico (☎ *561/832– 9203*) are family fashions and accessories by Lily Pulitzer. ⊠ *700 S. Rosemary Ave.* ☎ *561/366–1000* ⊕ *www.cityplace.com.*

NIGHTLIFE AND THE ARTS

NIGHTLIFE

Blue Martini. CityPlace comes alive at this bar, where eclectic music attracts a diverse crowd. ⊠ *550 S. Rosemary Ave.* ☎ *561/835–8601.*

Dr. Feelgood's Rock Bar & Grill. There are guitars hanging above the bar and a DJ booth made from a 1957 Chevy. Vince Neil, Mötley Crüe's lead singer, is the owner. ⊠ *219 Clematis St.* ☎ *561/833–6500.*

ER Bradley's Saloon. People of all ages congregate to hang out and socialize at this open-air restaurant and bar to gaze at the Intracoastal Waterway. ⊠ *104 Clematis St.* ☎ *561/833–3520.*

THE ARTS

Palm Beach Opera. Five productions, including the Vocal Competition Grand Finals, are staged from December to April at the Kravis Center with English translations projected above the stage. The family opera series includes matinee performances such as *Hansel & Gretel*; tickets are $20 to $165. ⊠ *415 S. Olive Ave.* ☎ *561/833–7888* ⊕ *www. pbopera.org.*

★ **Raymond F. Kravis Center for the Performing Arts.** This center stars amid the treasury of local arts attractions and the crown jewel is the 2,193-seat Dreyfoos Hall, a glass, copper, and marble showcase just steps from the restaurants and shops of CityPlace. The center also boasts the 300-seat Rinker Playhouse and the Gosman Amphitheatre, which holds 1,400 in seats and on the lawn. A packed year-round schedule unfolds here with drama, dance, and music. Kravis on Broadway features a blockbuster lineup of Broadway's biggest touring productions; Miami City Ballet, the Palm Beach Pops, and Florida Stage, a theater company that presents new and emerging plays, also perform here. ⊠ *701 Okeechobee Blvd.* ☎ *561/832–7469* ⊕ *www.kravis.org.*

WHERE TO EAT

$ ✕ **Havana**. Decorated with vintage travel posters of its namesake city,
CUBAN this two-level restaurant serves such authentic Cuban specialties as
roast-pork sandwiches and chicken slowly cooked in Spanish sauce.
Lunch and dinner dishes are enhanced by the requisite black beans
and rice. Open until 1 am Friday and Saturday, this friendly place
attracts a late-night crowd. The popular walk-up window serves strong
Cuban coffee, sugary fried churros, and fruit juices in exotic flavors like
mamey, mango, papaya, guava, and *guanabana*. ✉ *6801 S. Dixie Hwy.*
☎ *561/547–9799* ⊕ *www.havanacubanfood.com.*

$ ✕ **Howley's**. Since 1950 this diner's eat-in counter and "cooked in sight,
AMERICAN it must be right" motto has made a congenial setting for meeting old
friends and making new ones. Forgo the counter for the 1950s-style
tables or sit out on the patio. The café attracts a loyal clientele for breakfast, lunch, and dinner with such specialties as turkey and dressing,
burgers, and chicken salad. ✉ *4700 S. Dixie Hwy.* ☎ *561/833–5691.*

$$ ✕ **Il Bellagio**. In the center of CityPlace, this European-style bistro offers
ITALIAN Italian specialties and a wide variety of fine wines. The menu includes
classics like chicken parmigiana, risotto, and fettuccine Alfredo. Pizzas
from the wood-burning oven are especially tasty. Service is friendly and
efficient, but the overall noise level tends to be high. Sit at the outdoor
tables next to the main plaza's dancing fountains. ✉ *CityPlace, 600 S.
Rosemary Ave.* ☎ *561/659–6160* ⊕ *www.ilbellagiocityplace.com.*

¢ ✕ **Middle East Bakery**. This hole-in-the-wall Middle Eastern bakery, deli,
MEDITERRANEAN and market is packed at lunchtime with regulars who are on a first-name
basis with the gang behind the counter. From the nondescript parking
lot the place doesn't look like much, but inside, delicious hot and cold
Mediterranean treats await. Choose from traditional gyro sandwiches
and lamb salads with sides of grape leaves, tabbouleh, and couscous.
✉ *327 5th St., at Olive Ave.* ☎ *561/659–7322* ◔ *Closed Sun.*

WHERE TO STAY

For expanded hotel reviews, visit Fodors.com.

$$$ ▥ **Grandview Gardens Bed & Breakfast**. This 1923 Spanish-style bed-and-
B&B/INN breakfast, housed in a cheery yellow building, is conveniently located
★ next to Howard Park, across from the Armory Art Center, and a short
walk from the Convention Center, CityPlace, and the Kravis Center.
Pros: private entrances; pool; multilingual owners. **Cons:** not close to
the beach; steps to climb. **TripAdvisor:** "excellent upkeep," "everything
is charming," "pool is gorgeous." ✉ *1608 Lake Ave.* ☎ *561/833–9023*
⊕ *www.grandview-gardens.net* ⫝ *5 rooms, 1 cottage* ⌂ *In-room: a/c,
Internet. In-hotel: pool, parking* ⎝⎠ *Breakfast.*

$$$$ ▥ **Hampton Inn & Suites in Wellington**. The four-story hotel, about 10 mi
HOTEL west of downtown West Palm Beach, has the feeling of a ritzy clubhouse, with rich wood paneling, hunt prints, and elegant chandeliers.
Pros: complimentary hot breakfast; free high-speed Internet access;
near shopping. **Cons:** no restaurant. **TripAdvisor:** "great location for
concerts," "bed here was sumptuous," "nice pool and pool deck."
✉ *2155 Wellington Green Dr.* ☎ *561/472–9696* ⊕ *www.hamptoninn.*

com ⌐ *122 rooms, 32 suites* ⚇ *In-room: a/c, Wi-Fi. In-hotel: pool, gym* ⟦◯⟧ *Breakfast.*

$$$ ⌂ **Hotel Biba.** In the El Cid historic district, this 1940s-era motel has got-
HOTEL ten a fun stylish revamp from designer Barbara Hulanicki: each room
has a vibrant mélange of colors, along with handcrafted mirrors, mosaic
bathroom floors, and custom mahogany furnishings. **Pros:** cool design;
popular wine bar. **Cons:** water pressure is weak; bathrooms are tiny;
noisy when the bar is open late. **TripAdvisor:** "rooms are a bit small,"
"room smelled like mildew," "adorable little hotel." ⌧ *320 Belvedere
Rd.* ☎ *561/832–0094* ⊕ *www.hotelbiba.com* ⌐ *43 rooms* ⚇ *In-room:
a/c, Wi-Fi. In-hotel: bar, pool* ⟦◯⟧ *No meals.*

SOUTH TO BOCA RATON

Strung together by Route A1A, the towns between Palm Beach and
Boca Raton are notable for their variety, from high-rise condominiums
to small-town public beaches. In one town you'll find a cluster of art
galleries and fancy dining, and the very next town will yield mostly
hamburger joints and mom-and-pop stores.

LAKE WORTH

2 mi south of West Palm Beach, off I–95 or Federal Hwy.

For years, tourists looked here mainly for inexpensive lodging and easy
access to Palm Beach, since a bridge leads from the mainland to a barrier
island with Lake Worth's beach. Now Lake Worth has several blocks of
restaurants, nightclubs, shops, and art galleries, making this a worthy
destination on its own.

GETTING HERE AND AROUND

To drive to Lake Worth from West Palm Beach, drive 2 mi south on
Interstate 95 or Federal Highway.

ESSENTIALS

Visitor Information Lake Worth Chamber of Commerce (⌧ *501 Lake Ave.*
☎ *561/582–4401*).

EXPLORING

Museum of Polo & Hall of Fame. Start here for an introduction to polo. See
polo memorabilia, art, and a film on the history of the sport. ⌧ *9011
Lake Worth Rd.* ☎ *561/969–3210* ⊕ *www.polomuseum.com* ⌧ *Free*
☉ *May–Dec., weekdays 10–4; Jan.–Apr., weekdays 10–4, Sat. 10–2.*

WHERE TO EAT

¢ ✕ **Benny's on the Beach.** Perched on the Lake Worth Pier, Benny's has
AMERICAN diner-style food that's cheap and filling, but the spectacular view of
the sun glistening on the water and the waves crashing directly below
is what dining here is all about. Get here early—it doesn't serve din-
ner. ⌧ *10 Ocean Ave.* ☎ *561/582–9001* ⊕ *www.bennysonthebeach.com*
☉ *No dinner.*

$ ✕ **Bizaare Avenue Café.** Decorated with a mix of artwork and antiques,
ECLECTIC this cozy bistro, inspired by TV's *Friends,* fits right into downtown
Lake Worth's groovy, eclectic scene. Artwork and furnishings can be

The posh Palm Beach area has its share of luxury villas on the water; many are Mediterranean in style.

purchased. Daily specials are available on both the lunch and dinner menus, where crepes, pizzas, pastas, and salads are the staples. ⊠ *921 Lake Ave.* ☎ *561/588–4488* ⊕ *www.bizaareavecafe.com.*

$$$
ITALIAN ✕ **Paradiso.** Arguably downtown Lake Worth's finest Italian restaurant, this is the place to go for a romantic evening. Veal chops, seafood, cheese ravioli, and risotto are all good choices. Don't miss the chocolate Grand Marnier soufflé for dessert. As the name implies, the food is heavenly. ⊠ *625 Lucerne Ave.* ☎ *561/547–2500* ⊕ *www.paradisolakeworth.com.*

WHERE TO STAY

For expanded hotel reviews, visit Fodors.com.

$$$–$$$$
B&B/INN
★ 🏠 **Mango Inn.** It's only a 15-minute walk to the beach from this B&B dating from 1915. **Pros:** close to shops and restaurants; breakfasts served poolside; some suites have whirlpool tubs. **Cons:** some rooms are quite small. **TripAdvisor:** "beautifully landscaped garden and pool," "delicious breakfast," "relaxing retreat." ⊠ *128 N. Lakeside Dr.* ☎ *561/533–6900 or 888/626–4619* ⊕ *www.mangoinn.com* ⇲ *7 rooms, 3 suites, 1 cottage* ⌂ *In-room: a/c, kitchen, Internet. In-hotel: pool, some age restrictions* ⫶◯⫶ *Breakfast.*

$$$
B&B/INN
★ 🏠 **Sabal Palm House.** Built in 1936, this two-story B&B is a short walk from the Intracoastal Waterway, and each room is inspired by a different artist—including Renoir, Dalí, Norman Rockwell, and Chagall. **Pros:** fresh flowers in guest rooms; extra pillows; close to shops and restaurants. **Cons:** no pool. **TripAdvisor:** "professionally decorated," "breakfasts were memorable," "rooms are comfortable and quiet." ⊠ *109 N. Golfview Rd.* ☎ *561/582–1090 or 888/722–2572* ⊕ *www.*

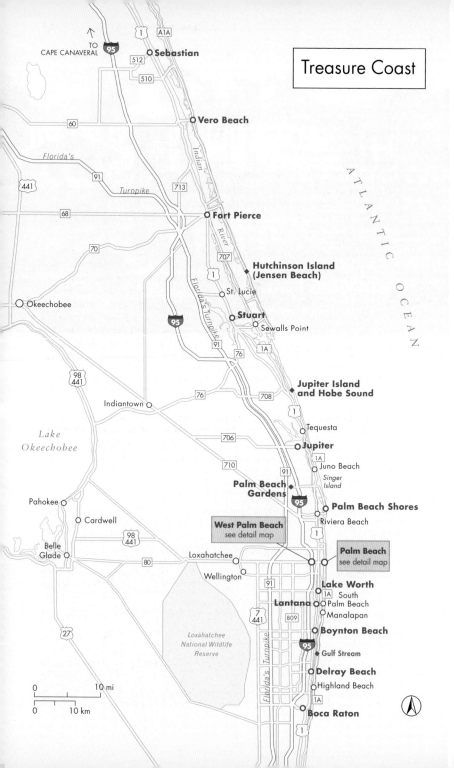

sabalpalmhouse.com ↻ *5 rooms, 2 suites* ⚭ *In-hotel: some pets allowed* ❙○❙ *Breakfast.*

LANTANA

2 mi south of Lake Worth, off I–95 or Federal Hwy.

Lantana—just a bit farther south from Palm Beach than Lake Worth—has inexpensive lodging and a bridge connecting the town to its own beach on a barrier island. Tucked between Lantana and Boynton Beach is **Manalapan,** a tiny but posh residential community.

ESSENTIALS

Visitor Information Lantana Chamber of Commerce (✉ *212 Iris Ave.* ☎ *561/585–8664*).

BEACHES

Lantana Public Beach. Ideal for sprawling, beachcombing, or power-walking, Lantana is also worthy for its proximity to one of the most popular food concessions in town, the **Dune Deck Café.** Here the choices are standard, but the food is particularly fresh and the portions are hearty. Try an omelet with a side of fries and melon wedges, Greek salad, homemade yogurt with seasonal fruit topped with honey, or a side of banana-nut bread. There are daily breakfast and lunch specials; dining is outdoors under yellow canopies perched over the beach. ✉ *100 N. Ocean Ave.* ☎ *561/582–0472* 🅿 *Parking $1.50 for 1 hr* ⊙ *Daily 9–4:45.*

SPORTS AND THE OUTDOORS

FISHING

B-Love Fleet. Three deep-sea fishing excursions depart daily: 8–noon, 1–5, and 6:30–10:30. No reservations are needed; just show up 30 minutes before the boat is scheduled to leave. The cost is $37 per person and includes fishing license, bait, and tackle. ✉ *314 E. Ocean Ave.* ☎ *561/588–7612.*

WHERE TO EAT AND STAY

For expanded hotel reviews, visit Fodors.com.

$$$
SEAFOOD
✕ **Old Key Lime House.** Overlooking the Intracoastal Waterway, the 1889 Lyman family house has grown in spurts over the years and its latest addition is the Manatee Observation Deck. This is an informal seafood house covered by a chickee hut built by the Seminole Indians. It's the largest viewing home for Gator Football. The panoramic water views are the main appeal here for adults—kids love to feed the fish and rock in the glider seats on the dock. Don't miss key lime pie—the house specialty was featured in *Bon Appetite* magazine. ✉ *300 E. Ocean Ave.* ☎ *561/533–5220* ⊕ *www.oldkeylimehouse.com.*

$$$
SEAFOOD
✕ **Station House.** The best Maine lobster in South Florida might well reside at this delicious dive, where all the seafood is cooked to perfection. Sticky seats and tablecloths are an accepted part of the scene, so don't wear your best duds. Although it's casual and family-friendly, reservations are recommended since it's a local favorite. Station Grill, across the street, is less seafood oriented but every "bite" as good.

✉ *233 Lantana Rd.* ☎ *561/547–9487* ⊕ *www.stationhouserestaurants. com* ⊗ *No lunch.*

$$$$ 🛎️ **Ritz-Carlton, Palm Beach.** A huge double-sided marble fireplace domi-
RESORT nates the elegant lobby of this hotel (which is actually in Manalapan)
★ and foreshadows the luxury of the guest rooms, which have richly
upholstered furnishings and marble tubs. **Pros:** gorgeous rooms; magnificent ocean views; shops across the street. **Cons:** not close to golf course;
15-minute drive to Palm Beach. **TripAdvisor:** "amazing spa," "way too
expensive," "rooms service views are all of the highest order." ✉ *100 S.
Ocean Blvd., Manalapan* ☎ *561/533–6000 or 800/241–3333* ⊕ *www.
ritz-carlton.com* ⤸ *310 rooms* ⚬ *In-room: a/c, Internet, Wi-Fi. In-hotel:
restaurants, bars, tennis courts, pools, spa, beach, water sports, children's programs, business center, parking* ¶⊙ *No meals.*

BOYNTON BEACH

3 mi south of Lantana, off I–95 or Federal Hwy.

In 1884, when fewer than 50 settlers lived in the area, Nathan Boynton, a Civil War veteran from Michigan, paid $25 for 500 acres with a
mile-long stretch of beachfront thrown in. How things have changed,
with today's population at about 118,000 and property values still on
an upswing. Far enough from Palm Beach to remain low-key, Boynton
Beach has two parts, the mainland and the barrier island—the town of
Ocean Ridge—connected by two bridges.

GETTING HERE AND AROUND

From Lantana, drive south 3 mi on Interstate 95 or south on Federal
Highway (U.S. 1) to reach Boynton Beach.

ESSENTIALS

Visitor Information Boynton Beach Chamber of Commerce (✉ *1880 N. Congress Ave., Suite 106* ☎ *561/732–9501*).

EXPLORING

Arthur R. Marshall–Loxahatchee National Wildlife Refuge. The most robust
part of the Everglades, this 221-square-mi refuge is one of three huge
water-retention areas accounting for much of the Everglades outside
the national park. These areas are managed less to protect natural
resources, however, than to prevent flooding to the south. Start from the
visitor center, where there is a marsh trail to a 20-foot-high observation
tower overlooking a pond. The boardwalk takes you through a dense
cypress swamp. There's also a 5½-mi canoe trail, best for experienced
canoeists since it's overgrown. Wildlife viewing is good year-round,
and you can fish for bass and panfish. ✉ *10216 Lee Rd., off U.S. 441
between Rte. 804 and Rte. 806* ☎ *561/734–8303* ⤸ *$5 per vehicle,
pedestrians $1* ⊗ *Daily sunrise–sunset; visitor center, weekdays 9–4,
weekends 9–4:30.*

ⓒ **Schoolhouse Children's Museum.** Boynton Beach's history is highlighted
★ through interactive exhibits that make the museum a kid-and-parent
pleaser. In this 1913 schoolhouse children can milk a mock cow or
pick and wash plastic vegetables at the Pepper Patch Farm. Kids can
buy tickets and dress up for a "time travel" train ride that immerses

them in Boynton's history. A great outdoor playground castle is adjacent to the museum. ⊠ *129 E. Ocean Ave.* ☎ *561/742–6780* ⊕ *www. schoolhousemuseum.org* ⊠ *$5* ☉ *Tues.–Sat. 10–5.*

BEACH

Boynton Beach Oceanfront Park. An inviting beach, boardwalk, concessions, grills, and playground await. ⊠ *6415 Ocean Blvd.* ☎ *No phone* ⊠ *Parking $10 per day* ☉ *Daily 7:30 am–11 pm.*

SPORTS AND THE OUTDOORS

FISHING

Arthur R. Marshall–Loxahatchee National Wildlife Refuge. West of Boynton Beach, fish the canal. There's a boat ramp, and the waters are decently productive, but bring your own equipment. ⊠ *10119 Lee Rd., off U.S. 441 between Rte. 804 and Rte. 806* ☎ *561/734–8303.*

Boynton Beach Inlet Pier. Here you can catch fish swimming between the Atlantic and Intracoastal Waterway. ⊠ *6990 N. Ocean Blvd.* ☎ *No phone.*

GOLF

Links at Boynton Beach. Find both an 18-hole course and 9-hole executive course; greens fees $27–$39 champion course, $39–$49 family course (rates vary with time of day; it's busier and costs more in the morning). ⊠ *8020 Jog Rd.* ☎ *561/742–6500.*

WHERE TO EAT

$ ✕ **Banana Boat.** A mainstay for local boaters who cruise up and down
AMERICAN the Intracoastal Waterway, Banana Boat is easily recognizable by the lighthouse on its roof. On weekends, casual crowds clad in tank tops, flip-flops, and bikinis dance to live island music while downing frozen drinks. The kitchen serves fish-and-chips, burgers, and ribs. ⊠ *739 E. Ocean Ave.* ☎ *561/732–9400* ⊕ *www.bananaboatboynton.com.*

DELRAY BEACH

2 mi south of Gulf Stream via I–95 or Federal Hwy.

A onetime artists' retreat with a small settlement of Japanese farmers, Delray has grown into a sophisticated beach town. Atlantic Avenue, the once dilapidated main drag, has evolved into a more-than-a-mile-long stretch of palm-dotted sidewalks, lined with stores, art galleries, and dining establishments. Running east–west and ending at the beach, it's a pleasant place for a stroll, day or night. Another active pedestrian way begins at the eastern edge of Atlantic Avenue and runs along the big, broad swimming beach that extends north to George Bush Boulevard and south to Casuarina Road.

GETTING HERE AND AROUND

To get to Delray Beach from Boynton Beach, drive 2 mi south on Interstate 95 or Federal Highway (U.S. 1).

ESSENTIALS

Visitor Information Delray Beach Chamber of Commerce (⊠ *64-A S.E. 5th Ave.* ☎ *561/278–0424*).

Morikami Museum and Japanese Gardens gives a taste of the Orient through its exhibits and tea ceremonies.

EXPLORING

Colony Hotel. The chief landmark along Atlantic Avenue since 1926 is this Mediterranean revival–style hotel, which is a member of the National Trust for Historic Preservation. Walk through the lobby to the parking lot of the hotel where original stable "garages" still stand—relics of the days when hotel guests would arrive via horse and carriage. ⊠ *525 E. Atlantic Ave.* ☎ *561/276–4123.*

Fodor's Choice ★ **Morikami Museum and Japanese Gardens.** Out in the boonies west of Delray Beach seems an odd place to encounter the East, but this is exactly where you can find a cultural and recreational facility heralding the Yamato Colony of Japanese farmers. The on-site Cornell Café serves light Asian fare. If you don't get your fill of orchids, the American Orchid Society's 20,000-square-foot headquarters is across the street. ⊠ *4000 Morikami Park Rd.* ☎ *561/495–0233* ⊕ *www.morikami.org* 🏷 *$12* ⊙ *Tues.–Sun. 10–5.*

Old School Square Cultural Arts Center. Just off Atlantic Avenue is this cluster of several museums set in restored school buildings dating from 1913 and 1926. The **Cornell Museum of Art & History** offers ever-changing art exhibits. During its season, the **Crest Theatre** showcases performances by local and touring troupes in the restored 1925 Delray High School building. ⊠ *51 N. Swinton Ave.* ☎ *561/243–7922* ⊕ *www. oldschool.org* 🏷 *$6* ⊙ *Tues.–Sat. 10:30–4:30, Sun. 1–4:30.*

BEACHES

Delray Beach Municipal Beach. A scenic walking path follows the main stretch of this public beach, which stretches 2 mi, half of it supervised by lifeguards. Reefs off the coast are popular with divers. ⊠ *Atlantic Ave. at Rte. A1A*

★ **Seagate Beach.** Enjoy many types of water-sports rentals—sailing, kayaking, windsurfing, Boogie boarding, surfing, snorkeling—or scuba diving at a sunken Spanish galleon less than ½ mi offshore. ⊠ *½ mi south of Atlantic Ave. at Rte. A1A.*

SPORTS AND THE OUTDOORS

BIKING

There's a bicycle path in Barwick Park and a special oceanfront lane along Route A1A.

Richwagen's Bike & Sport. Rent bikes by the hour or day and they'll come along with locks, baskets, helmets, and maps. ⊠ *298 N.E. 6th Ave.* ☎ *561/276–4234.*

WATERSKIING

Lake Ida Park. You can water-ski whether you're a beginner or a veteran. The park has a boat ramp, a slalom course, and a trick ski course. ⊠ *2929 Lake Ida Rd.*

SHOPPING

Atlantic Avenue. This charming area, from Swinton Avenue east to the ocean, has maintained much of its small-town integrity. It showcases art galleries, shops, and restaurants.

Escentials Apothecaries. In the historic Colony Hotel, this shop is packed with all things good smelling for your bath, body, and home. ⊠ *533 Atlantic Ave.* ☎ *561/276–7070.*

Snappy Turtle. Mackenzie-Childs and Lilly Pulitzer mingle with other fun fashions for the home and family. ⊠ *1100 Atlantic Ave.* ☎ *561/ 276–8088.*

NIGHTLIFE

Boston's on the Beach. Groove to reggae on Monday night and live music from jazz to country to rock most other nights. ⊠ *40 S. Ocean Blvd.* ☎ *561/278–3364.*

Dada. Bands play in the living room of a historic house. It's a place where those who don't drink will also feel comfortable. ⊠ *52 N. Swinton Ave.* ☎ *561/330–3232.*

Delux. A young hip crowd dances all night long. ⊠ *16 E. Atlantic Ave.* ☎ *561/279–4792.*

WHERE TO EAT

$$$ ✗ **32 East.** Although restaurants come and go on a trendy street like
AMERICAN   Atlantic Avenue, 32 East remains one of the best restaurants in Delray
★   Beach. A daily menu of wood-oven pizzas, salads, soups, seafood, and meat is all based on what is fresh and plentiful. Dark-wood accents and dim lighting make this large restaurant seem cozy. There's a packed bar in front and an open kitchen in back. ⊠ *32 E. Atlantic Ave.* ☎ *561/276– 7868* ⊕ *www.32east.com* ☾ *No lunch.*

$$ BRITISH **Blue Anchor.** Yes, this pub was actually shipped from England, where it stood for 150 years in London's historic Chancery Lane. There it was a watering hole for famed Englishmen, including Winston Churchill. The Delray Beach incarnation has stuck to authentic British pub fare. Chow down on a ploughman's lunch (a chunk of Stilton cheese, a hunk of bread, and pickled onions), shepherd's pie, fish-and-chips, and bangers and mash (sausages with mashed potatoes). Don't be surprised to find a rugby game on TV. English beers and ales are on tap and by the bottle. It's a late-night place open until at least 2. Classic rock and swing music are featured on Thursday nights. ✉ *804 E. Atlantic Ave.* ☎ *561/272–7272* 🌐 *www.theblueanchor.com.*

¢ AMERICAN ★ **Old School Bakery.** This place concentrates on sandwich making at its best. Particularly worthy is the cherry chicken salad sandwich with Brie on multigrain. Apart from sandwiches and soups served for lunch every day, order from a diverse baked-goods menu with artisan breads, pastries, several kinds of cookies, and even biscotti. The bakery is primarily takeout, but there are a few small tables in an adjacent open-air courtyard. ✉ *814 E. Atlantic Ave.* ☎ *561/243–8059.*

WHERE TO STAY

For expanded hotel reviews, visit Fodors.com.

$$$ HOTEL **Colony Hotel & Cabana Club.** In the heart of downtown Delray, this charming building dates back to 1926. **Pros:** great location; close to restaurants; shuttle to the beach. **Cons:** pool is a car or tram ride away at the beach club; breakfast buffet servings are repetitious. **TripAdvisor:** "charming but could do with some updates," "beautifully decorated lobby," "historic gem." ✉ *525 E. Atlantic Ave.* ☎ *561/276–4123 or 800/552–2363* 🌐 *www.thecolonyhotel.com* *69 rooms* *In-room: a/c, Internet, Wi-Fi. In-hotel: bar, pool, beach, parking* *Breakfast.*

$$$$ HOTEL **Delray Beach Marriott.** By far the largest property in Delray Beach, this five-story hotel has a stellar location at the east end of Atlantic Avenue. **Pros:** great location; near nightlife; luxurious spa. **Cons:** sprawling resort; chain-hotel feel; service can be impersonal. **TripAdvisor:** "nice and comfortable," "defines casual elegance," "great location." ✉ *10 N. Ocean Blvd.* ☎ *561/274–3200* 🌐 *www.delraybeachmarriott.com* *269 rooms, 84 suites* *In-room: a/c, Wi-Fi. In-hotel: restaurants, bars, pool, gym, spa, beach, laundry facilities, parking* *No meals.*

$$$ B&B/INN ★ **Sundy House.** Just about everything in this bungalow-style B&B is executed to perfection. **Pros:** beautiful property; excellent restaurant; quiet area. **Cons:** not on the beach. **TripAdvisor:** "nice but expected more," "found the value to be incredible," "unique place for brunch." ✉ *106 Swinton Ave.* ☎ *561/272–5678 or 877/434–9601* 🌐 *www.sundyhouse.com* *11 rooms* *In-room: Wi-Fi. In-hotel: restaurant, bar, pool* *Breakfast.*

BOCA RATON

6 mi south of Delray Beach, off I–95.

Less than an hour south of Palm Beach and anchoring the county's south end, upscale Boca Raton has much in common with its fabled cousin. Both reflect the unmistakable architectural influence of Addison

2

Mizner, their principal developer in the mid-1920s. The meaning of the name Boca Raton (pronounced boca rah-*tone*) often arouses curiosity, with many folks mistakenly assuming it means "rat's mouth." Historians say the probable origin is Boca Ratones, an ancient Spanish geographical term for an inlet filled with jagged rocks or coral. Miami's Biscayne Bay had such an inlet, and in 1823 a mapmaker copying Miami terrain confused the more northern inlet, thus mistakenly labeling this area Boca Ratones. No matter what, you'll know you've arrived in the heart of downtown when you spot the town hall's gold dome on the main street, Federal Highway.

GETTING HERE AND AROUND

To get to Boca Raton from Delray Beach, drive south 6 mi on Interstate 95 or Federal Highway (U.S. 1).

TOURS **Boca Raton Historical Society.** Trolley tour city sites on Thursday. The tours are seasonal; call for information. ⊠ *71 N. Federal Hwy.* ☎ *561/395–6766* ⊕ *www.bocahistory.org.*

ESSENTIALS

Visitor Information Boca Raton Chamber of Commerce (⊠ *1800 N. Dixie Hwy.* ☎ *561/395–4433*).

EXPLORING

2 East El Camino Real. Built in 1925 as the headquarters of the Mizner Development Corporation, this is an example of Mizner's characteristic Spanish-revival architectural style, with its wrought-iron grilles and handmade tiles. As for Mizner's grandiose vision of El Camino Real, the architect-promoter once prepared brochures promising a sweeping wide boulevard with Venetian canals and arching bridges. Camino Real is attractive, heading east to the Boca Raton Resort & Club, but don't count on feeling like you're in Venice. ⊠ *2 E. Camino Real.*

☺ ★ **Boca Raton Museum of Art.** An interactive children's gallery and changing exhibition galleries showcase internationally known artists at this museum in a spectacular building in the Mizner Park shopping center. The permanent collection upstairs includes works by Picasso, Degas, Matisse, Klee, and Modigliani, as well as notable pre-Columbian art. ⊠ *501 Plaza Real* ☎ *561/392–2500* ⊕ *www.bocamuseum.org* ☞ *$8* ☾ *Tues. 10–5, Wed. 10–9, Thurs. and Fri. 10–7, Sat. noon–7, Sun. noon–5.*

☺ **Children's Science Explorium.** This hands-on science center offers interactive exhibits, programs, and camps designed to enhance 5- to 12-year-old explorers' understanding of everyday physical sciences. The Explorium is in Sugar Sand Community Center. ⊠ *300 S. Military Trail* ☎ *561/347–3912* ⊕ *www.scienceexplorium.org* ☞ *Suggested donaton: $5* ☾ *Weekdays 9–6, weekends 10–5.*

☺ **Gumbo Limbo Nature Center.** A big draw for kids, this nifty nature center has four huge saltwater tanks brimming with sea life—from coral to stingrays—and a boardwalk through dense forest with a 40-foot tower you can climb to overlook the tree canopy. In spring and early summer, staffers lead nocturnal turtle walks: you can watch nesting females come ashore and lay eggs. (Purchase tickets in advance; see Web site for details.) A great hiking spot, the park has a sturdy boardwalk and a 40-foot observation tower. Spend a little time there and you're likely to see brown pelicans and osprey. Kids love the aquariums, insect tanks, and the butterfly garden. ⊠ *1801 N. Ocean Blvd.* ☎ *561/338–1473* ⊕ *www.gumbolimbo.org* ⊠ *Free but $3 donation suggested; turtle walks $5* ⊙ *Mon.–Sat. 9–4, Sun. noon–4; turtle walks May–July, Mon.–Thurs. 9 pm–midnight.*

Old Floresta. This residential area was developed by Addison Mizner starting in 1925 and landscaped with palms and cycads. It includes houses that are mainly Mediterranean in style, many with balconies supported by exposed wood columns. Home tours are held twice a year. ⊠ *Behind Boca Raton Art School on Palmetto Park Rd.*

BEACHES

Red Reef Park. The beach comes with a playground, picnic tables, and grills. The reef is close to shore, so this is a good snorkeling spot. ⊠ *1400 N. Rte. A1A.*

South Beach Park. This pretty stretch of sand is popular with sunbathers. ⊠ *400 N. Rte. A1A.*

Spanish River Park. In addition to its beach, the park has picnic tables, grills, and a large playground. ⊠ *3001 N. Rte. A1A.*

SPORTS AND THE OUTDOORS

BOATING

Palm Breeze Charters. For the thrill of blasting across the water at up to 80 mph, choose a trip from the variety of weekly cruises and boat charters. ⊠ *107 E. Palmetto Park Rd., Suite 330* ☎ *561/368–3566.*

GOLF

Boca Raton Resort & Club. Visit two championship courses and the Dave Pelz Golf School at this country club. Greens fees are $214, including a cart with GPS. ⊠ *501 E. Camino Real* ☎ *561/447–3078.*

SHOPPING

★ **Mizner Park.** This distinctive 30-acre shopping center intersperses apartments and town houses among its gardenlike retail and restaurant spaces. Some three dozen stores, including national and local retailers, mingle with fine restaurants, sidewalk cafés, galleries, a movie theater, a museum, and an amphitheater. ⊠ *Federal Hwy., 1 block north of Palmetto Park Rd.*

NIGHTLIFE

Rustic Cellar. Warm and intimate, this is perhaps the best wine bar in Palm Beach County. More than 300 hand-selected vintages from across the globe are served. ⊠ *409 S.E. Mizner Blvd., Royal Palm Place, Boca Raton* ☎ *561/392–5237* ⊕ *www.rusticcellar.com.*

WHERE TO EAT

$$$$
AMERICAN

✕ **Racks Downtown Eatery & Tavern.** Whimsical indoor–oudoor decor and comfort food with a twist help define this popular eatery in tony Mizner Park. Instead of dinner rolls, pretzel bread and mustard get things started. Share plates like house-smoked salmon bits and sea bass lettuce cups to promote convivial social dining. Happy hour is 4–7 and offers half-price drinks and appetizers. ⊠ *402 Plaza Real, Mizner Park Boca Raton* ☎ *561/395–1662* ⊕ *www.grrestaurant.com.*

$$$

ITALIAN

✗ **Tiramisu.** The food is an extravaganza of taste treats; veal chops, tuna, and anything with mushrooms draw raves, but count on hearty fare rather than a light touch. Start with the portobello mushroom with garlic or the Corsican baby sardines in olive oil. For a main course, try ricotta ravioli; scaloppine of veal stuffed with crabmeat, lobster, and Gorgonzola; or Tuscan fish stew. Enjoy it all in an intimate setting as Andrea Bocelli music plays in the background. ⊠ *170 W. Camino Real* ☎ *561/338–9692* ☾ *No lunch.*

$$$$

SEAFOOD

✗ **Truluck's.** This popular chain is so serious about seafood that it boasts its own fleet of 16 boats. Stone crabs are the signature dish, and you can have all you can eat on Monday night from December to May. Other recommended dishes include jalapeño salmon topped with blue crabmeat, hot-and-crunchy trout, crab cakes, and bacon-wrapped shrimp. Portions are huge, so you might want to make a meal of appetizers. The place comes alive each night with its popular piano bar. ⊠ *Mizner Park, 351 Plaza Real* ☎ *561/391–0755* ⊕ *www.trulucks.com.*

$$$

CHINESE

✗ **Uncle Tai's.** The draw at this upscale eatery is some of the best Szechuan food on Florida's east coast. Specialties include sliced duck with snow peas and water chestnuts in a tangy plum sauce, and orange beef delight—flank steak stir-fried until crispy and then sautéed with pepper sauce, garlic, and orange peel. They'll go easy on the heat on request. The service is quietly efficient. ⊠ *5250 Town Center Circle* ☎ *561/368–8806* ⊕ *www.uncle-tais.com* ☾ *No lunch Sun.*

WHERE TO STAY

For expanded hotel reviews, visit Fodors.com.

$$$$

RESORT

★

🛏 **Boca Raton Resort & Club.** Addison Mizner built this Mediterranean-style hotel in 1926, and additions over time have created a sparkling, sprawling resort with many lodging options. **Pros:** historical property; loaded with luxury; plenty of activities. **Cons:** all this luxury is costly; conventions crowd common areas. **TripAdvisor:** "tennis and spa facilities are excellent," "classic old world resort stay," "huge disappointment." ⊠ *501 E. Camino Real* ☎ *561/447–3000 or 800/327–0101* ⊕ *www.bocaresort.com* ⤵ *1,047 rooms, 134 suites, 60 2-bedroom bungalows* ♿ *In-room: a/c, kitchen (some), Wi-Fi. In-hotel: restaurants, bars, golf course, tennis courts, pools, gym, water sports, children's programs, parking* ⭐❙*No meals.*

$$$$

HOTEL

🛏 **Boca Raton Waterfront Bridge Hotel.** This boutique hotel on the Intracoastal Waterway has views of Lake Boca and the ocean that can't be beat, especially from Carmine's, the top-floor restaurant. **Pros:** great location; affordable rates; pet-friendly. **Cons:** can be noisy if you're near the bridge. **TripAdvisor:** "excellent value and location," "view was beautiful," "great view of the intercoastal." ⊠ *999 E. Camino Real* ☎ *561/368–9500 or 800/333–3333* ⊕ *www.bocaratonbridgehotel.com* ⤵ *121 rooms, 25 suites* ♿ *In-room: a/c, Internet. In-hotel: restaurants, bars, pool, gym, beach, laundry facilities, parking* ⭐❙*No meals.*

$

HOTEL

🛏 **Ocean Breeze Inn.** If golf is your game, this smaller resort is an excellent choice because guests can play the outstanding course at the adjoining Ocean Breeze Golf & Country Club, otherwise available only to club members. **Pros:** great spot for golfers; bargain rates. **Cons:** rooms are dated. ⊠ *5800 N.W. 2nd Ave.* ☎ *561/994–0400 or 800/344–6995* ⊕ *www.oceanbreezegolf.com* ↝ *46 rooms* ⓒ *In-room: a/c. In-hotel: restaurant, golf course, tennis courts, pool, laundry facilities, parking* ⏻ *No meals.*

THE TREASURE COAST

In contrast to the Gold Coast—as the Palm Beach/West Palm Beach area is known—is the more rural Treasure Coast, covering northernmost Palm Beach County, plus Martin, St. Lucie, and Indian River counties. Along the coast are barrier islands all the way to Sebastian and beyond. Inland there's cattle ranching in tracts of pine and palmetto scrub, along with sugar and citrus production. Shrimp farming uses techniques for acclimatizing shrimp from saltwater—land near seawater is costly—to freshwater, all the better to serve demand from restaurants popping up all over the region. Despite a growing number of malls and beachfront condominiums, much of the Treasure Coast remains largely blissfully undeveloped.

PALM BEACH SHORES

7 mi north of Palm Beach, on Singer Island.

Rimmed by mom-and-pop motels, this residential town is at the southern tip of Singer Island, across Lake Worth Inlet from Palm Beach. To travel between the two, however, you must cross over to the mainland before returning to the beach.

GETTING HERE AND AROUND

The best way to drive to Palm Beach Shores from West Palm Beach is to head 7 mi north on Interstate 95. Head east on Blue Heron Boulevard/Route 708 across the Intracoastal Waterway to Atlantic Avenue. Head south and you'll be in Palm Beach Shores.

ESSENTIALS

Visitor Information **Northern Palm Beach County Chamber of Commerce** (⊠ *800 N. U.S. 1, Jupiter* ☎ *561/746–7111* ⊕ *www.npbchamber.com*).

SPORTS AND THE OUTDOORS

Peanut Island. In the Intracoastal Waterway between Palm Beach Shores and Riviera Beach, this 79-acre island was opened in 1999 as a recreational park. There's a 20-foot-wide walking path surrounding the island, a 19-slip boat dock, a 170-foot T-shape fishing pier, six picnic pavilions, a visitor center, and 20 overnight campsites. The small **Palm Beach Maritime Museum** (☎ *561/832–7428*) is open daily except Friday and showcases the "Kennedy Bunker," a bomb shelter prepared for President John F. Kennedy. Call for tour hours. To get to the island, you can take a water taxi. ☎ *561/339–2504* ⊕ *www.pbmm.org* ✉ *$2 donation* ⊘ *Daily dawn–dusk for noncampers.*

Florida's Sea Turtles: The Nesting Season

From May to October it's turtle-nesting season all along the Florida coast. Female loggerhead, Kemp's ridley, and other species living in the Atlantic Ocean or Gulf of Mexico swim up to 2,000 mi to the Florida shore. By night they drag their 100- to 400-pound bodies onto the beach to the dune line. Then each digs a hole with her flippers, drops in 100 or so eggs, covers them up, and returns to sea.

The babies hatch about 60 days later. Once they burst out of the sand, the hatchlings must get to sea rapidly or risk becoming dehydrated from the sun or being caught by crabs, birds, or other predators.

Instinctively, baby turtles head toward bright light, probably because for millions of years starlight or moonlight reflected on the waves was the brightest light around, serving to guide hatchlings to water. But now light from beach development can lead the babies in the wrong direction, toward the street rather than the water. To help, many coastal towns enforce light restrictions during nesting months. Florida home owners are requested to dim their lights on behalf of baby sea turtles.

At night, volunteers walk the beaches, searching for signs of turtle nests. Upon finding telltale scratches in the sand, they cordon off the sites, so beachgoers will leave the spots undisturbed. Volunteers also keep watch over nests when babies are about to hatch and assist if the hatchlings get disoriented.

It's a hazardous world for baby turtles. They can die after eating tar balls or plastic debris, or they can be gobbled by sharks or circling birds. Only about one in a thousand survives to adulthood. After reaching the water, the babies make their way to warm currents. East Coast hatchlings drift into the Gulf Stream, spending years floating around the Atlantic.

Males never return to land, but when females attain maturity, in 15–20 years, they return to shore to lay eggs. Remarkably, even after migrating hundreds and even thousands of miles out at sea, most return to the very beach where they were born to deposit their eggs. Each time they nest, they come back to the same stretch of beach. In fact, the more they nest, the more accurate they get, until eventually they return time and again to within a few feet of where they last laid their eggs. These incredible navigation skills remain for the most part a mystery despite intense scientific study. To learn more, check out the Sea Turtle Survival League's and Caribbean Conservation Corporation's website at ⊕ www.cccturtle.org.

—Pam Acheson

2

FISHING

Sailfish Marina and Resort. Book a full or half day of deep-sea fishing for up to six people with the seasoned captains and large fleet of 28- to 60-foot boats. ⊠ *98 Lake Dr.* 🕾 *561/844–1724* ⊕ *www. sailfishmarina.com.*

WORD OF MOUTH

"Palm Beach Gardens is quiet and undiscovered. Lots of local golf. Very low key. It is convenient to Juno Beach—the most gorgeous Florida Beach with free beachside parking."   —LindaBrinck

WHERE TO EAT AND STAY
For expanded hotel reviews, visit Fodors.com.

$$

SEAFOOD

✕ **Sailfish Marina Restaurant.** This waterfront restaurant overlooking Peanut Island is a great place to chill out after a long day of mansion gawking, boating, or beach-bumming. Choose a table in the dining room or under an umbrella on the terrace and enjoy mainstays like conch chowder or grilled swordfish. More upscale entrées—this, after all, is still Palm Beach County—include lobster tail and baby sea scallops sautéed in garlic-and-lemon butter. Breakfast is a winner here, too. Sportfishing charters are available at Sailfish's store. ⊠ *98 Lake Dr.* 🕾 *561/842–8449* ⊕ *www.sailfishmarina.com.*

$$

HOTEL

🄷 **Sailfish Marina Resort.** This waterfront lodging has a marina with deep-water slips and accommodations that include motel-style rooms, efficiencies, and even a three-bedroom house. **Pros:** inexpensive rates; on the Intracoastal Waterway; water taxi stops here. **Cons:** can be noisy; area attracts a party crowd; dated rooms. **TripAdvisor:** "very dirty," "room rates were very reasonable," "very outdated." ⊠ *98 Lake Dr.* 🕾 *561/844–1724 or 800/446–4577* ⊕ *www.sailfishmarina.com* ⬎ *30 units* ⬧ *In-room: a/c, kitchen (some), Internet. In-hotel: restaurant, bar, pool, parking* 🍴 *No meals.*

PALM BEACH GARDENS

5 mi north of West Palm Beach, off I–95.

About 15 minutes northwest of Palm Beach is this relaxed, upscale residential community known for its high-profile golf complex, the PGA National Resort & Spa. Although not on the beach, the town is less than a 15-minute drive from the ocean.

GETTING HERE AND AROUND
To reach Palm Beach Shores from West Palm Beach, head north for 5 mi on Interstate 95.

ESSENTIALS
Visitor Information Northern Palm Beach County Chamber of Commerce (⊠ *800 N. U.S. 1, Jupiter* 🕾 *561/746–7111* ⊕ *www.npbchamber.com*).

SPORTS AND THE OUTDOORS
GOLF
PGA National Resort & Spa. If you're the kind of traveler who takes along a set of clubs, this is the place for you. The resort has five championship courses that are challenging enough for the pros. Among them are the Champion Course, designed by Tom Fazio and Jack Nicklaus (greens

fee $350); the General Course, designed by Arnold Palmer ($250); the Haig Course, the first course opened at the resort ($210); the Estate Course, with a practice range and putting green ($210); and the Tom Fazio–designed Squire Course ($210). Lessons are available at the Golf Digest Academy. ⊠ *1000 Ave. of the Champions* ☎ *561/627–1800.*

EN ROUTE

John D. MacArthur Beach State Park & Nature Center. Almost 2 mi of beach, good fishing and shelling, and one of the finest examples of subtropical coastal habitat remaining in southeast Florida are among the treasures here. To learn about what you see, take an interpretive walk to a mangrove estuary along the upper reaches of Lake Worth. The nature center, open daily 9–5, has exhibits on the coastal environment. ⊠ *10900 Rte. A1A, North Palm Beach* ☎ *561/624–6950* ⊕ *www.macarthurbeach.org* ☞ *$5 per vehicle, up to 8 people* ☉ *Daily 8–sundown.*

WHERE TO EAT

$$$
AMERICAN
★

✕**Café Chardonnay.** At the end of a strip mall, Café Chardonnay is surprisingly elegant. Soft lighting, warm woods, and cozy banquettes set the scene for a quiet lunch or romantic dinner. The place consistently receives praise for its innovative menu and outstanding wine list. Starters include wild-mushroom strudel and truffle-stuffed diver sea scallops. Entrées might include Gorgonzola-crusted filet mignon or pan-seared veal scaloppine with rock shrimp. ⊠ *4533 PGA Blvd.* ☎ *561/627–2662* ⊕ *www.cafechardonnay.com* ☉ *No lunch weekends.*

$$$
AMERICAN

✕**Ironwood Grille.** Chef Kenny Gilbert of TV's *Top Chef* oversees the kitchen at this contemporary eatery, located at the PGA National Resort & Spa. The menu features beef and seafood dishes made with locally grown organic produce. Choices include she-crab soup with sherry and grilled filet mignon. The chic lobby restaurant and the adjoining bar share an extensive wine cellar and a room for private wine tastings. On Thursday nights, a DJ plays music from 6 until 9. ⊠ *400 Ave. of the Champions* ☎ *561/627–2000* ⊕ *www.ironwoodgrille.com.*

$$
SEAFOOD

✕**Spoto's.** If you like oysters, head to this place where black-and-white photographs of oyster fisherman adorn the walls. The polished tables give the eatery a country club look. Spoto's serves up a delightful bowl of New England clam chowder and an impressive variety of oysters and clams. The prime-rib Caesar salad with crispy croutons never disappoints. Sit outside on the patio to take advantage of the area's perfect weather. ⊠ *4560 PGA Blvd.* ☎ *561/776–9448* ⊕ *www. spotosoysterbar.com.*

WHERE TO STAY

For expanded hotel reviews, visit Fodors.com.

$$$$
RESORT
★

⊡**PGA National Resort & Spa.** Golf draws in about 40% of the guests here, but the rest come for amenities, such as the extensive sports facilities, excellent dining, and 240-acre nature preserve. **Pros:** a golfer's paradise; short drive to shopping; large rooms. **Cons:** not on the beach. **TripAdvisor:** "classy," "great food," "upscale but great value for the money." ⊠ *400 Ave. of the Champions* ☎ *561/627–2000 or 800/633–9150* ⊕ *www.pgaresort.com* ⮑ *280 rooms, 59 suites* ☖ *In-room: a/c, kitchen (some), Wi-Fi. In-hotel: restaurants, bars, golf courses, tennis courts, pools, gym, spa, parking* ⦿ *No meals.*

Away from developed shorelines, Blowing Rocks Preserve on Jupiter Island lets you wander the dunes.

JUPITER

12 mi north of Palm Beach Shores via I–95 and Rte. 706.

Jupiter is one of the few little towns in the region not fronted by an island. Beaches here are part of the mainland, and Route A1A runs for almost 4 mi along the beachfront dunes and beautiful estates.

ESSENTIALS

Visitor Information Northern Palm Beach County Chamber of Commerce
(⊠ *800 N. U.S. 1, Jupiter* ☎ *561/746–7111* ⊕ *www.npbchamber.com*).

EXPLORING

★ **Jupiter Inlet Lighthouse.** Designed by Civil War hero General George Meade, this brick lighthouse has been operated by the Coast Guard since 1860. Tours of the 105-foot-tall landmark unfold every half hour. (Children must be at least 4 feet tall to go to the top.) There's a small museum that tells about efforts to restore this graceful spire to the way it looked from 1860 to 1918. ⊠ *500 Capt. Armour's Way, U.S. 1 and Beach Rd.* ☎ *561/747–8380* ⊕ *www.jupiterlighthouse.org* 🎫 *Tour $9* ⏲ *Tues.–Sun. 10–5; last tour at 4.*

BEACHES

Carlin Park. A beach is just one of the draws here. The park also has picnic pavilions, hiking trails, a baseball diamond, a playground, six tennis courts, and fishing sites. The Lazy Loggerhead Café, serving snacks and burgers, is open daily 9–5. ⊠ *A1A at Juno Beach* ☎ *561/799–0185* ⏲ *Daily dawn–dusk.*

Juno Beach. A 990-foot pier and a bait shop are the big draws here, but a section is available for surfing, and there's a snack bar, too. ⊠ *14775 S. Rte. A1A* ☎ *561/624–0065* ☼ *Daily dawn–dusk*.

SPORTS AND THE OUTDOORS

BASEBALL

Roger Dean Stadium. Both the St. Louis Cardinals and the Florida Marlins train at the 7,000-seat stadium. ⊠ *4751 Main St.* ☎ *561/775–1818*.

CANOEING

Canoe Outfitters of Florida. See animals, from otters to eagles, along 8 miles of the Loxahatchee River. Canoe or kayak rental for two to three hours is $25, including drop-off and pickup. ⊠ *9060 W. Indiantown Rd.* ☎ *561/746–7053*.

GOLF

Abacoa Golf Club. This 18-hole course is a good alternative to nearby private courses; greens fee $60/$119. ⊠ *105 Barbados Dr.* ☎ *561/ 622–0036*.

Golf Club of Jupiter. There are 18 holes of varying difficulty; greens fee $49/$69. ⊠ *1800 Central Blvd.* ☎ *561/747–6262*.

Jupiter Dunes Golf Club. Head for the 18-hole golf course named Little Monster and a putting green near the Jupiter River estuary; greens fee $36/$65. ⊠ *401 Rte. A1A* ☎ *561/746–6654*.

WHERE TO EAT

$$ ✕ **Food Shack**. This local favorite is a bit tricky to find, but worth the
SEAFOOD search. The fried-food standards you might expect at such a casual place are not found on the menu; instead there are fried-tuna rolls with basil and fried grouper cheeks with a fruity slaw. A variety of beers are fun to pair with the creatively prepared seafood dishes that include wahoo, mahimahi, and snapper. ⊠ *103 South U.S. 1* ☎ *561/741–3626* ⊕ *www. littlemoirsfoodshack.com* ☼ *Closed Sun*.

$$ ✕ **Guanabanas**. Expect a wait for dinner, which is not necessarily a bad
SEAFOOD thing at this island paradise of a waterfront restaurant and bar. Take the wait time to explore the bridges and trails of this open-air oasis and nibble on really good conch fritters. Try the lemon-butter hogfish for dinner and stick around for the live music. The waterfront eatery is next to the Jupiter Outdoor Center, where you can rent a kayak and burn some calories after lunch or breakfast. ⊠ *960 N. A1A, Jupiter* ☎ *561/747–8878* ⊕ *www.guanabanas.com*.

$$$ ✕ **Sinclair's Ocean Grill**. This popular spot in the Jupiter Beach Resort
SEAFOOD has sunlight streaming through the glass doors overlooking the pool. The menu has a daily selection of fresh fish, such as cashew-encrusted grouper, Cajun-spice tuna, and mahimahi with pistachio sauce. There are also thick juicy steaks—filet mignon is the house specialty—and chicken and veal dishes. The Sunday buffet is a big draw. ⊠ *5 N. Rte. A1A* ☎ *561/745–7120* ⊕ *www.jupiterbeachresort.com*.

$$ ✕ **Taste Casual Dining**. Located in the center of historic Hobe Sound, this
AMERICAN cozy dining spot with a pleasant, screened-in patio offers piano dinner music on Fridays and an occasional band on Saturday nights. Locals like to hang out at the old, English-style wine bar, but the food is the biggest draw here. Try a lobster roll and some Gorgonzola salad for lunch, and

prime rib or any fish dish for dinner. ✉ *11750 S.E. Dixie Hwy., Hobe Sound* ☎ *772/546–1129* ⊕ *www.tastehobesound.com.*

WHERE TO STAY

For expanded hotel reviews, visit Fodors.com.

$$$$ ⊞ **Jupiter Beach Resort.** This time-share resort has a 7,500-square-foot
RESORT spa and a nine-story tower filled with Caribbean-style rooms containing mahogany sleigh beds and armoires. **Pros:** fabulous views; good location; family-friendly. **Cons:** very high beds; pricey rates. ✉ *5 N. Rte. A1A* ☎ *561/746–2511 or 800/228–8810* ⊕ *www.jupiterbeachresort. com* ↘ *133 rooms, 44 suites* ⚒ *In-room: a/c, Wi-Fi. In-hotel: restaurants, bars, tennis court, pool, gym, spa, beach, water sports, laundry facilities, parking* |◎| *No meals.*

JUPITER ISLAND AND HOBE SOUND

5 mi north of Jupiter, off Rte. A1A.

Northeast across the Jupiter Inlet from Jupiter is the southern tip of Jupiter Island. Here expansive and expensive estates often retreat from the road behind screens of vegetation, and at the north end of the island turtles come to nest in a wildlife refuge. To the west, on the mainland, is the little community of Hobe Sound.

GETTING HERE AND AROUND

The best way to get to Jupiter Island and Hobe Sound from Jupiter is to drive north 5 mi on Interstate 95 to Indiantown Road. From there, head east to Federal Highway (U.S. 1), then north on U.S. 1.

EXPLORING

Blowing Rocks Preserve. Protected within this 73-acre preserve are plants native to beachfront dune, coastal strand (the landward side of the dunes), mangrove forests, and tropical hardwood forests. The best time to visit is when high tides and strong offshore winds coincide, causing the sea to blow spectacularly through holes in the eroded outcropping. Park in the lot; police ticket cars parked along the road. ✉ *574 S. Beach Rd., Rte. 707, Jupiter Island* ☎ *561/744–6668* ☒ *$2* ☉ *Daily 9–4:30.*

Hobe Sound National Wildlife Refuge. Two tracts make up this refuge: 232 acres of sand-pine and scrub-oak forest in Hobe Sound, and 735 acres of coastal sand dune and mangrove swamp on Jupiter Island. Trails are open to the public in both places. Turtle's nest and shells wash ashore on the 3½-mi-long beach, which has been severely eroded by high tides and strong winds. ✉ *13640 S.E. Federal Hwy., Hobe Sound* ☎ *772/546–6141* ☒ *$5 per vehicle* ☉ *Daily dawn–dusk.*

☂ **Hobe Sound Nature Center.** It's located in the Hobe Sound National Wildlife Refuge, but this nature center is an independent organization. Its museum, which has baby alligators and crocodiles and a scary-looking tarantula, is a child's delight. A ½-mi trail winds through a forest of sand pine and scrub oak—one of Florida's most unusual and endangered plant communities. It lost its original building in 2004 due to hurricanes and moved into a new building in 2007. A new visitor center opened in 2009. ✉ *13640 S.E. Federal Hwy., Hobe Sound* ☎ *772/546–2067*

⊕ *www.hobesoundnaturecenter.com* ⊠ *Donation suggested* ⊙ *Trail daily dawn–dusk; nature center weekdays 9–3.*

Jonathan Dickinson State Park. From Hobe Mountain, an ancient dune topped with a tower, you are treated to a panoramic view of this park's 10,285 acres of varied terrain and the Intracoastal Waterway. The Loxahatchee River, which cuts through the park, is home to manatees in winter and alligators all year. Two-hour boat tours of the river depart daily at 9, 11, 1, and 3 and cost $20 per person. Among amenities are a dozen cabins for rent, tent sites, bicycle and hiking trails, a campground, and a snack bar. ⊠ *16450 S.E. Federal Hwy., Hobe Sound* ☎ *772/546–2771* ⊠ *$6 per vehicle* ⊙ *Daily 8–dusk.*

SPORTS AND THE OUTDOORS
OUTFITTER
Jonathan Dickinson's River Tours. Boat tours of the Loxahatchee River are offered, as are canoe, kayak, and boat rentals from 9 to 5 daily. ⊠ *Jonathan Dickinson State Park, 16450 S.E. Federal Hwy., Hobe Sound* ☎ *561/746–1466.*

STUART

7 mi north of Hobe Sound.

This compact little town on a peninsula that juts out into the St. Lucie River has a remarkable amount of shoreline for its size and also has a charming historic district. The ocean is about 5 mi east.

GETTING HERE AND AROUND
To get to Stuart from Jupiter and Hobe Sound, drive north on Federal Highway (U.S. 1).

ESSENTIALS
Visitor Information **Stuart Main Street** (⊠ *201 S.W. Flagler Ave.* ☎ *772/286–2848*).**Stuart/Martin County Chamber of Commerce** (⊠ *1650 S. Kanner Hwy.* ☎ *772/287–1088*).

EXPLORING
Strict architectural and zoning standards guide civic-renewal projects. Stuart has antiques shops, restaurants, and more than 50 specialty shops within a two-block area. A self-guided walking-tour pamphlet is available at assorted locations downtown to clue you in on this once-small fishing village's early days.

★ **Maritime & Yachting Museum.** Linking the watery past with a permanent record of maritime and yachting events contributing to Treasure Coast lore, this museum near a marina has many old ships as well as historic exhibits to explore. Among those leading Saturday tours is a retired ship captain who has many interesting stories to share. ⊠ *1707 N.E. Indian River Dr.* ☎ *772/692–1234* ⊕ *www.mcbmfl.org* ⊠ *$5* ⊙ *Mon.– Sat. 10–5, Sun. 1–5.*

BEACHES

Stuart Beach. With its ever-vigilant lifeguards, this is a good spot for beginning surfers. More experienced wave riders enjoy the challenges of the choppy waters. Fishing and shelling are also draws. ⊠ *801 N.E. Ocean Blvd.* ☎ *772/221–1418.*

SPORTS AND THE OUTDOORS

FISHING

Sailfish Marina. Nab a deep-sea charter here. ⊠ *3565 S.E. St. Lucie Blvd.* ☎ *772/221–9456.*

SHOPPING

More than 60 restaurants and shops with antiques, art, and fashion have opened downtown along Osceola Street.

B&A Flea Market. Operating for more than two decades the oldest and largest such enterprise on the Treasure Coast has a street-bazaar feel, with shoppers happily scouting for the practical and unusual. ⊠ *2885 S.E. Federal Hwy.* ☎ *772/288–4915* 🎟 *Free* ⊘ *Weekends 8–3.*

THE ARTS

Lyric Theatre. On the National Register of Historic Places, this theater has been revived for live performances. A gazebo has free music performances. ⊠ *59 S.W. Flagler Ave.* ☎ *772/286–7827* ⊕ *www.lyrictheatre.com.*

WHERE TO EAT AND STAY

For expanded hotel reviews, visit Fodors.com.

$$
\begin{array}{l}
\end{array}
$$

$$ · **✕ Courtine's.** A husband-and-wife team oversees this quiet and hospitable restaurant under the Roosevelt Bridge. French and American influences are clear in the Swiss chef's dishes, from rack of lamb with Dijon mustard to grilled filet mignon stuffed with Roquefort and fresh spinach. The formal dining room has subtly elegant touches, such as fresh flowers on each table. A more casual menu is available at the bar. ⊠ *514 N. Dixie Hwy.* ☎ *772/692–3662* ⊕ *www.courtines.com* ⊘ *Closed Sun. and Mon. No lunch.*

FRENCH

$$ · **✕ Finz Waterfront Grille.** Located on the southern end of the Manatee Pocket in Port Salerno, the popular island-style restaurant is surrounded by boatyards and a lively gallery scene. Sit on the covered dock and take in the breeze while eating the tastiest crab cakes south of Chesapeake Bay. The kitchen also serves up savory teriyaki-marinated steak tips, Maryland crab soup, peel-and-eat shrimp, and maple-glazed salmon. There's live island music on Sunday afternoons 2–5 and entertainment every weekend night. ⊠ *4290 S.E. Salerno Rd.* ☎ *772/283–1929* ⊕ *www.finzwaterfrontgrille.com.*

SEAFOOD

$$$ · 🏨 **Pirate's Cove Resort & Marina.** On the banks of the St. Lucie River, this cozy enclave is the perfect place to recoup after a day at sea. The resort is relaxing and casual but packed with plenty of recreational activities. **ros:** pretty location; great for boaters. **Cons:** lounge gets noisy at night. **TripAdvisor:** "nice funky little place," "would definitely recommend," "good value friendly service." ⊠ *4307 S.E. Bayview St., Port Salerno* ☎ *772/287–2500 or 800/332–1414* ⊕ *www.piratescoveresort.net* ⟿ *48 rooms, 2 suites* ⚇ *In-room: a/c, Wi-Fi. In-hotel: restaurant, bar, pool, parking* 🍽 *Breakfast.*

RESORT

HUTCHINSON ISLAND (JENSEN BEACH)

5 mi northeast of Stuart.

The down-to-earth town of Jensen Beach, occupying the core of the island, stretches across both sides of the Indian River. Between late April and August more than 600 turtles come here to nest along the town's Atlantic beach. Area residents have taken pains to curb the runaway development that has created the commercial crowding found to the north and south, although some high-rises have popped up along the shore.

GETTING HERE AND AROUND

The best way to reach Jensen Beach from Stuart is to drive north on Federal Highway (U.S. 1) to Northwest Jensen Boulevard, then east on Jensen Beach Boulevard.

ESSENTIALS

Visitor Information **Jensen Beach Chamber of Commerce** (✉ *1900 N.E. Ricou Terr., Jensen Beach* ☎ *772/334–3444*).

EXPLORING

Elliott Museum. This pastel-pink museum was erected in 1961 in honor of Sterling Elliott, inventor of an early automated-addressing machine and a four-wheel cycle. The museum, with its antique cars, dolls, toys, and vintage baseball cards, is a nice stop for anyone fond of nostalgic goods. There are also antique fixtures from an early general store, blacksmith shop, and apothecary shop. ✉ *825 N.E. Ocean Blvd., Jensen Beach* ☎ *772/225–1961* ⊕ *www.elliottmuseumfl.org* ☞ *$8* ☾ *Mon.–Sat. 10–4, Sun. 1–4.*

★ **Florida Oceanographic Coastal Center.** Explore a ½-mi interpretive boardwalk through coastal hardwood and mangrove forest. Guided nature walks through trails and stingray feedings are offered at various times during the day. Dolphins, manatees, and turtles are often seen on the boat tour, for which reservations are required. ✉ *890 N.E. Ocean Blvd., Jensen Beach* ☎ *772/225–0505* ⊕ *www.floridaoceanographic.org* ☞ *$8* ☾ *Mon.–Sat. 10–5, Sun. noon–4; guided nature walks Mon.–Sat. 11 and 3, Sun. at 2.*

Gilbert's House of Refuge Museum. Built in 1875 on Hutchinson Island, the museum is the only remaining building of nine such structures built by the U.S. Life-Saving Service (a predecessor of the Coast Guard) to aid stranded sailors. Exhibits include antique lifesaving equipment, maps, artifacts from nearby wrecks, and boatbuilding tools. ✉ *301 S.E. MacArthur Blvd., Jensen Beach* ☎ *772/225–1875* ☞ *$6* ☾ *Mon.–Sat. 10–4, Sun. 1–4.*

BEACHES

Bathtub Reef Park. At the north end of the Indian River Plantation, is this ideal swimming spot for children because the waters are shallow and usually calm. At low tide you can walk to the reef. Facilities include restrooms and showers. ✉ *MacArthur Blvd., off Rte. A1A, Jensen Beach.*

2

SPORTS AND THE OUTDOORS
BASEBALL
Tradition Field. The **New York Mets** train here, and it's also the home of the St. Lucie Mets Minor League Team. ✉ *525 N.W. Peacock Blvd., Port St. Lucie* ☎ *772/871–2115.*

GOLF
Hutchinson Island Marriott Golf Club. There are 18 holes for members and hotel guests; greens fee $60 for 18 holes. ✉ *555 N.E. Ocean Blvd., Jensen Beach* ☎ *772/225–6819.*

PGA Golf Club at the PGA Villages. The PGA–operated public facility designed by Pete Dye and Tom Fazio has three separate courses; greens fee $62/$111. ✉ *1916 Perfect Dr., Port St. Lucie* ☎ *772/467–1300 or 800/800–4653.*

WHERE TO EAT AND STAY
For expanded hotel reviews, visit Fodors.com.

$$$
CONTINENTAL
★
✕ **11 Maple Street.** This cozy spot is as good as it gets on the Treasure Coast. Soft music and a friendly staff set the mood in the antiques-filled dining room, which holds only 20 tables. Appetizers run from panfried conch to crispy calamari, and entrées include seared rainbow trout, wood-grilled venison with onion-potato hash, and beef tenderloin with white-truffle-and-chive butter. Desserts like white-chocolate custard with blackberry sauce are seductive, too. ✉ *3224 Maple Ave., Jensen Beach* ☎ *772/334–7714* ⊕ *www.11maplestreet.net* ⌂ *Reservations essential* ☉ *Closed Mon. and Tues. No lunch.*

$
SEAFOOD
✕ **Conchy Joe's.** Like a hermit crab sliding into a new shell, Conchy Joe's moved up from West Palm Beach in 1983. Built in the 1920s, this rustic stilt house is full of antique fish mounts, gator hides, and snakeskins. It's a popular tourist spot, but the waterfront location, casual vibe, and delicious seafood attract locals, too. Staples include grouper marsala, broiled sea scallops, and fried cracked conch. There's live reggae Thursday through Sunday. ✉ *3945 N.E. Indian River Dr., Jensen Beach* ☎ *772/334–1130* ⊕ *www.conchyjoes.com.*

$$$–$$$$
RESORT
Hutchinson Island Marriott Beach Resort & Marina. With a 77-slip marina, a full water-sports program, a golf course, tennis courts, and a wide range of restaurants, this self-contained resort is excellent for families. **Pros:** attentive staff; challenging golf course. **Cons:** no children's program. **TripAdvisor:** "food was good value," "great for families," "needs some updating." ✉ *555 N.E. Ocean Blvd., Hutchinson Island* ☎ *772/225–3700 or 800/775–5936* ⊕ *www.marriott.com* ⟿ *213 rooms, 70 suites* ⌂ *In-room: a/c, kitchen (some), Internet. In-hotel: restaurants, bars, golf course, tennis courts, pools, gym, spa, beach, laundry facilities, parking, some pets allowed* ❂ *No meals.*

FORT PIERCE

11 mi north of Stuart, off Federal Hwy. (U.S. 1).

About an hour north of Palm Beach, this community has a distinctive rural feel, focusing on ranching and citrus farming. There are several worthwhile stops, including those easily seen while following Route 707.

GETTING HERE AND AROUND

You can reach Fort Pierce from Stuart by driving 11 mi north on Federal Highway (U.S. 1).

ESSENTIALS

Visitor Information St. Lucie County Tourist Development Council (⊠ *2300 Virginia Ave.* ☎ *800/344–8443*).

EXPLORING

Heathcote Botanical Gardens. Take a self-guided tour of this 3½-acre park, which includes a palm walk, a Japanese garden, and an orchid house. There is also a gift shop with whimsical and botanical knick-knacks. Guided tours are available Tuesday through Saturday by appointment. ⊠ *210 Savannah Rd.* ☎ *772/464–4672* ⊕ *www.heathcotebotanicalgardens.org* ☜ *$6* ☯ *May–Oct., Tues.–Sat. 9–5; Nov.–Apr., Tues.–Sat. 9–5, Sun. 1–5.*

★ **Navy SEAL Museum.** Commemorating more than 3,000 troops who trained here during World War II, the museum has weapons and equipment on view and exhibits depicting the history of the Underwater Demolition Teams. Patrol boats and vehicles are displayed outdoors. ⊠ *3300 N. Rte. A1A* ☎ *772/595–5845* ⊕ *www.navysealmuseum.com* ☜ *$6* ☯ *Tues.–Sat. 10–4, Sun. noon–4.*

☾ **Savannas Recreation Area.** Once a reservoir, the 550 acres have been returned to a natural state. Today the wilderness area has campsites, boat ramps, and trails. ⊠ *1400 E. Midway Rd.* ☎ *772/464–7855* ☯ *Daily 8–6.*

☾ **Smithsonian Marine Ecosystems Exhibit.** Run by the Smithsonian Institute and housed in the St. Lucie County Marine Center, this is where scientists come to study local ecosystems. A highlight is the 3,000-gallon coral-reef tank, originally shown in the Smithsonian's National Museum of Natural History in Washington, D.C. The parklike setting, where children love to play, makes it an ideal picnic destination. ⊠ *420 Seaway Dr.* ☎ *772/462–3474* ☜ *$3, free 1st Tues. of month* ☯ *Tues.–Sat. 10–4.*

BEACHES

Fort Pierce Inlet State Recreation Area. Sand dunes and coastal forests cover this 340-acre reserve. The park has swimming, surfing, picnic facilities, and a self-guided nature trail. ⊠ *905 Shorewinds Dr.* ☎ *772/468–3985* ☜ *$6 per vehicle* ☯ *Daily 8–dusk.*

Fort Pierce State Park. Accessible only by footbridge, the reserve has 4 mi of trails around Jack Island. The 1½-mi Marsh Rabbit Trail across the island traverses a mangrove swamp to a 30-foot-tall observation tower overlooking the Indian River. ⊠ *Rte. A1A* ☎ *772/468–3985* ☜ *$4 for one, $6 for a vehicle* ☯ *Daily 8–5:30.*

SPORTS AND THE OUTDOORS

FISHING

Dockside Harborlight Resort. For charter boats and fishing guides, contact the dockmaster. ⊠ *1160 Seaway Dr.* ☎ *772/461–4824.*

SCUBA DIVING
Urca de Lima Underwater Archaeological Preserve. On North Hutchinson Island, 200 yards from shore and under 10–15 feet of water, this preserve contains remains of a flat-bottom, round-bellied store ship. Once part of a treasure fleet bound for Spain, it was destroyed by a hurricane. ⊠ *3375 N. A1A.*

THE ARTS
A.E. "Bean" Backus Museum & Gallery. Works of one of Florida's foremost landscape artists are on display at this museum, which is also home to the Treasure Coast Art Association. It also mounts changing exhibits and offers exceptional buys on work by local artists. ⊠ *500 N. Indian River Dr.* ☎ *772/465–0630* ⊕ *www.backusgallery.com* 🎫 *Free but $2 donation suggested* ⊙ *Wed.–Sun. 10–4.*

WHERE TO EAT AND STAY
For expanded hotel reviews, visit Fodors.com.

$$$ ✕ **Mangrove Mattie's.** This upscale spot on Fort Pierce Inlet provides daz-
SEAFOOD zling waterfront views and delicious seafood. Dine on the terrace or in the dining room, and don't forget to try the coconut-fried shrimp or the chicken and scampi. Happy hour (weekdays 4–7) features roast beef or ham sandwiches, or oysters, clams and shrimp. Many locals come by for the Champagne Sunday brunch. ⊠ *1640 Seaway Dr.* ☎ *772/466–1044* ⊕ *www.mangrovematties.com.*

$ 🛏 **Dockside Harborlight Resort Inn.** Formerly two adjacent motels, this
RESORT resort is the best of the lodgings lining the Fort Pierce Inlet along Seaway Drive. **Pros:** good value; good spot for anglers; reasonable rates at marina. **Cons:** basic decor; some steps to climb. **TripAdvisor:** "loved sitting on the deck," "rundown and smells really bad," "tons of charm." ⊠ *1160 Seaway Dr.* ☎ *772/468–3555 or 800/286–1745* ⊕ *www.docksideinn.com* ⤺ *72 rooms, 4 apartments* ⚬ *In-room: a/c, kitchen (some). In-hotel: restaurant, pools, laundry facilities, parking* ⊙ *Breakfast.*

VERO BEACH

12 mi north of Fort Pierce.

Tranquil and charming, this Indian River County town has a strong commitment to the environment and the arts. There are plenty of outdoor activities here, even though many visitors to the area opt to do little at all. In the town's exclusive Riomar Bay area, roads are shaded by massive live oaks, and a popular cluster of restaurants and shops is just off the beach.

GETTING HERE AND AROUND
To get here, you have two options—Route A1A, along the coast, or Route 605 (also called Old Dixie Highway), on the mainland. As you approach Vero on the latter, you pass through an ungussied landscape of small farms and residential areas. On the beach route, part of the drive is through an unusually undeveloped section of the Florida coast.

ESSENTIALS

Visitor Information Indian River Chamber of Commerce (✉ *1216 21st St.* ☎ *772/567–3491*).

EXPLORING

Environmental Learning Center. In addition to aquariums filled with Indian River creatures, the 51 acres here have a 600-foot boardwalk through the mangrove shoreline and a 1-mi canoe trail. The center is on the northern edge of Vero Beach, and the pretty drive is worth the trip. ✉ *255 Live Oak Dr.* ☎ *772/589–5050* ⊕ *www.elcweb.org* ✑ *$5* ☾ *Tues.–Fri. 10–4, Sat. 9–4, Sun. 1–4.*

Heritage Center and Indian River Citrus Museum. You'll learn that more grapefruit is shipped from the Indian River area than anywhere else in the world at this museum. The memorabilia harks back to when families washed and wrapped the luscious fruit to sell at roadside stands, and oxen hauled citrus-filled crates with distinctive Indian River labels to the rail station. ✉ *2140 14th Ave.* ⊕ *www.veroheritage.org* ☎ *772/770–2263* ✑ *Free* ☾ *Tues.–Fri. 10–4.*

Fodor's Choice
★ **McKee Botanical Garden.** On the National Register of Historic Places, the 18 acres here are both a tropical garden and a horticulture museum. The historic Hall of Giants, a rustic structure built from cedar and hearts of pine, features a beautiful stained glass, bronze bells, and the world's largest single-plank mahogany table. There's a 529-square-foot bamboo pavilion, a gift shop, and the Garden Café, which serves tasty snacks and sandwiches and locally grown tea. This is the place to see spectacular water lilies. ✉ *350 U.S. 1* ☎ *772/794–0601* ⊕ *www.mckeegarden.org* ✑ *$9* ☾ *Tues.–Sat. 10–5, Sun. noon–5.*

Vero Beach Museum of Art. Part of a 26-acre campus dedicated to the arts, the museum is where a full schedule of exhibitions, art movies, lectures, workshops, and classes are hosted. The museum's five galleries and sculpture garden make it the largest art facility in the Treasure Coast. ✉ *3001 Riverside Park Dr.* ☎ *772/231–0707* ⊕ *www.verobeachmuseum.org* ✑ *Free* ☾ *Mon.–Sat. 10–4:30, Sun. 1–4:30.*

BEACHES

Treasure Shores Park. There are picnic tables, restrooms, and a nice playground for kids. ✉ *11300 A1A, 3 mi north of County Rd. 510* ☎ *772/581–4997.*

Wabasso Beach Park. Lifeguards, restrooms, a boardwalk, and showers make this a pleasant beach to visit. ✉ *County Rd. 510, east of A1A* ☎ *772/581–4998.*

SPORTS AND THE OUTDOORS

GOLF

Sandridge Golf Club. These two public 18-hole courses were designed by Ron Garl; greens fee $42. ✉ *5300 73rd St.* ☎ *772/770–5000.*

SHOPPING

Along Ocean Drive near Beachland Boulevard, a shopping area includes art galleries, antiques shops, and upscale clothing stores. The eight-block area of Oceanside has an interesting mix of boutiques, specialty shops, and eateries.

DID YOU KNOW?

Vero Beach is known for its arts. But like many of Florida's coastal towns, some of the top attractions here are the natural offerings, from Vero Beach's citrus trees to its beautiful sunrises.

Outlets at Vero Beach. Just west of Interstate 95 is a discount shopping destination with 70 brand-name stores, including Ann Taylor, Ralph Lauren Polo, and Jones New York. ✉ *1824 94th Dr.* ☎ *772/770–6097.*

THE ARTS

Riverside Children's Theatre. A series of professional touring and local productions are staged here. ✉ *Agnes Wahlstrom Youth Playhouse, 3280 Riverside Park Dr.* ☎ *772/234–8052* ⊕ *www.riversidetheatre.com.*

Riverside Theatre. Five productions go up each season at the 650-seat Mainstage and three at its 200-seat Second Stage. ✉ *3250 Riverside Park Dr.* ☎ *772/231–6990* ⊕ *www.riversidetheatre.com.*

WHERE TO EAT AND STAY

For expanded hotel reviews, visit Fodors.com.

$$$
SEAFOOD
✕ **Ocean Grill.** Opened as a hamburger shack in 1938, the Ocean Grill combines its ocean view with Tiffany-style lamps, wrought-iron chandeliers, and paintings of pirates. Count on at least three kinds of seafood any day on the menu, along with steaks, pork chops, soups, and salads. The house drink is "Pusser's Painkiller"—a curious blend first mixed by British sailors in the Virgin Islands and rationed in a tin cup. It commemorates the 1894 wreck of the *Breconshire*, which occurred offshore and from which 34 British sailors escaped. ✉ *Sexton Plaza, 1050 Ocean Dr.* ☎ *772/231–5409* ⊕ *www.ocean-grill.com* ⊙ *Closed 2 wks after Labor Day. No lunch weekends.*

$$
RESORT
🛏 **Aquarius Oceanfront Resort.** Right on beautiful South Beach, this small unpretentious resort has loyal guests who book a year in advance. **Pros:** relaxed vibe; great location; faces the beach. **Cons:** steps to climb; nothing too fancy. ✉ *1526 Ocean Dr.* ☎ *772/231–5218 or 877/767–1526* ⊕ *www.aquariusverobeach.com* ⟿ *28 rooms* ⚬ *In-room: a/c, kitchen (some). In-hotel: pool, beach, laundry facilities, parking* ⭐*No meals.*

$$$
HOTEL
🛏 **Costa d'Este.** Many people know this hotel because of its famous owners, singer Gloria Estefan and producer Emilio Estefan, who brought in a new design and a lively ambience. **Pros:** great location; huge showers; faces the beach. **Cons:** marble floors can be cold. **TripAdvisor:** "peaceful pool area," "noise at night," "not too expensive with good service." ✉ *3244 Ocean Dr.* ☎ *772/562–9919* ⊕ *www.costadeste.com* ⟿ *90 rooms, 4 suites* ⚬ *In-room: a/c, Wi-Fi. In-hotel: restaurant, pool, gym, spa, parking* ⭐*No meals.*

$$$$
RESORT
🛏 **Disney's Vero Beach Resort.** This oceanfront, family-oriented retreat operates as a hotel and a Disney Vacation Club. **Pros:** fun for families; lots to do for kids. **Cons:** not the best place if you don't have children; a bit kitschy. **TripAdvisor:** "much to offer for people of all ages," "great place to relax," "loved the location." ✉ *9250 Island Grove Terr.* ☎ *772/234–2000 or 800/359–8000* ⊕ *www.disneybeachresorts.com* ⟿ *161 rooms, 14 suites, 6 cottages* ⚬ *In-room: a/c, kitchen (some), Internet. In-hotel: restaurants, bar, tennis courts, pool, gym, beach, children's programs, laundry facilities, parking* ⭐*No meals.*

$$$
RESORT
🛏 **Driftwood Resort.** On the National Register of Historic Places, this 1935 inn was built entirely from ocean-washed timbers and decorated with such artifacts as ship bells, Spanish tiles, and a cannon from a 16th-century Spanish galleon. **Pros:** great seaside location; near restaurants

and shops. **Cons:** older property; rooms can be musty. **TripAdvisor:** "dated yet it had everything we needed," "bed was comfortable," "eclectic resort with lots of personality." ✉ *3150 Ocean Dr.* ☎ *772/231–0550* ⊕ *www.thedriftwood.com* ⤹ *96 1- and 2-bedroom suites, 4 hotel rooms* ⟲ *In-room: a/c, kitchen. In-hotel: restaurant, bar, pools, beach, parking* ❍ *No meals.*

$$$$
RESORT

🔆 **The Vero Beach Hotel & Spa.** This comfortable five-story hotel is right on the beach and near restaurants and boutiques. **Pros:** great ocean views; fabulous pool. **Cons:** spa under construction until fall 2010. ✉ *3500 Ocean Dr.* ☎ *772/231–5666* ⊕ *www.verobeachhotelandspa.com* ⤹ *32 rooms, 32 studios, 15 1-bedroom suites and 23 2-bedroom suites* ⟲ *In-room: a/c, Wi-Fi. In-hotel: restaurant, bar, pool, beach, parking* ❍ *No meals.*

SEBASTIAN

14 mi north of Vero Beach, off Federal Hwy. (U.S. 1).

One of the few sparsely populated areas on Florida's east coast, this fishing village has as remote a feeling as you're likely to find between Jacksonville and Miami Beach. That adds to the appeal of the recreation area around Sebastian Inlet, where you can walk for miles along quiet beaches and catch some of Florida's best waves for surfing.

ESSENTIALS

Visitor Information Sebastian Chamber of Commerce (✉ *700 Main St.* ☎ *772/589–5969*).

EXPLORING

McLarty Treasure Museum. A National Historic Landmark, this museum underscores this credo: "Wherever gold glitters or silver beckons, man will move mountains." It has displays of coins, weapons, and tools salvaged from a fleet of Spanish treasure ships that sank in the 1715 storm, leaving some 1,500 survivors struggling to shore between Sebastian and Fort Pierce. The museum's last video showing begins at 3:15. ✉ *13180 N. Rte. A1A* ☎ *772/589–2147* 🎟 *$2* ☉ *Daily 10–4.*

Mel Fisher's Treasures. You'll really come upon hidden loot when you enter this museum operated by the late Mel Fisher's family. See some of what was recovered in 1985 from the Spanish treasure ship *Atocha* and its sister ships of the 1715 fleet. The museum certainly piques one's curiosity about what is still buried at sea: treasures continue to be discovered each year. ✉ *1322 U.S. 1* ☎ *772/589–9875* ⊕ *www.melfisher.com* 🎟 *$6.50* ☉ *Mon.–Sat. 10–5, Sun. noon–5.*

Pelican Island National Wildlife Refuge. Within the Indian River Lagoon and on the barrier island across from Sebastian, Pelican Island was founded in 1903 by President Theodore Roosevelt as the nation's first national wildlife refuge. The island is a closed wilderness area. The historic Pelican Island rockery is viewable from a distance by commercial boat and kayak tours and from a public observation tower on the adjacent barrier island. The Refuge has more than 6 mi of foot trails through the barrier island habitats. A boardwalk and observation tower enable visitors to see birds, endangered species, and habitats. ✉ *1339 20th St.* ☎ *772/562–3909 Ext. 275* 💳 *Free* ☉ *Daily 7:30–sunset.*

Sebastian Inlet State Recreation Area. Because of the highly productive fishing waters of Sebastian Inlet, this 578-acre property at the north end of Orchid Island is one of the Florida park system's biggest draws. Both sides of the high bridge spanning the inlet—views are spectacular—attract anglers as well as those eager to enjoy the fine sandy shores, known for having some of the best waves in the state. A concession stand on the inlet's north side sells short-order food, rents various craft, and has a small apparel and surf shop. There's a boat ramp, and not far away is a dune area that's part of the **Archie Carr National Wildlife Refuge.** ✉ *9700 S. Rte. A1A, Melbourne Beach* ☎ *321/984–4852* ⊕ *www. floridastateparks.org* 💳 *$5 per vehicle* ☉ *Daily 7–sunset.*

SPORTS AND THE OUTDOORS
FISHING
Big Easy Fishing Charters. For sportfishing, try this outfitter. ✉ *Capt. Hiram's Restaurant, 1606 N. Indian River Dr.* ☎ *772/664–4068.*

Incentive Charter Fishing. This outfit will set you up for bottom-fishing. ✉ *Capt. Hiram's Restaurant, 1606 N. Indian River Dr.* ☎ *321/676–1948.*

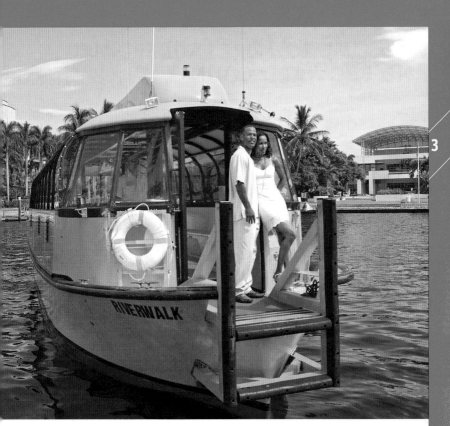

Fort Lauderdale and Broward County

WORD OF MOUTH

"I think you'll enjoy Fort Lauderdale. The Riverwalk/Las Olas area has lots of good restaurants—you can take a water taxi there from just about anywhere on the Intracoastal waterway."

—321go

WELCOME TO FORT LAUDERDALE AND BROWARD COUNTY

TOP REASONS TO GO

★ **Blue Waves:** Sparkling Lauderdale beaches spanning Broward County's entire coast were Florida's first to capture Blue Wave Beach status from the Clean Beaches Council.

★ **Inland Waterways:** More than 300 mi of inland waterways, including downtown Fort Lauderdale's historic New River, create what's known as the Venice of America.

★ **Everglades Access:** Just minutes from luxury hotels and golf courses, the rugged Everglades tantalize with alligators, colorful birds, and other wildlife.

★ **Vegas-Style Gaming:** Since Vegas-style slots and blackjack tables hit Hollywood's glittering Seminole Hard Rock Hotel & Casino in 2008, smaller competitors seem to be following this lucrative trend on every square inch of Indian territory.

★ **Cruise Gateway:** Port Everglades—homeport for *Allure* and *Oasis of the Seas*, the world's largest cruise vessels—hosts cruise ships from major lines

1 **Fort Lauderdale.** Anchored by the fast-flowing New River and its attractive Riverwalk, Fort Lauderdale embraces high-rise condos along with single-family homes, museums, parks, and attractions. Las Olas Boulevard, lined with boutiques, sidewalk cafés, and restaurants, links downtown and the beaches.

2 **North on Scenic A1A.** Stretching north on Route A1A, seaside attractions range from high-rise Galt Ocean Mile to low-rise resort communities—and a glimpse of a lighthouse, inspiration for the community of Lighthouse Point.

3 **South Broward.** From Hollywood's beachside Broadwalk and historic Young Circle (the latter transformed into an Arts Park) to Seminole gaming, South Broward provides grit, glitter, and diversity in attractions.

GETTING ORIENTED

Along the southeast's Gold Coast, Fort Lauderdale and Broward County anchor a delightfully chic middle ground between the posh and elite Palm and West Palm beaches and the international hubbub of Miami. From downtown Fort Lauderdale, it's about a four-hour drive to either Orlando or Key West, but there's plenty to keep you in Broward. All told, Broward boasts 31 communities from Deerfield Beach to Hallandale Beach along the coast, and from Coral Springs to Southwest Ranches closer to the Everglades. Big—in fact, huge—shopping options await in Sunrise, home of Sawgrass Mills, the upscale Colonnade Outlets at Sawgrass, and IKEA Sunrise.

FORT LAUDERDALE AND BROWARD COUNTY BEACHES

A wave-capped, 20-mi shoreline with wide ribbons of golden sand for beachcombing and sunbathing remains the anchor draw for Fort Lauderdale and Broward County.

Fort Lauderdale isn't just for spring breakers. In fact, ever since investors started pouring money into the waterfront scene, beginning in the '90s, the beach has lured a more upscale clientele. That said, it still has great people-watching and opportunities for partying.

Beyond the city, Broward County's beachfront extends for miles without interruption, although character of communities along the shoreline varies. To the south in Hallandale, the beach is backed by towering condominiums, while tee times and nightlife beckon in Hollywood. Deerfield Beach and Lauderdale-by-the-Sea to the north are magnets for active families, and nearby Pompano Beach attracts anglers. Many places along Broward shorelines—blessedly, for purists—are uncluttered with nothing but sand and turquoise waters.

SAFETY TIPS

⚠ **Avoid unguarded waters, and be aware of color codes.** In Fort Lauderdale, double red flags mean water is closed to the public, often because of lightning or sharks; a lone red flag signals strong currents; purple indicates the presence of marine pests like men-of-war, jellyfish, or sea lice; green means calm conditions. In Hollywood, orange signals rip currents with easterly onshore winds; blue warns of marine life like jellyfish; red means hazardous; green signals good conditions.

FORT LAUDERDALE'S BEST BEACHES

FORT LAUDERDALE BEACH

Alone among Florida's major beach-front communities, Fort Lauderdale's beach remains gloriously open and uncluttered. A wave theme unifies the Fort Lauderdale Beachfront setting— from the low, white, wave-shape wall between the beach and beachfront promenade to the widened and bricked inner promenade in front of shops, restaurants, and hotels. Walkways line both sides of the beach roadway, and traffic has been trimmed to two gently curving northbound lanes, where in-line skaters skim past slow-moving cars. On the beach side, a low masonry wall doubles as an extended bench, separating sand from the promenade. At night the wall is accented with pretty ribbons of fiber-optic color, often on the blink despite an ongoing search for a permanent fix. The beach is most crowded between Las Olas and Sunrise boulevards.

HOLLYWOOD'S BROADWALK

The name might be Hollywood, but there's nothing hip or chic about Hollywood North Beach Park, which sits at the north end of Hollywood (Route A1A and Sheridan Street). And that's a good thing. It's just a laid-back, old-fashioned place to enjoy the sun, sand, and sea. No high-rises overpower the scene here. Parking is $5. The main part of the Broadwalk is quite a bit more fashionable. Thanks to a $14 million makeover, this popular beach has spiffy new features like a pedestrian walk-way, a concrete bike path, a crushed-shell jogging path, an 18-inch decorative wall separating the Broadwalk from the sand, and places to shower off after a dip. Fido fans take note: the film *Marley & Me*, starring Jennifer Aniston and Owen Wilson and filmed in Greater Fort Lauderdale, spurred a comeback for dog beaches in South Florida, including the year-round Dog Beach of Hollywood.

LAUDERDALE-BY-THE-SEA

For a small village with a pier, Lauderdale-by-the-Sea packs a big punch for beach pleasure. Especially popular with divers and snorkelers, this laid-back stretch of sand provides great access to lovely coral reefs. When you're not down in the waters, look up and you'll likely see a pelican flying by. Gentle trade winds make this an utterly relaxing retreat from the hubbub of the Fort Lauderdale party scene. Things do liven up with nightly entertainment at a couple of local watering holes, but L-B-T-S, as it's known, still provides a small-town, easygoing, family-friendly feel.

Updated by
Paul Rubio

Collegians of the 1960s returning to Fort Lauderdale would be hard-pressed to recognize the onetime "Sun and Suds Spring Break Capital of the Universe." Back then, Fort Lauderdale's beachfront was lined with T-shirt shops, and downtown consisted of a lone office tower and dilapidated buildings waiting to be razed.

The beach and downtown have since exploded with upscale shops, restaurants, and luxury resort hotels equipped with enough high-octane amenities to light up skies all the way to western Broward's Alligator Alley. At risk of losing small-town 45-rpm magic in iPod times—when hotel parking fees alone eclipse room rates of old—Greater Fort Lauderdale somehow seems to meld disparate eras into *nouveau* nirvana, seasoned with a little Gold Coast sand.

The city was named for Major William Lauderdale, who built a fort at the river's mouth in 1838 during the Seminole Indian wars. It wasn't until 1911 that the city was incorporated, with only 175 residents, but it grew quickly during the Florida boom of the 1920s. Today's population hovers around 150,000, and suburbs keep growing—1.6 million live in Broward County's 31 municipalities and unincorporated areas. As elsewhere, many speculators busily flipping property here got caught when the sun-drenched real-estate bubble burst, leaving Broward's foreclosure rate to skyrocket.

Despite economic downturns, gaming options have expanded. South Florida's Indian tribes have long offered bingo, poker, and machines resembling slots. In 2005, Broward became Florida's first county to offer gambling with true slot machines at four wagering facilities referred to as racinos: Gulfstream Park Racing & Casino, the Mardi Gras Racetrack & Gaming, Dania Jai Alai Casino, and the Isle Casino & Racing of Pompano Park. In 2008, Hollywood's Seminole Hard Rock Hotel & Casino, which ranks as the most glittering example of Vegas-style gaming with a tropical twist, cut a deal with the state to replace bingo-style machines with genuine Vegas-style slots.

FORT LAUDERDALE PLANNER

WHEN TO GO

Peak season runs Thanksgiving through April, when concert, art, and entertainment seasons go full throttle. Expect rain, heat, and humidity in summer. Hurricane winds come most notably in August and September. Golfing tee-time waits are longer on weekends year-round. Fort Lauderdale sunshine can burn even in cloudy weather.

3

TOP FESTIVALS

Fort Lauderdale International Boat Show. In late October Fort Lauderdale hosts the world's largest boat show, the end-all, be-all of marine envy, with more than $2 billion worth of boats, yachts, superyachts, electronics, engines, and thousands of accessories from every major marine manufacturer and builder worldwide. ☎ 954/764–7642 ⊕ *www.showmanagement.com.*

Seminole Hard Rock Winterfest Boat Parade. Weeks of pre-events culminate in the largest one-day spectator event in Florida each December, drawing a crowd of 1 million onlookers as a stampede of 1,500 jaw-dropping yachts cruise 10 mi of Fort Lauderdale's waterways, complete with original themes and decorations. Over the years, celebrity grand marshals have included Joan Rivers, Brooke Burke, and Kim Kardashian. ☎ 954/767–0686 ⊕ *www.winterfestparade.com.*

GETTING HERE AND AROUND

AIR TRAVEL

Serving more than 21 million travelers a year, **Fort Lauderdale–Hollywood International Airport** is 3 mi south of downtown Fort Lauderdale, just off U.S. 1 between Fort Lauderdale and Hollywood, and near Port Everglades and Fort Lauderdale Beach. Other options include **Miami International Airport,** about 32 mi to the southwest, and the far less chaotic **Palm Beach International Airport,** about 50 mi to the north. All three airports link to **Tri-Rail,** a commuter train operating seven days through Palm Beach, Broward, and Miami-Dade counties.

BUS TRAVEL

Broward County Transit operates bus route No. 1 between the airport and its main terminal at Broward Boulevard and Northwest 1st Avenue, near downtown Fort Lauderdale. Service from the airport is every 20 minutes and begins at 5:22 am on weekdays, 5:37 am Saturday, and 8:41 am Sunday; the last bus leaves the airport at 11:38 pm Monday–Saturday and 9:41 pm Sunday. The fare is $1.75. ⚠ The Northwest 1st Avenue stop is in a crime-prone part of town. Exercise special caution there, day or night. Better yet, take a taxi to and from the airport. Broward County Transit (BCT) also covers the county on 303 fixed routes. The fare is $1.75. Service starts around 5 am and continues to 11:30 pm, except on Sunday.

CAR TRAVEL

Renting a car to get around Fort Lauderdale is highly recommended. Taxis are scarce and costly. Traditional public transportation is rarely used, but a water taxi makes transport between waterfront destinations quite easy (albeit slow).

TRAIN TRAVEL

Amtrak provides daily service to Fort Lauderdale and stops at Deerfield Beach and Hollywood.

By car, access to Broward County from north or south is via Florida's Turnpike, Interstate 95, U.S. 1, or U.S. 441. Interstate 75 (Alligator Alley, requiring a toll despite being part of the nation's interstate-highway system) connects Broward with Florida's west coast and runs parallel to State Road 84 within the county. East–west Interstate 595 runs from westernmost Broward County and links Interstate 75 with Interstate 95 and U.S. 1, providing handy access to the airport and seaport. Route A1A, designated a Florida Scenic Highway by the state's Department of Transportation, parallels the beach.

ESSENTIALS

Airport information **Fort Lauderdale–Hollywood International Airport** (*FLL* ☎ 866/435-9355 ⊕ www.broward.org/airport). **Miami International Airport** (*MIA* ☎ 305/876-7000 ⊕ www.miami-airport.com). **Palm Beach International Airport** (*PBI* ☎ 561/471-7420 ⊕ www.pbia.org). **Tri-Rail** (☎ 800/874-7245 ⊕ www.tri-rail.com).

Bus information **Broward County Transit** (☎ 954/357-8400 ⊕ www.broward. org/BCT).

ABOUT THE RESTAURANTS

References to "Fort Liquordale" from spring-break days of old have given way to au courant allusions for the decidedly cuisine-oriented "Fork Lauderdale." Greater Fort Lauderdale offers some of the finest, most varied dining of any U.S. city its size, spawned in part by the advent of new luxury hotels and upgrades all around. From among more than 4,000 wining-and-dining establishments in Broward, choose from basic Americana or cuisines of Asia, Europe, or Central and South America, and enjoy more than just food in an atmosphere with sub-tropical twists.

ABOUT THE HOTELS

Not as posh as Palm Beach or as deco-trendy as Miami Beach, Fort Lauderdale has a growing roster of more-than-respectable lodging choices, from beachfront luxury suites to intimate bed-and-breakfasts to chain hotels along the Intracoastal Waterway. Relatively new on the luxury beachfront are the Atlantic, the Hilton Fort Lauderdale Beach Resort, the Ritz-Carlton, Fort Lauderdale, and W resort, and more upscale places to hang your hat are on the horizon while smaller family-run lodging spots disappear. If you want to be *on* the beach, be sure to ask specifically when booking your room, since many hotels advertise "waterfront" accommodations that are along inland waterways or overlooking the beach from across Route A1A.

WHAT IT COSTS					
	¢	$	$$	$$$	$$$$
Restaurants	under $10	$10–$15	$15–$20	$20–$30	over $30
Hotels	under $80	$80–$100	$100–$140	$140–$220	over $220

Restaurant prices are per person for a main course at dinner. Hotel prices are for a standard double room, excluding 6% sales tax (more in some counties) and 1%–5% tourist tax.

BOAT TOURS

For a similar experience to these tours but with a local flair, explore Fort Lauderdale's waterways on the public water taxis. ⇨ *See Exploring the Venice of America, below, for more information.*

Carrie B. Board a 300-passenger day cruiser for a 90-minute tour on the New River and Intracoastal Waterway. Cruises depart at 11, 1, and 3 daily November through May and Thursday–Monday between June and October. The cost is $19.95. ⊠ *440 N. New River Dr. E, Fort Lauderdale* ☎ *954/768–9920* ⊕ *www.carriebcruises.com.*

Fort Lauderdale Duck Tours. This outfitter provides 90 minutes of land/water family fun on a 45-passenger amphibious Hydra-Terra, cruising Venice of America neighborhoods, historic areas, and the Intracoastal Waterway. Several tours depart daily (schedule varies) and cost $30. ⊠ *17 S. Fort Lauderdale Beach Blvd., at Beach Pl., Fort Lauderdale* ☎ *954/761–4002* ⊕ *www.fortlauderdaleducktours.com.*

Jungle Queen. The *Jungle Queen III* and *Jungle Queen IV* tour boats seat more than 550 for cruises up New River through the heart of Fort Lauderdale. Sightseeing cruises at 9:30 and 1:30 cost $17.50, and the 6 pm all-you-can-eat BBQ dinner cruise costs $39.95. ⊠ *Bahia Mar Beach Resort, 801 Seabreeze Blvd., Fort Lauderdale* ☎ *954/462–5596* ⊕ *www.junglequeen.com.*

Sea Experience. Glass-bottom-boat and snorkeling combination trips on the *Sea Experience I* explore Fort Lauderdale's offshore reefs. Daily two-hour trips at 10:15 am and 2:15 pm cost $28 for the ride or $35 to snorkel, equipment provided. ⊠ *Bahia Mar Beach Resort, 801 Seabreeze Blvd., Fort Lauderdale* ☎ *954/770–3483* ⊕ *www.seaxp.com.*

FORT LAUDERDALE

Like many southeast Florida neighbors, Fort Lauderdale has long been revitalizing. In a state where gaudy tourist zones often stand aloof from workaday downtowns, Fort Lauderdale exhibits consistency at both ends of the 2-mi Las Olas corridor. The sparkling look results from upgrades both downtown and on the beachfront. Matching the downtown's innovative arts district, cafés, and boutiques is an equally inventive beach area, with hotels, cafés, and shops facing an undeveloped

GREAT ITINERARIES

Many Broward County attractions are close, so you can pack a lot into a day—if you have wheels. Catch the history, museums, and shops and bistros in Fort Lauderdale's down-town and along Las Olas Boulevard. Then if you feel like hitting the beach, head east to the intersec-tion of Las Olas and Route A1A and you're there. Neighboring communi-ties like Lauderdale-by-the-Sea and Pompano Beach (to the north) or Dania Beach and Hollywood (to the south) have attractions of their own, and you may not realize when you've crossed municipal lines. As a result, you'll be able to cover most high points in three days.

3 DAYS
With a bigger concentration of hotels, restaurants, and attractions

than its suburbs, Fort Lauderdale makes a logical base for any visit. On your first day, see downtown, especially **Las Olas Boulevard** between Southeast 3rd and South-east 15th avenues. After lunch at a sidewalk café, head for the nearby Arts and Science District and the downtown **Riverwalk**, which you can enjoy at a leisurely pace in half a day or less. On your second day, spend time at the **Fort Lauderdale Beachfront**, sunbathing or having a cooling libation at an oceanfront lounge. Tour the waterways on the third day, either on a rented boat from one of the marinas along Route A1A, or via the Water Taxi.

shoreline, and new resort-style hotels replacing faded icons of yester-year. Despite wariness of pretentious overdevelopment, city leaders have allowed a striking number of glittering high-rises. Nostalgic locals and frequent visitors fret over the diminishing vision of sailboats bobbing in waters near downtown, now that a boxy high-rise has erased one of the area's oldest marinas. Sharp demographic changes are also altering the faces of Greater Fort Lauderdale communities, increasingly cosmopoli-tan with more minorities, including Hispanics and people of Caribbean descent, as well as gays and lesbians. In Fort Lauderdale, especially, a younger populace is growing, whereas longtime residents are heading north, to a point where one former city commissioner likens the change to that of historic New River—moving with the tide and sometimes appearing at a standstill. "The river of our population is at still point, old and new in equipoise, one pushing against the other."

GETTING HERE AND AROUND

The Fort Lauderdale metro area is laid out in a grid system, and only myriad canals and waterways interrupt the mostly straight-line path of streets and roads. Nomenclature is important here. Streets, roads, courts, and drives run east–west. Avenues, terraces, and ways run north–south. Boulevards can (and do) run any which way. For visitors, trendy Las Olas Boulevard is one of the most important east–west thorough-fares from the beach to downtown, whereas Route A1A—referred to as Atlantic Boulevard, Ocean Boulevard, and Fort Lauderdale Beach along some stretches—runs along the north–south oceanfront. These names can confuse visitors, since there are separate streets called Atlantic and

Ocean in Hollywood and Pompano Beach. Boulevards, composed of either pavement or water, give Fort Lauderdale its distinct "Venice of America" character.

The city's transportation system, though less congested than elsewhere in South Florida, suffers from traffic overload. Interstate 595 connects the city and suburbs and provides a direct route to the Fort Lauderdale–Hollywood International Airport and Port Everglades, but lanes slow to a crawl during rush hours. The Intracoastal Waterway, paralleling Route A1A, is the nautical equivalent of an interstate highway. It runs north–south between downtown Fort Lauderdale and the beach and provides easy boating access to neighboring beach communities.

The major taxi company serving the area is Yellow Cab, with vehicles equipped for major credit cards.

TOURS   Honeycombed with some 300 mi of navigable waterways, Fort Lauderdale is home port for about 44,000 privately owned vessels, but you don't need to be a boat owner to ply the waters. For a scenic way to really see this canal-laced city, simply hop on a Water Taxi, sometimes called a Water Bus, part of Fort Lauderdale's water-transportation system, made up of a fleet of vessels carrying up to 70 passengers each. Providing transport and quick, narrated tours, a water taxi is a good way to bar-hop or access many waterfront hotels and restaurants. Larger, multiple-deck touring vessels and motorboat rentals for self-guided adventure are other sightseeing options.

Boats won't get you everywhere; you may need to call for taxi service when getting to and from the airport, seaport, or major hotels. Meters run at rates of $4.50 for the first mile and $2.40 for each additional mile; waiting time is 40¢ per minute. There's a $10-fare minimum from seaport or airport, and an additional $2 service charge when you are collected from the airport.

Catch an orange-bottomed, yellow-topped Sun Trolley, running every 15 minutes, free on Friday and for 50¢ each way, on any route. Sun Trolley's *Convention Connection*, 50¢ per person, runs round-trip from Cordova Road's Harbor Shops near Port Everglades (where you can park free) to past the Convention Center, over the 17th Street Causeway, and north along Route A1A to Beach Place. Wave at trolley drivers— yes, they will stop—for pickups anywhere along the route.

ESSENTIALS

Transportation Contacts Sun Trolley (☎ *954/761–3543* ⊕ *www.suntrolley. com*). **Water Taxi** (☎ *954/467–0008* ⊕ *www.watertaxi.com*). **Yellow Cab** (☎ *954/565–5400*).

Visitor Information Greater Fort Lauderdale Convention and Visitors Bureau (☎ *954/765–4466* ⊕ *www.sunny.org*).

This couple tours Fort Lauderdale via a three-wheeled scooter; photo by rockindom, Fodors.com member.

EXPLORING

DOWNTOWN AND LAS OLAS

The jewel of downtown along New River is the Arts and Entertainment District, with Broadway shows, ballet, and theater at the riverfront Broward Center for the Performing Arts. Clustered within a five-minute walk are the Museum of Discovery & Science, the expanding Fort Lauderdale Historical Museum, and the Museum of Art, home to stellar touring exhibits. Restaurants, sidewalk cafés, bars, and blues, folk, jazz, reggae, and rock clubs flourish along Las Olas and its downtown extension. Tying these areas together is the Riverwalk, extending 2 mi along the New River's north and south banks. Tropical gardens with benches and interpretive displays fringe the walk on the north, boat landings on the south.

TOP ATTRACTIONS

Fort Lauderdale History Center. Surveying city history from the Seminole era to more recent times, the Fort Lauderdale Historical Society's museum has expanded into several adjacent buildings, including the historic King-Cromartie House (typical early 20th-century style Fort Lauderdale home), the 1905 New River Inn (Broward's oldest remaining hotel building), and the Hoch Heritage Center, a public research facility archiving original manuscripts, maps, and more than 250,000 photos. Daily docent-led tours run on the hour 1 pm–3 pm. ✉ *231 S.W. 2nd Ave.* ☎ *954/463–4431* ⊕ *www.oldfortlauderdale.org* 💲 *$10* ⊙ *Tues.–Sun. noon–4.*

★ **Las Olas Boulevard.** What Lincoln Road is to South Beach, Las Olas Boulevard is to Fort Lauderdale. The terrestrial heart and soul of Broward

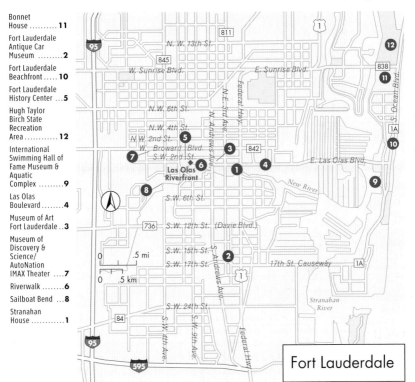

Fort Lauderdale

County, Las Olas is the premiere street for restaurants, art galleries, shopping, and people-watching. From west to east the landscape of Las Olas transforms from modern downtown high-rises to original boutiques and ethnic eateries. Beautiful mansions and traditional Floridian homes line the Intracoastal and define Fort Lauderdale. The streets of Las Olas connect to the pedestrian friendly Riverwalk, which continues to the edge of the New River on Avenue of the Arts. ⊕ *www. lasolasboulevard.com.*

Museum of Art Fort Lauderdale. Currently in an Edward Larrabee Barnes–designed building that's considered an architectural masterpiece, activists started this museum in a nearby storefront about 50 years ago. MOAFL now coordinates with Nova Southeastern University to host world-class touring exhibits and has an impressive permanent collection of 20th-century European and American art, including works by Picasso, Calder, Dalí, Mapplethorpe, Warhol, and Stella, as well as works by celebrated Ashcan School artist William Glackens. ⊠ *1 E. Las Olas Blvd.* ☎ *954/763–6464* ⊕ *www.moafl.org* ☛ *$10* ☙ *Tues.–Wed., Fri., and Sat. 11–5, Thurs.11–8, Sun. noon–5.*

☺ **Museum of Discovery & Science/AutoNation IMAX Theater.** With more
★ than 200 interactive exhibits, the aim here is to entertain children—*and* adults—with wonders of science. Exhibits include Kidscience,

encouraging youngsters to explore the world; and Gizmo City, a look at how gadgets work. Florida Ecoscapes has a living coral reef, plus sharks, rays, and eels. *Runways to Rockets* offers stimulating trips to Mars and the moon while nine different cockpit stimulators let you try out your pilot skills. The AutoNation IMAX theater, part of the complex, shows films, some in 3-D, on an 80-foot by 60-foot screen with 15,000 watts of digital surround sound broadcast from 42 speakers. ⊠ *401 S.W. 2nd St.* ☎ *954/467–6637 museum, 954/463–4629 IMAX* ⊕ *www.mods.org* ⊠ *Museum $11, $16 with one IMAX show (not including full-length feature films)* ۞ *Mon.–Sat. 10–5, Sun. noon–6.*

★ **Riverwalk.** Lovely views prevail on this paved promenade on the New River's north bank. On the first Sunday of every month a free jazz festival attracts visitors as does an organic, urban farmers' market each Saturday from 9 to 1. From west to east, the Riverwalk begins at the residential New River Sound, passes through the Arts and Science District, then the historic center of Fort Lauderdale, and wraps around the New River until it meets with Las Olas Boulevard's shopping district.

Stranahan House. The city's oldest residence, on the National Register of Historic Places, and increasingly dwarfed by high-rise development, was once home for businessman Frank Stranahan, who arrived in 1892. With his wife, Ivy, the city's first schoolteacher, he befriended and traded with Seminole Indians, and taught them "new ways." In 1901 he built a store that would later become his home after serving as a post office, a general store, and a restaurant. Frank and Ivy's former residence is now a museum, with many period furnishings, and tours. The historic home remains Fort Lauderdale's principal link to its brief 110-year history. Note that self-guided tours are not allowed. ⊠ *335 S.E. 6th Ave., at Las Olas Blvd.* ☎ *954/524–4736* ⊕ *www.stranahanhouse.org* ⊠ *$12* ۞ *Tours daily at 1, 2, and 3 pm; closed Sept.*

QUICK BITES

Kilwin's of Las Olas. The sweet smell of waffle cones lures pedestrians to an old-fashioned confectionery that also sells hand-paddled fudge and scoops of homemade ice cream. ⊠ *809 E. Las Olas Blvd.* ☎ *954/523-8338.*

WORTH NOTING

Fort Lauderdale Antique Car Museum. Retired floral company owner Arthur O. Stone set up a foundation to preserve these eyepoppers. Nostalgia includes around two dozen Packards (all in running condition) from 1900 to the 1940s, along with a gallery saluting Franklin Delano Roosevelt. This sparkling museum sports everything from grease caps, spark plugs, and gearshift knobs to Texaco Oil signage, plus a newer wing and an enlarged library. ⊠ *1527 S.W. 11th Ave. (Packard Ave.)* ☎ *954/779–7300* ⊕ *www.antiquecarmuseum.net* ⊠ *$8* ۞ *Weekdays 10–4, Sat. 10–3.*

Sailboat Bend. Between Las Olas and the river lies a neighborhood with a character reminiscent of Key West's Old Town and Miami's Coconut Grove. Although without shops or much in the way of services, it's still worth a visit to be reminded of bygone days. The circa-1927 Fire Station No. 3, designed by local architect Francis Abreu and now housing the

THE GHOSTS OF STRANAHAN HOUSE

These days the historic Stranahan House is equally famous for its nighttime ghost tours as it is for its daytime history tour. Originally built as a trading post in 1901 and later expanded into a town hall, a post office, a bank, and the personal residence of Frank Stranahan and wife, Ivy Cromartie, the historic Stranahan House was more than plagued by a number of tragic events and violent deaths, including Frank's tragic suicide. After financial turmoil, Stranahan tied himself to a concrete sewer grate and jumped into New River, leaving his widow to carry on. Sunday nights at 7:30, house staff reveal the multiple tragic tales from the Stranahan crypt during the River House Ghost Tour ($25) and help visitors communicate with "the other side." Using special tools and snapping photos to search for orbs, guests are encouraged to field energy from the supposed five ghosts in the house. Given the high success rate of reaching out to the paranormal, the Stranahan House has become a favorite campground for global ghost hunters and television shows. Advance reservations are required.

Fort Lauderdale Fire Museum, is at the corner of West Las Olas Boulevard and Southwest 11th Avenue. Across the river lies the tree-lined Tarpon River neighborhood, alluding to the canal-like river looping off New River from the southeast quadrant and running to the southwest section, returning to New River near Sailboat Bend.

ALONG THE BEACH

★ **Bonnet House.** A 35-acre oasis in the heart of the beach area, this subtropical estate on the National Register of Historic Places stands as a tribute to the history of Old South Florida. This charming home, built in the roaring '20s, was the winter residence of the late Frederic and Evelyn Bartlett, artists whose personal touches and small surprises are evident throughout. For architecture, artwork, or the natural environment, this place is special. After admiring the fabulous gardens, be on the lookout for playful monkeys swinging from trees. Hours can vary, so call first. ⊠ *900 N. Birch Rd.* ☎ *954/563–5393* ⊕ *www.bonnethouse. org* ⊠ *$20 for house tours, $10 for grounds only* ☾ *Tues.–Sat. 10–4, Sun. 11–4. Closed Sept.*

Fodor's Choice **Fort Lauderdale Beachfront.** Fort Lauderdale's increasingly stylish beach-
★ front offers easy access not only to a wide band of downy sands but also to restaurants and shops. Heading north for 2 mi, beginning at the Bahia Mar yacht basin along Route A1A, you'll have clear ocean views (typically across rows of colorful beach umbrellas) to ships passing in and out of nearby Port Everglades. If you're on the beach, gaze back on an exceptionally graceful promenade.

Hugh Taylor Birch State Recreation Area. Amid the tropical greenery of this 180-acre park, stroll along a nature trail, visit the Birch House Museum, picnic, play volleyball, or paddle a rented canoe. Since parking is limited on Route A1A, park here and take a walkway underpass to the beach (which can be accessed 9–5, daily). ⊠ *3109 E. Sunrise Blvd.*

☎ *954/564–4521* ⊕ *www.floridastateparks.org* ✉ *$6 per vehicle, $2 per pedestrian* ☾ *Daily 8–sunset.*

International Swimming Hall of Fame Museum. This monument to underwater accomplishments has photos, medals, and other souvenirs from major swim events, and the Huizenga Theater provides an automated video experience where you can select vintage-Olympic coverage or old films such as Esther Williams' *Million Dollar Mermaid*. Connected to the museum, the **Fort Lauderdale Aquatic Complex**(⊕ *www.ci.ftlaud. fl.us/flac*) has two 50-meter pools plus a dive pool open daily to the public (except mid-December to mid-January). ✉ *501 Sea Breeze Blvd., 1 block south of Las Olas at Rte. A1A* ☎ *954/462–6536 or 954/828–4580* ⊕ *www.ishof.org* ✉ *Museum $8, pool $4* ☾ *Museum daily 9–5; pool 8–4 daily, plus 6 pm–8 pm weekday evening.*

NEED A
BREAK?

Casablanca Café. For respite from the sun, duck in for a nice glass of chardonnay. ✉ *3049 Alhambra St.* ☎ *954/764–3500.*

Steak 954. Recover from a long day in the sun with a much-deserved, refreshing cocktail. ✉ *401 N. Fort Lauderdale Beach Blvd.* ☎ *954/414–8333.*

Starbucks addicts can get their iced coffee fix at the beachfront outpost at the Westin Hotel, smack-dab in the center of Fort Lauderdale beach.

WESTERN SUBURBS AND BEYOND

West of Fort Lauderdale is ever-growing suburbia, with most of Broward's golf courses, landlocked attractions, and shopping. As you head farther west, the terrain takes on more characteristics of the Everglades, and you'll occasionally see alligators sunning on canal banks. Eventually, you reach the Everglades themselves after hitting the airboat outfitters on the park's periphery. Tourists flock to these airboats, but the best way of seeing the Everglades is to visit the National Park itself.

☾ **Big Cypress Seminole Reservation.** On the way to the Everglades from Fort Lauderdale is this reservation's two very different attractions.

At the **Billie Swamp Safari**, experience the majesty of the Everglades firsthand. Daily tours of wildlife-filled wetlands and hammocks yield sightings of deer, water buffalo, raccoons, wild hogs, hawks, eagles, and alligators. Sighting of the rare Florida panther are limited to the two captive felines on-site. Animal and reptile shows entertain audiences. Ecotours are conducted aboard motorized swamp buggies, and airboat rides are available, too. The on-site Swamp Water Café serves gator nuggets, frogs' legs, catfish, and Indian fry bread with honey. ✉ *Big Cypress Seminole Indian Reservation, 30000 Gator Tail Trail, Clewiston* ☎ *863/983–6101 or 800/949–6101* ⊕ *www.swampsafari. com* ✉ *Swamp Safari Day Package (ecotour, shows, exhibits, and airboat ride) $49.95* ☾ *Daily 10–5.*

A couple of miles from Billie Swamp Safari is **Ah-Tah-Thi-Ki Museum**, whose name means "a place to learn, a place to remember." This museum documents the traditions and culture of the Seminole Tribe

FORT LAUDERDALE SPAS

Most of Fort Lauderdale's upscale spas are located within elegant beachfront hotels but remain open to the public. During low season (September and October), top spas offer $99 treatments during the "Spa Chic" promotion (⊕ www.sunny.org/spachic).

Bliss Spa, W Fort Lauderdale. The menu at this quiet respite matches that of other Bliss spas and features Bliss products. A local favorite is the "carrot and sesame body buff"—a carrot mulch and hot oil rubdown, warm milk and honey drizzle, skin-softening wrap, sesame seed and sea salt scrub, and Vichy shower.

Body Treatments: Massage: Swedish, aromatherapy, stone, couples massage, Ashiatsu, deep tissue, mother-to-be massage, hydromassage, reflexology, exfoliation.

Beauty Treatments: Anti-aging treatments, anti-cellulite, facials, manicure, pedicure, waxing.

Prices: Body Treatments, $70–$235. Facials, $80–$280. Manicure/Pedicure, $25–$90. Waxing, $15–$220.

✉ W Fort Lauderdale, 401 N. Fort Lauderdale Beach Blvd., Along the beach, Fort Lauderdale ☎ 954/414–8200 ⊕ www.blissworld.com.

The Spa at the Ritz-Carlton, Fort Lauderdale. The expansive 8,500-foot hideaway exudes tranquillity and relaxation, from the seashell color palate to the magical hands of Fort Lauderdale's top therapists.

Body Treatments: Massage options run the gamut, including Swedish, aromatherapy, stone, couples massage, deep tissue, hydrotherapy, reflexology, Thai massage, mother-to-be, and Sea Spray.

Beauty Treatments: Dermatologist-developed skincare treatments, anti-cellulite treatments, anti-aging treatments, facials, manicure, pedicure, and waxing.

Prices: Body Treatments, $130–$230. Facials, $75–$195. Manicure/Pedicure, $45–$110. Waxing, $30–$90.

✉ The Ritz-Carlton, Fort Lauderdale, 1 N. Fort Lauderdale Beach Blvd., Along the beach, Fort Lauderdale ☎ 954/465–2300 ⊕ www.RitzCarlton.com/FortLauderdale.

Spa Atlantic. The 10,000-foot Spa Atlantic boasts a relaxed glamour and offers a menu of perfected core spa services. Many treatments are rooted in India, Arabia, the Orient, and the Mediterranean but alongside are modern approaches, like the health-boosting beer scrubs and beer hair treatments.

Body Treatments: Swedish, aromatherapy, stone, couples massage, deep tissue, hydrotherapy, reflexology, mother-to-be, Thai, and chair massage. Baths, body wraps, body glows (exfoliation).

Beauty Treatments: Skincare enhancements, anti-aging treatments, facials, manicure, pedicure, waxing, hair, makeup.

Prices: Body Treatments, $75–$330. Facials, $75–$175. Manicure/Pedicure, $26–$70. Waxing, $20–$90.

✉ The Atlantic Hotel, 601 N. Fort Lauderdale Beach Blvd., Along the beach, Fort Lauderdale ☎ 954/567–8085 ⊕ www.atlantichotelfl.com.

of Florida through artifacts, exhibits, and reenactments of rituals and ceremonies. The 60-acre site includes a living-history Seminole village, nature trails, and a wheelchair-accessible boardwalk through a cypress swamp. ✉ *34725 W. Boundary Rd., Clewiston* ☎ *863/902–1113* ⊕ *www.ahtahthiki.com* 🖅 *$9* ⊙ *Tues.–Sun. 9–5.*

Sawgrass Mills. Twenty-six million visitors a year flock to this mall, 10 mi west of downtown Fort Lauderdale, making it Florida's second-biggest tourist attraction (after the one with the mouse). The ever-growing complex has a basic alligator shape, and walking it all amounts to about a 2-mi jaunt. Count on 11,000 self-parking spaces (note your location, or you'll be working those soles), valet parking, and two information centers. More than 400 shops—many manufacturer's outlets, retail outlets, and name-brand discounters—include Chico's Outlet, Super Target, and Ron Jon Surf Shop. Chain restaurants such as P.F. Chang's, the Cheesecake Factory, Grand Lux Cafe, and Rainforest Café are on-site. Wannado City, an "interactive-empowerment environment" is geared toward ages four and up. The adjacent Shops at Colonnade cater to well-heeled patrons with a David Yurman jewelry outlet and other shops including Valentino, Prada, Burberry, Kate Spade New York, and Barneys New York. ✉ *12801 W. Sunrise Blvd., at Flamingo Rd., Sunrise.*

Sawgrass Recreation Park. For Everglades thrills, take a half-hour airboat ride here. You'll see all manner of plants and wildlife, from birds and alligators to turtles, snakes, and fish. Besides the ride, your entrance fee covers admission to an Everglades nature exhibit; a native Seminole village; and exhibits on alligators, other reptiles, and birds of prey. ✉ *1006 N. U.S. Hwy. 27, Weston* ☎ *888/424–7262* ⊕ *www.evergladestours. com* 🖅 *$19.50* ⊙ *Airboat rides daily 9–5.*

SPORTS AND THE OUTDOORS

BIKING

Among the most popular routes are Route A1A and Bayview Drive, especially in early morning before traffic builds, and a 7-mi bike path that parallels State Road 84 and New River and leads to Markham Park, which has mountain bike trails. ■TIP➔ Alligator alert: Do not dangle your legs from seawalls.

BIRD-WATCHING

Evergreen Historic Cemetery. North of Fort Lauderdale's 17th Street Causeway, amid a Gothic setting, lies an avid bird-watchers' haven. The circa 1879 graveyard, shaded by gumbo limbo and strangler figs, doubles as a place of fleeting repose for Bahama mockingbirds and other species winging through urban Broward. Warblers are big here, and there are occasional sightings of red-eyed vireos, northern waterthrushes, and scarlet tanagers. ✉ *1300 S.E. 10th Ave.* ☎ *954/745–2140* ⊕ *www.browardcemeteries.com.*

EXPLORING THE VENICE OF AMERICA

While a number of tour outfitters offer an opportunity to journey the aqua back lots of Fort Lauderdale, the best way to experience the multimillion-dollar homes, hotels, and seafood restaurants along Fort Lauderdale's waterways is via the public Water Taxi. An unlimited day pass serves as both a tour and a means of transportation between Fort Lauderdale's most notable sights.

For sightseeing, the Water Taxi can pick you up at any of several docks along the Intracoastal Waterway or New River, and you can stop off at attractions like the Performing Arts Center, Beach Place, and the Stranahan House. For lunch or dinner, sail away to restaurants on Las Olas Boulevard, Las Olas Riverfront, or Fort Lauderdale beach. Water taxis are also a superb way to barhop, letting your pilot play the sober role of designated driver. Even just cruising on the water taxi for an afternoon is a fun way to take in the waterfront sights. Captains and helpers tend to be real characters, indulging guests in fun factoids about Fort Lauderdale, white lies about the city's history, and bizarre tales about the celebrity homes along the Intracoastal.

The Water Taxi has a direct pickup point at Hyatt Regency 66 and two stops a few minutes walk from the Ritz-Carlton, the Atlantic, and the W Fort Lauderdale. Since the service runs hourly, check the schedule before setting off to begin your tour.

The water-transport venture was started by Bob Bekoff, a longtime Broward resident and outspoken tourism promoter, who decided to combine the need for transportation with one of the area's most captivating features: waterways that make Fort Lauderdale the Venice of America.

Ride all you want with a day pass, purchased onboard or at a kiosk at the Gallery at Beach Place, 10:30 am–12:30 am, for $20. Family allday passes for two adults and up to three youths are $55, and after 7 pm, passes are $7. The taxis have fourteen scheduled stops.

In addition to regular service throughout Fort Lauderdale, the winter season brings the much-welcomed South Beach Express Water Taxi service. This express service first travels south 45 minutes to Hollywood, then continues another hour to the Art Deco District of Miami Beach ($38). From mid-December through February, the service leaves Fort Lauderdale at 10:15 am, returning by 6:30 pm. From early March through April, the service leaves Fort Lauderdale at 10:45 am, returning at 7 pm. To get around town by boat, contact **Water Taxi** (☎ 954/467–6677 ⊕ www.watertaxi.com).

FISHING

Bahia Mar Beach Resort. If you're interested in a saltwater charter, check out the offerings at this resort. Sportfishing and drift-fishing bookings can be arranged. ⊠ *801 Seabreeze Blvd.* ☎ *954/627–6357.*

Sand can sometimes be forgiving if you fall, and bicyclists also appreciate the ocean views.

SCUBA DIVING AND SNORKELING

Lauderdale Diver. This PADI–affiliated outfit arranges dive charters up and down Broward's shoreline. Dive trips typically last four hours. Nonpackage reef trips are open to divers for around $50; scuba gear is extra. ⊠ *1334 S.E. 17th St. Causeway* ☎ *954/467–2822.*

Pro Dive. The area's oldest diving operation has downsized and joined forces with another company, Sea Experience. Snorkelers can go out for $35 on a two-hour snorkeling trip, including equipment, with Sea Experience. Pro Dive offers daily trips for scuba divers to Broward's natural coral reefs or over two-dozen shipwrecks including the famous "Mercedes I." Expect to pay $55 if using your own gear or $115 with full scuba gear included. Pro Dive: ⊠ *801 Seabreeze Blvd.* ☎ *954/776–3483* ⊕ *www.prodiveusa.com.* Sea Experience: ⊠ *Bahia Mar Beach Resort, 801 Seabreeze Blvd., Fort Lauderdale* ☎ *954/770–3483* ⊕ *www.seaxp.com.*

SHOPPING

MALLS

Galleria Mall. Just west of the Intracoastal Waterway, the split-level emporium entices with Neiman Marcus, Dillard's, and Macy's, plus 150 specialty shops for anything from cookware to exquisite jewelry. Recent upgrades include marble floors and fine dining options. Chow down at Capital Grille, Truluck's, Blue Martini, P.F. Chang's or Seasons 52, or head for the food court, which will defy expectations with its international food-market feel. Galleria is open 10–9 Monday through

Saturday, noon–5:30 Sunday. ⊠ *2414 E. Sunrise Blvd.* ☎ *954/564–1015* ⊕ *www.galleriamall-fl.com.*

Sawgrass Mills. This alligator-shape megamall draws 26 million dollars a year to its collection of 400 outlet stores and name-brand discounters. Themed restaurants keep the whole family fed and entertained. If the kids (or even the adults) would rather not shop til they drop, they can have their own kind of fun at Wannado City, an "interactive-empowerment environment" (four and up) while the shopaholics do their thing. ⊠ *12801 W. Sunrise Blvd., at Flamingo Rd., Sunrise.*

Swap Shop. The South's largest flea market, with 2,000 vendors, is open daily. While exploring this indoor–outdoor entertainment-and-shopping complex, hop on the carousel or stick around for movies at the 14-screen Swap Shop drive-in. ⊠ *3291 W. Sunrise Blvd.*

SHOPPING DISTRICTS

Las Olas Boulevard. The city's best boutiques plus top restaurants and art galleries line a beautifully landscaped street. Window shopping allowed. ⊠ *1 block off New River east of Andrews Ave.* ⊕ *www.lasolasboulevard.com.*

NIGHTLIFE AND THE ARTS

For the most complete weekly listing of events, check "Showtime!" the *South Florida Sun-Sentinel*'s tabloid-sized entertainment section and events calendar published on Friday. "Weekend," in the Friday Broward edition of the *Herald,* also lists area happenings. The weekly *City Link* is principally an entertainment and dining paper with an "underground" look. *New Times* is a free alternative weekly circulating a Broward–Palm Beach County edition.

THE ARTS

Broward Center for the Performing Arts. More than 500 events unfold annually at the 2,700-seat architectural gem, including Broadway-style musicals, plays, dance, symphony, opera, rock, film, lectures, comedy, and children's theater. An enclosed elevated walkway links the centerpiece of Fort Lauderdale's arts district to a parking garage across the street. ⊠ *201 S.W. 5th Ave.* ☎ *954/462–0222* ⊕ *www.browardcenter.org.*

★ **Chef Jean-Pierre Cooking School.** Catering to locals, seasonal snowbirds, and folks winging in for even shorter stays, Jean-Pierre Brehier (former owner of the much-missed Left Bank Restaurant on Las Olas) teaches the basics, from boiling water onward. The enthusiastic Gallic transplant has appeared on NBC's *Today* and CNN's *Larry King Live.* For souvenir hunters, this fun cooking facility also sells nifty pots, pastas, oils, and other great items. ⊠ *1436 N. Federal Hwy.* ☎ *954/563–2700* ⊕ *www.chefjp.com* ⊠ *$65 per demonstration class, $125 hands-on class* ☉ *Store Mon.–Sat. 10–7, class schedules vary.*

Cinema Paradiso. This art-house movie theater operates out of a former church, south of New River near the county courthouse. The space doubles as headquarters for FLIFF, the Fort Lauderdale International Film Festival. ⊠ *503 S.E. 6th St.* ☎ *954/525–3456.*

NIGHTLIFE

BARS AND LOUNGES

The majority of Fort Lauderdale nightlife takes place near downtown though some of the high-end bars and clubs along Fort Lauderdale beach's luxury row have become popular. Nightlife options begin in the heart of downtown on Himmarshee Street (2nd Street), continuing on to the Riverfront and then to Las Olas Boulveard. Fort Lauderdale's gay nightlife is concentrated in the Wilton Manors area.

The Downtown Riverfront tends to draw a younger demographic somewhere between underage teens and late twenties. On Himmarshee Street, a half dozen rowdy bars entice a wide range of partygoers, ranging from the seedy to the sophisticated.

Coyote Ugly. Pick up where the film left off with wild girls and wild nights. ⊠ *214 S.W. 2nd St.* ☎ *954/764–8459* ⊕ *www.coyoteuglysaloon. com.*

Living Room. This dance palladium, near the Riverfront, is Fort Lauderdale's hottest Saturday club experience. Friday nights are alternative/gay night. The club is also open on Thursday for ladies night, where ladies drink free and get in free. ⊠ *300 S.W. 1st Ave, Suite 200, 2nd fl.* ☎ *888/992–7555* ⊕ *www.livingroomclub.com.*

O Lounge. This lounge and two adjacent establishments, **Yolo** and **Vibe,** on Las Olas and under the same ownership, cater to Fort Lauderdale's sexy yuppies, business men, desperate housewives, and hungry cougars letting loose during happy hour and on the weekends. Crowds alternate between Yolo's outdoor fire pit, O Lounge's chilled atmosphere and lounge music, and Vibe's more intense beats. Expect flashy cars in the driveway. ⊠ *333 E. Las Olas Blvd.* ☎ *954/523–1000* ⊕ *www. yolorestaurant.com.*

Tarpon Bend. Expect casual fun along with a few beers and some great bar food at this consistently busy joint. ⊠ *200 S.W. 2nd St.* ☎ *954/523–3233* ⊕ *www.tarponbend.com.*

Voodoo Lounge. The party gets going late at night. The lounge plays the latest club music and packs the house for ladies night on Wednesday and the gay-straight mixer, "Life's a Drag" on Sunday. ⊠ *111 S.W. 2nd Ave.* ☎ *954/522–0733* ⊕ *www. voodooloungeflorida.com.*

WHERE TO EAT

ALONG THE BEACH

$$$
ECLECTIC
✕ **Casablanca Cafe.** You'll get a fabulous ocean view and a good meal to boot at this historic two-story Moroccan-style villa, built in the 1920s by local architect Francis Abreu. This piano bar's menu is a potpourri with both tropical and Asian influence (try the Korean-style roasted duck) along with North African specialties like lamb shank and couscous. There's a deck for outside dining. It's a lively spot with friendly service. ⊠ *3049 Alhambra St.* ☎ *954/764–3500* ⊕ *www. casablancacafeonline.com.*

$$$
ITALIAN
✕ **Da Campo Osteria.** Todd English makes his Fort Lauderdale debut with this upscale Tuscan-inspired restaurant. On the ground floor of the

sleek Il Lugano hotel, the stylish restaurant impresses with its tableside mozzarella showcase and exceptional array of antipasti, primi, and secondi. The mozzarella barista makes the cheese fresh at your table from raw ingredients and then provides a choice of six toppings, including heirloom tomatoes and sweet basil or green and olive tapenade. Five pastas are handcrafted in house daily, usually two special ones and the three staples—spaghetti, tagliatelle, and *angnolotti*. ✉ *3333 N.E. 32nd Ave., Along the beach,Fort Lauderdale* ☎ *954/225–5002* ⊕ *www. dacampoosteria.com* ⌕ *Reservations essential.*

$$$
MEXICAN
Fodor'sChoice
★

✕ **Dos Caminos.** After taking over the Manhattan Mexican dining scene, Dos Caminos has settled into its Florida home, bringing the robust flavors of Mexico and the hospitality culture of NYC to Fort Lauderdale. Rounds of traditional and nontraditional margaritas (like the Pineapple Brown Sugar Margarita) begin an evening of new flavors and foodie fantasia. Chips are served with a trio of authentic salsas, usually followed by chunky guacamole, made to order. The ceviches vary from classic Mexican preparations, like the "Snapper Ceviche Veracruz" and the more modern, Asian-influenced "Tuna Ceviche Chino-Latino" and the "Shrimp Ceviche Yucateco," marinated in citrus and coconut foam. The house specialties, tacos, quesadillas, and enchiladas impress with a commingling of truly traditional Mexican dishes and neo-Mexican cuisine reinvented with an American flair. For example, the "Grilled Shrimp Quesadilla" is a creative tour de force—an open-faced crispy flour tortilla topped with chile-marinated shrimp, Mexican cheeses, wild mushrooms, and oven-dried tomatoes. Basically, heaven on a plate! ✉ *Sheraton Fort Lauderdale Beach Resort,1140 Seabreeze Blvd., Along the beach,Fort Lauderdale* ☎ *954/727–7090* ⊕ *www.doscaminos.com.*

$$$$
STEAKHOUSE
Fodor'sChoice
★

✕ **Steak 954.** Steak 954 has quickly become an institution for Fort Lauderdale's foodies and visitors alike. It's not just the steaks that impress here. The lobster and crab-coconut ceviche and the red snapper tiradito are divine; the butter-poached Maine lobster is perfection; and the raw bar showcases only the best and freshest seafood on the market. Located on the 1st floor of the swanky W Fort Lauderdale, Steak 954 offers spectacular views of the ocean for those choosing outdoor seating; or a sexy, sophisticated ambience for those choosing to dine in the main dining room, with bright tropical colors balanced with dark woods and an enormous jellyfish tank spanning the width of the restaurant. Sunday brunch is very popular, so arrive early for the best views. ✉ *401 N. Fort Lauderdale Beach Blvd., Along the beach,Fort Lauderdale* ☎ *954/414–8333* ⊕ *www.steak954.com.*

DOWNTOWN AND LAS OLAS

$$$
ECLECTIC

✕ **Big City Tavern.** A Las Olas landmark, Big City Tavern is the boulevard's most consistent spot for good food, good spirits, and good times. The diverse menu commingles Asian entrées like pad thai, Italian options like homemade meatballs and cheese ravioli, and American dishes like the grilled skirt steak Cobb salad. The Asian Calamari with peanuts, apricots, and sweet-and-sour sauce and the Pistachio Brown Butter Bundt Cake with honey-roasted spiced peaches and pistachio gelato are two of the tavern's best creations. Big City is open late night for drinks, desserts, and even offers a late-night menu. ✉ *609 E. Las Olas Blvd., Downtown and Las Olas,Fort Lauderdale* ☎ *954/727–0307* ⊕ *www.bigtimerestaurants.com.*

$$$$
BRAZILIAN

✕**Chima.** Fort Lauderdale's snazzy Brazilian steak house is located at the far eastern end of Las Olas, in a lushly landscaped enclave. Similar to other restaurants of its type, Chima has an entourage of meat carvers parading around the restaurant with different cuts as well as a massive salad bar with seafood options, fancy greens, and grilled vegetables to accompany the never-ending plates of protein. ✉ *2400 E. Las Olas Blvd., Downtown and Las Olas,Fort Lauderdale* ☎ *954/712–0580* ⊕ *www.chima.cc* ☽ *No lunch.*

$$
AMERICAN

✕**Floridian.** This classic diner is plastered with photos of Monroe, Nixon, and local notables past and present in a succession of brightly painted rooms with funky chandeliers. The kitchen dishes up typical grease-pit breakfast favorites (no matter the hour), with oversize omelets that come with biscuits, toast, or English muffins, plus a choice of grits or tomato. The restaurant also has good hangover eats but don't expect anything exceptional (besides the location). It's open 24 hours—even during hurricanes, as long as the power holds out. ✉ *1410 E. Las Olas Blvd.* ☎ *954/463–4041* ▭ *No credit cards.*

$
ITALIAN

✕**Grand Forno Cafe.** The gamble of importing an entire Italian bakery direct from Brescia, Italy definitely paid off. Most days, the sandwiches, fresh baked breads, and pastries sell out even before lunchtime. All products are made fresh daily, beginning at 4 am, by a team of bakers who can be seen hard at work through the café's glass windows. Customers line up at the door early in the morning to get their piping-hot artisanal breads, later returning for the scrumptious paninis and decadent desserts. A second branch, five blocks east on Las Olas, called Grand Forno Pronto, serves a more limited menu. ✉ *1235 E. Las Olas Blvd., Downtown and Las Olas,Fort Lauderdale* ☎ *954/467–2244* ⊕ *www.granforno.com* ☽ *Tues.–Sun. 7:30–7; closed Mon.*

$$$
AMERICAN
Fodor's Choice
★

✕**Himmarshee Bar and Grill.** There's a reason that Himmarshee Bar and Grill has survived all of downtown Fort Lauderdale's ups and downs—the food is utterly fantastic. While the restaurant is constantly evolving based on customer feedback and the chef's ingenuity, it has perfected a number of dishes in its 15 years while pushing the envelope of flavorful American cuisine with its ever-changing menu. Some items, like the butternut squash purses and the buttermilk blue cheese stuffed dates, have been the talk of the town since the 1990s and remain a fixture with each seasonal menu. Thankfully, so does the amazing herb-seared rare tuna served over a ragout of white bean, wild mushroom, broccolini, shallot, oil poached tomato, and balsamic jus. However, by virtue of using fresh, seasonal products, some good things (or entrees) must come to an end; but on the flip side, it's a great reason to return with each passing season to discover a new favorite dish. ✉ *210 S.W. 2nd St., Downtown and Las Olas,Fort Lauderdale* ☎ *954/524–1818* ⊕ *www.himmarshee.com.*

$
AMERICAN
★

✕**ROK: BRG.** It took a while, but Fort Lauderdale finally welcomed its first personality-driven gastro pub in early 2011, giving the grown-ups something to enjoy in teenage-infested Downtown. The long and narrow venue, adorned with exposed brick walls and flat-screen TVs, serves up the city's best burgers from Angus beef monsters to the more en vogue sushi-grade ahi tuna burger. The hand-cut original fries and sweet potato fries are served in their own mini fryers, accompanied by a series of sauces made from scratch every day (try the Bourbon BBQ sauce). Scrumptious starters include hand-battered onion rings with jalapeño-cheddar sauce and "Lobster Corn Dogs." With several beers on tap, a huge cocktail menu, and a great vibe, ROK: BRGR is the perfect place for amazing cheap eats and good times, any night of the week. ⊠ *208 S.W. 2nd St., Downtown and Las Olas,Fort Lauderdale* ☎ *954/525–7656* ⊕ *www.rokbrgr.com.*

$$$ ✕**YOLO.** YOLO stands for "You Only Live Once," but you will defi-
AMERICAN   nitely want to eat here more than once. For Fort Lauderdale's bour-
geoisie, this is the place to see and be seen and to show off your hottest wheels in the driveway. For others, it's an upscale restaurant with affordable prices and a great ambience. The restaurant serves the full gamut of new American favorites like tuna sashimi, fried calamari, garden burgers, and short ribs with a sophisticated spin. For example, the Szechuan Calamari is flash fried, and then covered in garlic-chili sauce, chopped peanuts, and sesame seeds; the garden burger is made from bulgur wheat, cremini mushrooms, and cashews and served with thin-cut fries. ⊠ *333 E. Las Olas Blvd., Downtown, Fort Lauderdale* ☎ *954/523–1000* ⊕ *www.yolorestaurant.com.*

INTRACOASTAL AND INLAND

$$$$ ✕**Canyon Southwest Cafe.** Southwestern fusion fare helps you escape
SOUTHWESTERN   the ordinary at this small magical enclave. It's been run for the past
Fodor's Choice dozen years by owner and executive chef Chris Wilber. Order, for exam-
★   ple, bison medallions with scotch bonnets, a tequila-jalapeño smoked salmon tostada, coriander-crusted tuna, or blue-corn fried oysters. Chipotle, wasabi, mango, and red chilies accent fresh seafood and wild game. Start off with a signature prickly pear margarita or choose from a well-rounded wine list or beer selection. Save room for the divine chocolate bread pudding. ⊠ *1818 E. Sunrise Blvd.* ☎ *954/765–1950* ⊕ *www.canyonfl.com* ☉ *No lunch.*

$$$ ✕**Casa D'Angelo.** Owner-chef Angelo Elia has created a gem of a Tuscan-
ITALIAN   style white-tablecloth restaurant, tucked in the Sunrise Square shopping center. Casa D'Angelo's oak oven turns out marvelous seafood and beef dishes. The pappardelle with porcini mushrooms takes pasta to pleasant heights. Another favorite is the calamari and scungilli salad with garlic and lemon. Ask about the oven-roasted fish of the day or the snapper *oreganta* at market price. ⊠ *1201 N. Federal Hwy.* ☎ *954/564–1234* ⊕ *www.casa-d-angelo.com* ☉ *No lunch.*

$$$$ ✕**China Grill.** China Grill takes the best of Asian cuisine and adds an
ASIAN   American flair to create a pan-Asian eating extravaganza. This concept of global Asian fusion draws inspiration from Marco Polo and his descriptions of the Far East and its riches. While Marco Polo's travels are imprinted on the restaurant floor, the flavors of his destinations are all over the menu. Try the crackling calamari salad—a taste explosion of zest with crispy lettuce, calamari, and citrus in lime-miso dressing—or the Shanghai Lobster—a 2.5-pound female lobster, unbelievably soft

and tender, drenched in ginger and curry and accompanied by crispy spinach. ⊠ *1881 S.E. 17th St., Intracoastal and Inland,Fort Lauderdale* 🕾 *954/759–9950* ⊕ *www.chinagrillmgt.com.*

$$ ╳ **Giorgio's Brick Oven Pizza.** The delicious brick oven pizza lures cus-
PIZZA tomers to this tiny restaurant, but it's really the salads and sandwiches
Fodor'sChoice that provide the wow factor. The blackened chicken Caesar salad and
★ the monstrous grilled chicken sandwiches (with grilled peppers and fresh mozzarella on freshly baked bread) are both memorable. Nevertheless, the homemade seafood salad is still Giorgio's best seller, a healthy mix of baby squid, shrimp, calamari, and scallops in a light vinaigrette. All meals are served with piping hot rolls and homemade hummus. ⊠ *1499 S.E. 17th St., Intracoastal and Inland,Fort Lauderdale* 🕾 *954/767–8300.*

$$ ╳ **Old Heidelberg Restaurant & Deli.** Likened to a Bavarian mirage plucked
GERMAN from the Alps and plopped along State Road 84 near the airport and seaport, the Old Heidelberg's beer stein–cowbell–cuckoo-clock decor accents the Bavarian lamb shanks, various schnitzels, sauerkraut, and other specialties, from apple strudel to Black Forest cake. The restaurant boats a great selection of German beers on tap. Old Heidelberg Deli next door (open Tuesday through Saturday 9–6) stocks kielbasa, liver dumplings, Bitburger beer, breads, and nearly a dozen mustards. ⊠ *900 State Rd. 84* 🕾 *954/463–6747* ⊕ *www.oldheidelbergdeli.com* ☉ *Closed Mon. No lunch Sat.*

$ ╳ **Southport Raw Bar.** You can't go wrong at this unpretentious spot
SEAFOOD where the motto, on bumper stickers for miles around, proclaims, "eat fish, live longer, eat oysters, love longer, eat clams, last longer." Raw or steamed clams, raw oysters, and peel-and-eat shrimp are market priced. Sides range from Bimini bread to key lime pie, with conch fritters, beer-battered onion rings, and corn on the cob in between. Order wine by the bottle or glass, and beer by the pitcher, bottle, or can. Eat outside overlooking a canal, or inside at booths, tables, or in the front or back bars. Limited parking is free, and a grocery-store parking lot is across the street. ⊠ *1536 Cordova Rd.* 🕾 *954/525–2526* ⊕ *www. southportrawbar.com.*

$$$ ╳ **Sublime.** Pamela Anderson and her celebrity pals are not the only
VEGETARIAN vegetarians that love this vegan powerhouse. The vegan sushi, the portobello stack, and innovative pizzas and pastas surprisingly satisfy carnivore cravings. All dishes are organic and void of any animal by-products, showing the world how vegan eating does not compromise flavor or taste. Even items like the key lime cheesecake, and chicken scaloppini use alternative ingredients and headline an evening of health-conscious eating. ⊠ *1431 N. Federal Hwy., Intracoastal and Inland, Fort Lauderdale* 🕾 *954/539–9000* ⊕ *www.sublimerestaurant. com* ☉ *Closed Mon.*

¢ ╳ **Zona Fresca.** A local favorite, Zona Fresca leads the healthy, Mexican
MEXICAN fast-food revolution with the best chips, salsas, and burritos in town.
Fodor'sChoice Everything is made fresh on premises, including the authentic salsas,
★ presented in a grand salsa bar. Known locally for its fantastic value and great products, Zona is busy seven days a week for both lunch and dinner and offers both indoor and outdoor seating. ⊠ *1635 N.*

Federal Hwy., Intracoastal and Inland,Fort Lauderdale ☎ *954/566–1777* ⊕ *www.zonafresca.com.*

WESTERN SUBURBS

$$
AMERICAN
✗ **Alligator Alley.** At this taproom and music hall big on nightly music from rockabilly to funk rock, chefs ladle up memorable gumbo, and alligator ribs so good they once were featured on the Food Network. Wash down your beer with Gator Bites or Buffalo Fingers, or for delicacy, go for an appetizer of scallopini of gator with Szechuan sauce. Vegetarians can bulk up on cheese fries, or keep trim with a garden salad. ⊠ *1321 E. Commercial Blvd.* ☎ *954/771–2220* ⊕ *www.alligatoralleyflorida.com.*

$$$$
IRISH
✗ **Ireland Steakhouse.** Don't let the name fool you. Ireland Steakhouse is not particularly Irish nor is it just a steak house. In fact, this restaurant is most popular for its sustainable seafood menu. Promoting a holistic philosophy of green eating, the restaurant meticulously chooses its ingredients and the purveyors that supply them, while staying true to the international "Seafood Watch" guide. The restaurant is a warm and woodsy enclave in the back corner of the Hyatt Bonaventure. In keeping with trends of other steak houses, hearty mains (like the Orange Glaze Wild Canadian Arctic Char and the Cherry Balsamic Yellowfin Tuna) are paired with loads of decadent sides made for sharing (like Lobster Mac n' Cheese and Lobster Fries). ⊠ *250 Racquet Club Rd., Weston* ☎ *954/349–5656* ⊕ *www.bonaventure.hyatt.com* ☾ *Dinner Tues.–Sat. 5:30–10:30 pm; closed Sun. and Mon.*

WILTON MANORS AND OAKLAND PARK

$
AMERICAN
✗ **Diner 24.** It's still a mystery why Fort Lauderdale's newest diner added the magic 2-4 to its name when it's open 24 hours on just Friday and Saturday, until 11 pm other nights. Regardless, the awesome diner favorites are served at rock-bottom prices, at nearly the same price as neighboring McDonald's. With promotions nightly, a kitsch fish shack decor, and a superwelcoming environment, Diner 24 merits a large following for the hours it is actually open. ⊠ *301 W. Oakland Park Blvd., Oakland Park,Fort Lauderdale* ☎ *954/765–6349.*

$$$
ASIAN
✗ **Galanga.** Serving both Thai and Japanese cuisine under one roof, Galanga manages to deliver authenticity and extreme satisfaction to patrons who often find it hard to choose between the fabulous sushi and the succulent coconut curries and Thai specialties. Located on the main strip in Wilton Manors, the restaurant offers a sophisticated and intimate ambience. ⊠ *2389 Wilton Dr., Wilton Manors,Fort Lauderdale* ☎ *954/202–0000* ⊕ *www.galangarestaurant.com.*

$$
AMERICAN
✗ **Rosie's Bar and Grill.** Rosie's is consistently lively, pumping out tons of pop tunes and volumes of joyous laughter to surrounding streets. The former Hamburger Mary's has become an institution in South Florida, as the go-to gay-friendly place for cheap drinks, decent bar food, and great times. Most of the fun at Rosie's is meeting new friends and engaging in conversation with the person seated next to you. Drink specials change daily. Sunday brunch with alternating DJ's is wildly popular. ⊠ *2449 Wilton Dr., Wilton Manors,Fort Lauderdale* ☎ *954/567–1320* ⊕ *www.rosiesbarandgrill.com.*

Lago Mar Resort & Club in Fort Lauderdale has its own private beach on the Atlantic Ocean.

$ ✕ **Stork's Café.** At the edge of Wilton Manors, Stork's Café stands out
CAFÉ as a gay-friendly, straight-friendly, and just plain friendly place to plot
sightseeing strategies (or catch up on local papers). Sit indoors or outside under tables with red umbrellas. Custom Barbie cakes (real dolls,
edible ball gowns) are Stork's signature as is the pistachio cheesecake.
Divine baked goods range from croissants, tortes, cakes, and pies to
"Monster Cookies," including gingersnap and snicker doodle. Pilgrim
(turkey) or Hello Kitty (tuna) sandwiches go with salads or made-from-
scratch soups like Vegan Split Pea. ⊠ *2505 N.E. 15th Ave., Wilton
Manors* ☎ *954/567–3220* ⊕ *www.storkscafe.com.*

WHERE TO STAY

For expanded hotel reviews, visit Fodors.com.

ALONG THE BEACH

$$$$ 🖥 **The Atlantic Hotel.** Functional but elegant, this luxury condo hotel
HOTEL overlooks the Atlantic Ocean. **Pros:** sophisticated lodging option; rooms
★ have high-tech touches. **Cons:** no complimentary water bottles in room;
expensive parking. **TripAdvisor:** "would definitely recommend," "a
great location," "a bit pricey." ⊠ *601 N. Fort Lauderdale Beach Blvd.*
☎ *954/567–8020 or 877/567–8020* ⊕ *www.atlantichotelfl.com* ⤴ *61
rooms, 58 suites, 4 penthouses* ⊘ *In-room: a/c, kitchen, Internet, Wi-Fi.
In-hotel: restaurants, bar, pool, gym, spa, parking* ❍| *No meals.*

$$ 🖥 **Lago Mar Resort and Club.** The sprawling Lago Mar, owned by the
RESORT Banks family since the early 1950s, has retained its sparkle thanks
☻ to frequent renovations. **Pros:** secluded setting; plenty of activities;
★ on the beach. **Cons:** not the easiest to find; far from restaurants and

beach action. **TripAdvisor:** "no wow factor," "a Florida classic," "spotlessly clean and spacious." ⊠ *1700 S. Ocean La.* ☎ *954/523–6511 or 800/524–6627* ⊕ *www.lagomar.com* ⟿ *52 rooms, 160 suites* ⚸ *In-room: a/c, kitchen, Wi-Fi. In-hotel: restaurants, tennis court, pool* ¶◎| *No meals.*

$$$–$$$$
RESORT
☺
★

🏨 **Pelican Grand Beach Resort.** Smack on the beach, this already lovely property has been transformed with a new tower, restaurant and lounge, an old-fashioned ice-cream parlor, and a circulating lazy-river pool that allows guests to float 'round and 'round. **Pros:** you can't get any closer to the beach in Fort Lauderdale. **Cons:** you'll need wheels to access Las Olas's beach-area action. **TripAdvisor:** "reasonably priced dining onsite that is oceanfront," "beautiful views from beachside rooms," "big bathroom." ⊠ *2000 N. Atlantic Blvd.* ☎ *954/568–9431 or 800/525–6232* ⊕ *www.pelicanbeach.com* ⟿ *121 rooms (remainder of 155 total are condominiums)* ⚸ *In-room: a/c, Internet, Wi-Fi. In-hotel: restaurant, bar, pool* ¶◎| *No meals.*

$$$
B&B/INN

🏨 **The Pillars Hotel at New River Sound.** A "small secret" kept by locals in the know, this gem is one block from the beach and on the Intracoastal Waterway. **Pros:** attentive staff; lovely decor; idyllic pool area. **Cons:** small rooms; not for families with young kids given proximity to dock and water with no lifeguard on duty. **TripAdvisor:** "room was very small," "own water taxi stop," "fabulous oasis." ⊠ *111 N. Birch Rd.* ☎ *954/467–9639* ⊕ *www.pillarshotel.com* ⟿ *17 rooms, 5 suites* ⚸ *In-room: a/c, Internet, Wi-Fi. In-hotel: restaurant, pool, some age restrictions* ¶◎| *No meals.*

$$$–$$$$
HOTEL
Fodor's Choice
★

🏨 **Ritz-Carlton, Fort Lauderdale.** It's an eyepopper, with 24 dramatically tiered, glass-walled stories rising behind a tropical sundeck and a pool looking out toward the ocean. **Pros:** golfers have privileges at the private Grande Oaks Golf Course, where *Caddyshack* was filmed. **Cons:** golf facilities off-site; no complimentary Wi-Fi in public spaces. **TripAdvisor:** "plush from beginning to end," "attention to detail of the interior decorating," "incredible disappointment all around." ⊠ *1 N. Fort Lauderdale Beach Blvd.* ☎ *954/465–2300* ⊕ *www.ritzcarlton.com* ⟿ *138 rooms, 54 suites* ⚸ *In-room: a/c, Wi-Fi. In-hotel: restaurants, bar, pool, gym, spa, parking* ¶◎| *No meals.*

$$$–$$$$
HOTEL
Fodor's Choice
★

🏨 **W Fort Lauderdale.** Fort Lauderdale's trendiest hotel, this pair of 23-story towers of the W Hotel rise over the Atlantic blues like a massive luxury boat at full sail. **Pros:** newest of the beach luxury leaders; tony scene; great spa. **Cons:** across highway from beach. **TripAdvisor:** "well designed and maintained," "bathroom is a good size," "great location." ⊠ *435 N. Fort Lauderdale Beach Blvd.* ☎ *954/462–1633* ⊕ *www.starwood.com* ⟿ *346 hotel rooms, 171 hotel condominiums* ⚸ *In-room: a/c, Internet, Wi-Fi. In-hotel: restaurants, bars, pools, gym, spa, parking, some pets allowed* ¶◎| *No meals.*

$$–$$$
HOTEL

The Worthington and the Alcazar. Side by side and sharing common amenities, the Worthington and the Alcazar are two of Fort Lauderdale beach's 27 clothing-optional resorts for gay men. **Pros:** fresh-squeezed orange juice in the morning; nice pool area. **Cons:** not on the beach; no view. **TripAdvisor:** "clientele is pretty cool and amicable," "really close to the ocean," "very lush Key West type feel." ✉ *543–555 N. Birch Rd.* ☎ *954/563–6819 or 954/567–2525* ⊕ *www.worthington.com, www.alcazarresort.com* ⤢ *17 rooms; 20 rooms and suites* ⟁ *In-room: a/c, kitchen (some). In-hotel: pool* ❑ *Breakfast.*

DOWNTOWN AND LAS OLAS

$$$
B&B/INN

Pineapple Point. Tucked a few blocks behind Las Olas Boulevard in the residential neighborhood of Victoria Park, Pineapple Point is a spectacular maze of tropical cottages and dense foliage catering to the gay community. **Pros:** superior service; tropical setting. **Cons:** away from the beach; need a vehicle. **TripAdvisor:** "personal and genuine service," "beautiful lush setting," "very special." ✉ *315 N.E. 16th Terrace, Victoria Park* ☎ *954/527–0094* ⊕ *www.pineapplepoint.com* ⤢ *25 rooms* ⟁ *In-room: a/c, kitchen (some), Wi-Fi. In-hotel: gym, spa, parking, some age restrictions* ❑ *Breakfast.*

$$$
HOTEL

Riverside Hotel. On Las Olas Boulevard, just steps from boutiques, restaurants, and art galleries, Fort Lauderdale's oldest hotel debuted in 1936, but frequent renovations have kept it looking great in true Tommy Bahamas style. **Pros:** historic appeal; in the thick of Las Olas action. **Cons:** no quick access to beach. **TripAdvisor:** "would highly recommend," "beautiful downtown location," "near great little shops and restaurants." ✉ *620 E. Las Olas Blvd.* ☎ *954/467–0671 or 800/325–3280* ⊕ *www.riversidehotel.com* ⤢ *203 rooms, 10 suites* ⟁ *In-room: a/c, Internet. In-hotel: restaurants, bars, pool* ❑ *No meals.*

INTRACOASTAL AND INLAND

$$$–$$$$
RESORT

Hyatt Regency Pier Sixty-Six Resort & Spa. The iconic 17-story tower dominates a lovely 22-acre spread that includes the full-service Spa 66. **Pros:** great views; plenty of activities; free shuttle to beach; easy water taxi access. **Cons:** not on the beach; '70s exterior. **TripAdvisor:** "pool was very large," "would definitely stay at this hotel again," "a great view." ✉ *2301 S.E. 17th St. Causeway* ☎ *954/525–6666* ⊕ *www.pier66.com* ⤢ *384 rooms and suites* ⟁ *In-room: a/c, Wi-Fi. In-hotel:*

ULTIMATE WINE TASTING

The seductive Wine Room and sensual Wine Vault at the Ritz-Carlton, Fort Lauderdale impress with 5,000 global bottles, classic elegance, and the haute design minutia that has given the Ritz-Carlton its flawless reputation. The surprisingly affordable "Take Flight in the Wine Vault" experience entails the hotel sommelier creating a private wine tasting for guests inside the signature wine vault. Experience a journey across France, Australia, Argentina, or California through six glasses of red or white wine while enjoying informative and fascinating lessons between sips! Reservations required, $50.

restaurants, bars, tennis courts, pools, gym, spa, water sports ♭⊙♭ *No meals.*

WESTERN SUBURBS

$$–$$$$ ⊡ **Hyatt Regency Bonaventure Conference Center & Spa.** This upscale venue
RESORT   targets conventioneers and business executives as well as vacationers
who value golf, Everglades, and shopping over beach proximity. **Pros:**
lush landscaping; pampering spa. **Cons:** in the suburbs; poor views
from some rooms. **TripAdvisor:** "property is quite pretty overlooking
a small lake and golf course," "large somewhat impersonal hotel,"
"big bathroom comfortable bed." ⊠ *250 Racquet Club Rd., Westin*
☎ *954/616–1234* ⊕ *www.bonaventure.hyatt.com* ⟿ *501 rooms* ♭ *In-room: a/c, Wi-Fi. In-hotel: restaurants, bars, golf courses, tennis courts,
pools, gym, spa, some pets allowed* ♭⊙♭ *No meals.*

NORTH ON SCENIC A1A

North of Fort Lauderdale's Birch Recreation Area, Route A1A edges
away from the beach through a stretch known as Galt Ocean Mile, and
a succession of ocean-side communities line up against the sea. Traf-
fic can line up, too, as it passes through a changing pattern of beach-
blocking high-rises and modest family vacation towns and back again.
As far as tourism goes, these communities tend to cater to a different
demographic than Fort Lauderdale. Europeans and cost-conscious fami-
lies head to Lauderdale-by-the-Sea, Pompano, and Deerfield for fewer
frills and longer stays.

Towns are shown on the Broward County map.

LAUDERDALE-BY-THE-SEA

5 mi north of Fort Lauderdale.

Just north of Fort Lauderdale's northern boundary, this low-rise fam-
ily resort town traditionally digs in its heels at mere mention of high-
rises. The result is choice shoreline access that's rapidly disappearing
in nearby communities. Without a doubt, Lauderdale-by-the-Sea takes
delight in embracing its small beach-town feel and welcoming guests
to a different world of years gone by.

GETTING HERE AND AROUND

Lauderdale-by-the-Sea is just north of Fort Lauderdale. If you're driv-
ing from Interstate 95, exit east onto Commercial Boulevard and head
over the Intracoastal Waterway. From U.S. 1 (aka Federal Highway),
turn east on Commercial Boulevard. If coming from A1A, just continue
north from Fort Lauderdale Beach.

ESSENTIALS

Visitor Information Lauderdale-by-the-Sea Chamber of Commerce
(⊠ *4201 N. Ocean Dr., Lauderdale-by-the-Sea* ☎ *954/776–1000* ⊕ *www.lbts.com*).

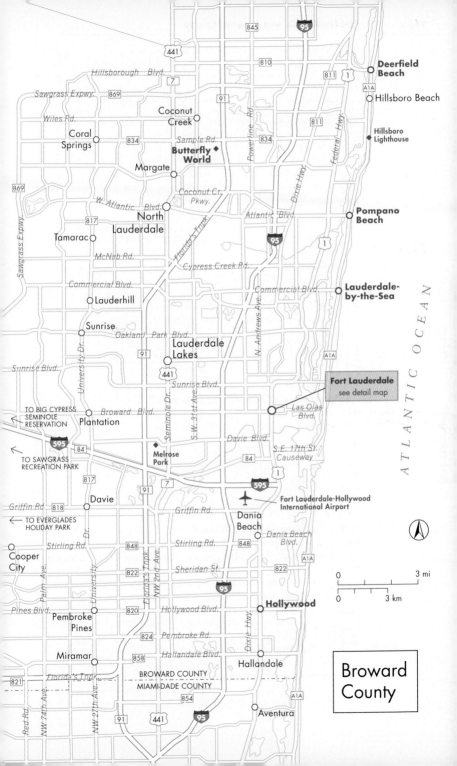

SPORTS AND THE OUTDOORS

★ **Anglin's Fishing Pier.** This longtime favorite for 24-hour fishing has a fresh, renovated appearance after shaking off repeated storm damage that closed the pier at intervals during the past decade. ☎ 954/491–9403.

WHERE TO EAT

$$ ✕ **Aruba Beach Café.** This massive, beachfront eatery is always crowded
CAFÉ and always fun. One of Lauderdale-by-the-Sea's most famous restaurants, Aruba Beach serves a wide range of American and Caribbean cuisine, including Caribbean conch chowder and conch fritters. There are also fresh tropical salads, sandwiches, and seafood. The café is famous for its divine fresh-baked Bimini Bread with Aruba Glaze (think challah with donut glaze). A band performs day and night, so head for the back corner with eye-popping views of the beach if you want conversation while you eat and drink. Sunday breakfast buffet starts at 9 am. ✉ *1 Commercial Blvd.* ☎ *954/776–0001* ⊕ *www. arubabeachcafe.com.*

$$$$ ✕ **Blue Moon Fish Company.** Most tables have stellar views of the Intra-
SEAFOOD coastal Waterway, but Blue Moon East's true magic comes from the
Fodor's Choice kitchen, where the chefs create moon-and-stars-worthy seafood dishes.
★ It's also the best deal in town with a two-for-one word-of-mouth lunch special Monday through Saturday. Start with whole roasted garlic and bread and continue on to the mussels, the langostino salad (with pecan-crusted goat cheese, spinach, and carmelized onions) or pan-seared fresh-shucked oysters. For Sunday champagne brunches book early, even in the off-season. ✉ *4405 W. Tradewinds Ave.* ☎ *954/267–9888* ⊕ *www.bluemoonfishco.com.*

$ ✕ **LaSpada's Original Hoagies.** The crew at this seaside hole-in-the-wall
AMERICAN puts on quite a show of ingredient-tossing flair while assembling take-out hoagies, subs, and deli sandwiches. Locals rave that they are the best around. Fill up on the foot-long Monster (ham, cheese, roast beef, and turkey, $10.95), Hot Meatballs Marinara ($8.50), or an assortment of salads. ✉ *4346 Seagrape Dr.* ☎ *954/776–7893* ⊕ *www. laspadashoagies.com.*

WHERE TO STAY

For expanded hotel reviews, visit Fodors.com.

$$–$$$ 🏨 **Blue Seas Courtyard.** Innkeeper Cristie Furth, with her husband,
B&B/INN Marc, runs this small motel in a quiet resort area across from the beach. **Pros:** south-of-the-border vibe; friendly owners; vintage stoves from 1971; memory foam mattress toppers. **Cons:** rooms lack ocean views; old bath tubs in some rooms. **TripAdvisor:** "tastefully decorated in Southwestern manner," "rooms were very clean," "quiet place." ✉ *4525 El Mar Dr.* ☎ *954/772–3336* ⊕ *www.blueseascourtyard.com* 🛏 *12 rooms* 🛁 *In-room: a/c, kitchen, Wi-Fi. In-hotel: pool, laundry facilities* ⊙ *Breakfast.*

$$–$$$ 🏨 **High Noon Beach Resort.** Family-run since 1961, this resort sits on
HOTEL 300 feet of beautiful beach, where you'll find a comfortable place to relax morning, noon, or night. **Pros:** smack on the beach; friendly vibe. **Cons:** early booking required. **TripAdvisor:** "grounds were beautiful," "owners take great care in treating their guests with respect," "a little

DID YOU KNOW?

Seagulls can drink both fresh and saltwater, and they can make short order of your lunch, since they eat everything from crabs and fish to bread, cookies, and potato chips.

oasis." ✉ *4424 El Mar Dr.* ☎ *954/776–1121 or 800/382–1265* ⊕ *www.highnoonresort.com* ⇌ *40 rooms* ⚇ *In-room: a/c, kitchen (some), Wi-Fi. In-hotel: pool, beach* ⦿ *Breakfast.*

$$–$$$ ⚏ **Sea Lord Hotel & Suites.** This attractive ocean-side hotel has undergone
HOTEL a major transformation in recent years, adding a pool deck, restaurant, lobby, sundeck, a new entranceway, a small fitness center, and room upgrades. **Pros:** terrific beach location; void of the moldy smell in other hotels. **Cons:** shaky elevators; limited parking. **TripAdvisor:** "right on the beach," "would recommend it to friends and family," "small quaint and a wonderful getaway." ✉ *4140 El Mar Dr.* ☎ *954/776–1505 or 800/344–4451* ⊕ *www.sealordhotel.com* ⇌ *47 rooms* ⚇ *In-room: a/c, kitchen (some), Wi-Fi. In-hotel: pool, laundry facilities, beach* ⦿ *Breakfast.*

$$–$$$ ⚏ **Tropic Seas Resort Motel.** This two-story property has an unbeatable
HOTEL location—directly on the beach, flanking 150 feet of pristine sands and sparkling blues. **Pros:** family-owned friendliness; great lawn furniture. **Cons:** must reserve far ahead; older style bathrooms **TripAdvisor:** "wonderful spot on the beach for the kids," "courtyard with pool is immaculate," "convenient to everything." ✉ *4616 El Mar Dr.* ☎ *954/772–2555 or 800/952–9581* ⊕ *www.tropicseasresort.com* ⇌ *16 rooms* ⚇ *In-room: a/c, kitchen (some), Wi-Fi. In-hotel: pool, beach* ⦿ *Breakfast.*

POMPANO BEACH

Pompano Beach is 3 mi north of Lauderdale-by-the-Sea.

As Route A1A enters this town directly north of Lauderdale-by-the-Sea the high-rise scene resumes. Sportfishing is big in Pompano Beach, as its name implies, but there's more to beachside attractions than the popular Fisherman's Wharf. Behind a low coral-rock wall, Alsdorf Park (also called the 14th Street boat ramp) extends north and south of the wharf along the road and beach.

GETTING HERE AND AROUND
From Interstate 95, Pompano Beach exits include Sample Road, Copans Road, or Atlantic Boulevard.

ESSENTIALS
Visitor Information Greater Pompano Beach Chamber of Commerce (☎ *954/941–2940* ⊕ *www.pompanobeachchamber.com*).

EXPLORING
Butterfly World. As many as 80 butterfly species from South and Central America, the Philippines, Malaysia, Taiwan, and other Asian nations are typically found within the serene 3-acre site inside Tradewinds Park, at the western edge of Pompano Beach, several miles inland. A screened aviary called North American Butterflies is reserved for native species. The Tropical Rain Forest Aviary is a 30-foot-high construction, with observation decks, waterfalls, ponds, and tunnels filled with thousands of colorful butterflies. Kids bug out at the bug zoo with Asian cockroaches as big as your hand. ✉ *3600 W. Sample Rd., Coconut Creek*

🕿 *954/977–4400* ⊕ *www.butterflyworld.com* 🖃 *$24.95* ⊗ *Mon.–Sat. 9–5, Sun. 11–5.*

SPORTS AND THE OUTDOORS

FISHING

Pompano Pier. The 24-hour pier extends more than 1,000 feet into the Atlantic. The pier tackle shop sells beer and snacks. Admission is $4 to fish, $1 to sightsee; rod-and-reel rental is $16.50 (including admission, plus a $20 deposit) for the day. Anglers brag about catching barracuda, jack, and snapper here in the same sitting, along with bluefish, cobia, and, yes, even pompano. 🕿 *954/226–6411.*

OUTFITTERS **Fish City Pride.** Morning, afternoon, and evening drift-fishing trips cost $37 and include fishing gear and bait. ⊠ *Fish City Marina, 2621 N. Riverside Dr., Pompano Beach* 🕿 *954/781–1211.*

Hillsboro Inlet Marina. The eight-boat fleet offers saltwater half-day charters for $550, six hours for $750, or a full day for $950, including gear for up to six anglers. ⊠ *2705 N. Riverside Dr., Pompano Beach* 🕿 *954/943–8222.*

SCUBA DIVING

SS *Copenhagen* State Underwater Archaeological Preserve. The wreck of the SS *Copenhagen* lies in 15- to 30-foot depths just outside the second reef on the Pompano Ledge, 3.6 mi south of Hillsboro Inlet. The 325-foot-long steamer's final voyage, from Philadelphia bound for Havana, began May 20, 1900, ending six days later when the captain—attempting to avoid gulf currents—crashed onto a reef off what's now Pompano Beach. In 2000, the missing bow section was identified a half mile to the south. The wreck, a haven for colorful fish and corals and a magnet for skin and scuba divers, became Florida's fifth Underwater Archaeological Preserve in 1994, listed on the National Register of Historic Places in 2001.

SHOPPING

Sugar Chest Antique Mall. Bargain hunters and antique junkies browse the 200 vendors' collectibles and antiques. ⊠ *906 N. Federal Hwy., Pompano Beach* 🕿 *954/942–8601* ⊕ *www.thesugarchestantiquemall.com.*

WHERE TO EAT

$$$$ ✕ **Cafe Maxx.** New-wave epicurean dining had its South Florida start
ECLECTIC here in the early 1980s, and Cafe Maxx remains fresh. The menu
★ changes nightly but showcases tropical appeal with jerk-spiced sea scallops or jumbo stone crab claws with honey-lime mustard sauce and black-bean-and-banana-pepper chili with Florida avocado. Appetizers include caviar pie and crispy sweetbreads. Desserts such as Trio of Sorbet (or ice cream) with a flurry of fruit sauces, including mango, stay the tropical course. Select from 300 wines by the bottle, and many by the glass. ⊠ *2601 E. Atlantic Blvd., Pompano Beach* 🕿 *954/782–0606* ⊕ *www.cafemaxx.com* ⊗ *No lunch.*

$$$ ✕ **Cap's Place.** On an island once a bootlegger's haunt, Lighthouse Point's
SEAFOOD ramshackle seafood spot reached by launch has served the famous as well as the infamous, including the likes of Winston Churchill, FDR, JFK, and Al Capone. Cap was Captain Theodore Knight, born in 1871, who, with partner-in-crime Al Hasis, floated a derelict barge to the area

in the 1920s. Broward's oldest restaurant, built on the barge, is run by Hasis's descendants. Sesame-crusted mahimahi is served with soy-ginger sauce, flaky rolls are baked fresh, and tangy lime pie is a great finale. Clams and oysters are shucked to order. Cap's is no cheapie; even a plate of linguine and clams will cost you $24. ⊠ *Cap's Dock, 2765 N.E. 28th Ct.* ☎ *954/941–0418* ⊕ *www.capsplace.com* ☉ *No lunch. Closed Mon. May–Dec.*

WHERE TO STAY
For expanded hotel reviews, visit Fodors.com.

$$–$$$
HOTEL
🛏 **Beachcomber Resort & Villas.** This property's beachfront location is close to most local attractions and a mile from the Pompano Pier. **Pros:** Old Florida feel; on the water. **Cons:** worn around the edges; moldy smell in some rooms. **TripAdvisor:** "can't wait to go back," "tiki bar was the best part," "food at the hotel restaurant was really good." ⊠ *1200 S. Ocean Blvd.* ☎ *954/941–7830 or 800/231–2423* ⊕ *www. beachcomberresort.com* ⇆ *143 rooms, 9 villas, 4 suites* 🖏 *In-room: a/c, Internet, Wi-Fi. In-hotel: restaurant, bar, pools, beach* ⍥❈ *No meals.*

EN ROUTE
Hillsboro Lighthouse. About 2 mi north of Pompano Beach you are afforded a beautiful view across Hillsboro Inlet to this lighthouse, often called the brightest lighthouse in the Southeast and used by mariners as a landmark for decades. When at sea you can see its light from almost halfway to the Bahamas. Although the octagonal-pyramid, iron-skeletal tower lighthouse is on private property inaccessible to the public, it's well worth a peek, even from afar. The Hillsboro Lighthouse Preservation Society offers tours about four times a year; call for schedule and tips on viewing vantage points. ☎ *954/942–2102* ⊕ *www. hillsborolighthouse.org.*

EN ROUTE
Hillsboro Mile. To the north, Route A1A traverses the so-called Hillsboro Mile (actually more than 2 mi), a millionaire's row of some of Broward's most beautiful and expensive homes. The road runs along a narrow strip of land between the Intracoastal Waterway and the ocean, with bougainvillea and oleander edging the way and yachts docked along both banks. Traffic often moves at a snail's pace, especially in winter, as vacationers (and sometimes even envious locals) gawk.

DEERFIELD BEACH

Deerfield Beach is 2 mi north of Pompano Beach.

As posh Hillsboro Mile comes to an end, Route A1A spills out onto Deerfield Beach, Broward's northernmost ocean-side community.

GETTING HERE AND AROUND
From Interstate 95, take the Hillsboro Boulevard exit east. From A1A, continue north past Pompano Beach and Hillsboro Beach.

ESSENTIALS
Visitor Information **Greater Deerfield Beach Chamber of Commerce** (☎ *954/427–1050* ⊕ *www.deerfieldchamber.com*).

EXPLORING

Quiet Waters Park. Its name belies what's in store for kids here. Splash Adventure is a high-tech water-play system with slides and tunnels, among other activities. A Rent-A-Tent program ($35 per night for up to four campers) provides already set-up tents or teepees. There's also cable water-skiing and boat rental on this county park's lake, and a skate park. Note that this space functions mostly as a public park for locals than as a tourist attraction and is located near a highway. ⊠ *401 S. Powerline Rd., Deerfield Beach* ☎ *954/360–1315* ⊕ *www.broward. org/parks* ▱ *Park $1 weekends, free weekdays* ⊘ *Apr.–Sept., daily 8–6; Oct.–Mar., daily 8–5:30.*

OFF THE BEATEN PATH

Deerfield Island Park. Reached only by boat (and with a new dock in the works for vessels longer than 25 feet), this officially designated Urban Wilderness Area showcases coastal hammock island and contains a mangrove swamp that provides a critical habitat for gopher tortoises, gray foxes, raccoons, and armadillos. County-operated boat shuttles run 10–3 on weekends (on the hour only). Amenities include a boardwalk, walking trails, and an observation tower. ⊠ *1720 Deerfield Island Park* ☎ *954/360–1320* ⊕ *www.broward.org/parks/ DeerfieldIslandPark* ▱ *Free.*

SPORTS AND THE OUTDOORS

FISHING

Deerfield Pier. This picturesque pier teems with fishermen and tourists. Admission is $4 to fish, $1 to sightsee. Common catches include king mackerel, snapper, blue fish, and barracuda. ☎ *954/426–9206.*

OUTFITTERS **Cove Marina**. The deep-sea charter fleet does excellent runs of sailfish, kingfish, dolphin, and tuna in winter. A half-day charter for six costs about $600, or $1,000 for a full day. ⊠ *Hillsboro Blvd. and Intracoastal Waterway, Deerfield Beach* ☎ *954/427–9747.*

SCUBA DIVING

Dixie Divers. Among the area's most popular dive operators, this outfit has morning and afternoon dives aboard the 48-foot *Lady-Go-Diver*, plus evening dives on weekends. Snorkelers and certified divers can explore the marine life of nearby reefs and shipwrecks. The cost is $60; ride-alongs are welcome for $35. ⊠ *Cove Marina, Hillsboro Blvd. and Intracoastal Waterway, Deerfield Beach* ☎ *954/420–0009* ⊕ *www. dixiedivers.com.*

WHERE TO EAT

$$$ ✕ **Brooks**. This is one of Broward's more elegant dining spots, thanks
FRENCH to French perfectionist Bernard Perron. Brooks is now run by Per-
★ ron's son-in-law John Howe. Updated Continental fare is served in a series of rooms filled with old-master replicas, cut glass, antiques, and floral wallpaper. Fresh ingredients go into distinctly Floridian dishes, including sautéed Key Largo yellowtail snapper. Roast rack of lamb is also popular. Put your order in early for the chocolate or Grand Marnier soufflé. ⊠ *500 S. Federal Hwy., Deerfield Beach* ☎ *954/427–9302* ⊕ *www.brooks-restaurant.com.*

$ ✕ **Olympia Flame Diner.** The family-owned Flame burned white-hot in
SEAFOOD   2009 when finance guru Suze Orman did a star turn as a waitress
★   here for an *Oprah* TV segment. Orman has a condo nearby, and her
fitness trainer—who dines here regularly—suggested the blue-awning
diner as an illuminated best bet for a hot, home-style meal accompanied by megawatt chatter. Greek specialties from spinach pie to
baklava dominate the menu, but you can order seafood, deli-style
sandwiches, and burgers along with beer or wine. And no, Oprah
and Orman mega-exposure hasn't changed the homey mood here at
all. ⊠ *80 S. Federal Hwy., Deerfield Beach* ☎ *954/480–8402* ⊕ *www.
olympiaflamediner.com.*

$$ ✕ **Whale's Rib.** For a casual, almost funky, nautical experience near the
SEAFOOD   beach, look no farther. If you want to blend in, order a fish special
★   with whale fries—thinly sliced potatoes that look like hot potato chips.
People come from near and far for the famous whale fries. Those with
smaller appetites can choose from salads and fish sandwiches, or raw-
bar favorites like Ipswich clams. ⊠ *2031 N.E. 2nd St., Deerfield Beach*
☎ *954/421–8880.*

WHERE TO STAY

For expanded hotel reviews, visit Fodors.com.

$ 🛏 **Carriage House Resort Motel.** This tidy motel, accredited as an SSL
HOTEL   (Superior Small Lodging), is less than a block from the ocean, and the
two-story, colonial-style building with black shutters has two sections
connected by a second-story sundeck. **Pros:** friendly staff; bargain rates.
Cons: nothing fancy. **TripAdvisor:** "relaxing peaceful and quiet," "basic
original Florida motel but well maintained," "clean inexpensive motel."
⊠ *250 S. Ocean Blvd.* ☎ *954/427–7670* ⊕ *www.carriagehouseresort.
com* 🛏 *6 rooms, 14 efficiencies, 10 apartments* ⌂ *In-room: a/c, Internet,
Wi-Fi. In-hotel: pool, laundry facilities.* 🍴 *No meals.*

SOUTH BROWARD

South Broward's roots are in early Florida settlements. Thus far it has
avoided some of the glitz and glamour of neighbors to the north and
south, and folks here like it that way. Still, there's plenty to see and
do—excellent restaurants in every price range, world-class pari-mutuels,
and a new focus on the arts.

HOLLYWOOD

Hollywood is 8 mi south of Fort Lauderdale.

Hollywood has had a face-lift, with more nips and tucks to come.
Young Circle, once down-at-heel, has become Broward's first Arts Park.
On Hollywood's western outskirts, the flamboyant Seminole Hard Rock
Hotel & Casino has permanently etched the previously downtrodden
section of State Road 7/U.S. 441 corridor on the map of trendy excite-
ment, drawing local weekenders, architecture buffs, and gamblers. But
Hollywood's redevelopment effort doesn't end there: new shops, res-
taurants, and art galleries open at a persistent clip, and the city has

spiffed up its Broadwalk (not Boardwalk)—a wide pedestrian walkway along the beach—where Rollerbladers are as commonplace as snow-birds from the north.

GETTING HERE AND AROUND
From Interstate 95, exit east on Sheridan Street or Hollywood Boulevard.

ESSENTIALS
Visitor Information **Hollywood Chamber of Commerce** (✉ *330 N. Federal Hwy., Hollywood* ☎ *954/923–4000* ⊕ *www.hollywoodchamber.org*).

3

EXPLORING

Art and Culture Center of Hollywood. This is a visual- and performing-arts facility with an art reference library, outdoor sculpture garden, and arts school. It's southeast of Young Circle, melding urban open space with a fountain, a 2,000-plus-seat amphitheater, and an indoor theater. Nearby, on trendy Harrison Street and Hollywood Boulevard, are chic lunch places, bluesy entertainment spots, and shops. ✉ *1650 Harrison St.* ☎ *954/921–3274* ⊕ *artandculturecenter.org* ⛵ *$7* ☾ *Tues.–Fri. 10–5, weekends noon–4. Closed Mon.*

BEACHES

☾ **Broadwalk.** With the Intracoastal Waterway to the west and the beach
Fodor's Choice and ocean immediately east, this spiffed-up 2-mi paved promenade
★ has lured pedestrians and cyclists since 1924. With a recent $14 mil-lion makeover, this stretch has taken on added luster for the buff, the laid-back, and the retired. Kids also thrive here: there are play areas, rental bikes, trikes, and other pedal-powered gizmos. Expect to hear French spoken here, since Hollywood Beach has long been a favorite getaway for Quebecois. Conversations in Spanish and Portuguese are also frequently overheard on this path. ✉ *Rte. A1A and Sheridan St.* ⛵ *Parking in public lots is $1.50 per hr.*

John U. Lloyd Beach State Recreation Area. The once pine-dotted natural area was restored to its natural state, thanks to government-driven efforts to pull out all but indigenous plants. Now native sea grape, gumbo-limbo, and other native plants offer shaded ambience. Nature trails and a marina remain are large draws as is canoeing on Whiskey Creek. ✉ *6503 N. Ocean Dr.* ☎ *954/923–2833* ⛵ *$6 per vehicle for 2 to 8 passengers, $4 for lone driver* ☾ *Daily 8–sunset.*

SPORTS AND THE OUTDOORS

☾ **West Lake Park.** Rent a canoe, kayak, or take the 40-minute boat tour at this park bordering the Intracoastal Waterway. At 1,500 acres, it is one of Florida's largest urban nature facilities. Extensive boardwalks traverse mangrove forests that shelter endangered and threatened spe-cies. A 65-foot observation tower showcases the entire park. At the free **Anne Kolb Nature Center,** named after Broward's late environmental advocate, there's a 3,500-gallon aquarium. The center's exhibit hall has 27 interactive displays. ✉ *751 Sheridan St.* ☎ *954/926–2480* ⛵ *Week-ends $1.50, weekdays free* ☾ *Daily 9–5.*

FISHING

Sea Leg's III. Drift-fishing trips run during the day and bottom-fishing trips at night. Trips cost $35–$38, including rod rental. ✉ *5398 N. Ocean Dr.* ☎ *954/923–2109*

GOLF

Diplomat Country Club & Spa. There are 18 holes and a spa; greens fee $69/$209. ✉ *501 Diplomat Pkwy., Hallandale* ☎ *954/883–4000.*

Emerald Hills. The course has 18 holes; greens fee $55/$190. ✉ *4100 N. Hills Dr.* ☎ *954/961–4000.*

NIGHTLIFE AND THE ARTS

THE ARTS

Harrison Street Art and Design District. In downtown Hollywood, this collection of galleries features original artwork (eclectic paintings, sculpture, photography, and mixed media). Friday night the artists' studios, galleries, and shops stay open later while crowds meander along Hollywood Boulevard and Harrison Street.

NIGHTLIFE

Although Hollywood has a small-town feel, it has an assortment of coffee shops, sports bars, martini lounges, and dance clubs.

Sushi Blues. Since 1989, this Japanese-American-theme establishment has served up revolving entertainment, especially on weekends. ✉ *2009 Harrison St.* ☎ *954/929–9560* ⊕ *www.sushiblues.com.*

Whisky Tango. The comfy couches are available nightly. ✉ *1903 Hollywood Blvd.* ☎ *954/925–2555* ⊕ *www.whiskeytangofl.com.*

WHERE TO EAT

$$$

ASIAN FUSION

Fodor's Choice

★

✕ **Azia.** Located on the Intracoastal across from the Westin Hollywood Diplomat, Azia remains somewhat a well-kept secret in greater Fort Lauderdale. Before the restaurant transforms into a chic and seductive Asian-inspired nightclub on the weekends, a phenomenal team presents an Asian fusion extravaganza seven nights a week. While classics are indeed on the menu, the chef puts a welcomed and successful twist on most dishes. For example, Azia's pad thai is infused with Tamarind sauce while the summer rolls are made with mango instead of shrimp. The shrimp tempura roll also has fried green tomatoes inside and the Lava Seafood appetizer mixes curried seafood with cream cheese to create mouth-watering heaven! The presentation is nothing less than spectacular. Even if you're not staying in Hollywood, Azia is worth the drive from Fort Lauderdale proper. ✉ *3660 S Ocean Dr., Hollywood* ☎ *954/602–8347* ⊕ *www.aiziahollywood.com.*

$$$

ITALIAN

✕ **Café Martorano.** Located within Hard Rock Hollywood's massive entertainment and restaurant zone, this Italian-American institution pays homage to anything and everything that has to do with the "Godfather" and impresses with massive family-style portions. Dishes run the full Italian-American gamut, from the classic parmigianas to the lobster and snapper francaise. The homemade mozzarella and fried calamari are excellent choices for starters. It's easy to gorge here since each dish is so succulent and savory. The ever-present "Godfather" motif is taken to the extreme—dinner is interrupted hourly with clips from the movie played on the surrounding flat screens. ⊠ *5751 Seminole Way, Hollywood* ☎ *954/584–4450* ⊕ *www.cafemartorano.com.*

$$$
SEAFOOD

✕ **Giorgio's Grill.** Good food and service are hallmarks of this expansive 400-seat restaurant overlooking the Intracoastal Waterway. Seafood is a specialty, but you'll also find pasta and meat dishes, and a solid Sunday brunch for around $20. A great watery view--especially around sunset--and friendly staff add to the experience, and there's a surprisingly extensive, reasonably priced wine list. ⊠ *606 N. Ocean Dr.* ☎ *954/929–7030* ⊕ *www.giorgiosgrill.com.*

$$$
ARGENTINE

✕ **Las Brisas.** Next to the beach, this cozy bistro offers seating inside or out, and the food is Argentine with Italian flair. A small pot, filled with *chimichurri*—a paste of oregano, parsley, olive oil, salt, garlic, and crushed pepper—for spreading on steaks, sits on each table. Grilled fish is a favorite, as are pork chops, chicken, and pasta entrées. Desserts include a flan like *mamacita* used to make. ⊠ *600 N. Surf Rd.* ☎ *954/923–1500* ☾ *No lunch.*

$$
AMERICAN

✕ **LeTub.** Formerly a Sunoco gas station, this quirky waterside saloon has an enduring affection for claw-foot bathtubs. Hand-painted porcelain is everywhere—under ficus, sea grape, and palm trees. If a potty doesn't appeal, there's a secluded swing facing the water north of the main dining area. Despite molasses-slow service and an abundance of flies at sundown, this eatery is favored by locals, and management seemed genuinely appalled when hordes of trend-seeking city slickers started jamming bar stools and tables after Oprah declared its thick, juicy Angus burgers the best around. A plain burger and small fries will run you around $15. ⊠ *1100 N. Ocean Dr.* ☎ *954/921–9425* ⊕ *www. theletub.com* ⊟ *No credit cards.*

$$
JAPANESE
Fodor's Choice
★

✕ **Sushi Blues Café.** Run by husband-and-wife-team Kenny Millions and Junko Maslak, this place proves that sushi has gone global. Japanese chefs prepare conventional and macrobiotic-influenced dishes, including lobster teriyaki and steamed snapper with miso sauce. Poached pears steamed in Cabernet sauce and cappuccino custard are popular desserts. Music is a big part of the appeal of this place, especially when the Sushi Blues Band performs on weekends. ⊠ *2009 Harrison St.* ☎ *954/929–9560* ⊕ *www.sushiblues.com.*

WHERE TO STAY

For expanded hotel reviews, visit Fodors.com.

$$–$$$
HOTEL
★

▦ **Manta Ray Inn.** Canadians Donna and Dwayne Boucher run this immaculate, affordable, two-story inn on the beach. **Pros:** on the beach; low-key atmosphere. **Cons:** no restaurant. **TripAdvisor:** "comfortable vacation spot," "good value," "really outstanding." ⊠ *1715 S. Surf Rd.* ☎ *954/921–9666 or 800/255–0595* ⊕ *www.mantarayinn.com* ⇲ *12 units* ⌂ *In-room: a/c, kitchen, Wi-Fi. In-hotel: beach, parking* ❑ *No meals.*

$$–$$$
HOTEL

▦ **Sea Downs.** Facing the Broadwalk and ocean, this three-story lodging is a good choice for families, as one-bedroom units can be joined to create two-bedroom apartments. **Pros:** facing ocean; reasonable rates. **Cons:** minimum stay often required. **TripAdvisor:** "clean comfortable and affordable," "enjoyed the kitchen setup," "the ability to literally walk out onto the sand." ⊠ *2900 N. Surf Rd.* ☎ *954/923–4968* ⊕ *www.*

seadowns.com ⤴ *4 efficiencies, 8 1-bedroom apartments* ⬧ *In-room: a/c, Internet. In-hotel: pool, laundry facilities, parking* ⊟ *No credit cards* ⦿ *No meals.*

$$$–$$$$

HOTEL

⌖ **Seminole Hard Rock Hotel & Casino.** On the flatlands of western Holly-wood, the Seminole Hard Rock Hotel & Casino serves as a magnet for pulsating Vegas-style entertainment. Poker unfolds at 40 tables, to the delight of spectators, near a phalanx of slot machines. **Pros:** nonstop entertainment; plenty of activities. **Cons:** not on the beach; endless entertainment can be exhausting. **TripAdvisor:** "this place has everything," "smoke in the casino permeates everything," "fun and lively." ⊠ *1 Seminole Way* ☎ *866/502–7529 or 800/937–0010* ⊕ *www.hardrock.com* ⤴ *395 rooms, 86 suites* ⬧ *In-room: a/c, Internet, Wi-Fi. In-hotel: restaurants, bars, pool, gym, spa* ⦿ *No meals.*

$$$–$$$$

RESORT

★

⌖ **The Westin Diplomat Resort & Spa.** This 39-story property has been instrumental in bringing new life and new style to Hollywood Beach with its massive, 60-foot high ceilinged atrium. **Pros:** heavenly beds for adults and kids now, too; in-room workouts and great spa; eye-popping architecture. **Cons:** beach is eroding. **TripAdvisor:** "clean hip and quite user friendly," "most outstanding features of this hotel are the outside pools," "beautiful property." ⊠ *1995 E. Hallandale Beach Blvd.* ☎ *954/602–6000 or 800/327–1212* ⊕ *www.starwoodhotels.com* ⤴ *900 rooms, 100 suites* ⬧ *In-room: a/c, Internet, Wi-Fi. In-hotel: restaurants, bars, golf course, tennis courts, pools, gym, spa* ⦿ *No meals.*

Miami and Miami Beach

WORD OF MOUTH

"South beach is perfect . . . plenty of shopping, beautiful beach . . . great restaurants, lots of fun."

—flep

WELCOME TO MIAMI AND MIAMI BEACH

TOP REASONS TO GO

★ **The Beach:** Miami Beach has been rated as one of the 10 best in the world. White sand, warm water, and bronzed bodies everywhere provide just the right mix of relaxation and people-watching.

★ **Dining Delights:** Miami's eclectic residents have transformed the city into a museum of epicurean wonders, ranging from Cuban and Argentine fare to fusion haute cuisine.

★ **Wee-Hour Parties:** A 24-hour liquor license means clubs stay open until 5 am, and after-parties go until noon the following day.

★ **Picture-Perfect People:** Miami is a watering hole for the vain and beautiful of South America, Europe, and the Northeast. Watch them—or join them—as they strut their stuff and flaunt their tans on the white beds of renowned art deco hotels.

★ **Art Deco District:** Iconic pastels and neon lights accessorize the architecture that first put South Beach on the map in the 1930s.

1 Downtown Miami. Weave through the glass-and-steel labyrinth of new condo construction to catch a Miami Heat game at the American Airlines Arena or a ballet at the spaceshiplike Adrienne Arsht Center for the Performing Arts. To the north is artsy and edgy Wynwood and the Design District.

2 South Beach. People-watch from sidewalk cafés along Ocean Drive, lounge poolside at posh Collins Avenue hotels, and party 'til dawn at the nation's hottest clubs.

3 Coral Gables. Dine and shop on family-friendly Miracle Mile, and take a driving tour of the Mediterranean-style mansions in the surrounding neighborhoods.

4 Mid-Beach. Home to the latest and greatest hotel trends and a booming restaurant scene, Mid-Beach is now rivaling South Beach as a trendy hotspot.

5 Coconut Grove. Catch dinner and a movie and listen to live music at CocoWalk, or cruise the bohemian shops and locals' bars in this hip neighborhood.

6 Key Biscayne. Pristine parks and tranquillity make this upscale enclave a total antithesis to the South Beach party.

GETTING ORIENTED

Long considered the gateway to Latin America, Miami is as close to Cuba and the Caribbean as you can get within the United States. The 36-square-mi city is located at the southern tip of the Florida peninsula, bordered on the east by Biscayne Bay. Over the bay lies a series of barrier islands, the largest being a thin 18-square-mi strip called Miami Beach. To the east of Miami Beach is the Atlantic Ocean. To the south are the Florida Keys.

LITTLE HAITI

N.W. 79th St. · 95 · JFK Causeway

9 · 441 · N.W. 62nd St. · 2nd Ave.

N.W. 54th St. · 944 · N. Miami Ave. · N.E. · Biscayne Blvd.

MIAMI BEACH

MID-BEACH · 4

Robert Frost Expwy. · 1

N.W. 36th St. · Julia Tuttle Causeway · 195

27 · 2

N.W. 20th St. · Art Center · Venetian Causeway · **SOUTH BEACH**

N.W. 17th Ave. · 395 · Watson Island · A1A

DOWNTOWN MIAMI · 95 · American Airlines Arena · 1 · MacArthur Causeway · Art Deco District · 41

W. Flagler St. · 12th Ave.

S.W. 8th St. · **LITTLE HAVANA** · S.W. 3rd. · 41

S.W. 22nd St. · Fisher Island

S. Dixie Hwy. · Marine Stadium

Rickenbacker Causeway · Virginia Key

COCONUT GROVE · 5 · Grove Isle

Coco Walk

Biscayne Bay

6 **KEY BISCAYNE**

ATLANTIC OCEAN

Cape Florida Lighthouse

MIAMI BEACHES

Almost every side street in Miami Beach dead-ends at the ocean. Sandy shores also stretch along the southern side of the Rickenbacker Causeway to Key Biscayne, where you'll find more popular beaches.

Beaches tend to have golden, light brown, or gray-tinted sand with coarser grains than the fine white stuff on Florida's Gulf Coast beaches. Although pure white-sand beaches are many peoples' idea of picture-perfect, darker beach sand is much easier on the eyes on a sunny day and—bonus!—your holiday photos (and the people in them) will have a subtle warm glow rather than harsh highlights.

Expect gentle waves, which can occasionally turn rough, complete with riptides, depending on what weather systems are lurking out in the ocean—always check and abide by the warnings posted on the lifeguard's station. One thing that isn't perfect here is shelling, but for casual shell collectors Bal Harbour Beach is the best bet; enter at 96th Street and Collins Avenue.

SOUTH BEACH PARKING TIPS

Several things are plentiful in South Beach. Besides the plethora of cell phones and surgically enhanced bodies, there are a lot of cars for a small area, and plenty of seriously attentive meter maids. On-street parking is scarce, tickets are given freely, and towing charges are high. Check your meter to see when you must pay to park; times vary. It's $1 per hour for meters north of 23rd Street (8 am–6 pm) and $1.50 per hour for meters south of 23rd Street (9 am–3 am). There are also public parking lots that accept cash and credit cards. Or, buy a Parking Meter Card at Miami Beach Visitors Center and Publix supermarkets for $25.

MIAMI'S BEST BEACHES

BILL BAGGS CAPE FLORIDA STATE PARK

At the end of Key Biscayne, at 1200 S. Crandon Boulevard, is a wide peachy-brown beach with usually gentle waves. The beach has been named several times in Dr. Beach's coveted America's Top Ten Beaches list. The picnic area is popular with local families on the weekends, but the beach itself never feels crowded. The park also includes miles of nature trails; bike, boat, beach chair, and umbrella rentals; and casual dining at the Lighthouse Café. You can fish off the piers by the marina, too. Come here for an escape from city madness.

CRANDON PARK BEACH

The 3-mi sliver of beach paradise is dotted with palm trees to provide a respite from the steamy sun, until it's time to take a dip in the clear-blue waters. On weekends, be prepared for a long hike from your car to the beach. There are bathrooms, outdoor showers, plenty of picnic tables, and concession stands. The family-friendly park offers abundant options for kids who find it challenging to simply sit and build sand castles. There are marine-theme play sculptures, a dolphin-shape spray fountain, an old-fashioned outdoor roller rink, and a restored carousel.

4

HAULOVER BEACH

Want to bare it all? Just north of Bal Harbour, at 10800 Collins Avenue in Sunny Isles, sits the only legal clothing-optional beach in the area. Haulover has more claims to fame than its casual attitude toward swimwear—it's also the best beach in the area for bodyboarding and surfing as it gets what passes for impressive swells in these parts. Plus the sand here is fine-grain white, unusual for the Atlantic coast. There's a section for families, singles, and a gay beach at Haulover.

MATHESON HAMMOCK PARK BEACH

Kids will love the gentle waves and warm water of the beach at 4000 Crandon Boulevard in Key Biscayne. The golden sands of this 3-mi beach are only part of the attraction: the park includes a playground, picnic areas, even a golf course. The man-made lagoon is perfect for inexperienced swimmers, and it's the best place in Miami for a picnic. But the water can be a bit murky, and with the emphasis on families, it's not the best place for singles.

SOUTH BEACH (LUMMUS PARK BEACH)

Want glitz and glamour? On South Beach's Ocean Drive from 6th to 14th streets, this beach is crowded with beautiful people working hard on their tans, muscle tone, and social lives. It's also the place for golden sands, blue water, and gentle waves.

Updated by
Paul Rubio

Even an ailing real estate market and plummeting property values have failed to dethrone Miami from its status as one of the world's trendiest and flashiest hotspots. In 2012, it almost feels as if the recession never happened. Downtown Miami's megamakeover, which began in 2006, and came to a screeching halt in 2008, was later resumed in 2010. No longer are high-end restaurants luring customers with three-course $30 specials nor are five-star hotels offering bargain basement $149/night rooms. Miami is back and with this revival of glam and economy return higher price tags and longer guest lists!

Luckily for visitors, South Beach is no longer the only place to stand and pose in Miami. The growing Design District is home to Miami's hipster and fashionista scene while South Beach continues to extend both north and west, with the addition of new venues north of 20th Street and along the bay on West Avenue. Following the reopening of the mammoth Fontainebleau and its enclave of nightclubs and restaurants along Mid-Beach, other globally renowned resorts have moved into the neighborhood, like the Soho Beach House and Canyon Ranch.

Visit Miami today and it's hard to believe that 100 years ago, it was a mosquito-infested swampland, with an Indian trading post on the Miami River. Then hotel builder Henry Flagler brought his railroad to the outpost known as Fort Dallas. Other visionaries—Carl Fisher, Julia Tuttle, William Brickell, and John Sewell, among others—set out to tame the unruly wilderness. Hotels were erected, bridges were built, the port was dredged, and electricity arrived. The narrow strip of mangrove coast was transformed into Miami Beach—and the tourists started to come. They haven't stopped since!

Greater Miami is many destinations in one. At its best it offers an unparalleled multicultural experience: melodic Latin and Caribbean tongues, international cuisines and cultural events, and an unmistakable joie de vivre—all against a beautiful beach backdrop. In Little Havana the air is tantalizing with the perfume of strong Cuban coffee. In Coconut Grove, Caribbean steel drums ring out during the Miami/Bahamas Goombay Festival. Anytime in colorful Miami Beach restless crowds wait for entry to the hottest new clubs.

Many visitors don't know that Miami and Miami Beach are really separate cities. Miami, on the mainland, is South Florida's commercial hub. Miami Beach, on 17 islands in Biscayne Bay, is sometimes considered America's Riviera, luring refugees from winter with its warm sunshine; sandy beaches; graceful, shady palms; and tireless nightlife. The natives know well that there's more to Greater Miami than the bustle of South Beach and its Art Deco District. In addition to well-known places such as Ocean Drive and Lincoln Road, the less reported spots—like the burgeoning Design District in Miami, the historic buildings of Coral Gables, and the secluded beaches of Key Biscayne—are great insider destinations.

MIAMI PLANNER

WHEN TO GO

Miami and Miami Beach are year-round destinations. Most visitors come November through April, when the weather is close to perfect; hotels, restaurants, and attractions are busiest; and each weekend holds a festival or event. "Season" kicks off in December with Art Basel Miami Beach, and hotel rates don't come down until after the college kids have left from spring break in late March.

It's hot and steamy from May through September, but nighttime temperatures are usually pleasant. Also, summer is a good time for the budget traveler. Many hotels lower their rates considerably, and many restaurants offer discounts—especially during **Miami Spice** in August, when slews of top restaurants offer special tasting menus at a steep discount (sometimes Spice runs for two months, check ⊕ *www.iLoveMiamiSpice. com* for details).

TOP EVENTS

Art Basel. The most prestigious art show in the United States is held every December. ⊕ *www.artbaselmiamibeach.com.*

South Beach Food and Wine Festival. The Food Network's star-studded weekend every February showcases the flavors and ingenuity of the country's top chefs. ⊕ *www.sobewineandfoodfest.com.*

Winter Music Conference. The largest DJ showcase in the world rocks Miami every March. ⊕ *www.wintermusicconference.com.*

GETTING HERE

Air Travel: Miami is serviced by Miami International Airport (MIA) 8 mi northwest of downtown and Fort Lauderdale-Hollywood International Airport (FLL) 26 mi northeast. Many discount carriers, like Spirit Airlines, Southwest Airlines, and AirTran fly into FLL, making it a smart bargain if you are renting a car. Otherwise, look for flights to MIA on American Airlines, Delta, and Continental. MIA recently underwent an extensive face-lift improving facilities, common spaces, and the overall aesthetic of the airport.

Car Travel: Interstate 95 is the major expressway connecting South Florida with points north; State Road 836 is the major east–west expressway and connects to Florida's Turnpike, State Road 826, and Interstate 95. Seven causeways link Miami and Miami Beach, Interstate 195 and Interstate 395 offering the most convenient routes; the Rickenbacker Causeway extends to Key Biscayne from Interstate 95 and U.S. 1. The high-speed lanes on the left hand side of I–95 require a prepaid toll gadget called a "Sunpass," available in most drug and grocery stores.

Remember U.S. 1 (aka Biscayne Boulevard)—you'll hear it often in directions. It starts in Key West, hugs South Florida's coastline, and heads north straight through to Maine.

Train Travel: Amtrak provides service from 500 destinations to the Greater Miami area. The trains make several stops along the way; north–south service stops in the major Florida cities of Jacksonville, Orlando, Tampa, West Palm Beach, and Fort Lauderdale. Note that these stops are often in less than ideal locations for immediate city access. For extended trips, or if you want to visit other areas in Florida, you can come via Auto Train (where you bring your car along) from Lorton, Virginia, just outside Washington, D.C., to Sanford, Florida, just outside Orlando. From there it's less than a four-hour drive to Miami. Fares vary, but expect to pay between $269 and $346 for a basic sleeper seat and car passage each way. ■ TIP➜ You must be traveling with an automobile to purchase a ticket on the Auto Train.

GETTING AROUND

Greater Miami resembles Los Angeles in its urban sprawl and traffic. You'll need a car to visit many attractions and points of interest. If possible, avoid driving during the rush hours of 7–9 am and 5–7 pm—the hour just after and right before the peak times also can be slow going. During rainy weather, be especially cautious of flooding in South Beach and Key Biscayne. Miami's main north and south thoroughfare, I–95, now offers an express lane to get more quickly between Miami and Fort Lauderdale. A prepaid Sunpass is required to use this lane.

Some sights are accessible via the public transportation system, run by the **Metro-Dade Transit Agency**, which maintains 740 Metrobuses on 90 routes; the 23-mi Metrorail elevated rapid-transit system; and the Metromover, an elevated light-rail system. Those planning on using public transportation should get an EASY Card or EASY Ticket available at any Metrorail station and most supermarkets. Fares are discounted and transfer fees are nominal. The bus stops for the **Metrobus** are marked with blue-and-green signs with a bus logo and route information. The fare is $2 (exact change only if paying cash). Cash-paying customers must pay for another ride if transferring. Some express routes carry a surcharge of 35¢. Elevated **Metrorail** trains run from downtown Miami north to Hialeah and south along U.S. 1 to Dadeland. The system operates daily 5 am–midnight. The fare is $2; 50¢ transfers to Metrobus are available only for EASY Card and EASY ticket holders. **Metromover** resembles an airport shuttle and runs on two loops around downtown Miami, linking major hotels, office buildings, and shopping areas. The system spans 4 mi, including the 1-mi Omni Loop and the 1-mi Brickell Loop. There is no fee to ride; transfers to Metrorail are $2.

Tri-Rail, South Florida's commuter-train system, stops at 18 stations north of MIA along a 71-mi route. There is a Metrorail transfer station 2 stops north of MIA. Prices range from $2.50 to $6.90 for a one-way ticket.

Transportation Information Metro-Dade Transit Agency (☎ 305/891–3131 ⊕ www.miamidade.gov/transit). **Tri-Rail** (☎ 800/874–7245 ⊕ www.tri-rail.com).

CAB IT

Except in South Beach, it's difficult to hail a cab on the street; in most cases you'll need to call a cab company or have a hotel doorman hail one for you. Fares run $4.50 for the first mile and $2.40 every mile thereafter; flat-rate fares are also available from the airport to a variety of zones. Many cabs now accept credit cards; inquire before you get in the car.

Taxi Companies Central Cabs (☎ 305/532–5555). **Diamond Cab Company** (☎ 305/545–5555). **Flamingo Taxi** (☎ 305/599–9999). **Metro Taxi** (☎ 305/888–8888). **Society Cab Company** (☎ 305/757–5523). **Super Yellow Cab Company** (☎ 305/888–7777). **Tropical Taxi** (☎ 305/945–1025). **Yellow Cab Company** (☎ 305/633–0503).

VISITOR INFORMATION

For additional information about Miami and Miami Beach, contact the city's visitor bureaus. You can also pick up a Free Miami Beach INcard at the Miami Beach Visitors Center 10 am–4 pm seven days a week, entitling you to discounts and offers at restaurants, shops, galleries, and more.

Visitor Information Coconut Grove Chamber of Commerce (✉ 2820 McFarlane Rd., Coconut Grove, Miami ☎ 305/444–7270 ⊕ www.coconutgrovechamber. com)). **Coral Gables Chamber of Commerce** (✉ 224 Catalonia Ave., Coral Gables ☎ 305/446–1657 ⊕ www.gableschamber.org). **Greater Miami Convention & Visitors Bureau** (✉ 701 Brickell Ave., Suite 2700, Miami ☎ 305/539–3000, 800/933–8448 in U.S. ⊕ www.miamiandbeaches.com). **Key Biscayne Chamber of Commerce and Visitors Center** (✉ 88 W. McIntyre St., Suite 100, Key Biscayne ☎ 305/361–5207 ⊕ www.keybiscaynechamber.org). **Miami Beach**

Visitors Center (✉ *1920 Meridian Ave., 1st fl., Miami Beach* ☎ *305/674–1300*
⊕ *www.miamibeachguestservices.com*).

EXPLORING MIAMI AND MIAMI BEACH

If you had arrived here 50 years ago with a guidebook in hand, chances are you'd be thumbing through listings looking for alligator wrestlers and you-pick strawberry fields or citrus groves. Things have changed. While Disney sidetracked families in Orlando, Miami was developing a unique culture and attitude that's equal parts beach town/big business, Latino/Caribbean meets European/American—all of which fuels a great art and food scene, as well as exuberant nightlife and myriad festivals.

To find your way around Greater Miami, learn how the numbering system works (or better yet, use a GPS). Miami is laid out on a grid with four quadrants—northeast, northwest, southeast, and southwest—which meet at Miami Avenue and Flagler Street. Miami Avenue separates east from west and Flagler Street separates north from south. Avenues and courts run north–south; streets, terraces, and ways run east–west. Roads run diagonally, northwest–southeast. But other districts—Miami Beach, Coral Gables, and Hialeah—may or may not follow this system, and along the curve of Biscayne Bay the symmetrical grid shifts diagonally. It's best to buy a detailed map, stick to the major roads, and ask directions early and often. However, make sure you're in a safe neighborhood or public place when you seek guidance; cabdrivers and cops are good resources.

DOWNTOWN MIAMI

Downtown Miami dazzles from a distance. The skyline is fluid, thanks to the sheer number of sparkling glass high-rises between Biscayne Boulevard and the Miami River. Business is the key to downtown Miami's daytime bustle. Traffic congestion from the high-rise offices and expensive parking tend to keep the locals away by day; however, downtown has become a nighttime hotspot in recent years.

The free, 23-mi, elevated commuter system known as the Metromover runs inner and outer loops through downtown and to nearby neighborhoods south and north. Many attractions are conveniently located within about a few blocks of a station.

Note that you can combine a visit to this neighborhood with one to Little Havana, which is just southwest of downtown. ⇨ *See our "Caribbean Infusion" spotlight for a map of Little Havana as well as one of Little Haiti in north Miami.*

TOP ATTRACTIONS

Adrienne Arsht Center for the Performing Arts. Lovers of culture and other artsy types are drawn to this stunning home of the Florida Grand Opera, Miami City Ballet, New World Symphony, Concert Association of Florida, and other local and touring groups, which have included Broadway hits like *Wicked* and *Jersey Boys*. Think of it as a sliver of savoir faire to temper Miami's often-over-the-top vibe. Designed

DOWNTOWN MIAMI ENCLAVES

The influx of massive, modern, and affordable condos has lured a young and trendy demographic to downtown, leading to the establishment of restaurant-centric enclaves and headlining eateries and nightclubs in hotels like the Viceroy and the Tempo.

Bayfront Park. Monuments dot this park, and both it and the streets that face it really pull in shoppers—particularly those from South America and especially those from Brazil. In the park's southwest corner is the white *Challenger* Memorial, commemorating the space shuttle that exploded in 1986. A little north is Plaza Bolivar, a tribute by Cuban immigrants to their adopted country; the JFK Torch of Friendship, a plaza with plaques representing all the South and Central American countries except Cuba; and the Bayside Marketplace entertainment, dining, and retail complex. *To get here:* Metromover to Bayfront Park, 1st Street, College/Basyide, or Freedom Tower stations.

Mary Brickell Village. This burgeoning neighborhood of low-rise condos and shops clustered around South Miami Avenue also has some rather popular restaurants, so you might want to plan a visit for some late-afternoon shopping followed by dinner. *To get here:* Metromover to 5th or 8th Street stops.

---

by architect César Pelli, the massive development contains a 2,400-seat opera house, 2,200-seat concert hall, a black-box theater, and an outdoor Plaza for the Arts. Restaurateur Barton G. opened up his pre-theater dining restaurant, **Prelude by Barton G.** (☎ *305/357–7900* ⊕ *www.preludebybartong.com*) in early 2010 to rave reviews. ⊠ *1300 Biscayne Blvd., at N.E. 13th St., Downtown* ☎ *305/949–6722* ⊕ *www. arshtcenter.org.*

Freedom Tower. In the 1960s this ornate Spanish-baroque structure was the Cuban Refugee Center, processing more than 500,000 Cubans who entered the United States after fleeing Fidel Castro's regime. Built in 1925 for the *Miami Daily News*, it was inspired by the Giralda, an 800-year-old bell tower in Seville, Spain. Preservationists were pleased to see the tower's exterior restored in 1988. Today, it is owned by Miami-Dade College, and continues to maintain the tower as a cultural and educational center, which includes a museum depicting Cuban history, the experiences of refugees, and the achievements of Cuban-Americans. ⊠ *600 Biscayne Blvd., at N.E. 6th St., Downtown* ☎ *305/237–7700* ⊗ *Tues.–Fri. noon–5.*

Miami-Dade Cultural Center. Containing three cultural resources, this fortresslike 3-acre complex is a downtown focal point. ⊠ *101 W. Flagler St., between N.W. 1st and 2nd Aves., Downtown.*

The **Miami Art Museum** (☎ *305/375–3000* ⊕ *www.miamiartmuseum. org* ⊐ *$8 [free for families every 2nd Sat.]* ⊗ *Tues.–Fri. 10–5, weekends noon–5*) is waiting to move into its new 120,000-square-foot home in Museum Park, which is to be completed in mid-2013. Meanwhile, the museum presents major touring exhibitions of work by international artists, with an emphasis on art since 1945. Every second Saturday, entrance is free for families.

Discover a treasure trove of colorful stories about the region's history at **HistoryMiami** (☎ 305/375–1492 ⊕ *www.historymiami.org* ✉ *$8 museum, $10 combo ticket art and history museums* ⊘ *Tues.–Fri. 10–5, weekends noon–5*), formerly known as the Historical Museum of Southern Florida. Exhibits celebrate Miami's multicultural heritage, including an old Miami streetcar, and unique items chronicling the migration of Cubans to Miami.

★ **Wynwood Art District.** Just north of downtown Miami, the funky, urban, and edgy Wynwood Art District is peppered with galleries, art studios, and private collections accessible to the public. Visit during Wynwood's monthly gallery walk on the second Saturday evening of each month when studios and galleries are all open at the same time.

Make sure a visit includes a stop at the **Margulies Collection at the Warehouse** (✉ *591 N.W. 27th St., between N.W. 5th and 6th Aves., Downtown* ☎ *305/576–1051* ⊕ *www.margulieswarehouse.com*). Martin Margulies's collection of vintage and contemporary photography, videos, and installation art in a 45,000-square-foot space makes for eye-popping viewing. Entrance fee is a $10 donation, which goes to a local homeless shelter for women and children. It's open November to April only, Wednesday to Saturday 11–4.

Fans of edgy art will appreciate the **Rubell Family Collection** (✉ *95 N.W. 29th St., between N. Miami and N.W. 1st Aves., Downtown* ☎ *305/573–6090* ⊕ *www.rfc.museum*). Mera and Don Rubell have accumulated work by artists from the 1970s to the present, including Jeff Koons, Cindy Sherman, Damien Hirst, and Keith Haring. Admission is $10, and the gallery is open December to August, Wednesday to Saturday 10–6.

WORTH NOTING

⊙ **Jungle Island.** Originally located deep in south Miami and known as Parrot Jungle, South Florida's original tourist attraction opened in 1936 and moved closer to Miami Beach in 2003. Located on Watson Island, a small stretch of land off of I–395 between Downtown Miami and South Beach, Jungle Island is far more than a park where cockatoos ride tricycles; this interactive zoological park is home to just about every unusual and endangered species you would want to see, including a rare albino alligator, a liger (lion and tiger mix), a 28-foot-long "crocosaur," and a myriad of exotic birds. The most intriguing offerings are the VIP animal tours, including the Lemur Experience ($45 for 45 minutes), in which the highly social primates make themselves at home on your lap or shoulders, and the Penguin Encounter ($30 for 30 minutes), where you can pet and feed warm-weather South African penguins. ✉ *1111 Parrot Jungle Trail, off MacArthur Causeway (I–395)* ☎ *305/400–7000* ⊕ *www.jungleisland.com* ✉ *$32.95, plus $8 parking* ⊘ *Weekdays 10–5, weekends 10–6.*

⊙ **Miami Children's Museum.** This Arquitectonica-designed museum, both imaginative and geometric in appearance, is directly across the MacArthur Causeway from Jungle Island. Twelve galleries house hundreds of

Downtown Miami

interactive, bilingual exhibits. Children can scan plastic groceries in the supermarket, scramble through a giant sand castle, climb a rock wall, learn about the Everglades, and combine rhythms in the world-music studio. ✉ *980 MacArthur Causeway* ☎ *305/373–5437* ⊕ *www. miamichildrensmuseum.org* ✉ *$15, parking $1/hr* ⊙ *Daily 10–6.*

MIAMI BEACH

The hub of Miami Beach is South Beach (better known as SoBe), with its energetic Ocean Drive, Collins Avenue, and Washington Avenue. Here, life unfolds 24 hours a day. Beautiful people pose in hotel lounges and sidewalk cafés, bronzed cyclists zoom past palm trees, and visitors flock to see the action. On Lincoln Road, café crowds spill onto the sidewalks, weekend markets draw all kinds of visitors and their dogs, and thanks to a few late-night lounges the scene is just as alive at night. A Mid-Beach renaissance is unfolding on Collins Avenue, with haute new hotels and restaurants popping up between 40th and 60th streets.

Quieter areas to the north on Collins Avenue are Surfside (from 88th to 96th streets), fashionable Bal Harbour (beginning at 96th Street), and Sunny Isles (between 157th and 197th streets). If you're interested in these areas and you're flying in, the Fort Lauderdale airport might be a better choice than Miami International.

SOUTH BEACH
TOP ATTRACTIONS

★ **Española Way.** There's a bohemian feel to this street lined with Mediterranean-revival buildings constructed in 1925. Al Capone's gambling syndicate ran its operations upstairs at what is now the Clay Hotel, a youth hostel. At a nightclub here in the 1930s, future bandleader Desi Arnaz strapped on a conga drum and started beating out a rumba rhythm. Visit this quaint avenue on a weekend afternoon, when merchants and craftspeople set up shop to sell everything from handcrafted bongo drums to fresh flowers. Between Washington and Drexel avenues the road has been narrowed to a single lane and Miami Beach's trademark pink sidewalks have been widened to accommodate sidewalk café's and shops selling imaginative clothing, jewelry, and art. ✉ *Española Way, between 14th and 15th Sts. from Washington to Jefferson Aves.*

★ **Holocaust Memorial.** A bronze sculpture depicts refugees clinging to a giant bronze arm that reaches out of the ground and 42 feet into the air. Enter the surrounding courtyard to see a memorial wall and hear the music that seems to give voice to the 6 million Jews who died at the hands of the Nazis. It's easy to understand why Kenneth Treister's dramatic memorial is in Miami Beach: the city's community of Holocaust survivors was once the second-largest in the country. ✉ *1933–1945 Meridian Ave., at Dade Blvd.* ☎ *305/538–1663* ⊕ *www.holocaustmmb. org* ✉ *Free (donations welcome)* ⊙ *Daily 9–9.*

☺ **Lincoln Road Mall.** A playful 1990s redesign spruced up this open-air
Fodor's Choice pedestrian mall, adding a grove of 20 towering date palms, five linear
★ pools, and colorful broken-tile mosaics to the once-futuristic 1950s

Continued on page151

Miami Beach and South Beach

MIAMI BEACH

27th St.

26th St.

A1

Miami Beach Dr.

23rd St.

22nd St.

Collins Ave.

Collins Park

21st St.

20th St.

19th

18th St.

Blvd.

Park Ave.

Liberty

James Ave.

Collins Canal

Prairie

Meridian Ave.

Prairie Ave.

Dade

907

Jefferson

17th St.

Lincoln

Rd.

16th St.

SOUTH BEACH

A1

Atlantic

Ocean

Lincoln Rd. Mall

Pennsylvania Ave.

Drexel

Way

6

16th

Meridian

Euclid

15th

Española

St.

5

14th

Lenox

Michigan

Flamingo Park

14th

13th

12th

St.

Ave.

4

Lummus Park

13th

12th

11th

Miami Beach

907

Alton

Rd.

Jefferson St.

12th

St.

ART DECO DISTRICT

Washington Ave.

Collins Ave.

Ocean Dr.

3

2

10th

9th

8th

Miami Beach

West

11th

10th St.

9th

8th

7th St.

Lummus Park

Ave.

7th

6th

6th St.

MacArthur Causeway

41

A1

4th

3rd St.

2nd St.

1st St.

5th St.

Collins

Ocean

5th

1

SOUTH POINTE

Ocean Front Park

Ocean Beach

Pier Park

9 10

Biscayne St.

Harley St.

Inlet Blvd.

Miami Beach Pier

South Pointe Park

SOUTH POINTE

0   400 yrds

0   400 meters

CARIBBEAN INFUSION

by Michelle Delio

Miami has sun, sand, and sea, but unlike some of Florida's other prime beach destinations, it also has a wave of cultural traditions that spice up the city.

It's with good reason that people in Miami fondly say that the city is an easy way for Americans to visit another country without ever leaving the United States. According to the U.S. Census Bureau, more than half of Miami's population is foreign born and more than 70% speak a language other than English at home (in comparison, only 36.7% of New York City residents were born in another country). The city's Latin/Caribbean immigrants and exiles make up the largest segments of the population.

Locals merrily merge cultural traditions, speaking "Spanglish" (a mix of Spanish and English), sipping Cuban coffee with Sicilian pastries, eating Nuevo Latino fusion food, and dancing to the beat of other countries' music. That said, people here are just as interested in keeping to their own distinct ways—think of the city as a colorful mosaic composed of separate elements rather than a melting pot.

Miami's diverse population creates a city that feels alive in a way that few other American cities do. Nothing is set in stone here, for better or worse, and there's always a new flavor to explore, a new holiday to celebrate, a new accent to puzzle over.

No visit to Miami would be complete without a stop at one of the two neighborhoods famed for their celebrations of cultural traditions— Little Haiti and Little Havana—places that have a wonderful foreign feel even amid cosmopolitan Miami.

Playing dominoes is a favorite pastime at Maximo Gomez Park in Little Havana (left).

LA PETITE HAÏTI—LITTLE HAITI

Little Haiti is a study in contrasts. At first glance you see the small buildings painted in bright oranges, pinks, reds, yellows, and turquoises, with signs, some handwritten, touting immigration services, lunch specials with *tassot* (fried cubed goat), and voodoo supplies.

But as you adjust to this dazzle of color, you become aware of the curious juxtapositions of poverty and wealth in this evolving neighborhood. Streets dip with potholes in front of trendy art galleries, and dilapidated houses struggle to survive near newly renovated soccer fields and arts centers.

Miami's Little Haiti is the largest Haitian community outside of Haiti itself, and while people of different ethnic backgrounds have begun to move to the neighborhood, people here tend to expect to primarily see other Haitians on these streets. Obvious outsiders may be greeted with a few frozen stares on the streets, but owners of shops and restaurants tend to be welcoming. Creole is commonly spoken, although some people—especially younger folks—also speak English.

WHEN TO GO

The neighborhood is best visited during the daytime, combined with a visit to the nearby Miami Design District, an 18-block section of art galleries, interior design showrooms, and restaurants between N.E. 41st Street and N.E. 36th Street, Miami Avenue, and Biscayne Boulevard.

CREOLE EXPRESSIONS

Creole, one of Haiti's two languages (the other is French), is infused with French, African, Arabic, Spanish, and Portuguese words.

Komon ou ye? How are you? *(also spelled Kouman)

N'ap boule! Great!

Kisa ou ta vla? What would you like?

Mesi. Thanks.

Souple. Please.

4

IN FOCUS CARIBBEAN INFUSION

MANGÉ KRÉYOL (HAITIAN FOOD)

Traditional Caribbean cuisines tend to combine European and African culinary techniques. Haitian can be a bit spicier—though never mouth-scorching hot—than many other island cuisines. Rice and beans are the staple food, enlivened with a little of whatever people might have: fish, goat, chicken, pork, usually stewed or deep-fried, along with peppers, plantains, and tomatoes.

Chez Le Bebe (✉ *114 N.E. 54th St.* ☎ *305/751–7639* ⊕ *www.chezlebebe. com*) offers Haitian home cooking—if you want to try stewed goat, this is the place to do it. Chicken, fish, oxtail, and fried pork are also on the menu; each plate comes with rice, beans, plantains, and salad for less than $12.

Tap Tap restaurant (✉ *819 Fifth St.* ☎ *305/672–2898*) is outside of Little Haiti, but this Miami institution will immerse you in the island's culture with an extensive collection of Haitian folk art displayed everywhere in the restaurant. On the menu is pumpkin soup, *spageti kreyol* (pasta, shrimp, and a Creole tomato sauce), goat stewed in Creole sauce (a mildly spicy tomato-based sauce), conch, and "grilled goat dinner." You can eat well here for $15 or less.

GETTING ORIENTED

Little Haiti, once a small farming community outside of Miami proper, is slowly becoming one of the city's most vibrant neighborhoods. Its northern and southern boundaries are 85th Street and 36th Street, respectively, with Interstate–95 to the west and Biscayne Boulevard to the east. The best section to visit is along North Miami Avenue from 54th to 59th streets. Driving is the best way to get here; parking is easy to find on North Miami Avenue. Public transit (☎ *305/891–3131*) is limited.

SHOPPING

The cluster of botanicas at N.E. 54th Street and N.E. 2nd Avenue offer items intended to sway the fates, from candles to plastic and plaster statues of Catholic saints that, in the voodoo tradition, represent African deities. While exploring, don't miss **Sweat Records** (✉ *5505 N.E. 2nd Ave.* ☎ *305/342–0953* ⊕ *www.sweatrecordsmiami.com*). Sweat sells a wide range of music—rock, pop, punk, electronic, hip-hop, and Latino. Check out the vegan-friendly organic coffee bar at the store, which is open from noon to 10 PM every day but Sunday.

LITTLE HAVANA

First settled en masse by Cubans in the early 1960s, after that country's Communist revolution, Little Havana is a predominantly working-class area and the core of Miami's Hispanic community. Spanish is the main language, but don't be surprised if the cadence is less Cuban than Salvadoran or Nicaraguan: the neighborhood is now home to people from all Latin American countries.

If you come to Little Havana expecting the Latino version of New Orleans's French Quarter, you're apt to be disappointed—it's not yet that picturesque. But if great, inexpensive food (not just Cuban; there's Vietnamese, Mexican, and Argentinean here as well), distinctive, affordable art, cigars, and coffee interest you, you'll enjoy your time in Little Havana. It's not a prefab tourist destination, so don't expect Disneyland with a little Latino flair—this is real life in Miami.

WHEN TO GO

The absolute best time to visit Calle Ocho is the last Friday evening of every month, between 6:30 and 11 PM on 8th Street from 14th to 17th avenues. Known as **Viernes Culturales** (⊕ *www.viernesculturales.com*), it's a big block party that everyone is welcome to attend. Art galleries, restaurants, and stores stay open late, and music, mojitos, and avant-garde street performances bring a young, hip crowd to the neighborhood where they mingle with locals.

If you come in mid-March, your visit may coincide with the annual **Calle Ocho festival** (⊕ *www.carnavalmiami.com*), which draws more than a million visitors in search of Latin music, food, and shopping.

LITTLE HAVANA

(Map)

El Pub Restaurant ✕
Calle Ocho
Walk of Stars ◆
Lily's Records
El Credito Cigar Factory
Tamiami Trail
Casa Panza Restaurant ✕
Los Pinareños Fruteria
El Rey de los Habanos
El Titan de Bronze
Dominio Park ◆

0 — 1/8 mile
0 — 1/8 km

SPANISH EXPRESSIONS

Qué deseaba? Can I help you?

Algo más? Anything else?

Muchas gracias! Thank you very much!

No hay de qué. / De nada. You're welcome.

No entiendo. I don't understand.

Oye! All-purpose word used to get attention or express interest, admiration, and appreciation.

GETTING ORIENTED

Little Havana's semi-official boundaries are 27th Avenue to 4th Avenue on the west, Miami River to the north, and S.W. 11th Street to the south. Much of the neighborhood is residential, but its heart and tourist hub is Calle Ocho (8th Street), between 14th and 18th avenues.

The best way to get here is by car. Park on the side streets off **Calle Ocho** (some spots have meters; most don't). Other options include the free **Metromover** (☎ 305/891–3131) and a cab ride. From Miami Beach the 15-minute ride should cost just under $30 each way.

THE SIGHTS

Stroll down Calle Oche from 12th to 17th avenues and look around you: cafés are selling guava pastries and rose petal flan, a botanica brims with candles and herbs to heal whatever ails you. Over there at a tropical fruit stand someone is hacking off the top of a coconut with a machete, while nearby, thimble-size cups of liquid energy (aka *café cubano*) are passed through the open windows of coffee shops. Small galleries showcasing modern art jostle up next to mom-and-pop food shops and high-end Cuban clothes and crafts. At Dominio Park (officially Maximo Gomez Park), guayabera-clad seniors bask in the sun and play dominoes, while at corner bodegas and coffee shops (particularly Versailles) regulars share neighborhood gossip and political opinions. A few steps away is the "Paseo de las Estrellas" (Walk of Stars). The Latin version of its Hollywood namesake, the strip of sidewalk embedded with stars honors many of the world's top Hispanic celebrities, among them the late salsa queen Celia Cruz, crooner Julio Iglesias, and superstar Gloria Estefan.

Calle Ocho Carnaval

Rolling cigars by hand in a Little Havana factory.

THE SOUNDS

Salsa and merengue pour out of storefronts and restaurants, while other businesses cater to the snap and shuffles of flamenco performances and Sevillana *tablaos* (dances performed on a wood-plank stage, using castanets). If you want to join in the merriment along Calle Ocho, dance with locals on the patio of **El Pub Restaurant** (near 15th Avenue), or snack on tapas at **Casa Panza Restaurant** (near 16th), where the background music is the restaurant owner's enthusiastic singing. Any time of day, you can hear the constant backbeat of people speaking Spanish and the occasional crowing of a stray, time-confused rooster. To take these sounds home with you, wander over to **Lily's Records** (✉ *1419 S.W. 8th St, near 14th* ☎ *305/856–0536*), for its huge selection of Latin music.

THE SCENTS

Bottled, the essence of Little Havana would be tobacco, café cubano, and a whiff of tropical fruit. To indulge your senses in two of these things, head to **Los Pinareños Fruteria** on Calle Ocho just west of 13th Avenue. Here you can sip a sweet, hot *cortadito* (coffee with milk), a *cafecito* (no milk), or a cool *coco frio* (coconut water). For more subsistence, dig into a Cuban-style tamale. There are stools out front of the shop, or take your drink to go and wander over to S.W. 13th Avenue, which has monuments to Cuban heroes, and sit under the ceiba trees. For cigars, head to Calle Ocho near 11th Avenue and visit any of these three stores: **El Credito Cigar Factory**, **El Rey de los Habanos**, and **El Titan de Bronze**. At these family-owned businesses employees deftly hand-roll millions of stogies a year.

TOURS

If a quick multicultural experience is your goal, set aside an hour or two to do your own self-guided walking tour of the neighborhood. For real ethnic immersion, allow more time; eating is a must, as well as a peek at the area's residential streets lined with distinctive homes.

Especially illuminating are **Little Havana tours by Dr. Paul George** (✉ *101 W. Flagler St.* ☎ *305/375–1621* ✎ *historictours@ hmsf.org*). A history professor at Miami Dade College and historian for the Historical Museum of Southern Florida, George covers architecture and community history on his tours. These take place only a few times a year. Private three-hour tours are available for groups of up to 20 people for $400 ($20 per person above 20 people).

For customized offerings, try **Miami Cultural Tours** (✉ *305/416-6868* ⊕ *www. miamiculturaltours.com*), interactive tours that introduce people to Little Havana and Little Haiti. Group and private tours are available, with prices ranging from $39 to $79 a person.

GREAT ITINERARIES

3 DAYS

Grab your lotion and head to the ocean, more specifically **Ocean Drive** on **South Beach**, and catch some rays while relaxing on the warm sands. Afterward, take a guided or self-guided tour of the **Art Deco District** to see what all the fuss is about, drop in at the News Café for breakfast anytime (or a snack), great coffee, and an outstanding selection of international magazines. Keep the evening free to socialize at Ocean Drive cafés or have a special dinner at one of the many Latin-European–fusion restaurants. The following day drive through **Little Havana** to witness the heartbeat of Miami's Cuban culture (stop for a high-octane Cuban coffee at Versaille's outside-counter window) on your way south to Coconut Grove's Vizcaya. Wrap up the evening a few blocks away in downtown **Coconut Grove**, enjoying its laid-back party mood and many nightspots. On the last day head over to **Coral Gables** to take in the eye-popping display of 1920s Mediterranean-revival architecture in the neighborhoods surrounding the city center and the majestic **Biltmore Hotel**; then take a dip in the fantastic thematic **Venetian Pool**. Early evening, stroll and shop Coral Gable's Miracle Mile—contrary to its name it's just a half mile, but every bit is packed with upscale shops, art galleries, and interesting restaurants.

5 DAYS

Follow the suggested three-day itinerary, and on Day 4 visit the beaches of **Virginia Key** and **Key Biscayne**. Take a diving trip or fishing excursion, learn to windsurf, or just watch the water. On Day 5, tour the 18-block Design District and browse its 130-plus art galleries, home-decor shops, and interesting restaurants, or explore the Fairchild Tropical Botanic Garden. Then return to **South Beach** for an evening of shopping, drinking, and outdoor dining at **Lincoln Road Mall**.

vision of Fontainebleau designer Morris Lapidus. Some of the shops are owner-operated boutiques with a delightful variety of clothing, furnishings, jewelry, and decorative design. Others are the typical chain stores of American malls. Remnants of tired old Lincoln Road—beauty supply and discount electronics stores on the Collins end of the strip—somehow fit nicely into the mix. The new Lincoln Road is fun, lively, and friendly for people old, young, gay, and straight—and their dogs. Folks skate, scoot, bike, or jog here. The best times to hit the road are during Sunday morning farmers' markets and on weekend evenings, when cafés bustle, art galleries open shows, street performers make the sidewalk their stage, and stores stay open late.

Two of the landmarks worth checking out at the eastern end of Lincoln Road are the massive 1940s keystone building at 420 Lincoln Road, which has a 1945 Leo Birchanky mural in the lobby, and the 1921 mission-style Miami Beach Community Church, at Drexel Avenue. The Lincoln Theatre (No. 541–545), at Pennsylvania Avenue, is a classical four-story art deco gem with friezes. The New World Symphony, a national advanced-training orchestra led by Michael Tilson Thomas, rehearses and performs here, and concerts are often broadcast via loudspeakers, to the delight of visitors. Just west, facing Pennsylvania, a fabulous Cadillac dealership sign was discovered underneath the facade of the Lincoln Road Millennium Building, on the south side of the mall. At Euclid Avenue there's a monument to Lapidus, who in his 90s watched the renaissance of his whimsical creation. At Lenox Avenue, a black-and-white art deco movie house with a Mediterranean

barrel-tile roof is now the Colony Theater (No. 1040), where live theater and experimental films are presented. ☒ *Lincoln Rd., between Collins Ave. and Alton Rd.* ⊕ *www.lincolnroad.org.*

QUICK BITES

Lincoln Road is a great place to cool down with an icy treat while touring South Beach. If you visit on a Sunday, stop at one of the many juice vendors, who will whip up made-to-order smoothies from mangoes, oranges, and other fresh local fruits.

Frieze Ice Cream Factory. Delight in homemade ice cream and sorbets—including Indian mango, key lime pie, cashew toffee crunch, and chocolate decadence. ☒ *1626 Michigan Ave., south of Lincoln Rd.* ☎ *305/538–2028* ⊕ *www.thefrieze.com.*

Gelateria Parmalat. Authentic Italian gelato (or the Spanish-inspired delicious *dulce de leche* gelato) is scooped up at this sleek glass-and-stainless-steel sweet spot. ☒ *670 Lincoln Rd., between Euclid and Pennsylvania Aves.* ☎ *786/276–9475.*

WORTH NOTING

Art Deco District Welcome Center. Run by the Miami Design Preservation League, the center provides information about the buildings in the district. An improved gift shop sells 1930s–50s art deco memorabilia, posters, and books on Miami's history. Several tours—covering Lincoln Road, Española Way, North Beach, and the entire Art Deco District, among others—start here. You can choose from a self-guided iPod audio tour or join one of the regular morning walking tours at 10:30 am, every day except Thursday when the tour takes place at 6:30 pm. Arrive at the center 15 minutes beforehand. All of the options provide detailed histories of the art deco hotels as well as an introduction to the art deco, Mediterranean revival, and Miami Modern (MiMo) styles found within the Miami Beach Architectural Historic District. Don't miss the special boat tours during Art Deco Weekend, in early January. (⇨ *For a map of the Art Deco District and info on some of the sites there, see the "A Stroll Down Deco Lane" in-focus feature.*) ☒ *1001 Ocean Dr., at Barbara Capitman Way (10th St.)* ☎ *305/763–8026* ⊕ *www.mdpl.org* 🎫 *Tours $20* ⊙ *Daily 9:30–7.*

Bass Museum of Art. The Bass, in historic Collins Park, is part of the Miami Beach Cultural Park, which includes the Miami City Ballet's Arquitectonica-designed facility and the Miami Beach Regional Library. The original building, constructed of keystone, has unique Maya-inspired carvings. The expansion designed by Japanese architect Arata Isozaki houses another wing and an outdoor sculpture garden. Special exhibitions join a diverse collection of European art. Works on permanent display include *The Holy Family*, a painting by Peter Paul Rubens; *The Tournament*, one of several 16th-century Flemish tapestries; and works by Albrecht Dürer and Henri de Toulouse-Lautrec. Special exhibits often cost a little extra. Docent tours are by appointment. ⌂ *2100 Collins Ave.* ☎ *305/673–7530* ⊕ *www.bassmuseum.org* ⌂ *$8* ⊗ *Wed.–Sun. noon–5.*

> **THE OCEAN DRIVE HUSTLE**
>
> As you stroll by the sidewalk restaurants lining Ocean Drive, don't be surprised if you are solicited by a pretty hostess, who will literally shove a menu in your face to entice you to her café—which is exactly like every other eatery on the strip. Be warned that reputable restaurants refrain from these aggressive tactics. If you are indeed enticed by the fishbowl drinks, use the chance to bargain. A request for free drinks with dinner may very well be accommodated!

Sanford L. Ziff Jewish Museum of Florida. Listed on the National Register of Historic Places, this former synagogue, built in 1936, contains art deco chandeliers, 80 impressive stained-glass windows, and a permanent exhibit, MOSAIC: Jewish Life in Florida, which depicts more than 235 years of the Florida Jewish experience. The museum, which includes a store filled with books, jewelry, and other souvenirs, also hosts traveling exhibits and special events. ⌂ *301 Washington Ave., at 3rd St.* ☎ *305/672–5044* ⊕ *www.jewishmuseum.com* ⌂ *$6, free on Sat.* ⊗ *Tues.–Sun. 10–5. Museum store closed Sat.*

★ **Wolfsonian–Florida International University.** An elegantly renovated 1926 storage facility is now a research center and museum showcasing a 120,000-item collection of modern design and "propaganda arts" amassed by Miami native Mitchell ("Micky") Wolfson Jr., a world traveler and connoisseur. Broad themes of the 19th and 20th centuries—nationalism, political persuasion, industrialization—are addressed in permanent and traveling shows. Included in the museum's eclectic holdings, which represent art deco, art moderne, art nouveau, Arts and Crafts, and other aesthetic movements, are 8,000 matchbooks collected by Egypt's King Farouk. ⌂ *1001 Washington Ave., at 10th St.* ☎ *305/531–1001* ⊕ *www.wolfsonian.org* ⌂ *$7, free after 6 pm Fri.* ⊗ *Mon., Tues., Thur., and weekends noon–6, Fri. noon–9. Closed Wed.*

World Erotic Art Museum (WEAM). The sexy collection of more than 4,000 erotic items, all owned by millionaire Naomi Wilzig, unfolds with unique art of varying quality—fertility statues from around the globe and historic Chinese *shunga* books (erotic art offered as gifts to new brides on the wedding night) share the space with some kitschy knickknacks. If this is your thing, an original phallic prop from Stanley

Kubrick's *A Clockwork Orange* and an over-the-top Kama Sutra bed is worth the price of admission, but the real standout is "Miss Naomi," who is usually on hand to answer questions and provide behind-the-scenes anecdotes. Kids 17 and under are not admitted. ✉ *1205 Washington Ave., at 12th St.* ☎ *305/532–9336* ⊕ *www.weam.com* ✉ *$15* ⊙ *Mon.–Thurs. 11 am–10 pm, Fri.–Sun. 11 am–midnight.*

CORAL GABLES

You can easily spot Coral Gables from the window of a Miami-bound jetliner—just look for the massive orange tower of the Biltmore Hotel rising from a lush green carpet of trees concealing the city's gracious homes. The canopy is as much a part of this planned city as its distinctive architecture, all attributed to the vision of George E. Merrick nearly 100 years ago.

The story of this city began in 1911, when Merrick inherited 1,600 acres of citrus and avocado groves from his father. Through judicious investment he nearly doubled the tract to 3,000 acres by 1921. Merrick dreamed of building an American Venice here, complete with canals and homes. Working from this vision, he began designing a city based on centuries-old prototypes from Mediterranean countries. Unfortunately for Merrick, the devastating no-name hurricane of 1926, followed by the Great Depression, prevented him from fulfilling many of his plans. He died at 54, an employee of the post office. Today Coral Gables has a population of about 45,000. In its bustling downtown, more than 150 multinational companies maintain headquarters or regional offices, and the University of Miami campus in the southern part of the Gables brings a youthful vibrancy to the area. A southern branch of the city extends down the shore of Biscayne Bay through neighborhoods threaded with canals.

EXPLORING
TOP ATTRACTIONS

★ **Biltmore Hotel.** Bouncing back stunningly from its dark days as an Army hospital, this hotel has become the jewel of Coral Gables—a dazzling architectural gem with a colorful past. First opened in 1926, it was a hot spot for the rich and glamorous of the Jazz Age until it was converted to an Army–Air Force regional hospital in 1942. Until 1968, the Veterans Administration continued to operate the hospital after World War II. The Biltmore then lay vacant for nearly 20 years before it underwent extensive renovations and reopened as a luxury hotel in 1987. Its 16-story tower, like the Freedom Tower in downtown Miami, is a replica of Seville's Giralda Tower. The magnificent pool, reportedly the largest hotel pool in the continental United States, is steeped in history—Johnny Weissmuller of Tarzan fame was a lifeguard here, and in the 1930s grand aquatic galas featuring alligator wrestling, synchronized swimming, and bathing beauties drew thousands. More recently it was President Clinton's preferred place to stay and golf. To the west is the Biltmore Country Club, a richly ornamented beaux arts–style structure with a superb colonnade and courtyard; it was reincorporated into the hotel in 1989. Sunday champagne brunch is a local legend; try to get a table in the courtyard. ✉ *1200 Anastasia Ave., near De Soto Blvd., Coral Gables* ☎ *305/445–1926* ⊕ *www.biltmorehotel.com.*

⟳ **Fairchild Tropical Botanic Garden.** With 83 acres of lakes, sunken gardens, a 560-foot vine pergola, orchids, bellflowers, coral trees, bougainvillea, rare palms, and flowering trees, Fairchild is the largest tropical botanical garden in the continental United States. The tram tour highlights the best of South Florida's flora; then you can set off exploring on your own. A 2-acre rain-forest exhibit showcases tropical plants from around the world complete with a waterfall and stream. The conservatory, Windows to the Tropics, is home to rare tropical plants, including the Titan Arum (*Amorphophallus titanum*), a fast-growing variety that attracted thousands of visitors when it bloomed in 1998. (It was only the sixth documented bloom in this country in the 20th century.) The Keys Coastal Habitat, created in a marsh and mangrove area in 1995 with assistance from the Tropical Audubon Society, provides food and shelter to resident and migratory birds. Check out the Montgomery Botanical Center, a research facility devoted to palms and cycads. Spicing up Fairchild's calendar are plant sales, afternoon teas, and genuinely special events year-round, such as the International Mango Festival the second weekend in July. The excellent bookstore–gift shop carries books on gardening and horticulture, and the Garden Café serves sandwiches and, seasonally, smoothies made from the garden's own crop of tropical fruits. ✉ *10901 Old Cutler Rd., Coral Gables* ☎ *305/667–1651* ⊕ *www.fairchildgarden.org* ☑ *$25* ⊙ *Daily 9:30–4:30.*

Fodor's Choice ★

Venetian Pool. Sculpted from a rock quarry in 1923 and fed by artesian wells, this 820,000-gallon municipal pool had a major face-lift in 2010. It remains quite popular because of its themed architecture—a fantasy version of a waterfront Italian village—created by Denman Fink. The pool has earned a place on the National Register of Historic Places and showcases a nice collection of vintage photos depicting 1920s beauty pageants and swank soirees held long ago. Paul Whiteman played here, Johnny Weissmuller and Esther Williams swam here, and you should, too (but no kids under 3). A snack bar, lockers, and showers make this must-see user-friendly as well. ✉ *2701 De Soto Blvd., at Toledo St., Coral Gables* ☎ *305/460–5306* ⊕ *www.gablesrecreation.com* ☑ *$11; free parking across De Soto Blvd.* ⊙ *Times vary month to month. Call ahead.*

WORTH NOTING

Coral Gables Congregational Church. With George Merrick as a charter member (he donated the land on which it stands) this parish was organized in 1923. Rumor has it that Merrick built Coral Gables's first church, in honor of his father, a congregational minister. It's only natural then that this was the first church in the state of Florida to be listed on the National Register of Historic Places. Nowadays, this functioning church is welcoming, regardless of age, sexual orientation, or faith. The original interior is still in magnificent condition. The church is located directly across from the Biltmore Hotel. ⊠ *3010 De Soto Blvd., at Anastasia Ave., Coral Gables* ☎ *305/448–7421* ⊕ *www. coralgablescongregational.org* ⊙ *Weekdays 8:30–5, Sun. services at 9 at Chapel and 11 at the Sanctuary.*

Coral Gables Merrick House and Gardens. In 1976 the city of Coral Gables acquired Merrick's boyhood home. Restored to its 1920s appearance, it contains Merrick family furnishings and artwork. The breezy veranda and coral-rock construction are details you'll see repeated on many of the grand homes along Coral Way. Note that the telephone is disconnected except during open hours. ⊠ *907 Coral Way, at Toledo St., Coral Gables* ☎ *305/460–5361* 🏷 *$5* ⊙ *45-min house tours Wed. and most Sun. at 1, 2, and 3.*

Miracle Mile. Even with competition from some impressive malls, this half-mile stretch of retail stores continues to thrive because of its intriguing mixture of unique boutiques, bridal shops, art galleries, charming restaurants, and upscale nightlife venues. ⊠ *Coral Way between S.W. 37th and S.W. 42nd Aves., Coral Gables* ⊕ *www.shopcoralgables.com.*

OFF THE BEATEN PATH

Zoo Miami. Don't miss a visit to this top-notch zoo, 14 mi southwest of Coral Gables. The only subtropical zoo in the continental United States, it has 320 plus acres that are home to more than 2,000 animals, including 40 endangered species, which roam on islands surrounded by moats. Take the monorail ($3 for an all-day pass) for a cool overview, then walk around for a closer look, including the latest attraction Amazon & Beyond, which encompasses 27 acres of simulated tropical rain forests showcasing 600 animals indigenous to the region, such as giant river otters, harpy eagles, anacondas, and jaguars. Other exhibits include Tiger Temple, where white tigers roam, and the African Plains exhibit, where giraffes, ostriches, and zebras graze in a simulated natural habitat. You can even feed veggies to the giraffes at Samburu Station. The Wings of Asia aviary has about 300 exotic birds representing 70 species flying free within the junglelike enclosure. There's also a petting zoo with a meerkat exhibit and interactive opportunities, such as those at Dr. Wilde's World and the Ecology Theater, where kids can touch Florida animals like alligators and opossums. An educational and entertaining wildlife show is given three times daily. ⊠ *12400 S.W. 152nd St., Richmond Heights, Miami* ☎ *305/251–0400* ⊕ *www.miamimetrozoo. com* 🏷 *$15.95, $11.95 children ages 3 to 12; 45-min tram tour $4.95* ⊙ *Daily 9:30–5:30, last admission 4.*

COCONUT GROVE

Eclectic and intriguing, Miami's Coconut Grove can be considered a loose tropical equivalent of New York's Greenwich Village. A haven for writers and artists, the neighborhood has never quite outgrown its image as a small village. During the day it's business as usual in Coconut Grove, much as in any other Miami neighborhood. But in the evening, especially on weekends, it seems as if someone flips a switch and the streets come alive. Locals and tourists jam into small boutiques, sidewalk cafés, and stores lodged in two massive retail-entertainment complexes. For blocks in every direction, students, families, and prosperous retirees flow in and out of a mix of galleries, restaurants, bars, bookstores, comedy clubs, and theaters. With this weekly influx of traffic, parking can pose a problem. There's a well-lighted city garage at 3315 Rice Street (behind the Mayfair and Cocowalk), or look for police to direct you to parking lots where you'll pay $10 and up for an evening's slot. If you're staying in the Grove, leave the car behind, and your night will get off to an easier start.

Nighttime is the right time to see Coconut Grove, but in the day you can take a casual drive around the neighborhood to see its diverse architecture. Posh estates mingle with rustic cottages, modest frame homes, and stark modern dwellings, often on the same block. If you're into horticulture, you'll be impressed by the Garden of Eden–like foliage that seems to grow everywhere without care. In truth, residents are determined to keep up the Grove's village-in-a-jungle look, so they lavish attention on exotic plantings even as they battle to protect any remaining native vegetation.

EXPLORING

Barnacle Historic State Park. A pristine bay-front manse sandwiched between cramped luxury developments, Barnacle is Miami's oldest house still standing on its original foundation. To get here, you'll hike along an old buggy trail through a tropical hardwood hammock and landscaped lawn leading to Biscayne Bay. Built in 1891 by Florida's first snowbird—New Yorker Commodore Ralph Munroe—the large home, built of timber that Munroe salvaged from wrecked ships, has many original furnishings, a broad sloping roof, and deeply recessed verandas that channel sea breezes into the house. If your timing is right, you may catch one of the monthly Moonlight Concerts, and the old-fashioned picnic on July 4 is popular. ⊠ *3485 Main Hwy.* ☎ *305/442–6866* ⊕ *www.floridastateparks.org/thebarnacle* ⊐ *$2 park entry, tours $3, concerts $7* ☉ *Fri.–Mon. 9–5; tours at 10, 11:30, 1, and 2:30; groups Wed. and Thurs.; closed Tues.; concerts Sept.–May on evenings near the full moon 6–9, call or check the Web site for date.*

Ⓒ **Miami Museum of Science and Planetarium.** This small fun museum is chock-full of hands-on sound, gravity, and electricity displays for children and adults alike. For animal lovers, its wildlife center houses native Florida snakes, turtles, tortoises, and birds of prey. Check the museum's schedule for traveling exhibits that appear throughout the year. If you're here the first Friday of the month—called Fabulous First Fridays—stick around for the free star show at 7:30 pm and then gaze at the planets through two powerful Meade telescopes at the Weintraub Observatory. Also enjoy a laser-light rock-and-roll show at either 9, 10, or 11 pm to the tunes of the Doors, the Beatles, or Pink Floyd to name a few. ⊠ *3280 S. Miami Ave.* ☎ *305/646–4200* ⊕ *www.miamisci.org* ⊐ *Museum exhibits, planetarium shows, and wildlife center $14.95, laser show $7* ☉ *Museum daily 10–6.*

Fodor's Choice ★ **Vizcaya Museum and Gardens.** Of the 10,000 people living in Miami between 1912 and 1916, about 1,000 of them were gainfully employed by Chicago industrialist James Deering to build this European-inspired residence. Once comprising 180 acres, this national historic landmark now occupies a 30-acre tract that includes a native hammock and more than 10 acres of formal gardens with fountains overlooking Biscayne Bay. The house, open to the public, contains 70 rooms, 34 of which are filled with paintings, sculpture, antique furniture, and other fine and decorative arts. The collection spans 2,000 years and represents the Renaissance, baroque, rococo, and neoclassical periods. The 90-minute self-guided Discover Vizcaya Audio Tour is available in both English and Spanish for an additional $5. Guided tours are also available. Moonlight tours, offered on evenings that are nearest the full moon, provide a magical look at the gardens; call for reservations. ⊠ *3251 S. Miami Ave.* ☎ *305/250–9133* ⊕ *www.vizcayamuseum.org* ⊑ *$15* ☾ *Wed.–Mon. 9:30–4:30.*

4

KEY BISCAYNE

Once upon a time, these barrier islands were an outpost for fishermen and sailors, pirates and salvagers, soldiers and settlers. The 95-foot Cape Florida Lighthouse stood tall during Seminole Indian battles and hurricanes. Coconut plantations covered two-thirds of Key Biscayne, and there were plans as far back as the 1800s to develop the picturesque island as a resort for the wealthy. Fortunately, the state and county governments set much of the land aside for parks, and both keys are now home to top-ranked beaches and golf, tennis, softball, and picnicking facilities. The long and winding bike paths that run through the islands are favorites for in-line skaters and cyclists. Incorporated in 1991, the village of Key Biscayne is a hospitable community of about 10,500; Virginia Key remains undeveloped at the moment, making these two playground islands especially family-friendly.

EXPLORING

Miami Seaquarium. This classic family attraction stages shows with sea lions, dolphins, and Lolita the killer whale. The Crocodile Flats exhibit has 26 Nile crocodiles. Discovery Bay, an endangered mangrove habitat, is home to sea turtles, alligators, herons, egrets, and ibis. You can also visit a shark pool, a tropical reef aquarium, and West Indian and Florida manatees. A popular interactive attraction is the Stingray Touch Tank, where you can touch and feed cow-nose rays and southern stingrays. Another big draw is the Swim with Our Dolphins program. For $199, a two-hour session allows you to touch, kiss, and swim with the gentle marine mammals on the Dolphin Odyssey, $139 ($99 for kids) to participate in the shallow water Dolphin Encounter. It may seem pricey but it does include park admission, towel, and a wet suit. Reservations required. ⊠ *4400 Rickenbacker Causeway, Virginia Key* ☎ *305/361–5705* ⊕ *www.miamiseaquarium.com* ⊑ *$37.95, children 3–9 $27.95, parking $8* ☾ *Daily 9–6, last admission 4:30; dolphin swim daily at 9:30, 10, 11:30, 1, and 2:30; dolphin encounter daily at 12:15 and 3:15.*

Old Rickenbacker Causeway Bridge. Here you can watch boat traffic pass through the channel, pelicans and other seabirds soar and dive, and dolphins cavort in the bay. Park at the bridge entrance, about a mile from the tollgate, and walk past anglers tending their lines to the gap

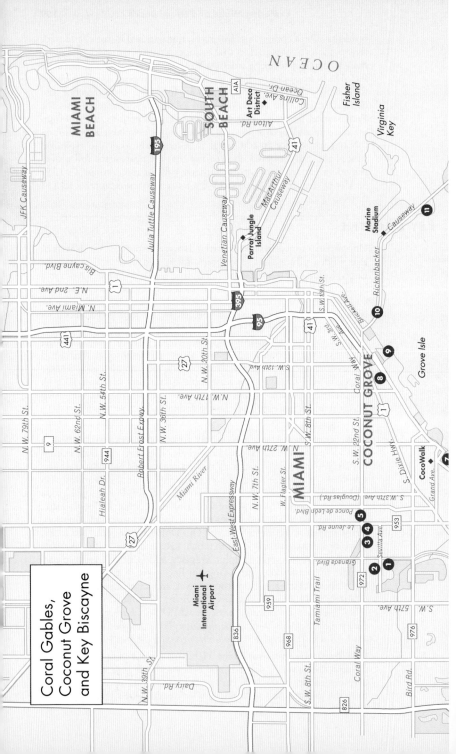

Coral Gables,
Coconut Grove
and Key Biscayne

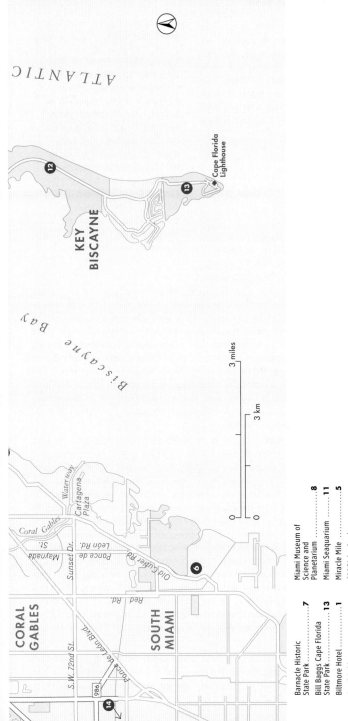

ATLANTIC

Biscayne Bay

KEY BISCAYNE

Cape Florida Lighthouse

CORAL GABLES

SOUTH MIAMI

Coral Gables

Maynada St.
Sunset Dr.
Ponce de León Rd.
Coral Gables Waterway
Cartagena Plaza
Old Cutler Rd.
Red Rd.
S.W. 72nd St.
Ponce de Léon Blvd.

0   3 km
0   3 miles

where the center draw span across the Intracoastal Waterway was removed. On the right, on cool, clear winter evenings, the water sparkles with dots of light from hundreds of shrimp boats. ⊠ *Rickenbacker Causeway south of Powell Bridge, east of Coconut Grove.*

BEACHES

MIAMI BEACH

NORTH BEACH AND AVENTURA

Haulover Beach Park. This popular clothing-optional beach is embraced by naturists of all ages, shapes, and sizes. Once you park in the North Lot, you'll walk through a short tunnel covered with trees and natural habitat until you emerge on the unpretentious beach, where nudity is rarely met by gawkers. There are volleyball nets, and plenty of beach chair and umbrella rentals to protect your birthday suit from too much exposure—to the sun, that is. The sections of beach requiring swimwear are popular, too, given the park's ample parking and relaxed atmosphere. Lifeguards stand watch. More active types might want to check out the kite rentals, charter-fishing excursions, and a par-3, 9-hole golf course. ⊠ *10800 Collins Ave., north of Bal Harbour in Sunny Isles* ☎ *305/947–3525* ⊕ *www.hauloverbeach.org* ☞ *$6 per vehicle if park in lot* ◷ *Daily sunrise–sunset.*

★ **Oleta River State Park.** Tucked away in North Miami Beach is a ready-made family getaway. Nature lovers will find it easy to embrace the 1,128 acres of subtropical beauty along Biscayne Bay. Swim in the calm bay waters and bicycle, canoe, kayak, and bask among egrets, manatees, bald eagles, and fiddler crabs. Dozens of picnic tables, along with 10 covered pavilions, dot the stunning natural habitat, which has recently been restored with red mangroves to revitalize the ecosystem and draw endangered birds, like the roseate spoonbill. There's a playground for tots, a mangrove island accessible only by boat, 15 mi of mountain-bike trails, a half-mile exercise track, concessions, and outdoor showers. If you want to continue the nature adventure into the evening, reserve an overnight stay in minimalist (but still air-conditioned) cabins, which run $55 per night. ⊠ *3400 N.E. 163rd St., North Miami Beach* ☎ *305/919–1844* ⊕ *www.floridastateparks.org/oletariver* ☞ *$6 per vehicle; $2 per person on foot or bike; free entrance if renting a cabin* ◷ *Daily 8–sunset.*

SOUTH BEACH

Fodor's Choice **South Beach.** A 10-block stretch of white sandy beach hugging the turquoise waters along Ocean Drive—from 5th to 15th streets—is one ★ of the most popular in America, known for drawing unabashedly

---

SAIL AWAY

If you can sail in Miami, do. Blue skies, calm seas, and a view of the city skyline make for a pleasurable outing—especially at twilight, when the fabled "moon over Miami" casts a soft glow on the water. Key Biscayne's calm waves and strong breezes are perfect for sailing and windsurfing, and although Dinner Key and the Coconut Grove waterfront remain the center of sailing in Greater Miami, sailboat moorings and rentals sit along other parts of the bay and up the Miami River.

Not all the fun is for grown-ups. With sandy shores great for kite flying, Miami beaches appeal to kids, too.

modelesque sunbathers and posers. With the influx of new luxe hotels and hotspots from 16th to 25th streets, the South Beach stand-and-pose scene is now bigger than ever. The beaches crowd quickly on the weekends with a blend of European tourists, young hipsters, and sun-drenched locals offering Latin flavor. Separating the sand from the traffic of Ocean Drive is palm-fringed Lummus Park, with its volleyball nets and chickee huts (huts made of palmetto thatch over a cypress frame) for shade. The beach at 12th Street is popular with gays, in a section often marked with rainbow flags. Locals hang out on 3rd Street beach, in an area called SoFi (South of Fifth) where they watch fit Brazilians play foot volley, a variation of volleyball that uses everything but the hands. Because much of South Beach leans toward skimpy sunning—women are often in G-strings and casually topless—many families prefer the tamer sections of Mid- and North Beach. Metered parking spots next to the ocean are a rare find. Instead, opt for a public garage a few blocks away and enjoy the people-watching as you walk to find your perfect spot on the sand. ⊠ Ocean Dr. from 5th to 15th Sts., then Collins Ave. to 25th St., Miami Beach ☎ 305/673–7714.

KEY BISCAYNE

Fodor'sChoice **Bill Baggs Cape Florida State Park.** Thanks to inviting beaches, sunsets, and
★ a tranquil lighthouse, this park at Key Biscayne's southern tip is worth the drive. In fact, the 1-mi stretch of pure beachfront has been ranked among Florida's best on several occasions. It has 19 picnic shelters, and two cafés that serve light lunches. A stroll or ride along walking and bicycle paths provides wonderful views of Miami's dramatic skyline.

From the southern end of the park you can see a handful of houses rising over the bay on wooden stilts, the remnants of Stiltsville, built in the 1940s and now protected by the Stiltsville Trust. The nonprofit group was established in 2003 to preserve the structures as they showcase the park's rich history.

Bill Baggs has bicycle rentals, a playground, fishing piers, and guided tours of the **Cape Florida Lighthouse,** South Florida's oldest structure. The lighthouse was erected in 1845 to replace an earlier one damaged in an 1836 Seminole attack, in which the keeper's helper was killed. The restored cottage and lighthouse offer free tours at 10 am and 1 pm Thursday to Monday. Be there a half hour beforehand. ⊠ *1200 S. Crandon Blvd., Key Biscayne* ☎ *305/361–5811* ⊕ *www.floridastateparks. org/capeflorida* ⊠ *$8 per vehicle; $2 per person on bicycle, bus, motorcycle, or foot* ⊙ *Daily 8–dusk.*

☺ **Crandon Park Beach.** This relaxing oasis in northern Key Biscayne is
★ popular with families. The sand is soft, there are no riptides, there's a great view of the Atlantic, and parking is both inexpensive and plentiful. The park is dotted with picnic tables and grills and cabanas are available for rent on a first-come, first-served basis.

Crandon Gardens at Crandon Park was once the site of a zoo. There are swans, waterfowl, and dozens of huge iguanas running loose. Nearby are a restored carousel (it's open weekends and major holidays 10–5, until 6 in summer, and you get three rides for $1), outdoor roller rink, and playground.

At the north end of the beach is the free **Marjory Stoneman Douglas Biscayne Nature Center** (☎ *305/361–6767* ⊙ *Daily 10–4*), where you can explore sea-grass beds on a tour with a naturalist; see red, black, and white mangroves; and hike along the beach and hammock in the Bear Cut Preserve. The park also sponsors hikes and tours.

⊠ *6747 Crandon Blvd., Key Biscayne* ☎ *305/361–5421* ⊕ *www. biscaynenaturecenter.org* ⊠ *$5 per vehicle* ⊙ *Daily 8–sunset.*

SPORTS AND THE OUTDOORS

Sun, sand, and crystal-clear water mixed with an almost nonexistent winter and a cosmopolitan clientele make Miami and Miami Beach ideal for year-round sunbathing and outdoor activities. Whether the priority is showing off a toned body, jumping on a Jet Ski, or relaxing in a tranquil natural environment, there's a beach tailor-made to please. But tanning and water sports are only part of this sun-drenched picture. Greater Miami has championship golf courses and tennis courts, miles of bike trails along placid canals and through subtropical forests, and skater-friendly concrete paths amidst the urban jungle. For those who like their sports of the spectator variety, the city offers up a bonanza of pro teams for every season. The Miami Dolphins remain the only NFL

MIAMI TOURS

BOAT TOURS

Duck Tours Miami. Amphibious vehicles make daily 90-minute tours of Miami that combine land and sea views. Comedy and music are part of the mix. Tickets are $18 for children 4–12. ✉ *1661 James Ave., Miami Beach* ☎ *305/673-2217* ⊕ *www.ducktourssouthbeach.com* 🍴 *$32.*

Island Queen, Island Lady, and Miami Lady. Double-decker, 140-passenger tour boats docked at Bayside Marketplace set sail daily for 90-minute narrated tours of the Port of Miami and Millionaires' Row. ✉ *401 Biscayne Blvd., Miami* ☎ *305/379-5119* ⊕ *www.islandqueencruises.com* 🍴 *$26.*

RA Charters. For something a little more private and luxe, sail out of the Dinner Key Marina in Coconut Grove. Full- and half-day charters include sailing lessons, with occasional extended trips to the Florida Keys.

For a romantic night, have Captain Masoud pack some gourmet fare and sail sunset to moonlight while you enjoy Biscayne Bay's spectacular skyline view of Miami. ☎ *305/666-7979 or 305/989-3959* ⊕ *www.racharters. com* 🍴 *Call for prices.*

WALKING TOURS

Art Deco District Tour. Operated by the Miami Design Preservation League, this is a 90-minute guided walking tour that departs from the league's welcome center at Ocean Drive and 10th Street. It starts at 10:30 am Friday through Wednesday, and at 6:30 pm Thursday. Alternatively, you can go at your own pace with the league's self-guided iPod audio tour, which takes roughly an hour and a half. ✉ *1001 Ocean Dr., South Beach, Miami Beach* ☎ *305/763-8026* ⊕ *www.mdpl.org* 🍴 *$20 guided tour, $15 audio tour.*

team to have ever played a perfect season (back in 1972), the scrappy Florida Marlins took the World Series title in 2003, and the Miami Heat were the 2006 NBA champions (hopes for more have risen with the dream three of Chris Bosch, Dwayne Wade, and LeBron James on the court). There's even a crazy ball-flinging game called jai alai that's billed as the fastest sport on earth.

In addition to contacting venues directly, get tickets to major events from **Ticketmaster** (☎ *800/745-3000* ⊕ *www.ticketmaster.com*).

BASEBALL

🌀 **Miami Marlins.** Miami's baseball team, formerly known as the Florida Marlins, is settling into its new home, Miami Ballpark—a 37,000-seat retractable-roof baseball stadium on the grounds of Miami's famous Orange Bowl. Go see the team that came out of nowhere to beat the New York Yankees and win the 2003 World Series. Home games are April through early October. ✉ *Miami Ballpark, 1501 N.W. 3rd St., 2 mi west of Downtown. Miami* ☎ *305/626-7378 or 877/627-5467* ⊕ *www.marlins.com* 🍴 *$10–$315, parking $10.*

BASKETBALL

Miami Heat. The 2006 NBA champs play at the 19,600-seat, water-front AmericanAirlines Arena. The state-of-the-art venue features restaurants, a wide patio overlooking Biscayne Bay, and a silver sun-shape special-effects scoreboard with rays holding wide-screen TVs. During Heat games, when the 1,100 underground parking spaces are reserved for season-ticket holders, you can park across the street at Miami's Bayside Marketplace ($20), at metered spaces along Biscayne Boulevard, or in lots on side streets, where prices range from $5 to $25, depending on the distance from the arena (a limited number of spaces for people with disabilities are available on-site for non-season-ticket holders). Better yet, take the Metromover to the Park West or Freedom Tower station. Home games are held November through April. ⊠ *AmericanAirlines Arena, 601 Biscayne Blvd., Downtown* ☎ *800/462–2849 ticket hotline* ⊕ *www.nba.com/heat* ✆ *$10–$500.*

BICYCLING

Perfect weather and flat terrain make Miami-Dade County a popular place for cyclists; however, biking here can also be quite dangerous. Be very vigilant when biking on Miami Beach, or better yet, steer clear and bike the beautiful paths of Key Biscayne.

Key Cycling. Rent bikes for $15 for two hours, $24 for the day, and $80 for the week. ⊠ *328 Crandon Blvd., Key Biscayne* ☎ *305/361–0061* ⊕ *www.keycycling.com.*

BOATING AND SAILING

Boating, whether on sailboats, powerboats, luxury yachts, Wave-Runners, or windsurfers, is a passion in greater Miami. The Intracoastal Waterway, wide and sheltered Biscayne Bay, and the Atlantic Ocean provide ample opportunities for fun aboard all types of watercraft.

The best windsurfing spots are on the north side of the Rickenbacker Causeway at Virginia Key Beach or to the south at, go figure, Windsurfer Beach. Kite surfing adds another level to the water-sports craze.

MARINAS

Bayshore Landing Marina. This bustling marina is home to a lively seafood restaurant that's good for viewing the nautical eye candy. ⊠ *2560 S. Bayshore Dr., Coconut Grove* ☎ *305/854–7997.*

Haulover Marine Center. It may be low on glamour, but this marina, with a bait-and-tackle shop and a 24-hour marine gas station, is high on service. ⊠ *15000 Collins Ave., north of Bal Harbour, Miami Beach* ☎ *305/945–3934* ⊕ *www.haulovermarinecenter.net.*

Miami Beach Marina. Near the Art Deco District there is plenty to entice sailors and landlubbers alike: restaurants, charters, boat rentals, a complete marine-hardware store, a dive shop, excursion vendors, a large grocery store, a fuel dock, concierge services, and 400 slips accommodating vessels of up to 250 feet. There's also a U.S. Customs clearing station and a charter service, Florida Yacht Charters. Picnic tables along the docks make this marina especially visitor-friendly. ✉ *MacArthur Causeway, 300 Alton Rd., Miami Beach* ☎ *305/673–6000* ⊕ *www. miamibeachmarina.com.*

OUTFITTERS AND EXPEDITIONS

Club Nautico. You can rent 18- to 34-foot powerboats and 52- to 54-foot yachts through this national boat rental company with two Miami locations. Half- to full-day rentals range from $399 to $3,600. ✉ *Miami Beach Marina, 300 Alton Rd., #112, Miami Beach* ☎ *305/673–2502* ⊕ *www.club-nautico.com* ✉ *Crandon Park Marina, 4000 Crandon Blvd., Key Biscayne.*

Playtime Watersports. A number of high-end hotels get their water-sports equipment, including WaveRunners and wind-driven devices, here. ☎ *786/234–0184 or 305/216-6967* ⊕ *www.playtimewatersport.com.*

Sailboards Miami. In addition to renting equipment, these friendly folks say they teach more windsurfers each year than anyone in the United States and promise to teach you to windsurf within two hours—for $79. Rentals average $30 for the first hour and $25 for each additional hour. ✉ *.7 mi after toll plaza on Rickenbacker Causeway, Key Biscayne* ☎ *305/361–7245* ⊕ *www.sailboardsmiami.com.*

FOOTBALL

Fodor's Choice ★ **Miami Dolphins.** The Dolphins have one of the largest average attendance figures in the league. September through January, on home-game days the Metro Miami-Dade Transit Agency runs buses to the stadium. ✉ *Sun Life Stadium, 2269 Dan Marino Blvd., 16 mi northwest of Downtown, between I–95 and Florida's Tpke.* ☎ *305/623–6100* ⊕ *www.miamidolphins.com.*

GOLF

Greater Miami has more than 30 private and public courses. Costs at most courses are higher on weekends and in season, but you can save by playing on weekdays and after 1 or 3 pm, depending on the course—call ahead to find out when afternoon-twilight rates go into effect. For information on most courses in Miami and throughout Florida, you can visit ⊕ *www.floridagolferguide.com.*

Biltmore Golf Course. The 18-hole, par-71 championship course, known for its scenic layout, has been restored to its original Donald Ross design, circa 1925. Greens fees in season range from $145 to $165 for nonresidents. The optional cart is $27. ✉ *1210 Anastasia Ave., Coral Gables* ☎ *305/460–5364* ⊕ *www.biltmorehotel.com.*

Crandon Golf. Overlooking the bay, this top-rated 18-hole, par-72 public course comes with a beautiful tropical setting. Nonresidents should expect to pay $180 for a round in season (December 15–April) and roughly half that off-season. Twilight rates apply after 3 pm. ✉ *6700 Crandon Blvd., Key Biscayne* ☎ *305/361–9129* ⊕ *www. crandongolfclub.com.*

Don Shula's Hotel & Golf Club. In northern Miami, this hotel has one of the longest championship courses in the area (7,055 yards, par 72), a lighted par-3 course, and a golf school. Greens fees are $134–$175, depending on the season. Hotel guests get discounted rates. You'll pay in the lower range on weekdays, more on weekends, and $45 after 3 pm. Golf carts are included. The par-3 course is $12 weekdays, $15 weekends. The club hosts more than 75 tournaments a year. ⊠ *7601 Miami Lakes Dr., 154th St. Exit off Rte. 826, Miami Lakes* ☎ *305/820–8106* ⊕ *www.donshulahotel.com.*

Fodor's Choice
★
Doral Golf Resort and Spa. Of its five courses and many annual tournaments this resort, just west of Miami proper, is best known for the par-72 Blue Monster course and the PGA's annual World Golf Championship. (The week of festivities planned around this tournament, which offers $8 million in prize money, brings hordes of pro-golf aficionados in late March.) Greens fees range from $65 to $325. Carts are not required. ⊠ *4400 N.W. 87th Ave., 36th St. Exit off Rte. 826, Doral, Miami* ☎ *305/592–2000 or 800/713–6725* ⊕ *www.doralresort.com.*

Miami Beach Golf Club. Hit the links in the heart of South Beach at a lovely 18-hole, par-72 course. Greens fees are $100 in summer, $200 in winter, including mandatory cart. ⊠ *2301 Alton Rd., Miami Beach* ☎ *305/532–3350* ⊕ *www.miamibeachgolfclub.com.*

SCUBA DIVING AND SNORKELING

Diving and snorkeling on the offshore coral wrecks and reefs on a calm day can be very rewarding. Chances are excellent you'll come face-to-face with a flood of tropical fish. One option is to find Fowey, Triumph, Long, and Emerald reefs in 10- to 15-foot dives that are perfect for snorkelers and beginning divers. On the edge of the continental shelf a little more than 3 mi out, these reefs are just ¼ mi away from depths greater than 100 feet. Another option is to paddle around the tangled prop roots of the mangrove trees that line the coast, peering at the fish, crabs, and other creatures hiding there. ⇨ *For the best snorkeling in Miami-Dade, head to Biscayne National Park. See the Everglades chapter for more information.*

Artificial Reefs. Perhaps the area's most unusual diving options are its artificial reefs. Since 1981, Miami-Dade County's Department of Environmental Resources Management has sunk tons of limestone boulders and a water tower, army tanks, and almost 200 boats of all descriptions to create a "wreckreational" habitat where divers can swim with yellow tang, barracudas, nurse sharks, snapper, eels, and grouper. Most dive shops sell a book listing the locations of these wrecks. Information on wreck diving can be obtained from the Miami Beach Chamber of Commerce. ⊠ *1920 Meridian Ave., Miami Beach* ☎ *305/672–1270.*

Divers Paradise of Key Biscayne. This complete dive shop and diving-charter service next to the Crandon Park Marina, includes equipment rental and scuba instruction with PADI and NAUI affiliation. Dive trips are offered Tuesday through Friday at 10 and 1, weekends 8:30 and 1:30. The trip is $60. ⊠ *4000 Crandon Blvd., Key Biscayne* ☎ *305/361–3483* ⊕ *www.keydivers.com.*

Continued on page 174

A STROLL DOWN

DECO LANE

by Susan MacCallum Whitcomb

"It was an age of miracles, it was an age of art,

it was an age of excess, and it was an age of satire."

—F. Scott Fitzgerald, *Echoes of the Jazz Age*

The 1920s and '30s brought us flappers and gangsters, plunging stock prices and soaring skyscrapers, and plenty of headline-worthy news from the arts scene, from talking pictures and the jazz craze to fashions where pearls piled on and sequins dazzled. These decades between the two world wars also gave us an art style reflective of the changing times: art deco.

Distinguished by geometrical shapes and the use of industrial motifs that fused the decorative arts with modern technology, art deco became the architectural style of choice for train stations and big buildings across the country (think New york's Radio City Music Hall and Empire State Building).

Using a steel-and-concrete box as the foundation, architects dipped into art deco's grab bag of accessories, initially decorating facades with spheres, cylinders, and cubes. They later borrowed increasingly from industrial design, stripping elements used in ocean liners and automobiles to their streamlined essentials.

The style was also used in jewelry, furniture, textiles, and advertising. The fact that it employed inexpensive materials, such as stucco or terrazzo, helped art deco thrive during the Great Depression.

MIAMI BEACH'S ART DECO DISTRICT

With its warm beaches and tropical surroundings, Miami Beach in the early 20th century was establishing itself as America's winter playground. During the roaring '20s luxurious hostelries resembling Venetian palaces, Spanish villages, and French châteaux sprouted up. In the 1930s, middle-class tourists started coming, and more hotels had to be built. Designers like Henry Hohauser chose Art Deco for its affordable yet distinctive design.

An antidote to the gloom of the Great Depression, the look was cheerful and tidy. And with the whimsical additions of portholes, colorful racing bands, and images of rolling ocean waves painted or etched on the walls, these South Beach properties created an oceanfront fantasy world for travelers.

Many of the candy-colored hotels have survived and been restored. They are among the more than 800 buildings of historical significance in South Beach's art deco district. Composing much of South Beach, the 1-square-mi district is bounded by Dade Boulevard on the north, the Atlantic Ocean on the east, 6th Street on the south, and Alton Road on the west.

Because the district as a whole was developed so rapidly and designed by like-minded architects—**Henry Hohauser, L. Murray Dixon, Albert Anis,** and their colleagues—it has amazing stylistic unity. Nevertheless, on this single street you can trace the evolution of period form from angular, vertically emphatic early deco to aerodynamically rounded Streamline Moderne. The relatively severe Cavalier and more curvaceous Cardozo are fine examples of the former and latter, respectively.

To explore the district, begin by loading up on literature in the **Art Deco Welcome Center** (⊠ *1001 Ocean Dr.* ☎*305/531–3484* ⊕ *www.mdpl.org*). If you want to view these historic properties on your own, just start walking. A four-block stroll north on Ocean Drive gets you up close to camera-ready classics: the **Clevelander** (1020), the **Tides** (1220), the **Leslie** (1244), the **Carlyle** (1250), the **Cardozo** (1300), the **Cavalier** (1320), and the **Winterhaven** (1400).

ART DECO TOURS

See the bold looks of classic Art Deco architecture along Ocean Drive.

SELF-GUIDED AUDIO TOURS

Expert insight on the architecture and the area's history is yours on the Miami Design Preservation League's (MDPL) 90-minute self-guided walks that use an iPod or cell phone and include a companion map. You can pick up the iPod version and companion map at the Art Deco Welcome Center from 9:30 AM to 5 PM daily; the cost is $15. The cell-phone option ($10) is available anytime by calling 786/312–1229 and charging the amount to your credit card; your payment allows you access to audio commentary for up to 24 hours after purchase.

WALKING TOURS

The MDPL's 90-minute "Ocean Drive and Beyond" group walking tour gives you a guided look at area icons, inside and out. (A number of interiors are on the itinerary, so it's a good chance to peek inside spots that might otherwise seem off-limits.) Morning tours depart at 10:30 AM from the Art Deco Welcome Center Gift Shop on Tuesday, Wednesday, Friday, Saturday, and Sunday. An evening tour departs at 6:30 PM on Thursdays. Reservations can't be made in advance, so arrive 15–20 minutes early to buy tickets ($20).

Celebrate the 1930s during Art Deco Weekend.

BIKE TOURS

Rather ride than walk? Three-hour cycling tours of the city's art deco history are organized daily for groups (5 or more) by **South Beach Bike Tours** (☎ 305/673–2002 ⊕ www.southbeachbiketours.com). The $59 cost includes equipment, snacks, and water.

ART DECO WEEKEND

Tours, lectures, film screenings, and dozens of other '30s-themed events are on tap every January, during the annual **Art Deco Weekend** (☎ 305/672–2014, ⊕ www.ArtDecoWeekend.com). Festivities—many of them free—kick off with a Saturday morning parade and culminate in a street fair. More than a quarter of a million people join in the action, which centers on Ocean Drive between 5th and 15th streets. The 2011 dates are Jan. 14–16.

ARCHITECTURAL HIGHLIGHTS

Cavalier Hotel

FRIEZE DETAIL, CAVALIER HOTEL
The decorative stucco friezes outside the Cavalier Hotel at 1320 Ocean Drive are significant for more than aesthetic reasons. Roy France used them to add symmetry (adhering to the "Rule of Three") and accentuate the hotel's verticality by drawing the eye upward. The pattern he chose also reflected a fascination with ancient civilizations engendered by the recent rediscovery of King Tut's tomb and the Chichén Itzá temples.

Park Central Hotel

LOBBY FLOOR, PARK CENTRAL HOTEL
Terrazzo—a compound of cement and stone chips that could be poured, then polished—is a hallmark of deco design. Terrazzo floors typically had a geometric pattern, like this one in the Park Central Hotel, a 1937 building by Henry Hohauser at 640 Ocean Drive.

CORNER FACADE, ESSEX HOUSE HOTEL
Essex House Hotel, a 1938 gem that appears permanently anchored at 1001 Collins Avenue, is a stunning example of Maritime deco (also known as Nautical Moderne). Designed by Henry Hohauser to evoke an ocean liner, the hotel is rife with marine elements, from the rows of porthole-style windows and natty racing stripes to the towering smokestack-like sign. With a prow angled proudly into the street corner, it seems ready to steam out to sea.

Essex House Hotel

NEON SPIRE, THE HOTEL
The name spelled vertically in eye-popping neon on the venue's iconic aluminum spire—Tiffany—bears evidence of the hotel's earlier incarnation. When the L. Murray Dixon–designed Tiffany Hotel was erected at 801 Collins Avenue in 1939, neon was still a novelty. Its use, coupled with the spire's rocket-like shape, combined to create a futuristic look influenced by the sci-fi themes then pervasive in popular culture.

The Hotel

ENTRANCE, JERRY'S FAMOUS DELI
Inspired by everything from car fenders to airplane noses, proponents of art deco's Streamline Moderne look began to soften buildings' hitherto boxy edges. But when Henry Hohauser designed Hoffman's Cafeteria in 1940 he took moderne to the max. The landmark at 1450 Collins Avenue (now Jerry's Famous Deli) has a sleek, splendidly curved facade. The restored interior echoes it through semicircular booths and rounded chair backs.

Jerry's Famous Deli

ARCHITECTURAL TERMS

The Rule of Three: Early deco designers often used architectural elements in multiples of three, creating tripartite facades with triple sets of windows, eyebrows, or banding.

Eyebrows: Small shelf-like ledges that protruded over exterior windows were used to simultaneously provide much-needed shade and serve as a counterpoint to a building's strong vertical lines.

Tropical Motifs: In keeping with the setting, premises were plastered, painted, or etched with seaside images. Palm trees, sunbursts, waves, flamingoes, and the like were particularly common.

Banding: Enhancing the illusion that these immobile structures were rapidly speeding objects, colorful horizontal bands (also called "racing stripes") were painted on exteriors or applied with tile.

Stripped Classic: The most austere version of art deco (sometimes dubbed Depression Moderne) was used for buildings commissioned by the Public Works Administration.

(top) Hotel Marlin; (left) Sherbrooke Hotel; (right) U.S. Post Office in Miami Beach.

For locals, the beach scene is often incorporated into daily life, from getting exercise to walking the dog.

South Beach Dive and Surf Center. The Discover Scuba course trains diving newcomers on Tuesday, Thursday, and Saturday at 8 am at a PADI-affiliated dive shop. Advance classes follow at 9:45 am. Night dives take place each Wednesday at 4:30, and wreck and reef dives on Sundays at 7:30 am and noon. The center also runs dives in Key Largo's Spiegel Grove, the second-largest wreck ever to be sunk for the intention of recreational diving, and in the Neptune Memorial Reef, inspired by the city of Atlantis and created in part using the ashes of cremated bodies. Boats depart from marinas in Miami Beach and Key Largo, in the Florida Keys. ⊠ *850 Washington Ave., Miami Beach* ☎ *305/531–6110* ⊕ *www.southbeachdivers.com.*

SHOPPING

Miami teems with sophisticated shopping malls and the bustling avenues of commercial neighborhoods. But this is also a city of tiny boutiques tucked away on side streets—such as South Miami's Red, Bird, and Sunset roads intersection—and outdoor markets touting unusual and delicious wares. Stroll through Spanish-speaking neighborhoods where shops sell clothing, cigars, and other goods from all over Latin America. At an open-air flea-market stall, score an antique glass shaped like a palm tree and fill it with some fresh Jamaican ginger beer from the table next door. Or stop by your hotel gift shop and snap up an alligator magnet for your refrigerator, an ashtray made of seashells, or a bag of gum balls shaped like Florida oranges. Who can resist?

People fly to Miami from all over the world just to shop, and the malls are high on their list of spending spots. Stop off at one or two of these climate-controlled temples to consumerism, many of which double as mega-entertainment centers, and you'll understand what makes Miami such a vibrant shopping destination.

If you're over the climate-controlled slickness of shopping malls and can't face one more food-court "meal," you've got choices in Miami. Head out into the sunshine and shop the city streets, where you'll find big-name retailers and local boutiques alike. Take a break at a sidewalk café to power up on some Cuban coffee or fresh-squeezed OJ and enjoy the tropical breezes.

Beyond the shopping malls and the big-name retailers, Greater Miami has all manner of merchandise to tempt even the casual browser. For consumers on a mission to find certain items—art deco antiques or cigars, for instance—the city streets burst with a rewarding collection of specialty shops.

Pass the mangoes! Greater Miami's farmers' markets and flea markets take advantage of the region's balmy weather and tropical delights to lure shoppers to open-air stalls filled with produce and collectibles.

COCONUT GROVE

MALLS

CocoWalk. This popular three-story indoor-outdoor mall has three floors of nearly 40 shops that stay open almost as late as its popular restaurants and clubs. Chain stores like Victoria's Secret and Gap blend with specialty shops like Koko & Palenki and Edward Beiner; the space blends the bustle of a mall with the breathability of an open-air venue. Kiosks with cigars, beads, incense, herbs, and other small items are scattered around the ground level, and restaurants and nightlife (Cheesecake Factory, Fat Tuesday, and a 16-screen AMC theater, to name a few) line the upstairs perimeter. Hanging out and people-watching is something of a pastime here. ✉ *3015 Grand Ave., Coconut Grove, Miami* ☎ *305/444–0777* ⊕ *www.cocowalk.net.*

SPECIALTY STORES
ANTIQUES

★ **Architectural Antiques.** Find an enormous selection of antique lighting, as well as large and eclectic items—railroad crossing signs, statues, English roadsters. There's also antique furniture, paintings, and silverware, all in a cluttered setting that makes shopping an adventure. ✉ *2520 S.W. 28th La., Coconut Grove* ☎ *305/285–1330* ⊕ *www.miamiantique.com.*

OUTDOOR MARKETS

★ **Coconut Grove Farmers' Market.** The most organic of Miami's outdoor markets specializes in a mouthwatering array of local produce as well as such ready-to-eat goodies as cashew butter, homemade salad dressings, and fruit pies (some of the offerings can taste stodgy to the nonorganic eater). If you are looking for a downright granola crowd and experience, pack your Birkenstocks because this is it. It's open Saturdays only, from 10 to 7, rain or shine. ✉ *3300 Grand Ave., Coconut Grove* ☎ *305/238–7747* ⊕ *www.glaserorganicfarms.com.*

CORAL GABLES

MALLS

Fodor'sChoice ★ **Village of Merrick Park.** At this Mediterranean-style shopping-and-dining venue, Neiman Marcus and Nordstrom anchor 115 specialty shops. Designers such as Etro, Tiffany & Co., Burberry, CH Carolina Herrera, and Gucci fulfill most high-fashion needs, and Brazilian contemporary-furniture designer Artefacto provides a taste of the haute-decor shopping options. International food venues like C'est Bon and a day spa, Elemis, offer further indulgences. ✉ *358 San Lorenzo Ave., Coral Gables* ☎ *305/529–0200* ⊕ *www.villageofmerrickpark.com.*

SHOPPING DISTRICTS

Miracle Mile. The centerpiece of the downtown Coral Gables shopping district, lined with trees and busy with strolling shoppers, is home to men's and women's boutiques, jewelry and home-furnishings stores, and a host of exclusive couturiers and bridal shops. Running from Douglas Road to LeJeune Road and Aragon Avenue to Andalusia Avenue, more than 30 first-rate restaurants offer everything from French to Indian cuisine, and art galleries and the Actors' Playhouse give the area a cultural flair. ✉ *Douglas Rd. to LeJeune Rd. and Aragon Ave. to Andalusia Ave., Coral Gables* ⊕ *www.shopcoralgables.com.*

SPECIALTY SHOPS

ANTIQUES

Valerio Antiques. This shop carries fine French art deco furniture, bronze sculptures, shagreen boxes, and original art glass by Gallé and Loetz, among others. ✉ *250 Valencia Ave., Coral Gables* ☎ *305/448–6779* ⊕ *www.valerioartdeco.com.*

BOOKS

Fodor'sChoice ★ **Books & Books, Inc.** Greater Miami's only independent English-language bookshops specialize in contemporary and classical literature as well as in books on the arts, architecture, Florida, and Cuba. At any of its three locations you can lounge at a café or, at the Coral Gables store, browse the photography gallery. All stores host regular poetry and other readings. ✉ *265 Aragon Ave., Coral Gables* ☎ *305/442–4408* ✉ *927 Lincoln Rd., South Beach, Miami Beach* ☎ *305/532–3222* ✉ *9700 Collins Ave., Bal Harbour* ☎ *305/864–4241* ⊕ *www.booksandbooks.com.*

CIGARS

Sabor Havana Cigars. Spanish wine helps patrons relax while browsing the selection of rare cigars. ✉ *2309 Ponce de León Blvd., Coral Gables* ☎ *305/444–1764* ⊕ *www.saborhavana.com.*

CLOTHING

★ **Silvia Tcherassi.** The Colombian designer's signature boutique in the Village of Merrick Park features feminine and frilly dresses and separates accented with chiffon, tulle, and sequins. ⊠ *350 San Lorenzo Ave., Coral Gables* ☎ *305/461–0009* ⊕ *www.silviatcherassi.com.*

JEWELRY

Jose Roca Fine Jewelry Designs. Jose Roca designs fine jewelry from precious metals and stones. If you have a particular piece that you would like to create, this is the place to have it meticulously executed. ⊠ *297 Miracle Mile, Coral Gables* ☎ *305/448–2808.*

OUTDOOR MARKETS

Coral Gables Farmers' Market. Some 25 local produce growers and plant vendors sell herbs, fruits, fresh-squeezed juices, chutneys, cakes, and muffins at this market between Coral Gables's City Hall and Merrick Park. Artists also join in. Regular events include gardening workshops, children's activities, and cooking demonstrations offered by Coral Gables's master chefs. The market opens on Saturday, mid-January through late March only. ⊠ *405 Biltmore Way, Coral Gables* ☎ *305/460–5311.*

4

DOWNTOWN MIAMI

MIAMI DESIGN DISTRICT

★ **Miami Design District.** Miami is synonymous with good design, and this visitor-friendly shopping district is an unprecedented melding of public space and the exclusive world of design. There are more than 200 showrooms and galleries, including Kartell, Ann Sacks, Poliform, and Luminaire. Restaurants like Michael's Genuine Food & Drink, Joey's, and Sra. Martinez also make this trendy neighborhood a hip place to dine. Unlike most showrooms, which are typically the beat of decorators alone, the Miami Design District's showrooms are open to the public and occupy windowed, street-level spaces. Bring your quarters, as all of the parking is on the street and metered. The neighborhood even has its own high school (of art and design, of course) and hosts street parties and gallery walks. Although in many cases you'll need a decorator to secure your purchases, browsers are encouraged to consider for themselves the array of rather exclusive furnishings, decorative objects, antiques, and art. ⊠ *N.E. 2nd Ave. and N.E. 40th St., Miami Design DistrictMiami* ⊕ *www.miamidesigndistrict.net.*

SPECIALTY SHOPS

ANTIQUES **Artisan Antiques Art Deco.** These purveyors of china, crystal, mirrors, and armoires from the French–art deco period also draw customers in with an assortment of 1930s radiator covers, which can double as funky sideboards. The shop is open weekdays. ⊠ *110 N.E. 40th St., Miami Design District, Miami* ☎ *305/573–5619* ⊕ *www.artisanartdeco.com.*

LITTLE HAVANA
SPECIALTY SHOPS

ONLY IN MIAMI **La Casa de las Guayaberas.** Like the name says, this shop sells custom-made guayaberas, the natty four-pocket dress shirts favored by Latin men. Hundreds are also available off the rack. ⊠ *5840 S.W. 8th St., Little Havana* ☎ *305/266–9683.*

CIGARS **Sosa Family Cigars.** There is a wide selection of premium and house cigars in a humidified shop, once known as Macabi. There's a selection of wines for purchase. Humidors and other accessories are also available. ⊠ *3475 S.W. 8th St., Little Havana* ☎ *305/446–2606.*

MIAMI BEACH

NORTH BEACH AND AVENTURA

Fodor'sChoice **Aventura Mall.** This three-story mall offers the ultimate in South Florida
★ retail therapy. Aventura houses many global top performers such as
MALLS the most lucrative Abercrombie & Fitch in the United States, a massive Crate & Barrel, the latest, greatest Nordstrom and Bloomingdale's, and 250 other shops, which together create the fifth-largest mall in the United States. This is the one-stop, shop-'til-you-drop retail palladium for locals, out-of-towners, and, frequently, celebrities. ⊠ *19501 Biscayne Blvd., Aventura* ☎ *305/935–1110* ⊕ *www.aventuramall.com.*

Fodor'sChoice **Bal Harbour Shops.** Local and international shoppers flock to this swank
★ collection of 100 high-end shops, boutiques, and department stores,
MALLS which include such names as Christian Dior, Gucci, Hermès, Salvatore Ferragamo, Tiffany & Co., and Valentino. Many European designers open their first North American signature store at this outdoor, pedestrian-friendly mall, and many American designers open their first boutique outside of New York here. Restaurants and cafés, in tropical garden settings, overflow with style-conscious diners. People-watching at outdoor café Carpaccio is the best in town. ⊠ *9700 Collins Ave., Bal Harbour* ☎ *305/866–0311* ⊕ *www.balharbourshops.com.*

SOUTH BEACH
SHOPPING DISTRICTS

★ **Collins Avenue.** Give your plastic a workout in South Beach shopping at the many high-profile tenants on this densely packed two-block stretch like Club Monaco, M.A.C., Kenneth Cole, Barney's Co-Op, and A/X Armani Exchange. Sprinkled among the upscale vendors are hair salons, spas, cafés, and such familiar stores as the Gap, Urban Outfitters, and Banana Republic. Be sure to head over one street east and west to catch the shopping on Ocean Drive and Washington Avenue. ⊠ *Collins Ave. between 5th and 10th Sts., South BeachMiami Beach.*

Fodor'sChoice **Lincoln Road Mall.** The eight-block-long pedestrian mall is the trendiest
★ place on Miami Beach. Home to more than 150 shops, 20-plus art galleries and nightclubs, about 50 restaurants and cafés, and the renovated Colony Theatre, Lincoln Road, between Alton Road and Washington Avenue, is like the larger, more sophisticated cousin of Ocean Drive. The see-and-be-seen theme is furthered by outdoor seating at every restaurant, where well-heeled patrons lounge and discuss the people

(and pet) parade passing by. An 18-screen movie theater anchors the west end of the street, which is where most of the worthwhile shops are; the far east end is mostly discount and electronics shops. Sure, there's a Pottery Barn, a Gap, and a Williams-Sonoma, but the emphasis is on emporiums with unique personalities, like En Avance, Chroma, Base, and Jonathan Adler. ⊠ *Lincoln Rd., between Alton Rd. and Washington Ave., South Beach,Miami Beach* ⊕ *www.lincolnroad.org.*

SPECIALTY SHOPS

★

CLOTHING

Base. Constantly evolving, this shop features an intriguing magazine section, an international CD station with DJ, and groovy home accessories. Stop here for men's and women's eclectic clothing, shoes, and accessories that mix Japanese design with Caribbean-inspired materials. The often-present house-label designer may help select your wardrobe's newest addition. ⊠ *939 Lincoln Rd., South Beach, Miami Beach* ☎ *305/531–4982* ⊕ *www.baseworld.com.*

Fodor's Choice
★
BEAUTY

Brownes & Co. An entire store dedicated to beauty, body, and soul, Brownes & Co. is a one-stop shop for pampering and high-end vanity. Cosmetics include Molton Brown, Nars, Le Clerc, and others. It also sells herbal remedies and upscale hair and body products from Bumble and bumble. Just try to resist something from the collection of French, Portuguese, and Italian soaps in various scents and sizes. There's also a fabulous spa and salon on-site. ⊠ *841 Lincoln Rd., South Beach, Miami Beach* ☎ *305/532–8703* ⊠ *87 N.E. 40 St., Design District* ☎ *305/538–7544* ⊕ *www.brownesbeauty.com.*

★
ONLY IN MIAMI

Dog Bar. Just north of Lincoln Road's main drag, this over-the-top pet boutique caters to enthusiastic animal owners with a variety of unique items for the pampered pet, including a luxurious pet sofa imported from Italy and offered in cowhide, leather, or vinyl fitted into a chrome frame. ⊠ *1684 Jefferson Ave., South Beach, Miami Beach* ☎ *305/532–5654* ⊠ *3301 N.E. 1st Ave., Midtown 4, Wynwood* ☎ *786/837–0904* ⊕ *www.dogbar.com.*

CLOTHING

Intermix. This modern New York–based boutique has the variety of a department store. You'll find fancy dresses, stylish shoes, slinky accessories, and trendy looks by sassy and somewhat pricey designers like Chloé, Stella McCartney, Marc Jacobs, Moschino, and Diane von Furstenberg. ⊠ *634 Collins Ave., South Beach, Miami Beach* ☎ *305/531–5950* ⊕ *www.intermixonline.com.*

★
JEWELRY

MIA Jewels. On Alton Road, this jewelry and accessories boutique is known for its colorful, gem- and bead-laden, gold and silver earrings, necklaces, bracelets, and brooches by lines such as Cousin Claudine, Amrita, and Alexis Bittar. This is a shoo-in store for everyone: you'll find things for trend lovers (gold-studded chunky Lucite bangles), classicists (long, colorful, wraparound beaded necklaces), and ice lovers (long Swarovski crystal cabin necklaces) alike. ⊠ *1439 Alton Rd., South Beach, Miami Beach* ☎ *305/532–6064* ⊠ *19575 Biscayne Blvd., Aventura* ☎ *305/931–2000*⊕ *www.miajewels.com.*

★
CLOTHING

Morgan Miller Shoes. Design your own couture stiletto or stylish sandal in just a half hour (cobblers are fast at work while you wait). The selection of materials is seemingly endless: wood, resin, or cork heels or sandals;

4

leather, alligator, snake, or ostrich straps in a myriad of vibrant colors; and more than 100 crystals and jewels to choose from. Prices range from a basic sandal with a denim strap for about $70 to an over-the-top pair of strappy lime-green, snakeskin stilettos laced with Swarovski crystals, colored tacks, and hanging jewels, topping $500. This is a great store for footwear fashionistas, but you don't have to be a shoe addict to enjoy finding the right fit here. ⊠ *618 Lincoln Rd., South Beach, Miami Beach* ☎ *305/672–8700* ⊕ *www.morganmillershoes.com.*

CLOTHING **South Beach Dive and Surf Center.** The one-stop shop for beach gear—from clothing and swimwear for guys and gals to wake-, surf-, and skate-boards—also offers multilingual surfing, scuba, snorkeling, and dive lessons and trips. ⊠ *850 Washington Ave., South Beach, Miami Beach* ☎ *305/531–6110* ⊕ *www.southbeachdivers.com.*

OUTDOOR MARKETS

★ **Lincoln Road Outdoor Antique and Collectibles Market.** Interested in picking up samples of Miami's ever-present modern and moderne furniture and accessories? This outdoor show takes place every other Sunday and offers eclectic goods that should satisfy postimpressionists, deco-holics, Edwardians, Bauhausers, Goths, and '50s junkies. ⊠ *Lincoln and Alton Rds., South Beach, Miami Beach* ⊕ *www.antiquecollectiblemarket.com.*

Lincoln Road Farmers' Market. With all the familiar trappings of a farmers' market (except for farmers—most of the people selling veggies appear to be resellers), this is a weekly South Beach Sunday (9–6:30) ritual. It brings local produce and bakery vendors to Lincoln Road and often features plant workshops, art sales, and children's activities. This is a good place to pick up live orchids, too. ⊠ *Lincoln Rd. between Meridian and Washington Aves., South Beach, Miami Beach* ☎ *305/531–0038* ⊕ *www.themarketcompany.org/mkts.html.*

NIGHTLIFE

One of Greater Miami's most popular pursuits is barhopping. Bars range from intimate enclaves to showy see-and-be-seen lounges to loud, raucous frat parties. There's a New York–style flair to some of the newer lounges, which are increasingly catering to the Manhattan party crowd who escape to South Beach for long weekends. No doubt, Miami's pulse pounds with nonstop nightlife that reflects the area's potent cultural mix. On sultry, humid nights with the huge full moon rising out of the ocean and fragrant night-blooming jasmine intoxicating the senses, who can resist Cuban salsa, Jamaican reggae, and Dominican merengue, with some disco and hip-hop thrown in for good measure? When this place throws a party, hips shake, fingers snap, bodies touch. It's no wonder many clubs are still rocking at 5 am. If you're looking for a relatively nonfrenetic evening, your best bet is one of the chic hotel bars on Collins Avenue.

The *Miami Herald* (⊕ *www.miamiherald.com*) is a good source for information on what to do in town. The Weekend section of the newspaper, included in the Friday edition, has an annotated guide to everything from plays and galleries to concerts and nightclubs. The "Ticket"

From salsa and merengue to disco and hip-hop, Miami's dance clubs cater to diverse styles of music.

column of this section details the week's entertainment highlights. Or, you can pick up the *Miami New Times* (⊕ *www.miaminewtimes.com*), the city's largest free alternative newspaper, published each Thursday. It lists nightclubs, concerts, and special events; reviews plays and movies; and provides in-depth coverage of the local music scene. "Night & Day" is a rundown of the week's cultural highlights. *Ocean Drive* (⊕ *www.oceandrive.com*), Miami Beach's model-strewn, upscale fashion and lifestyle magazine, squeezes club, bar, restaurant, and events listings in with fashion spreads, reviews, and personality profiles. Paparazzi photos of local party people and celebrities give you a taste of Greater Miami nightlife before you even dress up to paint the town.

The Spanish-language *El Nuevo Herald* (⊕ *www.elnuevoherald.com*), published by the *Miami Herald,* has extensive information on Spanish-language arts and entertainment, including dining reviews, concert previews, and nightclub highlights.

COCONUT GROVE

BARS AND LOUNGES

Monty's in the Grove. The outdoor bar here has Caribbean flair, thanks especially to live calypso and island music. It's very kid-friendly on weekends, when Mom and Dad can kick back and enjoy a beer and the raw bar while the youngsters dance to live music. Evenings bring a DJ and reggae music. ⊠ *2550 S. Bayshore Dr., at Aviation Ave.* ☏ *305/856–3992.*

THE VELVET ROPES

How to get past the velvet ropes at the hottest South Beach nightspots? First, if you're staying at a hotel, use the concierge. Decide which clubs you want to check out (consult *Ocean Drive* magazine celebrity pages if you want to be among the glitterati), and the concierge will email, fax, or call in your names to the clubs so you'll be on the guest list when you arrive. This means much easier access and usually no cover charge (which can be upward of $20) if you arrive before midnight. Guest list or no guest list, follow these pointers: make sure there are more women than men in your group. Dress up—casual chic is the dress code. For men this means no sneakers, no shorts, no sleeveless vests, and no shirts unbuttoned past the top button. For women, provocative and seductive is fine; overly revealing is not. Black is always right. At the door: don't name-drop—no one takes it seriously. Don't be pushy while trying to get the doorman's attention. Wait until you make eye contact, then be cool and easygoing. If you decide to tip him (which most bouncers don't expect), be discreet and pleasant, not big-bucks obnoxious—a $10 or $20 bill quietly passed will be appreciated, however. With the right dress and the right attitude, you'll be on the dance floor rubbing shoulders with South Beach's finest clubbers in no time.

CORAL GABLES

BARS AND LOUNGES

Bar at Ponce and Giralda. One of the oldest bars in South Florida, the old Hofbrau has been reincarnated and now serves vibrant, live reggae music on Saturday nights and a nontouristy vibe. ⊠ *172 Giralda Ave., at Ponce de León Blvd., Coral Gables* ☎ *305/442–2730.*

Globe. The centerpiece of Coral Gables's emphasis on nightlife draws crowds of twentysomethings who spill into the street for live jazz on Saturday evenings and a bistro-style menu nightly. Free appetizers and drink specials every weekday attract a strong happy-hour following. Outdoor tables and an art-heavy, upscale interior are comfortable, if you can find space to squeeze in. ⊠ *377 Alhambra Circle, at Le Jeune Rd.* ☎ *305/445–3555* ⊕ *www.theglobecafe.com.*

John Martin's Restaurant and Irish Pub. The cozy upscale Irish pub hosts an Irish cabaret on Saturday night with live contemporary and traditional music—sometimes by an Irish band—storytelling, and dancers. ⊠ *253 Miracle Mile, at Ponce de León Blvd.* ☎ *305/445–3777* ⊕ *www.johnmartins.com.*

DOWNTOWN MIAMI

BARS AND LOUNGES

Fodor'sChoice　★　**Tobacco Road.** Opened in 1912, this classic holds Miami's oldest liquor license: No. 0001! Upstairs, in a space that was occupied by a speakeasy during Prohibition, local and national blues bands perform nightly. There is excellent bar food, a dinner menu, and a selection of single-malt scotches, bourbons, and cigars. This is the hangout of grizzled journalists, bohemians en route to or from nowhere, and club kids seeking a way station before the real parties begin. Live blues, R&B, and jazz bands are on tap, along with food and drink, seven days a week. ⊠ *626 S. Miami Ave., Downtown Miami* ☎ *305/374–1198* ⊕ *www. tobacco-road.com.*

DANCE CLUBS

Fodor's Choice ★ **Space Miami.** Want 24-hour partying? Here's the place. Space revolutionized the Miami party scene 10 years ago and still gets accolades as one of the country's best dance clubs. Created from four downtown warehouses, it has two levels (one blasts house music; the other reverberates with hip-hop), an outdoor patio, a New York–style industrial look, and a 24-hour liquor license. It's open on weekends only, and you'll need to look good to be allowed past the velvet ropes. ⊠ *34 N.E. 11th St.* ☎ *305/375–0001* ⊕ *www.clubspace.com.*

> ### CULTURAL FRIDAYS
>
> On the last Friday of every month Little Havana takes its culture to the streets for *Viernes Culturales* (Cultural Friday ⊕ *www. viernesculturales.org*), held between 7 and 11 pm on 8th Street from 14th to 17th avenues. Art galleries and stores stay open late, and music, mojitos, and avant-garde street performances bring a young hip crowd to the neighborhood where they mingle with locals. The annual Calle Ocho festival, held in March, draws more than a million visitors in search of Latin music, food, and shopping.

SOUTH BEACH

BARS AND LOUNGES

B.E.D. Innocently standing for "beverages, entertainment, and dining," B.E.D. also offers king-pillow-strewn beds in place of tables. Not only were the sheets washed in 2010 but B.E.D. got an entire makeover, too, including new beds. ⊠ *929 Washington Ave., Miami Beach* ☎ *305/532–9070* ⊕ *www.bedmiami.com.*

★ **Buck 15.** This hidden lounge above popular Lincoln Road eatery Miss Yip Café is one of Miami's best-kept secrets. The tiny club manages to play amazing music—a rock-heavy mix of songs you loved but haven't heard in ages—and maintain a low-key, unpretentious attitude. It's a bit of a kitschy frat party for grown-ups. The drinks are reasonably priced, and the well-worn couches are great to dance on. The club attracts local hipsters. ⊠ *707 Lincoln Rd., Miami Beach* ☎ *305/538–3815* ⊕ *www. buck15.net.*

Club Deuce. Although it's completely unglam, this pool hall attracts a colorful crowd of clubbers, locals, celebs—and just about anyone else. Locals consider it the best spot for a cheap drink and one of the best dive bars. ⊠ *222 14th St., at Collins Ave., Miami Beach* ☎ *305/531–6200.*

Lost Weekend. Players at this pool hall are serious about their pastime, so it's hard to get a table on weekends. The full bar, which has 150 kinds of beer, draws an eclectic crowd, from yuppies to drag queens to slumming celebs like Lenny Kravitz. ✉ *218 Española Way, at Collins Ave., Miami Beach* ☎ *305/672–1707.*

Mynt Ultra Lounge. The name of this upscale nightclub, which opens its doors at midnight, is meant to be taken literally—not only are the walls bathed in soft green shades, but an aromatherapy system pumps out different fresh scents, including mint. Celebs like Enrique Iglesias, Angie Everhart, and Queen Latifah have cooled down here. ✉ *1921 Collins Ave., Miami Beach* ☎ *305/532-0727* ⊕ *www.myntlounge.com.*

★ **The National.** Don't miss a drink at the hotel's nifty wooden bar, one of many elements original to the 1939 building, which give it such a sense of its era that you'd expect to see Ginger Rogers and Fred Astaire hoofing it along the polished lobby floor. The adjoining Martini Room has a great collection of cigar and old airline stickers and vintage Bacardi ads on the walls. Don't forget to take a peek at the long, sexy pool. ✉ *1677 Collins Ave., Miami Beach* ☎ *305/532–2311* ⊕ *www. nationalhotel.com.*

Fodor'sChoice **Rose Bar at the Delano.** The airy lobby lounge at South Beach's trendiest
★ hotel manages to look dramatic but not cold, with long, snow-white, gauzy curtains and huge white pillars separating conversation nooks (this is where Ricky Martin shot the video for "La Vida Loca"). A pool table brings the austerity down to earth. There's also an expansive poolside bar, dotted with intimate poolside beds (bottle service required) and private cabanas to reserve for the evening—for a not-so-nominal fee, of course. ✉ *1685 Collins Ave., South Beach, Miami* ☎ *305/672–2000* ⊕ *www.delano-hotel.com.*

Fodor'sChoice **SkyBar at the Shore Club.** Splendor-in-the-garden is the theme at this haute
★ spot by the sea, where multiple lounging areas are joined together. Day-beds, glowing Moroccan lanterns, and maximum atmosphere make a visit to this chic outdoor lounge worthwhile. Groove to dance music in the Red Room, or enjoy an aperitif and Japanese bar bites at Nobu Lounge. The Red Room, Nobu Restaurant and Lounge, Italian restaurant Ago, and SkyBar all connect around the Shore Club's pool area. ✉ *1901 Collins Ave., Miami Beach* ☎ *305/695–3100* ⊕ *www.shoreclub. com.*

DANCE CLUBS

Fodor'sChoice **Cameo.** One of Miami's ultimate dance clubs, Cameo, formerly known
★ as Crobar, has emerged after a welcomed face-lift. Gone is the industrial feel, but all-star DJs and plentiful dance space remain, and plush VIP lounges have been added. If you can brave the velvet rope, Saturday-night parties are the best. ✉ *1445 Washington Ave.* ☎ *305/531–5535* ⊕ *www.cameomiami.com.*

Nikki Beach Club. Smack-dab on the beach, the full-service Nikki Beach Club was once a favorite of SoBe's pretty people and celebrities. Nowadays, it's filled with more suburbanites than the "in" crowd. Tepees and hammocks on the sand, dance floors both under the stars and inside, and beach parties make this a true South Beach experience circa 2003. ✉ *1 Ocean Dr.* ☎ *305/538–1111* ⊕ *www.nikkibeach.com/miami.*

Score. This popular bar is the see-and-be-seen central of Miami's gay community. DJs spin every night of the week except Sunday, a popular karaoke night where everything goes. Latin Tuesdays are popular as is the upstairs party at Crème Lounge on Thursday and the weekend dance offs. ✉ *727 Lincoln Rd.* ☎ *305/535–1111* ⊕ *www.scorebar.net.*

Twist. This longtime hot spot with the local gay clientele has two levels, an outdoor patio, and a game room that's crowded from 8 pm on, especially on Monday, Thursday (two-for-one), and Friday nights. ✉ *1057 Washington Ave., Miami Beach* ☎ *305/538–9478* ⊕ *www.twistsobe.com.*

LIVE MUSIC

★ **Jazid**. If you're looking for an unpretentious alternative to the velvet-rope nightclubs, this unassuming, live-music hot spot is a standout on the strip. Eight-piece bands play danceable Latin rhythms, as well as reggae, hip-hop, and fusion sounds. Get ready for a late night though, as bands are just getting started at midnight. They play every night of the week. Call ahead to reserve a table. ✉ *1342 Washington Ave.* ☎ *305/673–9372* ⊕ *www.jazid.net.*

4

WHERE TO EAT

Miami's restaurant scene has exploded in the last few years, with dozens of great new restaurants springing up left and right. The melting pot of residents and visitors has brought an array of sophisticated, tasty cuisine. Little Havana is still king for Cuban fare, while Miami Beach is swept up in a trend of fusion cuisine, which combines Asian, French, American, and Latin cuisine with sumptuous—and pricy—results. Downtown Miami and the Design District especially are home to some of the city's best spots, and they're all new. Since Miami dining is a part of the trendy nightlife scene, most dinners don't start until 8 or 9 pm, and may go well into the night. To avoid a long wait amongst the late night partiers at hot spots come before 7 or make reservations. Attire is usually casual-chic, but patrons like to dress to impress. Don't be surprised to see large tables of women in skimpy dresses—this is common in Miami. Prices tend to stay high in hot spots like Lincoln Road; but if you venture off the beaten path, you can find delicious food for reasonable prices. When you get your bill, check whether a gratuity is already included; most restaurants add between 15% and 18% (ostensibly for the convenience of, and protection from, the many Latin American and European tourists who are used to this practice in their homelands), but supplement it depending on your opinion of the service.

Use the coordinate (✛ C2) at the end of each review to locate a property on the Where to Eat in the Miami Area map.

WHAT IT COSTS					
	¢	$	$$	$$$	$$$$
AT DINNER	under $10	$10–$15	$15–$20	$20–$30	over $30

Price per person for a median main course or equivalent combination of smaller dishes.

COCONUT GROVE, CORAL GABLES, AND KEY BISCAYNE

COCONUT GROVE

$$$

PERUVIAN

Fodor's Choice

★

✕ **Jaguar Ceviche Spoon Bar & Grill.** A fabulous fusion of Peruvian and Mexican flavors, Jaguar is a gastronomic tour of Latin America in a single restaurant. As the name implies, there is a heavy emphasis on ceviches. The best option for experiencing this delicacy is the sampler, which includes six distinct Peruvian and Mexican ceviches served in oversized spoons. Meals come with blue corn tortilla and pita chips served with authentic Mexican salsa. Dishes, such the Mexican Tortilla Lasagna (chicken, poblano peppers, corn, tomato sauce, and cream, topped with melted cheese), are colorful, flavorful, and innovative. ✉ *3067 Grand Ave., Coconut Grove* ☎ *305/444–0216* ⊕ *www.jaguarspot.com.*

$$$

FRENCH

✕ **Le Bouchon du Grove.** This French bistro with a supercharged atmosphere is a great spot in the heart of the Grove. Waiters tend to lean on chairs while taking orders, and managers and owners freely mix with the clientele, making Le Bouchon perhaps the last remaining vestige of the Grove's bohemian days. The result is one big happy family, all enjoying traditional French pâtés, gratins, quiches, chicken fricassee, mussels, duck-leg confit, and steak frites. The lively mood inside is matched by the throngs that parade outside the French doors. Breakfast is served daily. ✉ *3430 Main Hwy.* ☎ *305/448–6060* ⊕ *www. lebouchondugrove.com* ✛ *5C.*

CORAL GABLES

$

CUBAN

✕ **Havana Harry's.** When Cuban families want a home-cooked meal but don't want to cook it themselves or go supercheap at the Cuban fast-food joint, Pollo Tropical, they come to this big, unassuming restaurant. In fact, you're likely to see whole families here, from babes in arms to grandmothers. The fare is traditional Cuban: the long thin steaks known as *bistec palomilla* (a panfried steak), roast chicken with citrus marinade, and fried pork chunks; contemporary flourishes—mango sauce and guava-painted pork roast—are kept to a minimum. Most dishes come with white rice, black beans, and a choice of ripe or green plantains. The sweet ripe ones offer a good contrast to the savory dishes. Start with the $5.95 *mariquitas* (plantain chips) with guacamole. ✉ *4612 Le Jeune Rd.* ☎ *305/661–2622* ⊕ *www.hharrys.com* ✛ *5C.*

$

SPANISH

✕ **Las Culebrinas.** Each of Las Culebrinas's five locations in Miami tends to draw throngs of adoring diners for Spanish tapas and Cuban steaks. Tapas here are not small; some are entrée size like the Frisbee-size Spanish *tortilla* (omelet). Our suggestion: indulge in a tender fillet of crocodile, fresh fish, or the grilled pork stuffed with mashed bananas, followed by a dessert of *crema Catalana*, caramelized at your table with a blowtorch—this is a good time to remind your kids not to touch. ✉ *4700 W. Flagler St., at N.W. 47th Ave.* ☎ *305/445–2337* ✉ *2890 S.W. 27 Ave., Coconut Grove* ☎ *305/448–4090* ⊕ *www.culebrinas.com* ✛ *4C.*

$$$$

CARIBBEAN

✕ **Ortanique on the Mile.** Cascading *ortaniques*, a Jamaican hybrid orange, are hand-painted on columns in this warm, welcoming yellow dining room. Food is vibrant in taste and color, as delicious as it is beautiful. Though there is no denying that the strong, full flavors are imbued with island breezes, chef-partner Cindy Hutson's personal cuisine goes beyond

BEST BETS FOR MIAMI DINING

Fodor's writers and editors have selected their favorite restaurants by price, cuisine, and experience in the Best Bets lists below. In the first column, Fodor's Choice designations represent the "best of the best" in every price category. Find specific details about a restaurant in the full reviews, listed alphabetically by neighborhood.

Fodor's Choice ★

Blue Door Fish, South Beach, p. 196

Bourbon Steak, Aventura, p. 194

Cecconi's, Mid-Beach, p. 192

Cioppino, Key Biscayne, p. 188

The Forge, Mid-Beach, p. 193

Jaguar Ceviche Spoon Bar & Grill, Coconut Grove, p. 186

Joe's Stone Crab Restaurant, South Beach, p. 196

Joey's, Wynwood, p. 189

Michael's Genuine Food & Drink, Design District, p. 189

Michy's, Mid-Beach, p. 194

NAOE, Sunny Isles Beach, p. 195

Palacio de los Jugos, Coral Gables, p. 188

Pascal's on Ponce, Coral Gables, p. 188

Perricone's Marketplace and Café, Downtown, p. 191

Sra. Martinez, Design District, p. 189

The Villa by Barton G—The Restaurant, South Beach, p. 203

By Price

¢

Palacio de los Jugos, Coral Gables, p. 188

$

Las Culebrinas, Coral Gables, p. 186

Tutto Pasta, Little Havana, p. 191

Versailles, Little Havana, p. 192

$$

Hy-Vong Vietnamese Cuisine, Little Havana, p. 192

Joey's, Wynwood, p. 189

Sra. Martinez, Design District, p. 189

$$$

Michael's Genuine Food & Drink, Downtown Miami, p. 189

$$$$

Cioppino, Key Biscayne, p. 188

The Forge, Mid-Beach, p. 193

Pascal's on Ponce, Coral Gables, p. 188

By Cuisine

AMERICAN

Big Pink, South Beach, p. 195

Joe Allen, South Beach, p. 196

Michael's Genuine Food & Drink, Downtown Miami, p. 189

ASIAN

Hakkasan, Mid-Beach, p. 193

SushiSamba Dromo, South Beach, p. 202

CUBAN

Havana Harry's, Coral Gables, p. 186

Versailles, Little Havana, p. 192

ITALIAN

Cecconi's, Mid-Beach, p. 192

Cioppino, Key Biscayne, p. 188

SEAFOOD

Chef Allen's, North Miami and Aventura, p. 194

Joe's Stone Crab Restaurant, South Beach, p. 196

STEAKHOUSE

Bourbon Steak, North Miami and Aventura, p. 194

The Forge, Mid-Beach, p. 193

Prime One Twelve, South Beach, p. 202

Red, the Steakhouse, South Beach, p. 202

By Experience

CHILD-FRIENDLY

Tutto Pasta, Little Havana, p. 191

Versailles, Little Havana, p. 192

HOT SPOTS

Blue Door Fish, South Beach, p. 196

Meat Market, South Beach, p. 197

Michael's Genuine Food & Drink, Downtown Miami, p. 189

4

Caribbean refinements. The menu centers on fish, since Hutson has a special way with it, and the Caribbean bouillabaisse is not to be missed. On Sunday there is live jazz. ⊠ *278 Miracle Mile* ☎ *305/446–7710* ⊕ *www. cindyhutsoncuisine.com* ☯ *No lunch weekends* ✦ *5C.*

¢ ✕**Palacio de los Jugos.** Nearby and to the west of Coral Gables, this
CUBAN joint is one of the easiest and truest ways to see Miami's local Latin life
Fodor's Choice in action. It's also one of the best fruit-shake shacks you'll ever come
★ across (ask for a juice of—*"jugo de"*—mamey, melón, or guanabana, a sweet-tart equatorial fruit, and you can't go wrong). Besides the rows and rows of fresh tropical fruits and vegetables, and the shakes you can make with any of them, this boisterous indoor-outdoor market has numerous food counters where you can get just about any Cuban food—tamales, rice and beans, a *pan con lechón* (roast pork on Cuban bread), fried pork rinds, or a coconut split before you and served with a straw. Order your food at a counter and eat it along with local families at rows of outdoor picnic-style tables next to the parking lot. It's disorganized, chaotic, and not for those cutting calories, but it's delicious and undeniably the real thing. ⊠ *5721 W. Flagler St.* ☎ *305/264–4557* ⊕ *www.elpalaciodelosjugosonline.com* ⊟ *No credit cards* ✦ *4B.*

$$$$ ✕**Pascal's on Ponce.** This French gem amid the Coral Gables restaurant
FRENCH district is always full, thanks to chef-proprietor Pascal Oudin's assured
Fodor's Choice and consistent cuisine. Oudin forgoes the glitz and fussiness often asso-
★ ciated with French cuisine, and instead opts for a simple, small, refined dining room that won't overwhelm patrons. The equally sensible menu includes a superb gnocchi appetizer (ask for mushrooms on top). The main course is a tough choice between oven-roasted duck with poached pears, milk-fed veal loin, and diver sea scallops with beef short rib. It opened in 2000. Ask your expert waiter to pair dishes with a selection from Pascal's impressive wine list, and, for dessert, order the bittersweet chocolate soufflé. ⊠ *2611 Ponce de León Blvd.* ☎ *305/444–2024* ⊕ *www.pascalmiami.com* ☯ *Closed Sun. No lunch Sat.* ✦ *5C.*

KEY BISCAYNE

$$ ✕**Cantina Beach.** Leave it to the Ritz-Carlton Key Biscayne to bring a
MEXICAN small sumptuous piece of coastal Mexico to Florida's fabulous beaches. The pool- and ocean-side Cantina Beach showcases authentic and divine Mexican cuisine, including fresh guacamole at your table. The restaurant also boasts the country's only *tequilier*, mixing and matching 85 high-end tequilas. It's no surprise then that Cantina Beach has phenomenal margaritas. And the best part is that you can enjoy them with your feet in the sand, gazing at the ocean. ⊠ *Ritz-Carlton, 455 Grand Bay Dr.* ☎ *305/365–4622* ⊕ *www.RitzCarlton.com/KeyBiscayne* ✦ *6E.*

$$$$ ✕**Cioppino.** Few visitors think to venture out to the far end of Key Bis-
ITALIAN cayne for dinner, but making the journey to the soothing grounds of this
Fodor's Choice quiet Ritz-Carlton property on the beach is well worth it. Choose your
★ view: the ornate dining room near the exhibition kitchen or the alfresco area with views of landscaped gardens or breeze-brushed beaches. Choosing your dishes may be more difficult, given the many rich, luscious Italian options, including imported cheeses, olive oils, risottos and fresh fish flown in daily. Items range from the creamy *burrata* mozzarella and authentic pasta dishes to tantalizing risotto with organic spinach

and roasted quail, all expertly matched with fine, vintage, rare, and boutique wines. An after-dinner drink and live music at the old-Havana-style RUMBAR inside the hotel is another treat. ⊠ *Ritz-Carlton, 455 Grand Bay Dr.* ☎*305/ 365–4156* ⊕ *www.RitzCarlton.com/ KeyBiscayne* ✢ *6E.*

MIAMI

DESIGN DISTRICT

$$ ✕ **Joey's.** This joyfully good and
ITALIAN merrily buzzing new place is literally
Fodor's Choice the only restaurant in Wynwood, an
★ emerging neighborhood to the south of the Design District. But this new restaurant already has that rarest of blessings—the sizzling vibe of a thriving neighborhood restaurant that everyone seems to adore. Its contagious charm begins with the service: informal but focused, very professional, and attentive. Then comes the food: Veneto native chef Ivo Mazzon does homage to fresh ingredients prepared simply and perfectly. A full line of flatbread pizzas contend for tops in Miami. The *dolce e piccante* has figs, Gorgonzola, honey, and hot pepper; it's unexpectedly sweet at first bite, and at bite 10 you'll be swearing it's the best you've ever had. The wine list is small but the product of much discernment. Because it's little and in a weird spot, Joey's makes you feel that you're the first to discover it, and that you've made a new friend in Miami—one you'll need to visit again very soon. ⊠ *2506 N.W. 2 Ave., Design District* ☎ *305/438–0488* ⊕ *www.joeyswynwood.com* ✢ *4D.*

$$$ ✕ **Michael's Genuine Food & Drink.** Michael's is often cited as Miami's
AMERICAN top restaurant. This indoor-outdoor bistro in Miami's Design District
Fodor's Choice relies on fresh ingredients and a hip but unpretentious vibe to lure
★ diners. Beautifully arranged combinations like crispy beef cheek with whipped celeriac, and sweet-and-spicy pork belly with kimchi explode with unlikely but satisfying flavor. Owner and chef Michael Schwartz aims for sophisticated American cuisine with an emphasis on local and organic ingredients. He gets it right. Portions are divided into small, medium, and large plates, and the smaller plates are more inventive, so you can order several and explore. Reserve two weeks in advance for weekend tables; also, consider brunch. ⊠ *130 N.E. 40th St., Design District* ☎ *305/573–5550* ⊕ *www.michaelsgenuine.com* ⚄ *Reservations essential* ⊗ *No lunch Sat.* ✢ *3D.*

$$ ✕ **Sra. Martinez.** For a good time with food, dial up Sra. Martinez.
SPANISH Michelle Bernstein's second restaurant (her, first, Michy's, is a must-visit
Fodor's Choice for Miami foodies); the name is a sly take on her name—her husband
★ is David Martinez—which is good, because something as artful as this

FULL-MOON DINNERS

The Moonrise Dinner Series at Cioppino is fun, romantic, geeky, and one of Miami's most memorable experiences. Held from October to May on the exact night of the full moon, the dinner is a four-course Italian gastronomic extravaganza under the magical path of the rising full moon. Tabletop telescopes serve as centerpieces. The restaurant's Constellation Connoisseur visits each table to point out key stars and constellations, and then invites guests to look at the moon through the mega telescope. Meanwhile the highly attentive staff serve the divine creations of Chef de Cuisine Ezio Gamba.

4

Daniel Boulud brings his celebrated take on French cuisine to Miami at db Bistro

new restaurant deserves a signature. Bernstein anchors her menu at Sra. Martinez in traditional Spanish cuisine, a brilliant jumping-off point for her wildly successful experiments in flavor, texture, and plate composition. Order several dishes from the Cold & Crisp ($5–$18) and Warm & Lush ($8–$23) sections, which feature small plates of takes on traditional tapas. The cuisine is modern, colorful and, above all, fun. Cocktail lovers will be delighted by the inventive, high-quality selections like the Jalisco Mule, a spicy take on the traditional Moscow Mule, made with tequila and ginger beer, and laced with chili syrup. It's no wonder this restaurant has already become one of the best and most exciting in the city. ⊠ *4000 N.E. 2 Ave., Design District* ☏ *305/573–5474* ⊕ *www.chefmichellebernstein.com* ☙ *Closed Sun. No Lunch Sat.* ✛ *3D.*

DOWNTOWN MIAMI

$$$$ ✕ db Bistro Moderne Miami. At long last, one of America's most celebrated
FRENCH French chefs, Daniel Boulud, brings his renowned cooking to the Miami scene. The menu of Boulud's latest outpost pays homage to the different cuisines and specialties of his homeland and surrounding regions, beginning with a fabulous raw bar alongside regional tasting plates such as the "Assiette Provencale" with mackerel escabeche, black olive tapenade, goat cheese with pear, and Swiss chard *barbajuan*. Moving on to the second course, chose from a dozen hot and cold small plates, like the signature "Daniel Boulud's Smoked Salmon," "Escargots Persillade" with wild burgundy snails simmered in parsley, garlic, salted butter with yellow tomatoes and wild mushrooms, and the "Tomato Tarte Tatin." For the main course, the authentic "Coq Au Vin" and the "Moules Piquante" are guaranteed crowd pleasers, channeling images

and/or memories of France through the tastes and smells of the restaurant's flagship dishes. ⊠ *255 Biscayne Boulevard Way, Downtown, Miami* ☎ *305/421–8800* ⊕ *www.danielnyc.com* ✢ *4D.*

$$
MEDITERRANEAN

✕ **Eos.** This restaurant at the snazzy Viceroy Hotel on Brickell is definitely worth a visit if you're downtown. Chef Michael Psilakis and restaurateur Donatella Arpaia are culinary superstars whose involvement gives this restaurant a lot of attention. The sophisticated, bold design is by Kelly Wearstler. The large menu of inexpensive light dishes is divided by ingredients—cheese and crostini; vegetable and potato; pasta; fish; and meats, poultry, and game. The influences are vast, with Greek, Italian, French, and Spanish flavors all evident. There's also a sushi and sashimi selection. ⊠ *485 Brickell Ave., Downtown Miami* ☎ *305/503–4400 or 866/781–9923* ⊕ *www.viceroymiami.com* ✢ *4D.*

$$
ARGENTINE

✕ **Novecento.** This Argentine eatery is the Financial District's answer to Ocean Drive: the people are still beautiful, but now they're wearing suits. Known for its empanadas (tender chicken or spinach and cheese), simple grilled meats (luscious grilled skirt steak with *chimichurri* sauce), and the innovative Ensalada Novecento (grilled skirt steak, french fries, and baby mixed greens), it's no wonder Novecento is Brickell Avenue's best power-lunch and happy-hour spot. Come for Sunday brunch and enjoy the signature *parillada*, a small grill with an assortment of steaks, sausages, and sweetbreads (not sweet bread, but rather the sweet pancreas of a lamb or calf). ⊠ *1414 Brickell Ave., Downtown Miami* ☎ *305/403–0900* ⊕ *www.novecento.com* ✢ *5D.*

$$
ITALIAN
Fodor'sChoice
★

✕ **Perricone's Marketplace and Café.** Brickell Avenue south of the Miami River is burgeoning with Italian restaurants, and this lunch place for local bigwigs is the biggest and most popular among them. It's housed partially outdoors and partially indoors in a 125-year-old Vermont barn. Recipes were handed down from generation to generation, and the cooking is simple and good. Buy your wine from the on-premises deli, and enjoy it (for a small corking fee) with homemade minestrone; a generous antipasto; linguine with a sauté of jumbo shrimp, scallops, and calamari; or gnocchi with four cheeses. The homemade tiramisu and cannoli are top-notch. ⊠ *Mary Brickell Village, 15 S.E. 10th St., Downtown Miami* ☎ *305/374–9449* ⊕ *www.perricones.com* ✢ *5D.*

$
AMERICAN

✕ **Tobacco Road.** If you like your food (or your drink) the way you like your blues—gritty, honest, and unassuming—then this almost-100-year-old joint will earn your respect. This is Miami's oldest bar and restaurant, and it manages to stay up the latest, too: 5 am. A live band plays daily, making this hangout one of Miami's low-key gems. The road burger is a popular choice, as are appetizers like nachos and chicken wings; the chili may induce a call for a fire hose. Fine single-malt scotches are stocked behind the bar. ⊠ *626 S. Miami Ave., Downtown Miami* ☎ *305/374–1198* ⊕ *www.tobacco-road.com* ✢ *4D.*

$
ITALIAN
🛈

✕ **Tutto Pasta.** Tourists might pay $30 for linguine elsewhere, but locals are more likely to frequent Tutto Pasta, where they feast on the delicious homemade pasta for less than $15. Start with fresh-baked goat-cheese focaccia with truffle oil. Then try the famous lobster ravioli garnished with plantain chips, or the tilapia sautéed with shrimp, calamari, scallops, and tomato sauce. Hop over to Tutto Pizza next door to enjoy innovative

4

Brazilian-inspired thin pizzas like the Portuguesa, topped with ham, mozzarella, black olives, eggs, and onions. Finish with Tutto chocolate cake or creamy Brazilian Pave. ⊠ *1751 S.W. 3rd Ave. at S.W. 18th Rd., Downtown Miami* ☎ *305/857–0709* ⊕ *www.tuttopasta.com* ✛ *5D.*

LITTLE HAVANA

$$$$

SPANISH

✕ **Casa Juancho.** This meeting place for the movers and shakers of the Cuban *exilio* community is also a haven for lovers of fine Spanish regional cuisine. Strolling balladeers serenade amid brown brick, rough-hewn dark timbers, hanging smoked meats, ceramic plates, and oil still lifes: a bit of old España dropped on Calle Ocho. Try the hake prepared in a fish stock with garlic, onions, and Spanish white wine or the *carabineros a la plancha* (jumbo red shrimp with head and shell on, split and grilled). For dessert, *crema Catalana* is a rich pastry custard with a delectable crust of burnt caramel. The house features one of the largest lists of reserve Spanish wines in the United States. Jackets are recommended for men at dinner. ⊠ *2436 S.W. 8th St., Little Havana* ☎ *305/642–2452* ⊕ *www.casajuancho.com* ✛ *5C.*

$$

VIETNAMESE

✕ **Hy-Vong Vietnamese Cuisine.** Spring springs forth in spring rolls of ground pork, cellophane noodles, and black mushrooms wrapped in homemade rice paper. People are willing to wait on the sidewalk for hours—come before 7 pm to avoid a wait—to sample the fish panfried with mango or with *nuoc man* (a garlic-lime fish sauce), not to mention the thinly sliced pork barbecued with sesame seeds, almonds, and peanuts. Beer-savvy proprietor Kathy Manning serves a half-dozen top brews (Double Grimbergen, Peroni, and Spaten, among them) to further inoculate the experience from the ordinary—well, as ordinary as a Vietnamese restaurant on Calle Ocho can be. ⊠ *3458 S.W. 8th St., Little Havana* ☎ *305/446–3674* ⊕ *www.hyvong.com* ⊗ *Closed Mon. No lunch* ✛ *5C.*

$

CUBAN

★

✕ **Versailles.** *¡Bienvenido a Miami!* To the area's Cuban population, Miami without Versailles is like rice without black beans. The storied eatery, where old émigrés opine daily about all things Cuban, is a stop on every political candidate's campaign trail, and it should be a stop for you as well. Order a heaping platter of *lechon asado* (roasted pork loin), *ropa vieja* (shredded beef), or *picadillo* (spicy ground beef), all served with rice, beans, and fried plantains. Battle the oncoming food coma with a cup of the city's strongest *cafecito,* which comes in the tiniest of cups but packs a lot of punch. Versailles operates a bakery next door as well—take some *pastelitos* home. ⊠ *3555 S.W. 8th St., between S.W. 35th and S.W. 36th Aves., Little Havana* ☎ *305/444–0240* ✛ *5C.*

MIAMI BEACH

MID-BEACH

$$$$

ITALIAN

Fodor's Choice

★

✕ **Cecconi's.** After the New York restaurant scene invaded Miami Beach, it was only a matter of time until L.A. made its way down southeast, too. With the unveiling of the new Soho House in Miami came the company's iconic Italian restaurant, Cecconi's. The wait for a table at this outpost is just as long as its West Hollywood counterpart, and the dining experience just as fabulous. Eating here is a real scene of who's who and who's eating what. Without a doubt, the truffle pizza, which servers shave huge hunks of black or white truffle onto table-side, is the restaurant's most talked about dish. The fish carpaccios are light and succulent while the classically hearty pastas and risottos provide authentic Italian fare. ✉ *4385 Collins Ave., Mid-Beach, Miami Beach* ☎ *786/507–7900* ⊕ *www.cecconismiamibeach.com* ⬥ *Reservations essential* ✛ *4F.*

$$$–$$$$
STEAKHOUSE
Fodor'sChoice
★

✕ **The Forge.** Legendary for its opulence, this restaurant has been wowing patrons since 1968. After a renovation, The Forge reemerged in 2010 more decadent than ever! It is a steak house, but a steak house the likes of which you haven't seen before. Antiques, gilt-framed paintings, a chandelier from the Paris Opera House, and Tiffany stained-glass windows from New York's Trinity Church are the fitting background for some of Miami's best steaks. The tried-and-true menu also includes prime rib, bone-in fillet, lobster *thermidor*, chocolate soufflé, and sinful side dishes like creamed spinach and roasted-garlic mashed potatoes. The focaccia bread is to die for. For its walk-in humidor alone, the over-the-top Forge is worth visiting. The automated wine machine spans the perimeter of the restaurant and allows you to pick your own pour and sample several wines throughout your meal. ✉ *432 Arthur Godfrey Rd., Mid-Beach, Miami Beach* ☎ *305/538–8533* ⊕ *www.theforge.com* ⬥ *Reservations essential* 🕑 *No lunch.* ✛ *4F.*

$$$$
CANTONESE

✕ **Hakkasan.** This stateside sibling of the Michelin-starred London restaurant is one of the best-looking restaurants on Miami Beach. Intricately carved, lacquered-black-wood Chinois panels divide seating sections, creating a deceptively cozy dining experience. The music is clubby, the waitresses' matching outfits are slinky, and the shadowy lighting is thoughtfully designed to make everyone look about as good as they can. Chef Alan Yau, a pioneer of the haute-Chinese-food movement, has collected mostly simple and authentic Cantonese recipes, many featuring fresh seafood. Don't overlook the tofu dishes in lieu of other proteins: this isn't supermarket soy. The braised tofu and aubergine claypot in black bean pairs glorious little pillows of silken tofu with expertly cooked eggplant in a perfectly seasoned, thick, funky sauce. ✉ *4441 Collins Ave., Mid-Beach, Miami Beach* ☎ *305/538–2000* ⊕ *www.hakkasan.com* ⬥ *Reservations essential* 🕑 *No lunch* ✛ *2F.*

$$$$
ARGENTINIAN

✕ **Las Vacas Gordas.** For more than 15 years, this Argentinean steak house has welcomed the who's who of Latin high society, fulfilling their wildest carnivore cravings. Recently expanded and reinvented as a glamorous enclave where the Pampas meets contemporary Miami, Vacas's grill sizzles day and nights to the troves of patrons who patiently wait to feast on mounds of fresh meat from the Argentinean lowlands. The reasonably priced house Malbecs complemented the high-end selections showcased in the floor-to-ceiling, glass-enclosed wine cellar. Those less enthused about massive meat slabs can opt for the Berecava (eggplant with tomato sauce and cheese), homemade pastas, grilled peppers, fish and shrimp, or fill up on homemade rolls with spicy chimmichurri. ✉ *933 Normandy Dr., Mid-Beach, Miami Beach* ☎ *305/867–1717* ⊕ *www.lasvacasgordas.com* ✛ *3F.*

4

$$$
MEDITERRANEAN
Fodor's Choice
★

✗ **Michy's.** Miami's homegrown star chef Michelle Bernstein made a huge splash with the shabby-chic decor and self-named restaurant on the north end of Miami's Design District. Bernstein serves exquisite French- and Mediterranean-influenced seafood dishes at over-the-causeway (read: non-tourist-trap) prices. Plates come in half portions and full portions, which makes the restaurant even more of a deal. Can't-miss entrées include the blue cheese and *jamón serrano* (serrano ham) *croquetas*, the beef short rib, and the steak frites au poivre. ⊠ *6927 Biscayne Blvd., Mid-Beach* ☎ *305/759–2001* ⊕ *www.chefmichellebernstein.com* ✆ *Closed Mon. No lunch* ✚ *3E.*

$
DELICATESSEN
☾

✗ **Roasters 'N Toasters.** This small Jewish delicatessen chain took over from Arnie and Richie's, a longtime family establishment, in 2008. Gone are the baskets of plastic silverware. The prices are slightly higher, but the faithful still come for the onion rolls, smoked whitefish salad, as well as the new "Corky's Famous Zaftig Sandwich," a deliciously juicy skirt steak served on twin challah rolls with a side of apple sauce. Service can be brusque, but it sure is quick. ⊠ *525 Arthur Goddrey Rd., Mid-Beach, Miami Beach* ☎ *305/531–7691* ⊕ *www.roastersntoasters. com* ✚ *3F.*

NORTH BEACH AND AVENTURA

$$$$
STEAKHOUSE
Fodor's Choice
★

✗ **Bourbon Steak.** Michael Mina's sole restaurant in the southeastern United States is arguably his best. The restaurant design is seductive, the clientele sophisticated, the wine list outstanding, the service phenomenal, and the food exceptional. Dinner begins with a skillet of fresh potato focaccia and chive butter. Mina then presents a bonus starter— his trio of famous fries (fried in duck fat) with three robust sauces. Appetizers are mainly seafood. The raw bar impresses and classic appetizers like the ahi tuna tartare are delightful and super fresh. Entrees like the Maine lobster pot pie and any of the dozen varieties of wood-grilled steaks (from natural, organic, hormone-free beef) are cooked to perfection. ⊠ *19999 W. Country Club Dr., Aventura, Miami* ☎ *786/279–6600* ⊕ *www.michaelmina.net* ⌔ *Reservations essential* ✚ *1F.*

$$$
ITALIAN

✗ **Café Prima Pasta.** If Tony Soprano lived in Miami, this is where you'd find him. This famous, bustling Italian eatery is infused with the energy of the Argentine Cea family, whose clan cooks, serves, and operates this place, while somehow finding the time to pose for photos with the hundreds of celebrities who have eaten here over the years (see them in the photos on the walls). It's on a busy street, yet the low light, soothing music, and intimate seating on this restaurant's outdoor veranda can make Café Prima Pasta a romantic spot. Everything is made in-house—from the fragrant rosemary butter to the pasta, which tastes best as crab-stuffed ravioli or as linguine dyed in squid ink and served with seafood in a lobster sauce. ⊠ *414 71st St., North Beach, Miami* ☎ *305/867–0106* ⊕ *www.primapasta.com* ✆ *No lunch* ✚ *3F.*

$$$
SEAFOOD

✗ **Chef Allen's.** Chef Allen Susser has long been a figure of Miami's culinary scene, a member of the original, self-designated "Mango Gang," who created contemporary American masterpieces from a global menu. Over the past couple of years, though, his namesake restaurant has been renovated with a new look and jolt of fresh energy as a "modern seafood bistro," focusing on sustainable fish. The restaurant is still the best in northern Miami. After trying the famous Devil's on a Horseback (manchego- and mango-stuffed dates wrapped in bacon), order a salad of baby greens and warm wild mushrooms or a rock-shrimp hash with roasted corn. Allen serves only locally caught seafood, so you may want to consider the swordfish with conch-citrus couscous, macadamia nuts, and lemon. It's hard to resist the dessert soufflé; order it when you order your appetizer to eliminate a mouthwatering wait at the end of your meal. ✉ *19088 N.E. 29th Ave., Aventura, Miami* ☎ *305/935–2900* ⊕ *www.chefallens.com* ⌖ *1F.*

$$$$
JAPANESE
Fodor'sChoice
★

✕ **NAOE.** Once in a rare while, you discover a restaurant so authentic, so special, yet still undiscovered by the masses. By virtue of its petite size (16 person max) and strict seating times (twice per night at 6:30 and 9:30), the Japanese gem, NAOE, will forever remain intimate and original. The menu changes daily, based on the day's best and freshest seafood. Beginning with a Bento Box and continuing on to rounds of Nigirizushi, every visit ushers in a new exploration of the senses. Chef Kevin Corey prepares the gastronomic adventure a few feet from his patrons, using only the best ingredients and showcasing family treasures, like the renowned products of his centuries' old family shoyu (soy sauce) brewery and sake brewery. From start to finish, you'll be transported to Japan through the stellar service, the tastes of bizarre sea creatures, the planching of live scallops, and the smoothness of spectacular sakes. ✉ *175 Sunny Isles Blvd., Sunny Isles Beach* ☎ *305/947–6263* ⊕ *www.naoemiami.com* ⌂ *Reservations essential* ⌖ *1F.*

$$$
ITALIAN
★

✕ **Timó.** Located in a glorified strip mall 5 mi north of South Beach, Timó (Italian for "thyme") is worth the trip from anywhere in South Florida. It's a kind of locals' secret that it's the best food in South Florida. The handsome bistro, co-owned by chef Tim Andriola and Rodrigo Martinez (former general manager and wine director at Norman's), has dark-wood walls, Chicago brick, and a stone-encased wood-burning stove. Andriola has an affinity for robust Mediterranean flavors: sweetbreads with bacon, honey, and aged balsamic vinegar; inexpensive, artisanal pizzas; and homemade pastas. Wood-roasted meats and Parmesan dumplings in a truffle broth are not to be missed. Every bite of every dish attests to the care given, and the service is terrific. ✉ *17624 Collins Ave., Sunny Isles* ☎ *305/936–1008* ⊕ *www.timorestaurant.com* ⊗ *No lunch weekends* ⌖ *1F.*

SOUTH BEACH

$
AMERICAN

✕ **Big Pink.** The decor in this innovative, superpopular diner may remind you of a roller-skating rink—everything is pink Lucite, stainless steel, and campy (think sports lockers as decorative touches)—and the menu is 3 feet tall, complete with a table of contents. Food is solidly all-American, with dozens of tasty sandwiches, pizzas, turkey or beef burgers, and side dishes, each and every one composed with gourmet flair. Big Pink also makes a great spot for brunch. ✉ *157 Collins Ave., South Beach* ☎ *305/532–4700* ⊕ *www.mylesrestaurantgroup.com* ⌖ *5H.*

$$$$
STEAKHOUSE

✕ **BLT Steak.** Miami suddenly has a plethora of good steak houses. This Ocean Drive favorite is in the light-filled, open lobby of the snazzy Betsy Hotel at the very northern end of South Beach and has the distinction of being open for breakfast daily—get the sensational steak and eggs.

The clever name stands for Bistro Laurent Tourondel, Mr. T being the highly regarded chef who created the chain of BLTs. You can count on the highest quality cuts of USDA prime, certified Black Angus, and American Wagyu beef, in addition to blackboard specials and raw-bar selections. The grilled Kobe beef–skirt salad is juicy and delicious. The popovers are even better. ⊠ *1440 Ocean Dr., South Beach* ☎ *305/673–0044* ⊕ *www.bltrestaurants.com* ✛ *2H.*

$$$$ ✕ **Blue Door Fish.** In a hotel where style reigns supreme, this high-profile
SEAFOOD restaurant at the Delano Hotel provides both glamour and solid cui-
Fodor'sChoice sine. Thankfully, Master Chef Claude Troisgros kept a dozen of the
★ most popular dishes from the restaurant's predecessor, Blue Door at the Delano, including the famous Crabavocat, Big Ravioli, Homard Banana and Boeuf Gorgonzola. He, also thankfully, added 50 inventive seafoodcentric items like Shrimp over Risotto with a saffron bouilla-baisse-style sauce and Scallops a la Plancha with brown butter sauce, garlic, lemon, parsley and pine nuts. The restaurant also serves sushi from its Philippe Starck countertop sushi bar across the hall, Blue Sea: remarkable creations include the Wild Coho Salmon Tartare (with olive and soy tapenade and fried ginger), the rice-less Smokey Roll (with four types of smoked fish and caviar), the Yakuza Roll (BBQ eel, avocado, and Boursin cheese with spicy *masago* and eel sauce), and California rolls with real blue or king crab. ⊠ *1685 Collins Ave., South Beach* ☎ *305/674–6400* ⌓ *Reservations essential* ✛ *2H.*

$$ ✕ **Emeril's.** "It's getting happy in here" is one of Emeril Lagasse's stock
SOUTHERN phrases, and now he has brought his brand of happy to Miami Beach. You can expect a different gumbo each day and other New Orleans spe-cialties at Lagasse's chain, which appears to have the winning formula down. The seafood naturally shines in these parts (an andouille-crusted redfish signals the imported Lagasse touch), and the chef has his own take on mango pie and banana-cream pie. As a bonus, the restaurant delivers without even a hint of South Beach attitude—though a view of the pool at its Loews hotel location is a perk. ⊠ *1601 Collins Ave., at Loews Miami Beach Hotel, South Beach* ☎ *305/695–4550* ⊕ *www. emerils.com* ✛ *2H.*

$$$ ✕ **Joe Allen.** Crave a good martini along with a terrific burger? Locals
AMERICAN head to this hidden hangout in an exploding neighborhood of condos, town houses, and stores. The eclectic crowd includes kids and grandpar-ents, and the menu has everything from pizzas to calves' liver to steaks. Start with an innovative salad, such as arugula with pear, prosciutto, and a Gorgonzola dressing, or roast-duck salad with blue cheese and pears. Home-style desserts include banana-cream pie and ice-cream-and-cookie sandwiches. Comfortable and homey, this is the perfect place to go when you don't feel like going to a restaurant. ⊠ *1787 Purdy Ave., South Beach* ☎ *305/531–7007* ⊕ *www.joeallenrestaurant. com* ✛ *4E.*

$$$$ ✕ **Joe's Stone Crab Restaurant.** In South Beach's decidedly new-money
SEAFOOD scene, the stately Joe's Stone Crab is an old-school testament to good
Fodor'sChoice food and good service. South Beach's most storied restaurant started
★ as a turn-of-the-century eating house when Joseph Weiss discovered succulent stone crabs off the Florida coast. Almost a century later,

Pink as cotton candy and bubble gum, the Big Pink diner fits right in with its art deco surroundings.

the restaurant stretches a city block and serves 2,000 dinners a day to local politicians and moneyed patriarchs. Stone crabs, served with legendary mustard sauce, crispy hash browns, and creamed spinach, remain the staple. Though stone crab season runs from October 15 to May 15, Joe's remains open year-round serving other phenomenal seafood dishes. Finish your meal with tart key lime pie, baked fresh daily. ■TIP→ Joe's famously refuses reservations, and weekend waits can be three hours long—yes, you read that correctly—so come early or order from Joe's Take Away next door. ⊠ *11 Washington Ave., South Beach* ☎ *305/673–0365, 305/673–4611 for takeout, 800/780–2722 for overnight shipping* ⊕ *www.joesstonecrab.com* ⚅ *Reservations not accepted* ⊙ *No lunch Wed.–Sun. Closed Mon. and Tues. May 15–Oct. 15* ⊹ *5G.*

$$$
STEAKHOUSE
★
✕ **Meat Market.** Yes, it's a great name for a steak-inspired restaurant, and a name seemingly destined for a place like this on Lincoln Road, where sexy people amble by in skimpy clothes year-round. But here's the great news: this is a sophisticated place with a large non-steak-house menu. Appetizers such as cedar-scented *hamachi* (yellowtail sashimi) topped with mango caviar, white truffle, fresh lime, and rice-paper tuna tacos with *guajillo* chili, cabbage, grilled watermelon, micro watercress, and roasted garlic are just the beginning of the incredible variety. The seafood selection, like the seared Florida grouper in browned goat butter and bacon-chipotle conch broth, is also excellent. Naturally, there are the steaks, which range from simple à la carte cuts to thoughtful creations like the braised prime brisket with coconut, mango, Cuban sweet potatoes, and wild mushrooms. ⊠ *915 Lincoln Rd., South Beach* ☎ *305/532–0088* ⊕ *www.meatmarketmiami.com* ⊙ *No lunch* ⊹ *2G.*

CUBAN FOOD

If the tropical vibe has you hankering for Cuban food, you've come to the right place. Miami is the top spot in the country to enjoy authentic Cuban cooking.

The flavors and preparations of Cuban cuisine are influenced by the island nation's natural bounty (yucca, sugarcane, guava), as well as its rich immigrant history, from near (Caribbean countries) and far (Spanish and African traditions). Chefs in Miami tend to stick with the classic versions of beloved dishes, though you'll find some variation from restaurant to restaurant as recipes have often been passed down through generations of home cooks. Try the popular **Versailles** (✉ 3555 S.W. 8th St. ☎ 305/444–0240) in Little Havana or Coral Gables's **Havana Harry's** (✉ 4612 Le Jeune Rd. ☎ 305/661–2622), appealing to families seeking a home-cooked, Cuban-style meal. The South Beach late- night institution **David's Café** (✉ 1058 Collins Ave. ☎ 305/534–8736 ✉ 1654 Meridian Ave. ☎ 305/672–8707) is a hole-in-the-wall with excellent eats.

THE CUBAN SANDWICH

A great *cubano* (Cuban sandwich) requires pillowy Cuban bread layered with ham, garlic-citrus-marinated slow-roasted pork, Swiss cheese, and pickles (plus salami, in Tampa; lettuce and tomatoes in Key West), butter and/or mustard. The sandwich is grilled in a sandwich press until the cheese melts and all the elements are fused together. Try one at **Enriqueta's Sandwich Shop** (✉ 186 N.E. 29th St. ☎ 305/573-4681 ⊙ Weekdays 6 am–4 pm, Sat. 6 am–2 pm) in the Design District, or **Exquisito Restaurant** (✉ 1510 S.W. 8th St. ☎ 305/643-0227 ⊙ Open daily 7 am–midnight) in Little Havana.

KEY CUBAN DISHES

ARROZ CON POLLO

This chicken-and-rice dish is Cuban comfort food. Found throughout Latin America, the Cuban version is typically seasoned with garlic, paprika, and onions, then colored golden or reddish with saffron or achiote (a seed paste), and enlivened with a sizable splash of beer near the end of cooking. Green peas and sliced, roasted red peppers are a standard topping.

BISTEC DE PALOMILLA

This thinly sliced sirloin steak is marinated with lime juice and garlic, and fried with onions. The steak is often served with chimichurri sauce, an olive oil, garlic, and cilantro sauce that is sometimes served with bread as a dip (slather bread with butter and dab on the chimichurri). Also try *ropa vieja*, a slow-cooked, shredded flank steak in a garlic-tomato sauce.

DESSERTS

Treat yourself to a slice of *tres leches* cake. The "three milks" come from the sweetened condensed milk, evaporated milk, and heavy cream that are poured over the cake until it's an utterly irresistible gooey mess. Also, don't miss the *pastelitos*, Cuban fruit-filled turnovers. Traditional flavors include plain guava, guava with cream cheese, and cream cheese with coconut. Yum!

DRINKS

Sip *guarapo* (gwa-RA-poh), a fresh sugarcane juice that isn't really as sweet as you might think, or grab a straw and enjoy a frothy *batido* (bah-TEE-doe), a Cuban-style milk shake made with tropical fruits like mango, *piña* (pineapple), or *mamey* (mah-MAY, a tropical fruit with a melon-cherry taste). For a real twist, try the *batido de trigo*—a wheat shake that will remind you of sugar-glazed breakfast cereal.

FRITAS

If you're in the mood for an inexpensive, casual Cuban meal, have a *frita*—a hamburger with distinctive Cuban flair. It's made with ground beef that's mixed with ground or finely chopped chorizo, spiced with pepper, paprika, and salt, topped with sautéed onions and shoe-string potato fries, and then served on a bun slathered with a special tomato-based ketchuplike sauce.

LECHON ASADO

Fresh ham or an entire suckling pig marinated in *mojo criollo* (parsley, garlic, sour orange, and olive oil) are roasted until fork tender and served with white rice, black beans, and *tostones* (fried plantains) or yucca (pronounced YU-kah), a starchy tuber with a mild nut taste that's often sliced into fat sticks and deep-fried like fries.

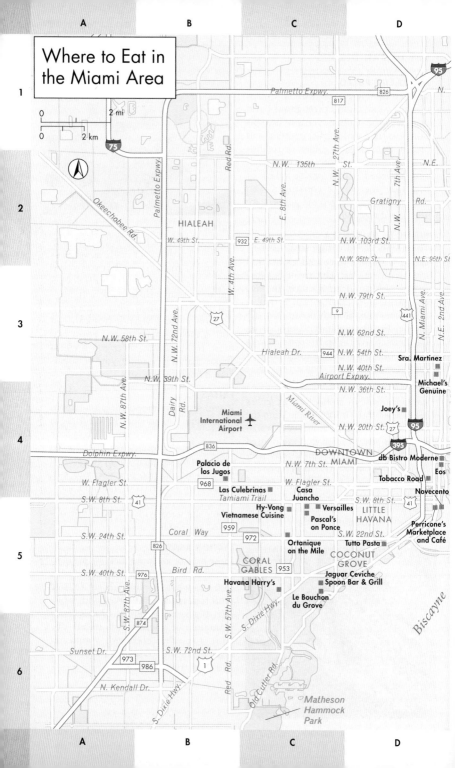

Where to Eat in the Miami Area

0 ___ 2 mi
0 ___ 2 km

Palmetto Expwy.

Okeechobee Rd.

HIALEAH

N.W. 135th St.

N.W. 27th Ave.

7th Ave.

N.E.

Gratigny Rd.

W. 49th St.   E. 49th St.   N.W. 103rd St.   N.E. 95th St.

N.W. 95th St.

E. 8th Ave.

W. 4th Ave.

N.W. 79th St.

N.W. 72nd Ave.

N.W. 62nd St.

N. Miami Ave.   N.E. 2nd Ave.

N.W. 58th St.

Hialeah Dr.   N.W. 54th St.   **Sra. Martinez**

N.W. 40th St.   **Michael's Genuine**

N.W. 87th Ave.   N.W. 39th St.   Airport Expwy.   N.W. 36th St.

Dairy Rd.

Miami River

Miami International Airport

N.W. 20th St.   **Joey's**

Dolphin Expwy.   DOWNTOWN MIAMI   **db Bistro Moderne**

N.W. 7th St.   **Eos**

Palacio de los Jugos

W. Flagler St.   W. Flagler St.   **Tobacco Road**

S.W. 8th St.   **Las Culebrinas**   **Casa Juancho**   **Novecento**

Tamiami Trail   S.W. 8th St.

Hy-Vong Vietnamese Cuisine   **Versailles**   LITTLE HAVANA

Coral Way   **Pascal's on Ponce**   **Perricone's Marketplace and Café**

S.W. 24th St.   S.W. 22nd St.

Ortanique on the Mile   **Tutto Pasta**   COCONUT GROVE

CORAL GABLES

S.W. 40th St.   Bird Rd.   **Jaguar Ceviche Spoon Bar & Grill**

S.W. 87th Ave.   **Havana Harry's**

S.W. 57th Ave.   **Le Bouchon du Grove**

Biscayne

Sunset Dr.

S.W. 72nd St.

N. Kendall Dr.

S. Dixie Hwy.

Red Rd.

Old Cutler Rd.

Matheson Hammock Park

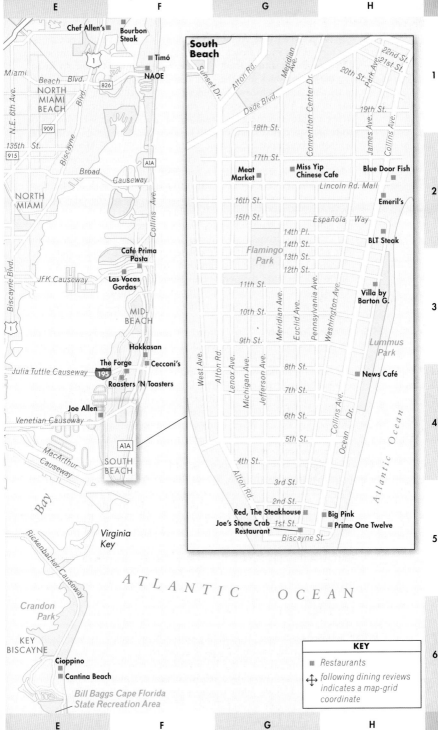

South Beach

KEY
- Restaurants
- following dining reviews indicates a map-grid coordinate

$$ ✕ **Miss Yip Chinese Cafe.** At the most popular of only a handful of Chinese
CHINESE restaurants on South Beach, the hip Miss Jennie Yip serves authentic
dim sum and steaming fresh Cantonese dishes just off Lincoln Road.
Try the Peking duck and the "Princess Jade" sea bass, made of cubes
of tender battered fish with Chinese mayo sauce. Wash it down with
one of Miss Yip's many specialty cocktails: a few favorites include the
lychee mojito and the ginger martini. A small market sells dozens of
sauce and spice mixes. The crowds here are lively, the design vividly col-
orful and contemporary, and the food flavorful. ✉ *1661 Meridian Ave.,
South Beach* ☎ *305/534–5488* ⊕ *www.missyipchinesecafe.com* ✛ *2G.*

$ ✕ **News Café.** No trip to Miami is complete without a stop at this Ocean
AMERICAN Drive landmark. The 24-hour café attracts a crowd with snacks, light
meals, drinks, periodicals, and the people-parade on the sidewalk out
front. Most prefer sitting outside, where they can feel the salt breeze
and gawk at the human scenery. Sea-grape trees shade a patio where
you can watch from a quiet distance. Offering a little of this and a
little of that—bagels, pâtés, chocolate fondue, sandwiches, and a ter-
rific wine list—this joint has something for everyone. Although service
can be indifferent to the point of laissez-faire and the food is mediocre
at best, News Café is just one of those places visitors just can't miss!
✉ *800 Ocean Dr., South Beach* ☎ *305/538–6397* ⊕ *www.newscafe.com*
🍴 *Reservations not accepted* ✛ *4H.*

$$$$ ✕ **Prime One Twelve.** This wildly busy steak house is particularly
STEAKHOUSE renowned for its highly marbleized prime beef (try the 30-ounce bone-
in rib eye for two, $68), creamed corn, truffle macaroni and cheese,
and buzzing scene: while you stand at the bar awaiting your table
(everyone has to wait—at least a little bit), you'll clamor for a drink
with all facets of Miami's high society, from the city's top real estate
developers and philanthropists to striking models and celebrities (Lenny
Kravitz, Jay-Z, and Matt Damon are among a big list of celebrity
regulars). ✉ *112 Ocean Dr., South Beach* ☎ *305/532–8112* ⊕ *www.
mylesrestaurantgroup.com* ✛ *5H.*

$$$$ ✕ **Red, the Steakhouse.** Just when it seemed that South Beach had become
STEAKHOUSE all too saturated with steak houses, Red arrived and raises the bar on
SoBe's steak house experience. The carnivore glamour den seduces with
its red and black dominatrix color scheme and overloads the senses
with the divine smells and tastes of the extensive menu. Red boasts an
equal number of seafood and traditional carnivorous offerings, each
delicately prepared, meticulously presented, and gleefully consumed.
Start with the tuna tartare, the mussels *diavolo*, or crisp chili calamari
and then continue with fresh lobster or the many variations of Angus
Beef Prime. And don't forget about the dozen or so sides, often the most
exciting part of any steak house experience. ✉ *119 Washington Ave.,
South Beach* ☎ *305/534–3688* ⊕ *www.redthesteakhouse.com* 🍴 *Reser-
vations essential* ✛ *4G.*

$$$ ✕ **SushiSamba Dromo.** This sibling to the New York City SushiSamba
JAPANESE makes an eclectic pairing of Japanese, Peruvian, and Brazilian cuisines.
The results are fabulous if a bit mystifying: miso-marinated sea bass,
hamachi *taquitos* (basically a yellowtail tartare), *mocqueca mista* (Brazilian seafood stew), and caramel–passion fruit sponge cake. Loaded

CHEAP EATS ON SOUTH BEACH

Miami Beach is notorious for overpriced eateries, but locals know better. **Half Moon Empanadas** (✉ *1616 Washington Ave., at Lincoln Rd.*) has the colorful and polished look of a national franchise but is a genuine local start-up serving 17 delicious flavors of baked (or fried) empanadas for $1.99 each. **Pizza Rustica** (✉ *8th St. and Washington Ave., 14th St. and Washington Ave., and at 667 Lincoln Rd.*) serves up humongous slices overflowing with mozzarella, steak, olives, and barbecue chicken until 4 am. **La Sandwicherie** (✉ *14th St. between Collins and Washington Aves.*) is a South Beach classic since 1988, serving gourmet French sandwiches, a delicious prosciutto salad, and healthy smoothies from a walk-up bar. **Lime Fresh Mexican Grill** (✉ *1439 Alton Rd. at 14th St.*) serves fresh and tangy fish tacos and homemade guacamole.

with customers in the heart of pedestrian Lincoln Road, colorful Sush-iSamba has a vibe that hurts the ears but warms the trendy heart. ✉ *600 Lincoln Rd., South Beach* ☎ *305/673–5337* ⊕ *www.sushisamba.com* ⌂ *Reservations essential* ✚ *2G.*

$$$$
ECLECTIC
Fodor's Choice
★
✕ **The Villa by Barton G.—the Restaurant.** Set within the glitz, the glamour, and the ostentation of Gianni Versace's former mansion, the Villa by Barton G. is an international destination. Famous for the area where Versace spent his last moments, the mansion provides a more intimate experience inside. Eating here or enjoying afternoon tea allows you to roam the front terrace, the inner courtyard, and the magical black pool garden of this historic Mediterranean fantasy home. Dinner is usually served in courses with suggested wine pairings. The avant-garde dishes served in the intimate 30-seat dining room are a gastronome's delight—Caesar salad with grilled artichokes and frozen Caesar dressing, vodka-cured salmon, and out-of-this-world clementine carrot veloute. Traditional afternoon tea, with a full spread of pastries and sandwiches, is served from 2:30 to 4 Thursday through Sunday in the Mosaic Garden ($55). ✉ *1116 Ocean Dr., South Beach* ☎ *305/576–8003* ⊕ *www.thevillabybartong.com* ⌂ *Reservations essential* ✚ *3H.*

WHERE TO STAY

For expanded hotel reviews, visit Fodors.com.

Room rates in Miami tend to swing wildly. In high season, which is January through May, expect to pay at least $150 per night, even at budget hotels. In summer, however, prices can be as much as 50% lower than the dizzying winter rates. You can also find great values between Easter and Memorial Day, which is actually a delightful time in Miami. Business travelers tend to stay in downtown Miami, while most vacationers stay on Miami Beach, as close as possible to the water. If money is no object, stay in one of the glamorous hotels lining Collins Avenue between 15th and 23rd streets. Otherwise, stay on the quiet beaches farther north, or in one of the small boutique hotels on Ocean Drive, Collins, or Washington avenues between 10th and 15th streets.

Two important considerations that affect price are balcony and view. If you're willing to have a room without an ocean view, you can sometimes get a much lower price than the standard rate. Mid-Beach and Downtown have taken the hotel scene by storm in the past few years, unveiling some of Miami's most avant-garde and luxurious properties to date.

Use the coordinate (⊕ C2) at the end of each review to locate a property on the Where to Stay in the Miami Area map.

WHAT IT COSTS					
	¢	$	$$	$$$	$$$$
FOR TWO PEOPLE	under $150	$150–$200	$200–$300	$300–$400	over $400

Prices for hotels are for two people in a standard double room in high season, excluding 12.5% city and resort taxes.

COCONUT GROVE, CORAL GABLES, AND KEY BISCAYNE

COCONUT GROVE

Coconut Grove is blessed with a number of excellent luxury properties. All are within walking distance of its principal entertainment center, Coco Walk, as well as its marinas. Although this area certainly can't replace the draw of Miami Beach or the business convenience of downtown, about 20 minutes away, it's an exciting bohemian-chic neighborhood with a gorgeous waterfront.

$$$
HOTEL
🔲 **Ritz-Carlton, Coconut Grove.** Overlooking Biscayne Bay, the hotel has rooms that are appointed with marble baths, a choice of down or nonallergenic foam pillows, and private balconies. **Pros:** best service in Coconut Grove; high-quality spa. **Cons:** of the three Miami Ritz-Carltons this one has the least interesting location and the fewest amenities. **TripAdvisor:** "bathroom was beautiful," "within walking distance to Coconut Grove shops," "great in service." ⊠ *3300 S.W. 27th Ave.* ☎ *305/644–4680 or 800/241–3333* ⊕ *www.ritzcarlton.com* ⟿ *88 rooms, 27 suites* ⌂ *In-room: a/c, Internet, Wi-Fi. In-hotel: restaurants, bar, pool, gym, spa, business center, parking, some pets allowed* ❄ *No meals* ⊕ *5D.*

CORAL GABLES

The beautiful Coral Gables is set around its beacon, the national landmark Biltmore Hotel. It also has a couple of big business hotels and one smaller boutique property. The University of Miami is nearby.

$$$
HOTEL
Fodor's Choice
★
🔲 **Biltmore Hotel.** Built in 1926, this landmark hotel has had several incarnations over the years—including a stint as a hospital during World War II—but through it all, this grande dame remains an opulent reminder of yesteryear, with its palatial lobby and grounds, enormous pool, and distinctive 315-foot tower, which rises above the canopy of trees shading Coral Gables. **Pros:** historic property; possibly best pool in the Miami area; great tennis and golf. **Cons:** far from Miami Beach. **TripAdvisor:** "the greatest pool an hotel can have," "health club is fantastic," "wonderful bathrooms." ⊠ *1200 Anastasia Ave.* ☎ *305/445–1926*

or 800/727–1926 ⊕ *www.biltmorehotel.com* ⊅ *241 rooms, 39 suites* ⏃ *In-room: a/c, Wi-Fi. In-hotel: restaurants, bars, golf course, tennis courts, pool, gym, spa, business center, parking* ⏃⏃ *No meals* ⊹ *5C.*

KEY BISCAYNE

There is probably no other place in Miami where slowness is lifted to a fine art. On Key Biscayne there are no pressures, there's no nightlife outside of the Ritz-Carlton's great live Latin music weekends, and the dining choices are essentially limited to the hotel (which has four dining options, including the languorous, Havana-style RUMBAR).

$$$
RESORT
Fodor's Choice
★

🏨 **Ritz-Carlton, Key Biscayne.** In this ultra-laid-back Key Biscayne setting, it's natural to appreciate the Ritz brand of pampering with luxurious rooms, attentive service, and ample recreational activities for the whole family. **Pros:** private beach; quiet, luxurious family retreat. **Cons:** it will be too quiet if you're looking for a party—so you have to drive to Miami for nightlife. **TripAdvisor:** "nice but nothing spectacular," "gorgeous views," "grounds were lovely." ⊠ *455 Grand Bay Dr.* ☎ *305/365–4500 or 800/241–3333* ⊕ *www.ritzcarlton.com/keybiscayne* ⊅ *365 rooms, 37 suites* ⏃ *In-room: a/c, Internet, Wi-Fi. In-hotel: restaurants, bars, tennis courts, pools, gym, spa, beach, water sports, business center, parking, some pets allowed* ⏃⏃ *No meals* ⊹ *6E.*

DOWNTOWN MIAMI

$$
HOTEL

🏨 **Doubletree Grand Hotel Biscayne Bay.** This elegant waterfront option is at the north end of downtown off a scenic marina, and near many of Miami's headline attractions: the Port of Miami, Bayside, the Arena, and the Carnival Center. **Pros:** great bay views; deli and market on-site. **Cons:** need a cab to get around. **TripAdvisor:** "furniture was a bit dated but clean," "fantastic pool area," "rooms were nice and spacious." ⊠ *1717 N. Bayshore Dr., Downtown Miami* ☎ *305/372–0313 or 800/222–8733* ⊕ *www.doubletree.com* ⊅ *152 suites* ⏃ *In-room: a/c, kitchen (some), Wi-Fi. In-hotel: restaurant, bar, pool, gym, spa, business center, parking* ⏃⏃ *No meals* ⊹ *4E.*

$$$
HOTEL

🏨 **Epic Hotel.** Located in the heart of downtown, alongside glittery high-rise condominiums, the Epic Hotel is a real gem. **Pros:** sprawling pool deck with a view of the water; complimentary wine in the lobby every day from 5 to 6 pm; complimentary in-room yoga mats and yoga television programming; tennis courts and golf courts available through partnerships with nearby tennis clubs and golf courses. **Cons:** not located directly near the beach; some rooms overlook tall condominiums and office buildings. **TripAdvisor:** "stylish spotlessly clean," "a wonderful hotel," "an eco-friendly hotel." ⊠ *270 Biscayne Blvd., Downtown Miami* ☎ *305/424–5226* ⊕ *www.epichotel.com* ⊅ *411 rooms* ⏃ *In-room: a/c, Wi-Fi. In-hotel: restaurant, bar, pool, gym, spa, water sports, children's programs, business center, parking, some pets allowed* ⏃⏃ *No meals* ⊹ *5D.*

$$$$
HOTEL
Fodor's Choice
★

🏨 **Four Seasons Hotel Miami.** Stepping off busy Brickell Avenue into this hotel, you see a soothing water wall trickling down from above, and the serenity continues in the yoga classes and poolside. **Pros:** sensational service; amazing gym and pool deck. **Cons:** no balconies. **TripAdvisor:**

BEST BETS FOR MIAMI LODGING

Fodor's offers a selective listing of quality lodging experiences in every price range, from the city's best budget beds to its most sophisticated luxury hotels. Here, we've compiled our top recommendations by price and experience. The very best properties are designated in the listings with the Fodor's Choice logo. Find specific details about a hotel in the full reviews, listed alphabetically by neighborhood.

"ambiance is heavenly," "wowed me with the little things," "high standards in service food and beverage." ✉ *1435 Brickell Ave., Downtown Miami* ☎ *305/358–3535 or 800/819–5053* ⊕ *www.fourseasons.com/miami* ⬅ *182 rooms, 39 suites* ⬳ *In-room: a/c. In-hotel: restaurant, bars, pools, gym, spa, business center, parking* †⊘ *No meals* ✛ *5D.*

$$$$ ⊡ **Mandarin Oriental, Miami.** Clandestinely hidden at the tip of Brickell Key in Biscayne Bay, the Mandarin feels as exclusive as it does glamorous. **Pros:** only beach (man-made) in downtown; intimate feeling; top luxury hotel. **Cons:** small pool; few beach cabanas. **TripAdvisor:** "turndown service every night was so nice," "rooms beginning to show their age," "well appointed bathroom and nice amenities." ✉ *500 Brickell Key Dr., Downtown Miami* ☎ *305/913–8288 or 866/888–6780* ⊕ *www.mandarinoriental.com* ⬅ *326 rooms, 31 suites* ⬳ *In-room: a/c, Internet. In-hotel: restaurants, bars, pool, gym, spa, children's programs, business center, parking* †⊘ *No meals* ✛ *5E.*

HOTEL

Fodor's Choice

★

$$ ⊡ **Tempo, A Rock Resort.** In the Marquis high-rise in downtown, Tempo, offers a splendid boutique experience steps from major venues such as the Arsht Performing Arts Center and the American Airlines Arena. **Pros:** spacious rooms; great restaurant; amazing bathrooms. **Cons:** some bathrooms do not have doors. **TripAdvisor:** "great price for the quality," "spectacular," "rooftop pool that is so peaceful." ✉ *1100 Biscayne Blvd., Downtown* ☎ *786/369–0300* ⊕ *www.tempomiami.rockresorts.com* ⬅ *56 rooms* ⬳ *In-room: a/c, Wi-Fi. In-hotel: restaurant, bar, pool, gym, spa, business center, parking* †⊘ *No meals* ✛ *4E.*

HOTEL

$$ ⊡ **Viceroy.** This hotel has a brash, supersophisticated South Beach attitude—something that distinguishes it wholly from every other Miami nonbeach hotel. **Pros:** sensationally designed spa area; fantastic pool deck; sleek rooms. **Cons:** downtown location rather than the beach; tiny lobby. **TripAdvisor:** "gorgeous hotel with great service," "fabulous massive pool deck," "liked the décor and the marble finish in the rooms." ✉ *485 Brickell Ave., Downtown Miami* ☎ *305/503–4400 or 866/781–9923* ⊕ *www.viceroymiami.com* ⬅ *150 rooms, 18 suites* ⬳ *In-room: a/c, kitchen (some), Wi-Fi. In-hotel: restaurant, bars, pools, gym, spa, business center, parking, some pets allowed* †⊘ *No meals* ✛ *5D.*

HOTEL

FISHER AND BELLE ISLANDS

$$$$ ⊡ **Fisher Island Hotel & Resort.** Assuming you don't have a private yacht, there are three ways to gain access to Fisher Island just off South Beach: you can either become a club member (initiation fee alone: $25,000), be one of the 750 equity members who have vacation places here (starting price: $8 million), or book a night at the club hotel (basic villa: $900 a night). **Pros:** great private beaches; exclusive surroundings; varied dining choices. **Cons:** expensive ferry rides take time. **TripAdvisor:** "a cool place," "very intimate," "truly an amazing experience." ✉ *1 Fisher Island Dr., Fisher Island* ☎ *305/535–6000 or 800/537–3708* ⊕ *www.fisherislandclub.com* ⬅ *5 junior suites, 50 condo units, 6 villas, 3 cottages* ⬳ *In-room: a/c, Wi-Fi. In-hotel: restaurants, golf course, tennis*

RESORT

Fodor's Choice

★

4

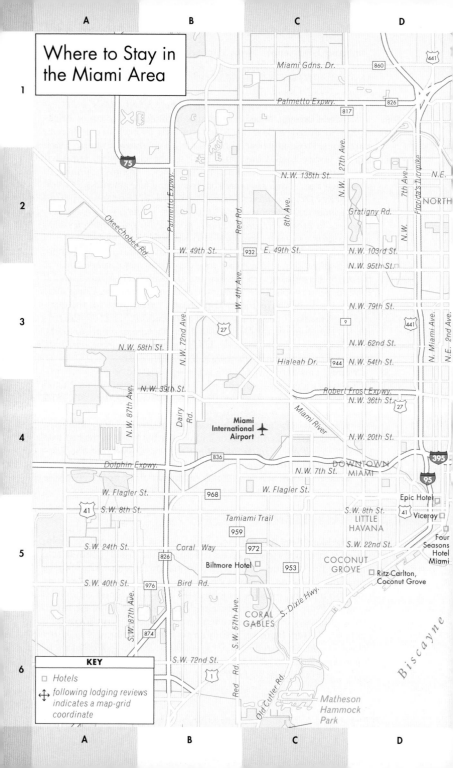

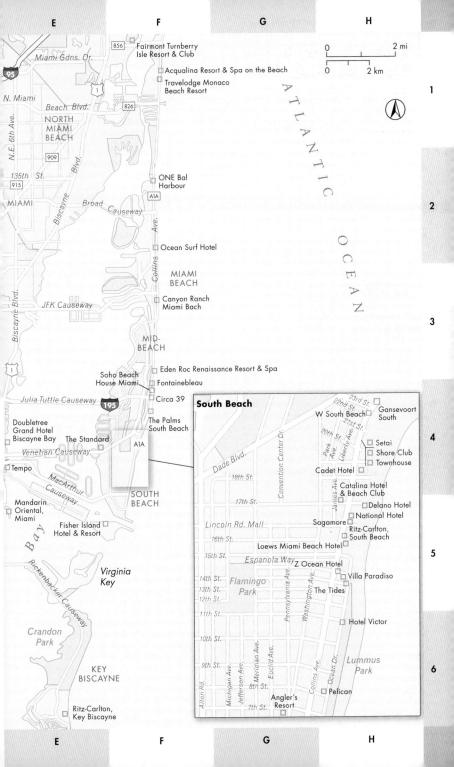

E · F · G · H

856 Fairmont Turnberry
Isle Resort & Club

Miami Gdns. Dr.

95

Acqualina Resort & Spa on the Beach

Travelodge Monaco
Beach Resort

N. Miami

Beach Blvd.

826

N. MIAMI
BEACH

N.E. 6th Ave.

NORTH
MIAMI
BEACH

909

135th St.
915

MIAMI

Biscayne Blvd.

Broad Causeway

Collins Ave.

ONE Bal
Harbour

A1A

ATLANTIC OCEAN

Ocean Surf Hotel

MIAMI
BEACH

Biscayne Blvd.

JFK Causeway

Canyon Ranch
Miami Bach

MID-
BEACH

1

Eden Roc Renaissance Resort & Spa

Soho Beach
House Miami   Fontainebleau

Julia Tuttle Causeway **195**

Circa 39

Doubletree
Grand Hotel
Biscayne Bay   The Standard

The Palms
South Beach

A1A

Venetian Causeway

Tempo

MacArthur Causeway

SOUTH
BEACH

Mandarin
Oriental,
Miami

Fisher Island
Hotel & Resort

BAY

Rickenbacker Causeway

Virginia
Key

Crandon
Park

KEY
BISCAYNE

Ritz-Carlton,
Key Biscayne

South Beach

23rd St.
22nd St.
20th St.   W South Beach   Gansevoort
South

Dade Blvd.

Convention Center Dr.

18th St.

Park Ave.
Liberty Ave.
21st St.

Setai
Shore Club
Townhouse

Cadet Hotel

17th St.

James Ave.

Catalina Hotel
& Beach Club

Delano Hotel

National Hotel

Sagamore

Ritz-Carlton,
South Beach

Lincoln Rd. Mall

16th St.

Loews Miami Beach Hotel

15th St.

Espanola Way   Z Ocean Hotel

14th St.
13th St.
12th St.

Flamingo
Park

Pennsylvania Ave.
Washington Ave.

Villa Paradiso

The Tides

11th St.

Hotel Victor

10th St.

9th St.

8th St.

7th St.

Alton Rd.
Michigan Ave.
Meridian Ave.
Jefferson Ave.
Euclid Ave.
Collins Dr.
Ocean Dr.

Lummus
Park

Pelican

Angler's
Resort

0   2 mi
0   2 km

E · F · G · H

courts, pools, gym, spa, beach, water sports, business center, parking, some pets allowed ❍| *No meals* ✛ *5E.*

$$
RESORT
🖵 **The Standard.** An extension of André Balazs's trendy, budget hotel chain, the Standard is a Hollywood newcomer that set up shop a few minutes from South Beach on an island just over the Venetian Causeway. **Pros:** interesting island location;

free bike and kayak rentals; swank pool scene; great spa; inexpensive. **Cons:** removed from South Beach nightlife; small rooms with no views. **TripAdvisor:** "very calming and civilized," "the real place to be relaxed," "rude and inattentive staff." ✉ *40 Island Ave., Belle Isle* ☎ *305/673–1717* ⊕ *www. standardhotel.com* ⤷ *104 rooms, 1 suite* ⟁ *In-room: a/c, Internet, Wi-Fi. In-hotel: restaurant, bars, pool, gym, spa, water sports, business center, parking, some pets allowed, some age restrictions* ❍| *No meals* ✛ *4E.*

MID-BEACH

Where does South Beach end and Mid-Beach begin? With the massive amount of money being spent on former 1950s pleasure palaces like the Fontainebleau and Eden Roc, it could be that Mid-Beach will soon just be considered part of South Beach. North of 24th Street, Collins Avenue curves its way to 44th Street, where it takes a sharp left turn after running into the Soho House Miami and then the Fontainebleau resort. The area between these two points—24th Street and 96th Street—is Mid-Beach. This stretch is undergoing a renaissance, as formerly rundown hotels are renovated and new hotels and condos are being built.

$$$
RESORT
🖵 **Canyon Ranch Miami Beach.** When you're not lounging around your well-appointed suite, with its 400-thread-count Mascioni linens and flat-panel HDTVs, or swimming in one of the hotel's four pools, take your meals at the Canyon Ranch Grill, where you can indulge in tasty cuisine with a healthy slant: each dish's nutritional information (including calories) is printed on the menu, and all wines served here are sustainable, organic, or biodynamic. **Pros:** located directly on the beach; spacious suites with kitchenettes (no smaller than 720 square feet); spa treatments exclusive to hotel guests. **Cons:** bit of a drive to the heart of South Beach. **TripAdvisor:** "great place but bring your wallet," "room was modern and had that spa-like tranquil yet cozy vibe," "food was delicious in addition to being healthy." ✉ *6801 Collins Ave., Mid-Beach* ☎ *305/514–7000* ⊕ *www.canyonranch.com* ⤷ *150 suites* ⟁ *In-room: a/c, kitchen, Wi-Fi. In-hotel: restaurants, pools, gym, spa, beach, business center, parking* ❍| *No meals* ✛ *3F.*

¢–$ ▦ **Circa 39 Hotel.** This stylish budget boutique hotel pays attention to
HOTEL   every detail and gets them all right. **Pros:** affordable; chic; intimate;
Fodor's Choice   beach chairs provided; art deco fireplace. **Cons:** not on the beach side
★   of Collins Avenue. **TripAdvisor:** "pleased with the rooms," "cute boutique hotel," "rooms are small." ✉ *3900 Collins Ave., Mid-Beach*
☎ *305/538–4900 or 877/824–7223* ⊕ *www.circa39.com* ↻ *96 rooms*
⚲ *In-room: a/c, kitchen, Internet. In-hotel: restaurant, bar, pool, gym,*
parking, some pets allowed ⦿ *No meals* ✛ *4F.*

$$$–$$$$ ▦ **Eden Roc Renaissance Resort & Spa.** This grand 1950s hotel designed by
RESORT   Morris Lapidus retains its old glamour while renovations have updated
and added sparkle to the rooms and grounds. **Pros:** all-new rooms
and facilities; great pools. **Cons:** too many rooms makes experience
feel impersonal. **TripAdvisor:** "not much sunshine in pool area," "hit
or miss," "good spot to catch a celebrity." ✉ *4525 Collins Ave., Mid-*
Beach ☎ *305/531–0000 or 800/327–8337* ⊕ *www.edenrocresort.com*
↻ *631 rooms* ⚲ *In-room: a/c, kitchen (some), Wi-Fi. In-hotel: restau-*
rants, bars, pools, gym, spa, beach, business center, parking ⦿ *No*
meals ✛ *3F.*

$$–$$$ ▦ **Fontainebleau.** This classic property is Miami's biggest hotel—twice
RESORT   the size of the Loews, with more than 1,500 rooms; 11 restaurants
and lounges, a huge nightclub, sumptuous pool with cabana islands, a
state-of-the-art fitness center, a 40,000-square-foot-spa, and more than
100,000 square feet of meeting and ballroom space come along with all
those rooms. **Pros:** historic design mixed with all-new facilities; fabulous
pools. **Cons:** away from the South Beach pedestrian scene; too big to
be intimate. **TripAdvisor:** "room was kind of rundown," "resort itself
is stunning," "phenomenal experience." ✉ *4441 Collins Ave., Mid-*
Beach ☎ *305/538–2000 or 800/548–8886* ⊕ *www.fontainebleau.com*
↻ *1,504 rooms* ⚲ *In-room: a/c, kitchen (some), Wi-Fi. In-hotel: res-*
taurants, bars, pools, gym, spa, water sports, business center, parking
⦿ *No meals* ✛ *4F.*

¢–$ ▦ **Ocean Surf Hotel.** Don't expect luxury in this colorful art deco lodge,
HOTEL   but if you want a cheap stay away from everybody and ideal beach
access, you can't beat the tiny Ocean Surf Hotel. **Pros:** adorable art
deco hotel; cheap. **Cons:** basic rooms; no Internet; spotty service.
TripAdvisor: "terrible hotel," "not too clean," "old filthy." ✉ *7436*
Ocean Terr., Mid-Beach ☎ *305/866–1648 or 800/555–0411* ⊕ *www.*
theoceansurfhotel.com ↻ *49 rooms* ⚲ *In-room: a/c. In-hotel: beach,*
parking ⦿ *No meals* ✛ *2F.*

$–$$ ▦ **The Palms South Beach.** Stay here if you're seeking an elegant, relaxed
HOTEL   property away from the noise but still near South Beach. **Pros:** tropi-
cal garden; relaxed and quiet. **Cons:** no balconies; away from South
Beach. **TripAdvisor:** "beach is directly in back of the hotel," "top
notch," "amenities were updated." ✉ *3025 Collins Ave., Mid-Beach*
☎ *305/534–0505 or 800/550–0505* ⊕ *www.thepalmshotel.com* ↻ *220*
rooms, 22 suites ⚲ *In-room: a/c, Wi-Fi. In-hotel: restaurant, bars, pool,*
beach, parking ⦿ *No meals* ✛ *4F.*

4

$$$$ [hotel icon] **Soho Beach House Miami.** Though a stay usually requires membership
HOTEL   to the House, if you are lucky enough to land a room through a sales
★   promotion, then do so! **Pros:** trendy; two pools; fabulous restaurant
Cons: patchy Wi-Fi; members have priority for rooms. **TripAdvisor:**
"great location with really nice relaxed feel," "pricey but worth every
penny," "older cheaper rooms aren't worth the money." ⊠ *4385 Collins
Ave., Mid-Beach, Miami* ☎ *786/507–7900* ⊕ *www.sohobeachhouse.
com* ⇦ *55 rooms* ☖ *In-room: a/c, Wi-Fi. In-hotel: restaurant, bar, pool,
gym, spa, beach, business center, parking* ⌾ *No meals* ✛ *4F.*

NORTH MIAMI BEACH AND AVENTURA

Nearing the 100th Street mark on Collins Avenue, Mid-Beach gives way
to North Beach. In particular, at 96th Street, the town of Bal Harbour
takes over Collins Avenue from Miami Beach. The town runs a mere
10 blocks to the north before the bridge to Sunny Isles. Bal Harbour is
famous for its outdoor upscale shops. If you take your shopping seriously, you'll probably want to stay in this area. At 106th Street, the
town of Sunny Isles is an appealing, calm, predominantly upscale choice
for families looking for a beautiful beach. There is no nightlife to speak
of in Sunny Isles, and yet the half-dozen megaluxurious skyscraper
hotels that have sprung up here since 2005 have created a niche-resort
town from the demolished ashes of much older, affordable hotels. Further west are the high-rises of Aventura.

$$$$ [resort icon] **Acqualina Resort & Spa on the Beach.** When it opened in 2006, this hotel
RESORT   raised the bar for luxury in Miami, and it stands as one of the city's
Fodor's Choice best hotels. **Pros:** in-room check-in; luxury amenities; huge spa. **Cons:**
★   no nightlife near hotel. **TripAdvisor:** "instantly fell in love with the
place," "they have taken their service to an entirely new level," "wonderful amenities." ⊠ *17875 Collins Ave., Sunny Isles* ☎ *305/918–8000*
⊕ *www.acqualinaresort.com* ⇦ *54 rooms, 43 suites* ☖ *In-room: a/c,
Wi-Fi. In-hotel: restaurants, bars, pools, gym, spa, beach, water sports,
children's programs, business center, parking* ⌾ *No meals* ✛ *1F.*

$$$$ [resort icon] **Fairmont Turnberry Isle Resort & Club.** Golfers and families will enjoy
RESORT   this upscale resort with one of the best service staffs in the city. **Pros:**
great golf, pools, and restaurants; free shuttle to Aventura Mall. **Cons:**
far from the beach; no nightlife. **TripAdvisor:** "ultra comfortable beds,"
"would definitely recommend this to families," "pools are so warm."
⊠ *19999 W. Country Club Dr., Aventura* ☎ *305/932–6200 or 800/327–
7028* ⊕ *www.turnberryisle.com* ⇦ *392 rooms, 41 suites* ☖ *In-room: a/c,
kitchen (some), Wi-Fi. In-hotel: restaurants, bars, golf courses, tennis
courts, pools, gym, spa, water sports, business center, parking, some
pets allowed* ⌾ *No meals* ✛ *1F.*

$$$$ [resort icon] **ONE Bal Harbour.** The tiny, tony town of Bal Harbour finally has a
RESORT   hotel worthy of its ultra-high-end mall. **Pros:** great views; beachfront;
great contemporary-art collection. **Cons:** pricey; limited lobby social-
izing; beach less attractive than that of its neighbors. **TripAdvisor:** "luxury and tranquility," "amazing hotel room bathroom," "luxury at its

finest." ⊠ *10295 Collins Ave., Bal Harbour* ☎ *305/455–5400* ⊕ *www. oneluxuryhotels.com* ⌁ *124 rooms, 63 suites* ⌂ *In-room: a/c, kitchen, Wi-Fi. In-hotel: restaurant, bar, tennis courts, pools, gym, spa, beach, water sports, parking* ⎮○⎮ *No meals* ✥ *2F.*

¢   ⛣ **Travelodge Monaco Beach Resort.** The last of a dying breed, the Trav-
HOTEL elodge Monaco is a no-frills step up from a youth hostel. **Pros:** steps to great beach; bottom-dollar cost; free shuttle to South Beach and Aventura. **Cons:** older rooms; not service-oriented; no Wi-Fi in room, and public Wi-Fi in hotel has a fee. ⊠ *17501 Collins Ave., Sunny Isles* ☎ *305/932–2100 or 800/227–9006* ⊕ *www.monacomiamibeachresort. com* ⌁ *110 rooms* ⌂ *In-room: a/c, kitchen (some). In-hotel: restaurant, bar, pool, beach, parking* ⎮○⎮ *No meals* ✥ *1F.*

SOUTH BEACH

$$ ⛣ **Angler's Boutique Resort.** Angler's has the feel of a sophisticated private
HOTEL Mediterranean villa community. **Pros:** gardened private retreat. **Cons:** on busy Washington Ave. **TripAdvisor:** "very special," "beautiful bed-rooms," "within walking distance of the beach." ⊠ *660 Washington Ave., South Beach* ☎ *305/534–9600* ⊕ *www.theanglersresort.com* ⌁ *24 rooms, 20 suites* ⌂ *In-room: a/c, kitchen (some), Wi-Fi. In-hotel: res-taurant, bar, pool, business center, parking, some pets allowed* ⎮○⎮ *No meals* ✥ *G6.*

¢   ⛣ **Cadet Hotel.** You can trace the fact that this is one of the sweetest, qui-
HOTEL etest hotels in South Beach to the ways of its independent female owner, a local doctor named Vilma Biaggi. **Pros:** well run with friendly service; lovely garden; great value. **Cons:** no pool. **TripAdvisor:** "loaded with character and very comfortable," "clean as a whistle," "great location." ⊠ *1701 James Ave., South Beach* ☎ *305/672–6688 or 800/432–2338* ⊕ *www.cadethotel.com* ⌁ *32 rooms, 3 suites* ⌂ *In-room: a/c, Wi-Fi. In-hotel: restaurant, bar* ⎮○⎮ *Breakfast* ✥ *4H.*

$–$$ ⛣ **Catalina Hotel & Beach Club.** The Catalina is the budget party spot in
HOTEL the heart of South Beach's hottest block. **Pros:** free drinks; free bikes; free airport shuttle; good people-watching. **Cons:** $15 wireless fee; ser-vice not a high priority; loud. **TripAdvisor:** "rates are excellent for what you get," "contemporary style," "funky in a charming sort of way." ⊠ *1732 Collins Ave., South Beach* ☎ *305/674–1160* ⊕ *www. catalinahotel.com* ⌁ *200 rooms* ⌂ *In-room: a/c, Wi-Fi. In-hotel: res-taurant, bars, pool, parking, some pets allowed* ⎮○⎮ *No meals* ✥ *5H.*

$$$$ ⛣ **Delano Hotel.** The decor of this grand hotel is inspired by Lewis Car-
HOTEL roll's *Alice in Wonderland*, and as you make your way from the sparse, busy, spacious lobby past cascading white curtains and through rooms dotted with strange, whimsical furniture pieces, you will feel like you are indeed falling down a rabbit hole. **Pros:** electrifying design; loung-ing among the beautiful and famous. **Cons:** crowded; scene-y; small rooms; expensive. **TripAdvisor:** "great swimming pool area," "sophis-ticated trendy atmosphere," "would definitely recommend." ⊠ *1685 Collins Ave., South Beach* ☎ *305/672–2000 or 800/555–5001* ⊕ *www.*

Fodor's Choice ★

Acqualina Resort & Spa on the Beach

Circa 39 Hotel

Biltmore Hotel

Delano Hotel

Ritz-Carlton, Key Biscayne

Four Seasons Hotel Miami

The Tides South Beach

Mandarin Oriental

delano-hotel.com ⤴ *184 rooms, 24 suites* ⌂ *In-room: a/c, Wi-Fi. In-hotel: restaurants, bars, pool, gym, spa, beach, business center, parking* ⍩ *No meals* ✢ *5H.*

$$$$ 🖵 **Gansevoort South.** For the well-heeled, party-seeking, jet-setting
RESORT   crowd, there's a South Beach hotel to toy with: this southern cousin
of New York's trendsetting Meatpacking District hotel is better than
the original, starting with a fantastic beachfront setting. **Pros:** spacious
rooms (averaging 700 square feet); big, fun setting with huge pool
deck and rooftop; fancy on-site restaurants. **Cons:** room views aren't
amazing; a few blocks too far from most SoBe foot traffic. **TripAdvisor:** "rooms are spacious and relatively accommodating," "pretty disappointed," "well worth a visit." ✉ *2377 Collins Ave., South Beach*
☎ *305/604–1000* ⊕ *www.gansevoortsouth.com* ⤴ *334 rooms* ⌂ *In-room: a/c, kitchen (some), Internet, Wi-Fi. In-hotel: restaurants, bar,
pool, gym, spa, beach, water sports, business center, parking* ⍩ *No
meals* ✢ *4H.*

$$$$ 🖵 **Hotel Victor.** The sleek look of the Hotel Victor was created by the Parisian
HOTEL   designer Jacques Garci and unusually organized rooms draw a sleek
set of customers. **Pros:** great design; views of Ocean Drive from the pool
deck; high hip factor; good service. **Cons:** small rooms; small pool. **TripAdvisor:** "not a party hotel," "rooms were really beautiful," "rooms
were very small but had a huge tub." ✉ *1144 Ocean Dr., South Beach*
☎ *305/428–1234 or 800/327–7028* ⊕ *www.hotelvictorsouthbeach.com*
⤴ *91 rooms* ⌂ *In-room: a/c, kitchen (some), Wi-Fi. In-hotel: restaurants, bar, pool, gym, spa, business center, parking, some pets allowed*
⍩ *No meals* ✢ *5H.*

$$$–$$$$ 🖵 **Loews Miami Beach Hotel.** Loews Miami Beach is marvelous for families,
HOTEL   businesspeople, groups, and pet-lovers. **Pros:** top-notch amenities
include a beautiful oceanfront pool and immense spa; pets welcome.
Cons: intimacy is lost due to its large size. **TripAdvisor:** "very clean
and modern," "large pool," "like feel of the whole place." ✉ *1601
Collins Ave., South Beach* ☎ *305/604–1601 or 800/235–6397* ⊕ *www.
loewshotels.com/miamibeach* ⤴ *733 rooms, 57 suites* ⌂ *In-room: a/c,
Internet, Wi-Fi. In-hotel: restaurants, bars, pool, gym, spa, beach, business center, parking, some pets allowed* ⍩ *No meals* ✢ *5H.*

$$ 🖵 **National Hotel.** This luxurious, beautiful hotel serves as a bastion
HOTEL   of calm in the sea of white-on-white mod decor and raucous reveling
Fodor's Choice   usually reserved for the beachfront masterpieces lining Collins Avenue
★   between 15th and 20th streets. **Pros:** stunning pool; perfect location.
Cons: tower rooms aren't impressive; neighboring hotels can be
noisy on the weekends. **TripAdvisor:** "beach area very nice," "rooms
were very small," "great location." ✉ *1677 Collins Ave., South Beach*
☎ *305/532–2311 or 800/327–8370* ⊕ *www.nationalhotel.com* ⤴ *143
rooms, 9 suites* ⌂ *In-room: a/c, Internet, Wi-Fi. In-hotel: restaurants,
bars, pools, gym, beach, business center, parking, some pets allowed*
⍩ *No meals* ✢ *5H.*

$$ 🖵 **Pelican.** The spirit of Diesel clothing company, which owns this
HOTEL   Ocean Drive boutique, permeates the hotel: Each room is completely

different, fashioned from a mix of antique and garage-sale furnishings selected by the designer of Diesel's clothing-display windows. **Pros:** unique, over-the-top design; central Ocean Drive location. **Cons:** rooms are so tiny that the quirky charm wears off quickly; no no-smoking rooms. **TripAdvisor:** "absolute comfort," "good choice," "creatively decorated." ✉ *826 Ocean Dr., South Beach* ☎ *305/673–3373 or 800/773–5422* ⊕ *www.pelicanhotel.com* ⇥ *28 rooms, 4 suites* ⌂ *In-room: a/c, Wi-Fi. In-hotel: restaurant, bar, beach, parking* ⏐○⏐ *No meals* ⊹ *6H.*

> **WORD OF MOUTH**
>
> "If you can get a hotel room at a good price than you should come to Miami during Art Basel week (first weekend in Dec.). It's a very, very cosmopolitan atmosphere. It will be busy but if you like being in a city then you'll enjoy the energy with all sorts of interesting people, art lovers, artists, celebrities, and art everywhere. It's the best week to feel alive in Miami."
> —SoBchBud1

$$$$ **Ritz-Carlton, South Beach.** A sumptuous affair, the Ritz-Carlton is the
HOTEL only truly luxurious property on the beach that *feels* like it's on the
Fodor'sChoice beach, because its long pool deck leads you right out to the water.
★ **Pros:** luxury rooms; great service; great location. **Cons:** too big to be intimate. **TripAdvisor:** "first impressions were favorable," "had such a good time," "good value." ✉ *1 Lincoln Rd., South Beach* ☎ *786/276–4000 or 800/241–3333* ⊕ *www.ritzcarlton.com* ⇥ *375 rooms* ⌂ *In-room: a/c, Wi-Fi. In-hotel: restaurants, bars, pools, gym, spa, beach, children's programs, business center, parking, some pets allowed* ⏐○⏐ *No meals* ⊹ *5H.*

$$ **Sagamore.** This supersleek, all-white hotel in the middle of the action
HOTEL looks and feels more like a Chelsea art gallery, filled with brilliant contemporary art. **Pros:** sensational pool; great location; quiet on weekdays; good rate specials. **Cons:** basic rooms are not as stylish as public areas; service can be spotty. **TripAdvisor:** "rooms are spacious," "our sanctuary," "close enough to walk to South Beach." ✉ *1671 Collins Ave.* ☎ *305/535–8088* ⊕ *www.sagamorehotel.com* ⇥ *93 suites* ⌂ *In-room: a/c, kitchen, Wi-Fi. In-hotel: restaurant, bars, pool, spa, beach, business center, parking* ⏐○⏐ *No meals* ⊹ *5H.*

$$$$ **Setai.** The place feels like an Asian museum, serene and beautiful,
HOTEL with heavy granite furniture lifted by orange accents, warm candlelight, and the soft bubble of seemingly endless pools and ponds. **Pros:** quiet and classy; beautiful grounds. **Cons:** somewhat cold aura; TVs are far from the beds. **TripAdvisor:** "delightful in every aspect," "every detail was taken care of," "more style than substance." ✉ *101 20th St., South Beach* ☎ *305/520–6000 or 888/625–7500* ⊕ *www.setai.com* ⇥ *110 rooms* ⌂ *In-room: a/c, Wi-Fi. In-hotel: restaurant, bars, pools, gym, spa, beach, business center, parking, some pets allowed* ⏐○⏐ *No meals* ⊹ *4H.*

$$$$ **Shore Club.** Shore Club is the perfect adult playground; in terms of
HOTEL lounging, people-watching, and poolside glitz, this is the best of South

Beach. **Pros:** good restaurants and bars; nightlife in your backyard. **Cons:** uninviting rooms. **TripAdvisor:** "best room service ever," "service was top notch," "able to walk to so many great locations." ✉ *1901 Collins Ave., South Beach* ☎ *305/695–3100 or 877/640–9500* 🌐 *www.shoreclub.com* *309 rooms, 79 suites* *In-room: a/c, Wi-Fi. In-hotel: restaurants, bars, pools, gym, spa, beach, business center, parking, some pets allowed* *No meals* ✣ *4H.*

$$$$ HOTEL **The Tides.** The Tides is arguably Miami's most exclusive Ocean Drive art deco hotel. **Pros:** superior service; great beach location; ocean views from all suites plus the terrace restaurant. **Cons:** tiny elevators; ubiquitous taxidermy. **TripAdvisor:** "you had to work hard to get the most out of your stay," "would definitely stay here again," "stellar customer service." ✉ *1220 Ocean Dr., South Beach* ☎ *305/604–5070 or 866/438–4337* 🌐 *www.thetideshotel.com* *45 suites* *In-room: a/c, Internet, Wi-Fi. In-hotel: restaurant, pool, gym, beach, business center, parking* *No meals* ✣ *5H.*

$ HOTEL ★ **Townhouse.** Though sandwiched between the Setai and the Shore Club—two of the coolest hotels on the planet—the Townhouse doesn't try to act all dolled up: it's comfortable being the shabby-chic, lighthearted, relaxed, no-frills, fun hotel on South Beach. **Pros:** a great budget buy for the style-hungry; direct beach access; hot rooftop lounge. **Cons:** no pool; small rooms not designed for long stays. **TripAdvisor:** "breakfast is good," "rooms are neat," "very good value for money." ✉ *150 20th St., east of Collins Ave., South Beach* ☎ *305/534–3800 or 877/534–3800* 🌐 *www.townhousehotel.com* *69 rooms, 2 suites* *In-room: a/c, Internet, Wi-Fi. In-hotel: restaurant, bar, laundry facilities, business center, parking* *Breakfast* ✣ *4H.*

¢ HOTEL **Villa Paradiso.** One of South Beach's best deals, Paradiso has huge rooms with kitchens and a charming tropical courtyard with benches for hanging out at all hours. **Pros:** great hangout spot in courtyard; good value; great location. **Cons:** no pool; no restaurant. **TripAdvisor:** "a jewel," "like we were staying at a friend's house," "clean spacious rooms." ✉ *1415 Collins Ave., South Beach* ☎ *305/532–0616* 🌐 *www.villaparadisohotel.com* *17 studios* *In-room: a/c, kitchen, Internet, Wi-Fi. In-hotel: some pets allowed* *No meals* ✣ *5H.*

$$$ HOTEL Fodor's Choice ★ **W South Beach.** Fun, fresh, and funky, this W is also the flagship for the brand's evolution towards young sophistication, which means less club music in the lobby, more lighting, and more attention to the $40 million art collection lining the lobby's expansive walls. **Pros:** pool scene; masterful design; ocean-view balconies in each room. **Cons:** not a classic art deco building. **TripAdvisor:** "pretentious staff," "spa was very small and disappointing," "beautiful hotel shame about the service." ✉ *2201 Collins Ave., South BeachMiami Beach* ☎ *305/938–3000* 🌐 *www.WHotels.com/SouthBeach* *334 rooms* *In-room: a/c, kitchen, Wi-Fi. In-hotel: restaurant, bars, pools, gym, spa, beach, business center, parking, some pets allowed* *No meals* ✣ *4H.*

$$ HOTEL **Z Ocean Hotel.** The lauded firm of Arquitectonica designed the rooms and suites at this glossy and bold hideaway that began as an über-exclusive Regent property, before changing hands a few times. **Pros:** incredible

balconies; huge rooms. **Cons:** gym is just a small "cardio room;" no spa; not much privacy on private decks. **TripAdvisor:** "large bathroom with huge shower," "pool deck was constantly cleaned and well stocked with towels," "in the heart of South Beach." ⊠ *1437 Collins Ave., South Beach* ☎ *305/672–4554* ⊕ *www.zoceanhotelsouthbeach.com* ⟳ *79 suites* ⚄ *In-room: a/c, Wi-Fi. In-hotel: restaurant, bar, pool, gym, parking* ⫟ *No meals* ✛ *5H.*

The Everglades

WORD OF MOUTH

"Sign up at the Ernest Coe Visitor Center or call the Flamingo Visitor Center for the free ranger-led canoe tour. . . . No experience necessary—maneuvering the long canoe through the twists and turns of the mangroves was a challenge, but very fun."

—JC98

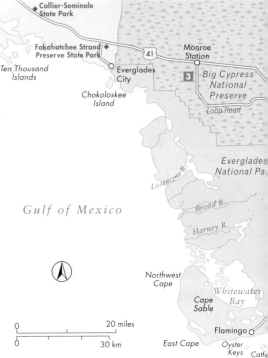

WELCOME TO THE EVERGLADES

TOP REASONS TO GO

★ **Fun Fishing:** Cast for some of the world's fight-ingest game fish—600 species of fish in all—in the Everglades' backwaters.

★ **Abundant Birdlife:** Check hundreds of birds off your life list, includ-ing—if you're lucky—the rare Everglades snail kite.

★ **Cool Kayaking:** Do a half-day trip in Big Cypress National Preserve or reach for the ultimate—the 99-mi Wilderness Trail.

★ **Swamp Cuisine:** Hankering for alligator tail and frogs' legs? Or how about swamp cabbage, made from hearts of palm? Better yet, try stone crab claws fresh from the traps.

★ **Great Gator-Spotting:** This is ground zero for alligator viewing in the United States, and there's a good bet you'll leave having spotted your quota.

1 **Everglades National Park.** Alligators, Florida panthers, black bears, mana-tees, dolphins, bald eagles, and roseate spoonbills call this vast habitat home.

2 **Biscayne National Park.** Mostly underwater, here's where the string of coral reefs and islands that form the Florida Keys begin.

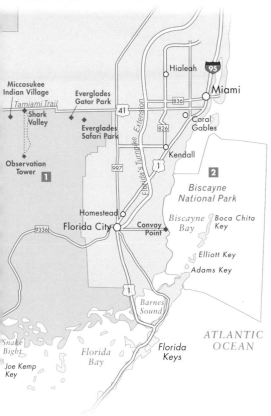

GETTING ORIENTED

The southern third of the Florida peninsula is largely taken up by protected government land that includes Everglades National Park, Big Cypress National Preserve, and Biscayne National Park. Miami lies to the northeast, while Naples and Marco Island are northwest. Land access to Everglades National Park is primarily by two roads. The park's main road traverses the southern Everglades from the gateway towns of Homestead and Florida City to the outpost of Flamingo, on Florida Bay. In the northern Everglades, Tamiami Trail (U.S. 41) runs from the Greater Miami area on the east coast or from Naples on the west coast to the western park entrance in Everglades City at Route 29.

5

3 Big Cypress National Preserve. Neighbor to Everglades National Park, it's an outdoor-lover's paradise.

THE FLORIDA
EVERGLADES

by Lynne Helm

Alternately described as elixir of life or swampland muck, the Florida Everglades is one of a kind—a 50-mi-wide "river of grass" that spreads across hundreds of thousands of acres. It moves at varying speeds depending on rainfall and other variables, sloping south from the Kissimmee River and Lake Okeechobee to estuaries of Biscayne Bay, Florida Bay, and the Ten Thousand Islands.

Today, apart from sheltering some 70 species on America's endangered list, the Everglades also embraces more than 7 million residents, 50 million annual tourists, 400,000 acres of sugarcane, and the world's largest concentration of golf courses.

Demands on the land threaten the Everglades' finely balanced ecosystem. Irrigation canals for agriculture and roadways disrupt natural water flow. Drainage for development leaves wildlife scurrying for new territory. Water runoff, laced with fertilizers, promotes unnatural growth of swamp vegetation. What remains is a miracle of sorts, given decades of these destructive forces.

Creation of the Everglades required unique conditions. South Florida's geology, linked with its warm, wet subtropical climate, is the perfect mix for a marshland ecosystem. Layers of porous, permeable limestone create water-bearing rock,

soil, and aquifers, which in turn affects climate, weather, and hydrology.

This rock beneath the Everglades reflects Florida's geologic history—its crust was once part of the African region. Some scientists theorize that continental shifting merged North America with Africa, and then continental rifting later pulled North America away from the African continent but took part of northwest Africa with it—the part that is today's Florida. The Earth's tectonic plates continued to migrate, eventually placing Florida at its current location as a land mass jutting out into the ocean, with the Everglades at its tip.

EXPERIENCING THE ECOSYSTEMS

Eight distinct habitats exist within Everglades National Park, Big Cypress National Preserve, and Biscayne National Park.

ECOSYSTEMS	EASY WAY	MORE ACTIVE WAY
COASTAL PRAIRIE: An arid region of salt-tolerant vegetation lies between the tidal mud flats of Florida Bay and dry land. **Best place to see it: The Coastal Prairie Trail**	Take a guided boat tour of Florida Bay, leaving from Flamingo Marina.	Hike the Coastal Prairie Trail from Eco Pond to Clubhouse Beach.
CYPRESS: Capable of surviving in standing water, cypress trees often form dense clusters called "cypress domes" in natural water-filled depressions. **Best place to see it: Big Cypress National Preserve**	Drive U.S. 41 (also known as Tamiami Trail—pronounced Tammy-Amee), which cuts across Southern Florida, from Naples to Miami.	Hike (or drive) the scenic Loop Road, which begins off Tamiami Trail, running from the Loop Road Education Center to Monroe Station.
FRESH WATER MARL PRAIRIE: Bordering deeper sloughs are large prairies with marl (clay and calcium carbonate) sediments on limestone. Gators like to use their toothy snouts to dig holes in prairie mud. **Best place to see it: Pahayokee Overlook**	Drive there from the Ernest F. Coe Visitor Center.	Take a guided tour, either through the park service or from permitted, licensed guides. You also can set up camp at Long Pine Key.
FRESH WATER SLOUGH AND HARDWOOD HAMMOCK: Shark River Slough and Taylor Slough are the Everglades' two sloughs, or marshy rivers. Due to slight elevation amid sloughs, dense stands of hardwood trees appear as teardrop-shaped islands. **Best place to see it: The Observation Tower**	Take a two-hour guided tram tour from the Shark Valley Visitor Center to the tower and back.	Walk or bike (rentals available) the route to the tower via the tram road and (walkers only) Bobcat Boardwalk trail and Otter Cave Hammock Trail.
MANGROVE: Spread over South Florida's coastal channels and waterways, mangrove thrives where Everglades fresh water mixes with salt water. **Best place to see it: The Wilderness Waterway**	Picnic at the area near Long Pine Key, which is surrounded by mangrove, or take a water tour at Biscayne National Park.	Boat your way along the 99-mi Wilderness Waterway. It's six hours by motorized boat, seven days by canoe.
MARINE AND ESTUARINE: Corals, sponges, mollusks, seagrass, and algae thrive in the Florida Bay, where the fresh waters of the Everglades meet the salty seas. **Best place to see it: Florida Bay**	Take a boat tour from the Flamingo Visitor Center marina.	Canoe or kayak on White Water Bay along the Wilderness Waterway Canoe Trail.
PINELAND: A dominant plant in dry, rugged terrain, the Everglades' diverse pinelands consist of slash pine forest, saw palmettos, and more than 200 tropical plant varieties. **Best place to see it: Long Pine Key trails**	Drive to Long Pine Key, about 6 mi off the main road from Ernest F. Coe Visitor Center.	Hike or bike the 28 mi of Long Pine Key trails.

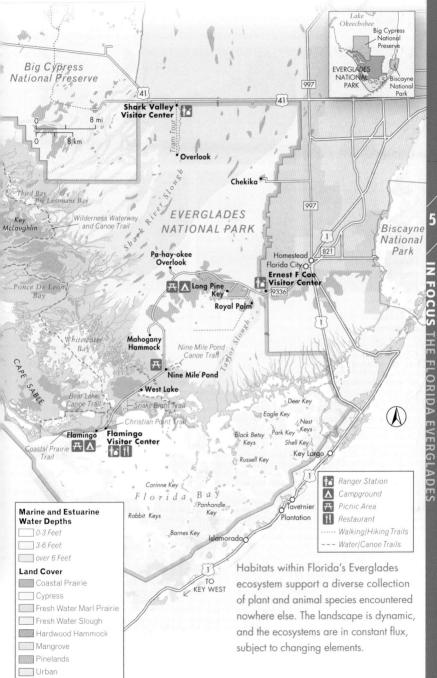

Lake Okeechobee

Big Cypress National Preserve

EVERGLADES NATIONAL PARK

Biscayne National Park

Big Cypress National Preserve

41

Shark Valley Visitor Center

Tram Tour

• Overlook

Chekika •

997

EVERGLADES NATIONAL PARK

Third Bay
Big Lostmans Bay

Key McLaughlin

Wilderness Waterway and Canoe Trail

Shark River Slough

0   8 mi
0   8 km

Ponce De Leon Bay

Pa-hay-okee Overlook

Long Pine Key

Royal Palm

Homestead
Florida City

821

Ernest F Coe Visitor Center

9336

1

Biscayne National Park

Whitewater Bay

Mahogany Hammock

Nine Mile Pond Canoe Trail

Taylor Slough

CAPE SABLE

Bear Lake Canoe Trail

Nine Mile Pond

• West Lake

Snake Bight Trail

Christian Point Trail

1

Flamingo

Flamingo Visitor Center

Coastal Prairie Trail

Deer Key

Eagle Key

Nest Keys

Black Betsy Keys

Park Key

Shell Key

Russell Key

Key Largo

Corinne Key

Florida Bay

Panhandle Key

Rabbit Keys

Barnes Key

Islamorada

Tavernier

Plantation

1

5

IN FOCUS THE FLORIDA EVERGLADES

Marine and Estuarine Water Depths

  ☐ 0-3 Feet
  ☐ 3-6 Feet
  ☐ over 6 Feet

Land Cover

  ☐ Coastal Prairie
  ☐ Cypress
  ☐ Fresh Water Marl Prairie
  ☐ Fresh Water Slough
  ☐ Hardwood Hammock
  ☐ Mangrove
  ☐ Pinelands
  ☐ Urban

🛈 Ranger Station
△ Campground
⛱ Picnic Area
🍴 Restaurant
·········· Walking/Hiking Trails
– – – Water/Canoe Trails

1
TO KEY WEST

Habitats within Florida's Everglades ecosystem support a diverse collection of plant and animal species encountered nowhere else. The landscape is dynamic, and the ecosystems are in constant flux, subject to changing elements.

FLORA

❶ Cabbage Palm

It's virtually impossible to visit the Everglades and not see a cabbage palm, Florida's official state tree. The cabbage palm (or sabal palm), graces assorted ecosystems and grows well in swamps. **Best place to see them:** At Loxahatchee National Wildlife Refuge (embracing the northern part of the Everglades, along Alligator Alley), throughout Everglades National Park, and at Big Cypress National Preserve.

❷ Sawgrass

With spiny, serrated leaf blades resembling saws, sawgrass inspired the term "river of grass" for the Everglades. **Best place to see them:** Both Shark Valley and Pahayokee Overlook provide terrific vantage points for gazing over sawgrass prairie; you also can get an eyeful of sawgrass when crossing Alligator Alley, even when doing so at top speeds.

❸ Mahogany

Hardwood hammocks of the Everglades live in areas that rarely flood because of the slight elevation of the sloughs, where they're typically found. **Best place to see them:** Everglades National Park's Mahogany Hammock Trail (which has a boardwalk leading to the nation's largest living mahogany tree).

❹ Mangrove

Mangrove forest ecosystems provide both food and protected nursery areas for fish, shellfish, and crustaceans. **Best place to see them:** Along Biscayne National Park shoreline, at Big Cypress National Preserve, and within Everglades National Park, especially around the Caple Sable area.

❺ Gumbo Limbo

Sometimes called "tourist trees" because of peeling reddish bark (not unlike sunburns). **Best place to see them:** Everglades National Park's Gumbo Limbo Trail and assorted spots throughout the expansive Everglades.

FAUNA

❶ American Alligator

In all likelihood, on your visit to the Everglades you'll see at least a gator or two. These carnivorous creatures can be found throughout the Everglades swampy wetlands.

Best place to see them: Loxahatchee National Wildlife Refuge (also sheltering the endangered Everglades snail kite) and within Everglades National Park at Shark Valley or Anhinga Trail. Sometimes (logically enough) gators hang out along Alligator Alley, basking in early morning or late-afternoon sun along four-lane I–75.

❷ American Crocodile

Crocs gravitate to fresh or brackish water, subsisting on birds, fish, snails, frogs, and small mammals.

Best place to see them: Within Everglades National Park, Big Cypress National Preserve, and protected grounds in or around Billie Swamp Safari.

❸ Eastern Coral Snake

This venomous snake burrows in underbrush, preying on lizards, frogs, and smaller snakes.

Best place to see them: Snakes typically shy away from people, but try Snake Bight or Eco Pond near Flamingo, where birds are also prevalent.

❹ Florida Panther

Struggling for survival amid loss of habitat, these shy, tan-colored cats now number around 100, up from lows of near 30.

Best place to see them: Protected grounds of Billie Swamp Safari sometimes provide sightings during tours. Signage on roadway linking Tamiami Trail and Alligator Alley warns of panther crossings, but sightings are rare.

❺ Green Tree Frog

Typically bright green with white or yellow stripes, these nocturnal creatures thrive in swamps and brackish water.

Best place to see them: Within Everglades National Park, especially in or near water.

● =Extremely Common ● =Very Common ● =Somewhat Common ● =Rare

BIRDS

❶ Anhinga

The lack of oil glands for waterproofing feathers helps this bird to dive as well as chase and spear fish with its pointed beak. The Anhinga is also often called a "water turkey" because of its long tail, or a "snake bird" because of its long neck.

Best place to see them: The Anhinga Trail, which also is known for attracting other wildlife to drink during especially dry winters.

❷ Blue-Winged Teal

Although it's predominantly brown and gray, this bird's powder-blue wing patch becomes visible in flight. Next to the mallard, the blue-winged teal is North America's second most abundant duck, and thrives particularly well in the Everglades.

Best place to see them: Near ponds and marshy areas of Everglades National Park or Big Cypress National Preserve.

❸ Great Blue Heron

This bird has a varied palate and enjoys feasting on everything from frogs, snakes, and mice to shrimp, aquatic insects, and sometimes even other birds! The all-white version, which at one time was considered a separate species, is quite common to the Everglades.

Best place to see them: Loxahatchee National Wildlife Refuge or Shark Valley in Everglades National Park.

❹ Great Egret

Once decimated by plume hunters, these monogamous, long-legged white birds with S-shaped necks feed in wetlands, nest in trees, and hang out in colonies that often include heron or other egret species.

Best place to see them: Throughout Everglades National Park, along Alligator Alley, and sometimes even on the fringes of Greater Fort Lauderdale.

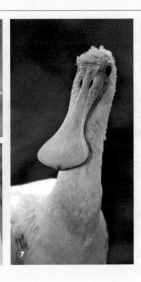

❺ Greater Flamingo

Flocking together and using long legs and webbed feet to stir shallow waters and mud flats, color comes a couple of years after hatching from ingesting shrimplike crustaceans along with fish, fly larvae, and plankton.

Best place to see them: Try Snake Bight or Eco Pond, near Flamingo Marina.

❻ Osprey

Making a big comeback from chemical pollutant endangerment, ospreys (sometimes confused with bald eagles) are distinguished by black eyestripes down their faces. Gripping pads on feet with curved claws help them pluck fish from water.

Best place to see them: Look near water, where they're fishing for lunch in the shallow areas. Try the coasts, bays, and ponds of Everglades National Park. They also gravitate to trees. You can usually spot them from the Gulf Coast Visitor Center, or you can observe them via boating in the Ten Thousand Islands.

❼ Roseate Spoonbill

These gregarious pink-and-white birds gravitate toward mangroves, feeding on fish, insects, amphibians, and some plants. They have long, spoon-like bills, and their feathers can have a touch of red and yellow. These birds appear in the Everglades year-round.

Best place to see them: Sandy Key, southwest of Flamingo, is a spoonbill nocturnal roosting spot, but at sunrise these colorful birds head out over Eco Pond to favored day hangouts throughout Everglades National Park.

❽ Wood Stork

Recognizable by featherless heads and prominent bills, these birds submerge in water to scoop up hapless fish. They are most common in the early spring and often easiest to spot in the morning.

Best place to see them: Amid the Ten Thousand Island areas, Nine Mile Pond, Mrazek Pond, and in the mangroves at Paurotis Pond.

5

IN FOCUS THE FLORIDA EVERGLADES

● =Extremely Common ● =Very Common ● =Somewhat Common ● =Rare

THE BEST EVERGLADES ACTIVITIES

HIKING

Top experiences: At Big Cypress National Preserve, you can hike along designated trails or push through unmarked acreage. (Conditions vary seasonally, which means you could be tramping through waist-deep waters.) Trailheads for the Florida National Scenic Trail are at Loop Road off U.S. 41 and Alligator Alley at mile marker 63.

What will I see? Dwarf cypress, hardwood hammocks, prairies, birds, and other wildlife.

For a short visit: A 6.5-mi section from Loop Road to U.S. 41 crosses Robert's Lake Strand, providing a satisfying sense of being out in the middle nowhere.

With more time: A 28-mi stretch from U.S. 41 to I–75 (Alligator Alley) reveals assorted habitats, including hardwood hammocks, pinelands, prairie, and cypress.

Want a tour? Big Cypress ranger-led exploration starts from the Oasis Visitor Center, late November through mid-April.

WALKING

Top experiences: Everglades National Park magnets: wheelchair accessible walkways at Anhinga Trail, Gumbo Limbo Trail, Pahayokee Overlook, Mahogany Hammock, and West Lake Trail.

What will I see? Birds and alligators at Anhinga; tropical hardwood hammock at Gumbo Limbo; an overlook of the River of Grass from Pahayokee's tower; a subtropical tree island with massive mahogany growth along Mahogany Hammock; and a forest of mangrove trees on West Lake Trail.

For a short visit: Flamingo's Eco Pond provides for waterside wildlife viewing.

With more time: Shark Valley lets you combine the quarter-mile Bobcat Boardwalk (looping through sawgrass prairie and a bayhead) with the 1-mi-long round-trip Otter Cave, allowing you to steep in subtropical hardwood hammock.

Want a tour? Pahayokee and Flamingo feature informative ranger-led walks.

The Anhinga Trail near the Royal Palm Visitor Center at Everglades National Park

BOATING

Top experiences: Launch a boat from the Gulf Coast Visitors Center or Flamingo Marina. Bring your own watercraft or rent canoes or skiffs at either location.

What will I see? Birds from bald eagles to roseate spoonbills, plus plenty of mangrove and wildlife—and maybe even some baby alligators with yellow stripes.

For a short visit: Canoe adventurers often head for Hells Bay, a 3-mi stretch about 9 mi north of Flamingo. Or put in at the Turner River alongside the Tamiami Trail in the Big Cypress National Preserve and paddle all the way (about eight hours) to Chocoloskee Bay at Everglades City.

With more time: Head out amid the Ten Thousand Islands and lose yourself in territory once exclusively the domain of only the hardiest pioneers and American Indians. If you've got a week or more for paddling, the 99-mi Wilderness Waterway stretches from Flamingo to Everglades City.

Want a tour? Sign on for narrated boat tours at the Gulf Coast or Flamingo visitor center.

BIRD WATCHING

Top experiences: Anhinga Trail, passing over Taylor Slough.

What will I see? Anhinga and heron sightings are a nearly sure thing, especially in early morning or late afternoon. Also, alligators can be seen from the boardwalk.

For a short visit: Even if you're traveling coast to coast at higher speeds via Alligator Alley, chances are you'll spot winged wonders like egrets, osprey, and heron.

With more time: Since bird-watching at Flamingo can be a special treat early in the morning or late in the afternoon, try camping overnight even if you're not one for roughing it. Reservations are recommended. (Flamingo Lodge remains under reconstruction from 2005 hurricane damage.)

Want a tour? Ranger-led walks at Pahayokee and from Everglades National Park visitor centers provide solid birding background for novices.

(top left) Tourists cruise the Everglades by airboat; (bottom left) Green Heron; (right) Eastern Meadowlark

THE BEST EVERGLADES ACTIVITIES

BIKING

Top experiences: Shark Valley (where bicycling is allowed on the tram road) is great for taking in the quiet beauty of the Everglades. Near Ernest F. Coe Visitor Center, Long Pine Key's 14-mi nature trail also can be a way to bike happily away from folks on foot.

What will I see? At Shark Valley, wading birds, turtles, and, probably alligators. At Long Pine Key, shady pinewood with subtropical plants and exposed limestone bedrock.

For a short visit: Bike on Shark Valley tram road but turn around to fit time schedule.

With more time: Go the entire 15-mi tram road route, which has no shortcuts. Or try the 22-mi route of Old Ingraham Highway near the Royal Palm Visitor Center, featuring mangrove, sawgrass, and birds (including hawks).

Want a tour? In Big Cypress National Preserve, Bear Island Bike Rides (8 mi round-trip over four to five hours) happen on certain Saturdays.

SNORKELING

Top experiences: Biscayne National Park, where clear waters incorporate the northernmost islands of the Florida Keys.

What will I see? Dense mangrove swamp covering the park shoreline, and, in shallow waters, a living coral reef and tropical fish in assorted colors.

For a short visit: Pick a sunny day to optimize your snorkeling fun, and be sure to use sunscreen.

With more time: Advanced snorkel tours head out from the park on weekends to the bay, finger channels, and around shorelines of the barrier islands. Biscayne National Park also has canoe and kayak rentals, picnic facilities, walking trails, fishing, and camping.

Want a tour? You can swim and snorkel or stay dry and picnic aboard tour boats that depart from Biscayne National Park's visitor center.

(top left) Biking near the Shark Valley Visitor Area. (top right) Snorkeling on the surface in the Atlantic Ocean.

DID YOU KNOW?

You can tell you're looking at a crocodile if you can see its lower teeth protruding when its jaws are shut, whereas an alligator shows no teeth when his mouth is closed. Gators are much darker in color—a grayish black—compared with the lighter tan color of crocodiles. Alligators' snouts are also much broader than their long, thin crocodilian counterparts.

THE STORY OF THE EVERGLADES

Dreams of draining southern Florida took hold in the early 1800s, expanding in the early 1900s to convert large tracts from wetlands to agricultural acreage. By the 1920s, towns like Fort Lauderdale and Miami boomed, and the sugar indus-try—which came to be known as "Big Sugar"—established its first sugar mills. In 1947 Everglades National Park opened as a refuge for wildlife.

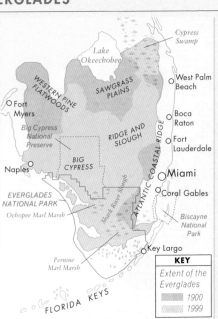

Cypress Swamp

Lake Okeechobee

WESTERN PINE FLATWOODS

SAWGRASS PLAINS

West Palm Beach

Fort Myers

Boca Raton

Big Cypress National Preserve

RIDGE AND SLOUGH

Fort Lauderdale

BIG CYPRESS

Naples

Miami

Coral Gables

EVERGLADES NATIONAL PARK

Ochopee Marl Marsh

ATLANTIC COASTAL RIDGE

Shark River Slough

Biscayne National Park

Key Largo

Pernine Marl Marsh

FLORIDA KEYS

KEY

Extent of the Everglades

1900

1999

Meanwhile, the sugar industry grew. In its infancy, about 175,000 tons of raw sugar per year was produced from fields totaling about 50,000 acres. But once the U.S. embargo stopped sugar imports from Cuba in 1960 and laws restricting acreage were lifted, Big Sugar took off. Less than five years later, the industry produced 572,000 tons of sugar and occupied nearly a quarter of a million acres.

Fast-forward to 2008, to what was hailed as the biggest conservation deal in U.S. history since the creation of the national parks. A trailblazing restora-tion strategy hinged on creating a water flow-way between Lake Okeechobee and the Everglades by buying up and flooding 187,000 acres of land. The country's largest producers of cane sugar agreed to sell the necessary 187,000 acres to the state of Florida for $1.75 billion. Environmentalists cheered.

But within months, news broke of a scaled-back land acquisition plan: $1.34 billion to buy 180,000 acres. By spring 2009, the restoration plan had shrunk to $536,000 to buy 73,000 acres. With the purchase still in limbo, critics claim the state might overpay for acreage appraised at pre-recession values and proponents fear dwindling revenues may derail the plan altogether.

The Big Sugar land deal is part of a larger effort to preserve the Everglades. In 2010, two separate lawsuits charged the state, along with the United States Environmental Protection Agency, with stalling Everglades cleanup that was supposed to begin in 2006. "Glacial delay" is how one judge put it. The state must reduce phosphorus levels in water that flows to the Everglades or face fines and sanctions for violating the federal Clean Water Act. The fate of the Ever-glades remains in the balance.

THE EVERGLADES PLANNER

WHEN TO GO

5

Updated by
Lynne Helm

Winter is the best, and busiest time to visit the Everglades. Temperatures and mosquito activity are more tolerable, low water levels concentrate the resident wildlife, and migratory birds swell the avian population. In late spring the weather turns hot and rainy, and tours and facilities are less crowded. Migratory birds depart, and you must look harder to see wildlife. Summer brings intense sun and afternoon rainstorms. Water levels rise and mosquitoes descend, making outdoor activity virtually unbearable, unless you swath yourself in netting. Mosquito repellent is a necessity any time of year.

FLYING IN

Miami International Airport (MIA) is 34 mi from Homestead and 47 mi from the eastern access to Everglades National Park. ⇨ *For MIA airline carrier information, refer to the Miami chapter.* Shuttles run between MIA and Homestead. Southwest Florida International Airport (RSW) in Fort Myers, a little over an hour's drive from Everglades City, is the closest major airport to the Everglades's western access. On-demand taxi transportation from the airport to Everglades City is available, and costs $150 for up to three passengers ($10 each for additional passengers).

ABOUT THE RESTAURANTS

Dining in the Everglades area centers on mom-and-pop places that serve hearty home-style food, and small eateries that specialize in fresh local fare: alligator, fish, stone crab, frogs' legs, and Florida lobster from the Keys. American Indian restaurants serve local favorites as well as catfish, Indian fry bread (a flour-and-water flatbread), and pumpkin bread. A growing Hispanic population around Homestead means plenty of authentic, inexpensive Latin cuisine, with an emphasis on Cuban and Mexican dishes. Restaurants in Everglades City, especially those along the river, have fresh seafood, particularly succulent, sustainable stone crab. These places are mostly casual to the point of rustic, and are often closed in late summer or fall. For finer dining, go to Marco Island or Naples.

ABOUT THE HOTELS

Accommodations near the parks range from inexpensive to moderate and offer off-season rates in summer, when rampant mosquito populations preclude spending much time outdoors, especially at dusk. If you're spending several days exploring the east coast Everglades, stay in one of the park's campgrounds; 11 mi away in Homestead–Florida City, where there are reasonably priced motels and RV parks; or in the Florida Keys or the Greater Miami–Fort Lauderdale area. Lodgings and campgrounds are also available on the Gulf Coast in Everglades City, Marco Island, and Naples, which has the most upscale accommodations in the area. Florida City's selection is mostly of the chain variety and geared toward business travelers.

WHAT IT COSTS					
	¢	$	$$	$$$	$$$$
Restaurants	under $10	$10–$15	$15–$20	$20–$30	over $30
Hotels	under $80	$80–$100	$100–$140	$140–$220	over $220

Restaurant prices are per person for a main course at dinner. Hotel prices are for a standard double room, excluding 6% sales tax (more in some counties) and 1%–5% tourist tax.

EVERGLADES NATIONAL PARK

More than 1.5 million acres of South Florida's 4.3 million acres of subtropical, watery wilderness were given national-park status and protection in 1947 with the creation of Everglades National Park. It is one of the country's largest national parks and is recognized by the world community as a Wetland of International Importance, an International Biosphere Reserve, and a World Heritage Site. Come here if you want to spend the day biking, hiking, or boating in deep, raw wilderness with lots of wildlife.

BISCAYNE NATIONAL PARK

To the east of Everglades National Park, Biscayne National Park brings forth a pristine, magical, subtropical Florida. It is the nation's largest marine park and the largest national park within the continental United States boasting living coral reefs. A small portion of the park's 172,000 acres consists of mainland coast and outlying islands, but 95% remains under water. Of particular interest are the mangroves and their tangled masses of stiltlike roots that thicken the shorelines. These "walking trees," as some locals call them, have curved prop roots, which arch down from the trunk, and aerial roots that drop from branches. The trees draw freshwater from saltwater and create a coastal nursery that sustains myriad types of marine life. You can see Miami's high-rise buildings from many of Biscayne's 44 islands, but the park is virtually undeveloped and large enough for escaping everything that Miami and the Upper Keys have become. To truly escape, don scuba diving or snorkeling gear, and lose yourself in the wonders of the coral reefs.

BIG CYPRESS NATIONAL PRESERVE

On the northern edge of Everglades National Park is Big Cypress National Preserve, one of South Florida's least-developed watersheds. Established by Congress in 1974 to protect the Everglades, it comprises extensive tracts of prairie, marsh, pinelands, forested swamps, and sloughs. Hunting is allowed, as is off-road-vehicle use. Come here if you like alligators. Stop at the Oasis Visitor Center to walk the boardwalk with alligators lounging underneath and then drive Loop Road for a backwoods experience. If time permits, kayak the Turner River. ■TIP→ Many activities in the parks and preserve are based on water, so be prepared to get a bit damp on the marshy trails.

NEARBY TOWNS

Surrounding the parks and preserve are several small communities: Everglades City, Florida City, and Homestead, home to many area outfitters.

⇨ *While outfitters are listed with the parks and preserve, see our What's Nearby section later in this chapter for information about each town.*

CAMPING IN THE EVERGLADES

For an intense stay in the "real" Florida, consider one of some four-dozen backcountry campsites deep in Everglades National Park, many inland, some on the beach. You'll have to carry in your food, water, and supplies, and carry out all your trash. You'll also need a site-specific permit, available on a first-come, first-served basis from the Flamingo or Gulf Coast visitors centers. Permits cost $10, plus $2 per person per night for sites, with a 14-night limit, and are only issued up to 24 hours in advance. Front-country camping fees at park campgrounds are $16 per night.

EVERGLADES NATIONAL PARK

45 mi southwest of Miami International Airport.

If you're heading across South Florida on U.S. 41 from Miami to Naples, you'll breeze right through the Everglades. Also known as Tamiami Trail, this mostly two-lane road along much of the route skirts the edge of Everglades National Park and cuts across the Big Cypress National Preserve. You'll also be near the park if you're en route from Miami to the Florida Keys on U.S. 1, which travels through Homestead and Florida City, two communities east of the main park entrance. Basically, if you're in South Florida you can't get away from at least fringes of the Everglades. With tourist strongholds like Miami, Naples, and the Florida Keys so close by, travelers from all over the world typically make day trips to the park.

Everglades National Park has three main entry points: the park headquarters at Ernest F. Coe Visitor Center, southwest of Homestead and Florida City; the Shark Valley area, in the northern reaches and accessed by Tamiami Trail (U.S. 41); and the Gulf Coast Visitor Center, just south of Everglades City to the west and closest to Naples.

You can explore on your own or participate in free ranger-led hikes, bicycle tours, bird-watching tours, and canoe trips; the number and variety of these excursions are greatest from mid-December through Easter, and some excursions (canoe trips, for instance) typically aren't offered in the sweltering summer. Among the more popular are the Anhinga Amble, a 50-minute walk around the Taylor Slough (departs from the Royal Palm Visitor Center), and the Early Bird Special, a 90-minute walk centered on birdlife (departs from Flamingo Visitor Center at 7:30 am). Ask at the visitor centers for details.

PARK ESSENTIALS

Admission Fees $10 per vehicle, $5 per pedestrian, bicycle, or motorcycle. Admission, payable at gates, is good for seven consecutive days at all park entrances. Annual passes are $25.

Admission Hours The park is open daily, year-round, and both the main entrance near Florida City and Homestead, and the Gulf Coast entrance are open 24 hours. The Shark Valley entrance is open 8:30 am to 6 pm.

COE VISITOR CENTER TO FLAMINGO

About 30 mi from Miami.

The most popular access to Everglades National Park is via the park headquarters entrance just southwest of Homestead and Florida City. If you're coming to the Everglades from Miami, the highway you'll take is Route 836 west to Route 826/874 south to the Homestead Extension of Florida's Turnpike, U.S. 1, and Krome Avenue (Route 997/old U.S. 27). To reach the Ernest F. Coe Visitor Center from Homestead, go right (west) from U.S. 1 or Krome Avenue onto Route 9336 (Florida's only four-digit route) in Florida City and follow signs to the park entrance.

EXPLORING

To explore this section of the park, follow Route 9336 from the park entrance to Flamingo; there are many opportunities to stop along the way, and an assortment of activities to pursue in the Flamingo area. The following is arranged in geographic order.

Ernest F. Coe Visitor Center. Don't just grab your park map and go; this visitor center's numerous interactive exhibits and films are well worth your time. The 15-minute film *River of Life*, updated frequently, provides a succinct park overview with emphasis on the river of grass. There is also a movie on hurricanes and a 35-minute wildlife film for children available upon request. A bank of telephones offers differing viewpoints on the Great Water Debate, detailing how last century's gung ho draining of swampland for residential and agricultural development also cut off water-supply routes for precious wetlands in the Everglades ecosystem. Here you'll also find a schedule of daily ranger-led activities, mainly walks and talks, and information on canoe rentals and boat tours at Flamingo. The Everglades Discovery Shop stocks books and jewelry including bird-oriented earrings, and you can browse through cool nature, science, and kids' stuff or pick up extra insect repellent. Coe Visitor Center, which has restrooms, is outside park gates, so you can stop in without paying park admission. ⊠ *11 mi southwest of Homestead at 40001 State Rd. 9336* ☎ *305/242–7700* ☾ *Daily 8–4:30; hrs sometimes shortened in off-season.*

Main road to Flamingo. Route 9336 travels 38 mi from the Ernest F. Coe Visitor Center southwest to the Florida Bay at Flamingo. It crosses a section of the park's eight distinct ecosystems: hardwood hammock, freshwater prairie, pinelands, freshwater slough, cypress, coastal prairie, mangrove, and marine-estuarine. Route highlights include a dwarf cypress forest, the transition zone between saw grass and mangrove forest, and a wealth of wading birds at Mrazek and Coot Bay ponds—where in early morning or late afternoon you can observe the hundreds of birds feeding. Boardwalks, looped trails, several short spurs, and observation platforms help you stay dry. You also may want to stop along the way to walk several short trails (each takes about 30 minutes): the popular, wheelchair-accessible **Anhinga Trail**, which cuts through saw grass marsh and allows you to see lots of wildlife (be on the lookout for alligators and the trail's namesake, water birds known as anhingas); and junglelike—yet, also wheelchair-accessible—**Gumbo-Limbo Trail**; the **Pinelands Trail,** where you can see the limestone bedrock that underlies the park; the **Pahayokee Overlook Trail,** which ends at an observation tower; and the **Mahogany Hammock Trail** with its dense growth.

■**TIP**➔ Before you head out on the trails, inquire about insect and weather conditions and plan accordingly, stocking up on bug repellent, sunscreen, and water as necessary. Also, even on seemingly nice days, it's probably smart to bring along rain gear.

★ **Royal Palm Visitor Center.** A must for anyone wanting to experience the real Everglades, and ideal for when there's limited time, this small center with a bookstore and vending machines permits access to the **Anhinga Trail boardwalk,** where in winter catching sight of alligators congregating in watering holes is almost guaranteed. Or follow the neighboring **Gumbo Limbo Trail** through a hardwood hammock. Both strolls are short (½ mi) and expose you to two Everglades ecosystems. Rangers conduct daily Anhinga Ambles in season (check for dates by calling ahead) starting at 10:30. At 1:30 the Glades Glimpse program takes place daily in season. Ask also about starlight walks and bike tours in season. ⊠ *4 mi west of Ernest F. Coe Visitor Center on Rte. 9336* ☎ *305/242–7700* ☾ *Daily 8–4:15.*

NEED A BREAK?

Good spots to pull over for a picnic lunch are **Paurotis Pond,** about 10 mi north of Florida Bay, or **Nine Mile Pond,** less than 30 mi from the main visitor center. Another option is along **Bear Lake,** 2 mi north of the Flamingo Visitor Center.

Flamingo. At the far end of the main road to Flamingo lies this community along Florida Bay, where you'll find a marina, visitor center, and campground, with nearby hiking and nature trails. Before hurricanes Katrina and Wilma washed them away in 2005, a lodge, cabins, and restaurants in Flamingo provided Everglades National Park's only accommodations. At press time, the rebuilding of Flamingo Lodge was projected to materialize sometime after 2012 (and has been for quite some time), but for now, you can still pitch a tent or bring an RV to the campground, where improvements include solar-hot-water showers and electricity for RV sites. A popular houseboat rental concession returned in December 2010. The 35-foot floating homes sleep six and are equipped with a shower, a toilet, bedding, pots, flatware, a stereo, and depth finder. Houseboats (thankfully air-conditioned) with 60-horsepower outboards rent for $350 per night, plus fuel.

Flamingo Visitor Center. Check the schedule here for ranger-led activities, such as naturalist discussions, hikes along area trails, and evening programs in the 100-seat campground amphitheater, which replaced the old gathering spot destroyed by hurricanes in 2005. Also, find natural history exhibits and pamphlets on canoe, hiking, and biking trails in the small Florida Bay Flamingo Museum on the 2nd floor of the visitor center. ⊠ *1 Flamingo Lodge Hwy., Flamingo* ☎ *239/695–2945, 239/695–3101 marina* ☉ *Exhibits are always open, staffed mid-Nov.– mid-Apr., daily 8–4:30.*

SPORTS AND THE OUTDOORS

BIRDING
Some of the park's best birding is in the Flamingo area.

BOATING
The 99-mi inland **Wilderness Trail** between Flamingo and Everglades City is open to motorboats as well as canoes, although, depending on the water level, powerboats may have trouble navigating the route above Whitewater Bay. Flat-water canoeing and kayaking are best in winter, when temperatures are moderate, rainfall diminishes, and mosquitoes back off—a little, anyway. You don't need a permit for day trips, although there is a seven-day, $5 launch fee for all motorized boats brought into the park. The Flamingo area has well-marked canoe trails, but be sure to tell someone where you're going and when you expect to return. Getting lost is easy, and spending the night without proper gear can be unpleasant, if not dangerous.

OUTFITTER **Flamingo Lodge, Marina, and Everglades National Park Tours.** The official Everglades National Park concessionaire runs tours and operates a marina. The 1.75-hour backcountry *Pelican* cruise ($26.50) winds through the water under a heavy canopy of mangroves, revealing abundant wildlife—from alligators, crocodiles, and turtles to herons, hawks, and egrets. A second boat, *Sawgrass*, follows the same route in peak season (November–April). Flamingo Marina charters boats, and rents 17-foot power skiffs from 7 am for $195 per day (eight hours, if returned by 4 pm), $150 per half day, $80 for two hours. Canoes for up to three paddlers rent for $16 for two hours (minimum), $22 for four hours, and $40 overnight. Family canoes for up to four rent for $20 for two hours (minimum), $30 for four hours, $40 for eight hours, and $50 for 24 hours. Two-person charter fishing trips can be arranged for weekends ($350 for a half day or $450 a day; each additional person pays $25). Cost includes tackle, ice, and license. The concessionaire also rents bikes, binoculars, rods, reels, and other equipment by the half and full day. Feeling sticky after a day in the 'Glades? Hot showers are $3. The Flamingo Lodge, a victim of massive hurricane damage in 2005, remains closed pending funding for a fresh start. ⊠ *1 Flamingo Lodge Hwy., on Buttonwood Canal, Flamingo* ☎ *239/695–3101.*

> ### GOOD READS
>
> ■ *The Everglades: River of Grass.* This circa-1947 classic by pioneering conservationist Marjory Stoneman Douglas (1890–1998) is a must-read.
>
> ■ *Everglades Wildguide.* Jean Craighead George gives an informative account of the park's natural history in this official National Park Service handbook.
>
> ■ *Everglades: The Park Story.* Wildlife biologist William B. Robertson Jr. presents the park's flora, fauna, and history.

WHERE TO CAMP

For expanded campground reviews, visit Fodors.com.

■ **TIP→** In the dry winter season, be careful with campfires and matches; this is when the wildfire-prone saw grass prairies and pinelands are most vulnerable.

★ 🏕 **Flamingo.** This campground has 234 drive-in sites; 55 have a water view, and nine of 64 walk-in sites are along water. *Flush toilets, dump station, drinking water, showers, general store ⤳ 234 drive-up sites, 64 walk-in sites* ☎ *877/444–6777 campsite reservations, 305/242–7700 park information, 239/695–0124 camping information* ⊕ *www.recreation.gov.*

¢ 🏕 **Long Pine Key.** About 6 mi west of the park's main entrance, Long Pine Key has drive-up sites for tents and RVs, several area hiking trails, and a pond for fishing (permit required). *Flush toilets, dump station, drinking water, picnic tables ⤳ 108 drive-up sites* ☎ *305/242–7700* ⊕ *www.nps.gov/ever.*

GULF COAST ENTRANCE

To reach the park's western gateway, take U.S. 41 west from Miami for 77 mi, turn left (south) onto Route 29, and travel another 3 mi through Everglades City to the Gulf Coast Ranger Station. From Naples on the Gulf Coast, take U.S. 41 east for 35 mi, then turn right onto Route 29.

Gulf Coast Visitor Center. The best place to bone up on Everglades National Park's watery western side is at this visitor center just south of Everglades City, where rangers are on hand to answer any of your questions. In winter, canoeists check in here for trips to the Ten Thousand Islands and 99-mi Wilderness Waterway Trail, nature lovers view interpretive exhibits on local flora and fauna while waiting for naturalist-led boat trip departures, and backcountry campers purchase permits. In season (Christmas through Easter), rangers lead bike tours and canoe trips. No direct roads run from here to other sections of the

Much skill is required to navigate boats through the shallow, muddy waters of the Everglades.

park, and admission is free only to this section of the park. ✉ *Rte. 29, Everglades City* ☎ *239/695–3311* ✆ *Mid-Nov.–mid-Apr., daily 8–4:30; mid-Apr.–mid-Nov., daily 9–4:30.*

OUTFITTERS

Everglades National Park Boat Tours. Operating in conjunction with boat tours at Flamingo, this company runs 1½-hour trips ($26.50) through the Ten Thousand Islands National Wildlife Refuge. Adventure-seekers often see dolphins, manatees, bald eagles, and roseate spoonbills. In peak season (November–April), 49-passenger boats run on the hour and half-hour daily. Mangrove wilderness tours are also conducted on smaller boats for up to six passengers. These one-hour, 45-minute trips ($35) are the best option to see alligators. The outfitter also rents canoes. ✉ *Gulf Coast Visitor Center, Everglades City* ☎ *239/695–2591 or 866/628–7275* ⊕ *evergladesnationalparkboattoursflamingo.com/index.php.*

Fodor's Choice **Everglades Rentals & Eco Adventures.** Inside the Ivey House Inn there is an
★ established, year-round source for canoes, sea kayaks, and guided Everglades paddling tours. Canoe rentals cost $35 the first day, $27 for each day thereafter. Day-long kayak rentals are from $65. All half-day rentals are from 1 to 5 pm. Shuttles deliver you to major launching areas such as Turner River ($30 for up to two people) and Collier-Seminole State Park ($60). Tour highlights include bird and gator sightings, mangrove forests, no-man's-land beaches, relics of hideouts for infamous and just-plain-reclusive characters, and spectacular sunsets. Longer adventures ($859 for two nights to $1,439 for six nights, per person with a two-person minimum) include canoe/kayak and equipment rental,

all necessary camping equipment, a guide, and meals. ✉ *Ivey House, 107 Camellia St., Everglades City* ⌂ *Box 5038, Everglades City 34139* ☎ *877/567–0679 or 239/695–3299* ⊕ *www.evergladesadventures.com.*

SHARK VALLEY

23½ mi west of Florida's Turnpike, off Tamiami Trail. Approximately 45 minutes west of Miami.

One thing you won't see at Shark Valley is sharks. The name comes from the Shark River, also called the River of Grass, which flows through the area. Several species of shark swim up this river from the coast (about 45 mi south of Shark Valley) to give birth. Young sharks (called pups), vulnerable to being eaten by adult sharks and other predators, gain strength in waters of the slough before heading out to sea to fend for themselves.

EXPLORING

Though Shark Valley is the national park's north entrance, no roads here lead directly to other parts of the park. However, it's still worth stopping here to take a tram tour. Be sure to stop at the halfway point and ascend to the top of the observation tower via a ramp.

Prefer to do the trail on foot? It takes a bit of nerve to walk the paved 15-mi loop in Shark Valley because in the winter months alligators lie on and alongside the road, basking in the sun—most, however, do move quickly out of the way.

You also can ride a bicycle (the outfitter here rents one-speed, well-used bikes daily 8:30–4 for $7 per hour) or take a two-hour guided tram tour (reservations recommended in winter). Just behind the bike-rental area a short boardwalk trail meanders through the saw grass, and another one passes through a tropical hardwood hammock. An underwater live camera in the canal behind the center (viewed from the gift shop) lets visitors sporadically see the alligators and otters.

Observation Tower. At the Shark Valley trail's end (really, the halfway point of the 15-mi loop), you can pause to navigate this tower, first built in 1984, spiraling 50 feet upward. Once on top, the River of Grass gloriously spreads out as far as your eye can see. Observe water birds as well as alligators, and perhaps even river otters crossing the road. The tower has a wheelchair-accessible ramp to the top.

Shark Valley Visitor Center. The small center has rotating exhibits, a bookstore, and park rangers ready for your questions. ✉ *23½ mi west of Florida's Turnpike, off Tamiami Trail* ☎ *305/221–8776* ☽ *Late Mar.– late Dec., daily 9:15–5:15; late Dec.–late Mar., daily 8:45–5:15; gate daily 8:30–6.*

TOURS

★ **Shark Valley Tram Tours.** Starting at the Shark Valley visitor center, two-hour, narrated tours ($18.25) follow a 15-mi loop road—especially good for viewing gators—into the interior, stopping at a 50-foot observation tower. Reservations are recommended December through April. ✉ *Valley Visitor Center* ☎ *305/221–8455* ⊕ *www.sharkvalleytramtours.com.*

com ✉ *$16.25 per person* ☉ *Tours Dec.–Apr., hourly 9–4; May–Nov., hourly 9–3.*

SPORTS AND THE OUTDOORS

BOATING

Many Everglades-area tours operate only in season, roughly November through April.

Buffalo Tiger's Airboat Tours. A former chief of Florida's Miccosukee tribe operates this Shark Valley area company. Though at 90 (or so) years old he no longer skippers the boat, the chief still gets out to

meet and greet customers when he can. Guides narrate the trip to an old Indian camp on the north side of Tamiami Trail from the American Indian perspective. Don't worry about airboat noise, since guides shut down the engines during informative talks. The 45-minute round-trip tours go 10–5 Saturday through Thursday and cost $30 per person for two, $20 per person for more than two, up to 12 people. Reservations are not required, but cash is—no credit cards accepted. ✉ *29708 S.W. 8th St., Miami, 5 mi east of Shark Valley, 25 mi west of Florida's Turnpike* ☎ *305/559–5250* ⊕ *www.buffalotigersairboattours.com.*

BIG CYPRESS NATIONAL PRESERVE

Through the 1950s and early 1960s the world's largest cypress-logging industry prospered in Big Cypress Swamp. As the industry died out, the government began buying parcels. Today, more than 729,000 acres, or nearly half of the swamp, form this national preserve. The word "big" refers not to the size of the trees but to the swamp, which juts into the north edge of Everglades National Park like a jigsaw-puzzle piece. Size and strategic location make Big Cypress an important link in the region's hydrological system, where rainwater first flows through the preserve, then south into the park, and eventually into Florida Bay. Its variegated pattern of wet prairies, ponds, marshes, sloughs, and strands provides a wildlife sanctuary, and thanks to a policy of balanced land use—"use without abuse"—the watery wilderness is devoted to recreation as well as research and preservation.

The preserve allows—in limited areas—hiking, hunting, and off-road-vehicle (airboat, swamp buggy, four-wheel-drive vehicles) use by permit. Compared with Everglades National Park, the preserve is less developed and hosts fewer visitors. That makes it ideal for naturalists, birders, and hikers who prefer to see more wildlife than humans.

Several scenic drives link from Tamiami Trail; some require four-wheel-drive vehicles, especially in wet summer months. A few lead to camping areas, and roadside picnic areas.

PARK ESSENTIALS

Admission Fees There is no admission fee to visit the preserve.

Admission Hours The park is open daily, year-round. Accessible only by boat, Adams Key is for day use only.

Contact Information Big Cypress National Preserve (⊞ *HCR 61, Box 11, Ochopee 34141* ☎ *239/695–1201* ⊕ *www.nps.gov/bicy*).

EXPLORING

Oasis Visitor Center. The big attraction here is the observation deck where you can view huge gators as well as fish, birds, and other wildlife. There's also a small butterfly garden where native plants seasonally attract winged wonders. Inside the information center you'll find a small exhibit area, a bookshop, and a theater that shows a dated but informative 15-minute film on the Big Cypress Preserve swamplands. ⊠ *24 mi east of Everglades City, 50 mi west of Miami, 20 mi west of Shark Valley* ☎ *239/695–1201* ⊕ *Free* ⊗ *Daily 9–4:30.*

Ochopee Post Office. This former irrigation pipe shed, on the south side of Tamiami Trail, is North America's smallest post office. Don't blink or you'll miss it. To help keep this picturesque outpost in business during times of governmental cutbacks and layoffs, buy a postcard of the one-room shack, and mail it to someone who would appreciate such a rustic spot. ⊠ *4 mi east of Rte. 29, at 38000 E. Tamiami Trail, Ochopee* ☎ *239/695–2099* ⊗ *Weekdays 10–noon and 1–4:30, Sat. 10–11:30.*

RANGER PROGRAMS

From the Oasis Visitor Center you can get in on one of the seasonal ranger-led or self-guided activities, such as campfire and wildlife talks, hikes, slough slogs, and canoe excursions. The 8-mi Turner River Canoe Trail begins nearby and crosses through Everglades National Park before ending in Chokoloskee Bay, near Everglades City. Rangers lead four-hour canoe trips and two-hour swamp walks in season; call for days and times. Bring shoes and long pants for the swamp walks and be prepared to wade at least knee-deep in water. Ranger program reservations are accepted up to 14 days in advance.

SPORTS AND THE OUTDOORS

There are three types of trails—walking (including part of the extensive Florida National Scenic Trail), canoeing, and bicycling. All three trail types are easily accessed from the Tamiami Trail near the preserve visitor center, and one boardwalk trail departs from the center. Canoe and bike equipment can be rented from outfitters in Everglades City, 24 mi west, and Naples, 40 mi west.

Hikers can tackle the Florida National Scenic Trail, which begins in the preserve and is divided into segments 6.5 to 28 mi each. Two 5-mi trails, Concho Billy and Fire Prairie, can be accessed off Turner River Road, a few miles east. Turner River Road and Birdon Road form a 17-mi gravel loop drive that's excellent for birding. Bear Island has about 32 mi of scenic, flat, looped trails that are ideal for bicycling. Most trails are hard-packed lime rock, but a few miles are gravel. Cyclists share the road with off-road vehicles, most plentiful from mid-November through December.

To see the best variety of wildlife from your car, follow 26-mi Loop Road, south of U.S. 41 and west of Shark Valley, where alligators, raccoons, and soft-shell turtles crawl around beside the gravel road, often swooped upon by swallowtail kites and brown-shouldered hawks. Stop at H. P. Williams Roadside Park, west of the Oasis, and walk along the boardwalk to spy gators, turtles, and garfish in the river waters.

WHERE TO CAMP

For expanded campground reviews, visit Fodors.com. For lodging options in the area, see the Where to Stay sections under each town in What's Nearby, later in this chapter.

ȼ   △ **Big Cypress National Preserve.** There are four no-fee primitive campgrounds within the preserve along Tamiami Trail and Loop Road, including Burns Lake, Bear Island, Pinecrest, and Mitchell's Landing. *Flush toilets, dump station, showers* ⤳ *40 sites at Burns Lake; 40 sites at Bear Island; 10 sites at Pinecrest; 15 sites at Mitchell's Landing; 10 tent, 26 RV sites at Monument Lake; 10 tent, 26 RV sites at Midway* ⊠ *Tamiami Trail (Hwy. 41), between Miami and Naples* ⓓ *HCR 61, Box 110, Ochopee 34141* ☎ *239/695–1201* ▭ *No credit cards.*

ȼ   △ **Trail Lakes Campground.** Close to Everglades City and Big Cypress National Preserve, Trail Lakes spreads out over 30 acres, is near a canoe launch, and has the added attraction of a nature park and wildlife exhibits. *Flush toilets, drinking water, electricity, public telephone, general store* ⤳ *80 RV sites, 25 tent sites* ⊠ *40904 E. Tamiami Trail (Hwy. 41), Ochopee* ☎ *239/695–2275* ⊕ *www.skunkape.info.*

BISCAYNE NATIONAL PARK

Occupying 172,000 acres along the southern portion of Biscayne Bay, south of Miami and north of the Florida Keys, this national park is 95% submerged, and its altitude ranges from 4 feet above sea level to 60 feet below. Contained within from shore to sea are four distinct zones: mangrove forest along the coast, Biscayne Bay, the undeveloped upper Florida Keys, and coral reefs. Mangroves line the mainland shore much as they do elsewhere along South Florida's protected bay waters. Biscayne Bay functions as a lobster sanctuary and a nursery for fish, sponges, and crabs. Manatees and sea turtles frequent its warm shallow waters.

GETTING HERE

To reach Biscayne National Park from Homestead, take Krome Avenue to Route 9336 (Palm Drive) and turn east. Follow Palm Drive for about 8 mi until it becomes S.W. 344th Street and follow signs to park headquarters in Convoy Point. The entry is 9 mi east of Homestead and 9 mi south and east of Exit 6 (Speedway Boulevard/S.W. 137th Avenue) off Florida's Turnpike.

PARK ESSENTIALS

Admission Fees There is no fee to enter Biscayne National Park, and you don't pay a fee to access the islands, but there is a $20 overnight camping fee that includes a $5 dock fee to berth vessels at some island docks. The park concessionaire charges for trips to the coral reefs and the islands (⇨ *see Outfitters and Expeditions*).

Admission Hours The park is open daily, year-round.

Contact Information Biscayne National Park (⌂ *Dante Fascell Visitor Center, 9700 S.W. 328th St., Homestead* ☎ *305/230–7275* ⊕ *www.nps.gov/bisc*).

EXPLORING

Biscayne is a great place if you want to dive, snorkel, canoe, camp, birdwatch, or learn about marine ecology. The best place to hike is Elliott Key (⇨ *see Islands, below*).

5

THE CORAL REEF

Biscayne's corals range from the soft, flagellant fans, plumes, and whips found chiefly in the shallower patch reefs to the hard brain corals, elkhorn, and staghorn forms that can withstand the depths and heavier wave action along the ocean's edge.

THE ISLANDS

To the east, about 8 mi off the coast, lie 44 tiny keys, stretching 18 nautical mi north–south and accessible only by boat. There's no commercial transportation between the mainland and the islands, and only a handful can be visited: Elliott, Boca Chita, Adams, and Sands keys. The rest are wildlife refuges, are too small, or have rocky shores or waters too shallow for boats. It's best to explore the Keys between December and April, when the mosquito population is less aggressive. Repellent is a must.

Adams Key. A stone's throw from the western tip of Elliott Key and 9 mi southeast of Convoy Point, the onetime site of the Cocolobo Club, a yacht club famous for once hosting presidents Harding, Hoover, Johnson, Nixon and other luminaries, is open for day use. It has picnic areas, restrooms, dockage, and a short trail that runs along the shore and through a hardwood hammock. Rangers live on-island. Access is by private boat, and no pets or overnight docking are allowed.

★ **Boca Chita Key.** Ten miles northeast of Convoy Point, this key was once owned by the late Mark C. Honeywell, former president of Honeywell Company. A ½-mi hiking trail curves around the south side of the island. Climb the 65-foot-high ornamental lighthouse (by ranger tour only) for a panoramic view of Miami or check out the cannon from the HMS *Fowey*. There's no freshwater, access is by private boat only, and no pets are allowed. Only portable toilets are on-site, and there are no sinks or showers. A $20 fee for overnight docking between 6 pm and 6 am covers a campsite; pay at the automated kiosk near the harbor. Boca Chita Key, about 12 mi south of the Cape Florida Lighthouse on Key Biscayne, is listed on the National Register of Historic Places for its 10 historic structures.

Elliott Key. The largest of the islands, 9 mi east of Convoy Point, has a mile-long loop trail on the bay side of the island at the north end of the campground. Boaters may dock at any of 36 slips, and a $20 fee for stays between 6 pm and 6 am covers a campsite. Take an informal, ranger-led nature walk or head out on your own to hike the 6-mi trail along so-called Spite Highway, a 225-foot-wide swath of green that developers mowed down in hopes of linking this key to the mainland. Luckily the federal government stepped in, and now it's a hiking trail through tropical hardwood hammock. Facilities include restrooms, picnic tables, fresh drinking water, cold (or, occasionally, lukewarm) water showers, grills, and a campground. Leashed pets are allowed in developed areas only, not on trails. A 30-foot-wide sandy shoreline about a mile north of the harbor on the west (bay) side of the key is the only one in the national park. Boaters like to anchor off it to swim. The beach, fun for families, is for day use only; it has picnic areas and a short trail that follows the shore and cuts through the hammock.

> ### BISCAYNE IN ONE DAY
>
> Most visitors come to snorkel or dive. Divers should plan to spend the morning on the water and the afternoon exploring the Convoy Point Visitor Center. The opposite is true for snorkelers, as snorkel trips (and one-tank shallow-dive trips) depart in the afternoon. If you want to hike as well, turn to the trails at Elliott Key—just be sure to apply insect repellent (and sunscreen, too, no matter what time of year).

VISITOR CENTER

★ **Dante Fascell Visitor Center.** Go outside on the wide veranda to take in views across mangroves and Biscayne Bay. Inside the museum, artistic vignettes and on-request videos including the 11-minute *Spectrum of Life* explore the park's four ecosystems, while the Touch Table gives both kids and adults a feel for bones, feathers, and coral. Facilities include the park's canoe and tour concessionaire, restrooms with showers, a ranger information area, gift shop with books, and vending machines. Various ranger programs take place daily during busy fall and winter seasons. On the second Sunday of each month from January through May, the Family Fun Fest program offers three hours of hands-on activities for kids and families. Rangers also give informal tours of Elliott and Boca Chita keys; arrange in advance. Outside are picnic tables and grills. A short trail and boardwalk lead to a jetty. This is the only area of the park accessible without a boat. ⊠ *9700 S.W. 328th St., Homestead/Convoy Point* ☎ *305/230–7275* ⊕ *www.nps.gov/bisc* ⊠ *Free* ☉ *Daily 9–4:30.*

SPORTS AND THE OUTDOORS

BIRD-WATCHING

More than 170 species of birds have been identified around the park. Expect to see flocks of brown pelicans patrolling the bay—suddenly rising, then plunging beak first to capture prey in their baggy pouches. White ibis probe exposed mud flats for small fish and crustaceans.

Although all the Keys are excellent for birding, Jones Lagoon (south of Adams Key, between Old Rhodes Key and Totten Key) is outstanding. It's approachable only by nonmotorized craft.

DIVING AND SNORKELING

Diving is great year-around, but best in summer, when calmer winds and smaller seas result in clearer waters. Ocean waters, another 3 mi east of the Keys, showcase the park's main attraction—the northernmost section of Florida's living tropical coral reefs. Some are the size of an office desk, others as large as a football field. You can take a glass-bottom-boat ride to see this underwater wonderland, but you really should snorkel or scuba dive to fully appreciate it.

A diverse population of colorful fish—angelfish, gobies, grunts, parrot fish, pork fish, wrasses, and many more—flits through the reefs. Shipwrecks from the 18th century are evidence of the area's international maritime heritage, and a Maritime Heritage Trail is being developed to link six of the major shipwreck and underwater cultural sites. Thus far, three sites, including a 19th-century wooden sailing vessel, have been plotted with GPS coordinates and marked with mooring buoys. Plastic dive cards are being developed that will contain navigational and background information.

WHERE TO CAMP

For expanded campground reviews, visit Fodors.com. For lodging options in the area, see the Where to Stay sections under each town in What's Nearby, later in this chapter.

- ⊄ ⚠ **Boca Chita Campground.** This small flat island has a grassy, waterside campground shaded by palms whispering in the breeze. *Flush toilets, picnic tables* ☁ *39 sites* ⊠ *Visitor center: 9700 S.W. 328th St., Homestead* ☎ *305/230–7275* ⊟ *No credit cards.*

- ⊄ ⚠ **Elliott Key Campground.** You'll need a private boat to get here, but grassy, beachfront tent sites with awesome views and populated with plenty of native hardwood trees make it worth the inconvenience. *Flush toilets, drinking water, showers, picnic tables, swimming (ocean)* ☁ *40 sites* ⊠ *Visitor center: 9700 S.W. 328th St., Homestead* ☎ *305/230–7275, 305/230–1100 transportation, 305/230–1144 Ext. 3074 for group campsite* ⊕ *www.nps.gov/bisc* ⊟ *No credit cards.*

WHAT'S NEARBY

EVERGLADES CITY

35 mi southeast of Naples and 83 mi west of Miami.

Aside from a chain gas station or two, Everglades City is perfect Old Florida. No high-rises (other than an observation tower) mar the landscape at this western gateway to Everglades National Park, just off the Tamiami Trail. It was developed in the late 19th century by Barron Collier, a wealthy advertising entrepreneur, who built it as a company town to house workers for his numerous projects including construction of the Tamiami Trail. It grew and prospered until the Depression and World War II. Today this ramshackle town draws adventure-seekers heading to the park for canoeing, fishing, and bird-watching excursions. Airboat tours, though popular, are banned within the preserve and park because of the environmental damage they cause to the mangroves. The Everglades Seafood Festival, going strong for nearly 40 years and held the first full weekend of February, draws crowds of up to 75,000 for delights from the sea, music, and craft displays. At quieter times, dining choices are limited to a handful of basic eateries. The town is small, fishing-oriented, and unhurried, making it excellent for boating, bicycling, or just strolling around. Pedal along the waterfront on a 2-mi ride along the strand out to Chokoloskee Island.

Visitor Information Everglades Area Chamber of Commerce (✉ *Rte. 29 and Tamiami Trail* ☎ *239/695–3172* ⊕ *www.evergladeschamber.com*).

EXPLORING

★ **Fakahatchee Strand Preserve State Park.** The ½-mi boardwalk through this linear swamp forest gives you an opportunity to see rare plants, bald cypress, nesting eagles, and North America's largest stand of native royal palms and largest concentration and variety of epiphytic orchids, including more than 30 varieties of threatened and endangered species blooming most extravagantly in hotter months. It's particularly famous for its ghost orchids (as featured in the novel *The Orchid Thief* by Susan Orlean), visible only on guided hikes. In your quest for ghost orchids, also keep a hopeful eye out for white-tailed deer, black bears, bobcats, and the Florida panther. For park nature on parade, take the 12-mi-long (one-way) W. J. Janes Memorial Scenic Drive, and, if you have the time, hike the spur trails leading off it. Rangers lead swamp walks and canoe trips November through April. ✉ *Boardwalk on north side of Tamiami Trail, 7 mi west of Rte. 29; W. J. Janes Scenic Dr., ¾ mi north of Tamiami Trail on Rte. 29; ranger station on W. J. Janes Scenic Dr.* ☎ *239/695–4593* ⊕ *www.floridastateparks.org/fakahatcheestrand* 🎟 *Free* ☉ *Daily 8 am–sunset.*

OFF THE BEATEN PATH

Collier-Seminole State Park. Nature trails, biking, hiking, camping, and canoeing into Everglades territory make this park a prime introduction to this often forbidding land. Of historical interest, a Seminole War blockhouse has been re-created to hold the interpretative center, and one of the "walking dredges"—a towering black machine invented to carve the Tamiami Trail out of the muck—stands silent on the grounds amid tropical hardwood forest. Campsites ($22 per night) include electricity, water, and picnic table. Restrooms have hot water, and one has laundry. ✉ *20200 E. Tamiami Trail, Naples* ☎ *239/394–3397* ⊕ *www.floridastateparks.org/collier-seminole* 🎟 *$5 per car, $4 with lone driver* ☉ *Daily 8–sunset.*

Museum of the Everglades. Through artifacts and photographs you can meet the American Indians, pioneers, entrepreneurs, and fishermen who played a role in the development of southwest Florida. Exhibits and a short film chronicle the tremendous feat of building the Tamiami Trail through the mosquito-ridden, gator-infested Everglades wetlands. In addition to the permanent displays, monthly exhibits rotate the work

Native plants along the Turner River Canoe Trail hem paddlers in on both sides, and alligators lurk nearby.

of local artists. ⊠ *105 W. Broadway* ☎ *239/695–0008* 🎫 *Free* ⏱ *Tues.– Sat. 10–4.*

SPORTS AND THE OUTDOORS
BOATING AND CANOEING

On the Gulf Coast explore the nooks, crannies, and mangrove islands of Chokoloskee Bay and Ten Thousand Islands National Wildlife Refuge, as well as the many rivers near Everglades City. The Turner River Canoe Trail, a pleasant day trip with a guarantee of bird and alligator sightings, passes through mangrove, dwarf cypress, coastal prairie, and freshwater slough ecosystems of Everglades National Park and Big Cypress National Preserve.

OUTFITTER **Glades Haven Marina.** Get on the water to explore the Ten Thousand Islands in 16-foot Carolina skiffs and 24-foot pontoon boats. Rates start at $150 a day, with half-day and hourly options. The outfitter also rents kayaks and canoes and has a 24-hour boat ramp and dockage for vessels up to 24 feet long. ⊠ *801 Copeland Ave. S, Everglades City* ☎ *239/695–2628* ⊕ *www.gladeshaven.com*

WHERE TO EAT

$$$ ✕ **City Seafood.** Owner Richard Wahrenberger serves up gems from the
SEAFOOD sea delivered fresh from his own boat. Even better, patrons can chow down on the delectable stone crabs—which come in sizes medium, large, jumbo, and colossal based on weight—with a clear conscience. The sustainable dishes are made only with the meaty claws, and the crabs are returned to the water where they grow new ones. Sure you can have lunch or dinner inside this rustic haven, but if you pick outdoor seating you can watch pelicans, gulls, tarpon, manatee, and the

occasional gator play off the dock in the Barron River. Relax with a beer or wine by the glass. Appetizers run from deep-fried corn to fried conch and sandwiches from hot dogs to pulled pork. But it's the stone crabs and the plates and baskets of smoked mullet, grouper, shrimp, oysters, blue crab, gator, or frog legs that keep people coming back. Got a cooler? Florida lobster tail, scallops, clams, and gator can be wrapped for the road. City Seafood's market also ships nationwide, and a gift shop sells cutesy crabby-style tanks, boxers and tees. ✉ *702 Begonia St., Everglades City* ☎ *239/695-4700* ⊕ *www.cityseafood1.com.*

$$-$$$ ✕ **Everglades Seafood Depot.** Count on an affordable, scenic breakfast,
SEAFOOD lunch, or dinner at this storied 1928 Spanish-style stucco structure fronting Lake Placid. Beginning life as the original Everglades train depot, the building later was deeded to the University of Miami for marine research, and appeared in scenes from the film Winds across the Everglades, before becoming a haven for assorted restaurants through the years. Well-prepared seafood including shrimp, frogs' legs, and alligator—much from local boats—dominates the menu. For big appetites, there are generously portioned entrées of steak and fish specials and combination platters that include warm, fresh-baked biscuits. All-you-can-eat specials, such as fried chicken, a taco bar, or a seafood buffet are staged on selected nights. There's also an all-you-can-eat salad bar. Save room for the coconut guava cake. Ask for a table on the back porch or for a window seat overlooking the lake. Bargain hunters arrive early for the 99¢ breakfast menu specials, served Friday and Saturday 5:30 am–10:30 am. ✉ *102 Collier Ave.* ☎ *239/695–0075* ⊕ *www. evergladesseafooddepot.com.*

$ ✕ **Havana Cafe.** Cuban specialties are a tasty change from the shanty sea-
CUBAN food houses of Everglades City; brightly painted walls and floral tablecloths make this little eatery with 10 indoor tables and four porch tables a cheerful spot. Service is order-at-the-counter for breakfast and lunch (8 am–3 pm; with dinner on Friday and Saturday nights in season). Jump-start your day with *café con leche* and a pressed-egg sandwich. For lunch, you'll find the ubiquitous Cuban sandwich, burgers, shrimp, grouper, steak, and pork plates with rice and beans and yucca. ✉ *191 Smallwood Dr., Chocoloskee* ☎ *239/695–2214* ▭ No credit cards ⊙ *No dinner Apr.–Oct. No dinner Sun.–Thurs. Nov.–Mar.*

$$ ✕ **Oyster House Restaurant.** One of the town's oldest and most old-fash-
SEAFOOD ioned fish houses, Oyster serves all the local staples—shrimp, gator
ↄ tail, frogs' legs, oysters, stone crab, and grouper—in a lodgelike setting where mounted wild game decorates walls and rafters. Shrimp and grouper smothered in tomatoes are among the few exceptions to fried preparation. Deep-frying remains an art in these parts, so if you're going to indulge, do it here. Consider the stone crab soup, in season, and try to dine at sunset for golden rays with your watery view. Outside, a 75-foot observation tower affords a terrific view of the Ten Thousand Islands. ✉ *Hwy. 29 S* ☎ *239/695–2073* ⊕ *www.oysterhouserestaurant.com.*

$$$ ✕ **Rod and Gun Club.** The striking, polished pecky-cypress woodwork
SEAFOOD in this historic building dates from the 1920s when wealthy hunters, anglers, and yachting parties from around the world arrived for the winter season. Presidents Hoover, Roosevelt, Truman, Eisenhower, and

Nixon have stopped by here, as have Ernest Hemingway, Burt Reynolds, and Mick Jagger. The main dining room holds the overflow from the popular, enormous screened porch overlooking the river. Like life in general here, friendly servers move slowly and upkeep is minimal. Fresh seafood dominates, from stone crab claws in season (October 15–May 15) to a surf-and-turf combo of steak and grouper, a swamp-and-turf combo of frogs' legs and steak, and seafood and pasta pairings. For $14.95 you can have your own catch fried, broiled, or blackened, and served with salad, veggies, and potato. Pie offerings include key lime and chocolate–peanut butter. Be aware separate checks are discouraged and there's a $5 plate-sharing charge. Yesteryear's main lobby is well worth a look—even if you plan to eat elsewhere. Arrive by boat or land. Adjacent cottages with private baths and air-conditioning run $95 to $140 depending on the season. ⊠ *200 Riverside Dr.* ☎ *239/695–2101* ⊕ *www.evergladesrodandgun.com* ⊟ *No credit cards.*

$ ✕ **Triad Seafood.** Along the Barron River, seafood houses, fishing boats,
SEAFOOD   and crab traps populate one shoreline; mangroves the other. Some of the seafood houses, selling fresh off the boat, added picnic tables and eventually grew into restaurants. Family-owned Triad is one, with a screened dining area seating 44, and additional outdoor seating under a breezeway and on a deck overhanging the scenic river where you can savor fresh seafood during stone crab season, October 15 to May 15. Nothing fancy (although smoked salmon and blue crab salad have been added to the lineup), but you'd be hard-pressed to find a better grouper sandwich. An all-you-can-eat fresh stone crab jumbo feast will set you back around $85; or $59.95 for large; $42, medium, with prices fluctuating. Hours for lunch and dinner vary but lunch starts at 10:30 am with fried shrimp, oyster, crab cake, and soft-shell blue crab baskets, plus Reubens, hamburgers, Philly cheesesteak sandwiches and, on Friday, smoked ribs. ⊠ *401 School Dr.* ☎ *239/695–0722* ⊕ *www. triadseafood.com* ⊗ *Closed May 16–Oct. 15.*

WHERE TO STAY

For expanded hotel reviews, visit Fodors.com.

$ ▦ **Glades Haven Cozy Cabins.** Bob Miller wanted to build a Holiday Inn
HOTEL   next to his Oyster House Restaurant on marina-channel shores, but when that didn't fly, he sent for cabin kits and set up mobile-home-size units around a pool on his property. **Pros:** good food options; convenient to ENP boating; free docking; marina. **Cons:** crowded trailer-park feel; no phones. **TripAdvisor:** "more like jail cells," "need a sense of humor to stay here," "check out other lodging." ⊠ *801 Copeland Ave.* ☎ *239/695–2746 or 888/956–6251* ⊕ *www.gladeshaven.com* ↘ *24 cabins, 4 3-bedroom houses* ⟳ *In-room: a/c, kitchen (some). In-hotel: restaurants, pool, laundry facilities* ⊺⊙⊺ *No meals.*

$$$ ▦ **Ivey House.** A remodeled 1928 boardinghouse originally for workers
B&B/INN   building the Tamiami Trail, Ivey House today fits many budgets. **Pros:**
Fodor'sChoice   canoe and kayak rentals and tours; pleasant; affordable. **Cons:** not
★   on water; some small rooms. **TripAdvisor:** "very eco-conscious," "felt very comfortable here," "was a pleasant surprise." ⊠ *107 Camellia St.* ☎ *877/567–0679 or 239/695–3299* ⊕ *www.iveyhouse.com* ↘ *30*

SHUTTLES FROM MIAMI

Airporter. Shuttle buses run three times daily and stop at the Ramada Inn in Florida City on the way between MIA and the Florida Keys. Shuttle service, which takes about an hour, runs 6:10 am–5:20 pm from Florida City, 7:30 am–6 pm from the airport. Reserve at least 48 hours in advance. Pickups can be arranged for all baggage-claim areas. The cost is $30 one-way. ☎ 800/830–3413

Super Shuttle. This 24-hour service runs 11-passenger air-conditioned vans between MIA and the Homestead-Florida City area; pickup is outside baggage claim and costs around $53 per person depending on your destination. For the return to MIA, reserve 24 hours in advance and know your pickup zip code for a price quote. Taxi fare from MIA to Everglades City runs about $115. ☎ 305/871–2000 ⊕ www.supershuttle.com.

5

rooms, 18 with bath; 1 2-bedroom cottage ⛺ In-room: a/c, Internet, Wi-Fi (some). In-hotel: pool, laundry facilities ⭐❰Breakfast.

FLORIDA CITY

3 mi southwest of Homestead on U.S. 1.

Florida's Turnpike ends in Florida City, the southernmost town on the peninsula, spilling thousands of vehicles onto U.S. 1 and eventually west to Everglades National Park, east to Biscayne National Park, or south to the Florida Keys. Florida City and Homestead run into each other, but the difference couldn't be more noticeable. As the last outpost before 18 mi of mangroves and water, this stretch of U.S. 1 is lined with fast-food eateries, service stations, hotels, bars, dive shops, and restaurants. Hotel rates increase significantly during NASCAR races at the nearby Homestead Miami Speedway. Like Homestead, Florida City is rooted in agriculture, with hundreds of acres of farmland west of Krome Avenue and a huge farmers' market that processes produce shipped nationwide.

VISITOR INFORMATION

Tropical Everglades Visitor Center (✉ *160 U.S. 1* ☎ *305/245–9180 or 800/388–9669* ⊕ *www.tropicaleverglades.com*).

SHOPPING

☾ **Robert Is Here.** This remarkable fruit stand sells vegetables, fresh-fruit
★ milk shakes (try the key lime shake), 10 flavors of honey, more than 100 types of jams and jellies, fresh juices, salad dressings, and some 30 kinds of tropical fruits, including (in season) carambola, lychee, egg fruit, monstera, sapodilla, dragonfruit, genipa, sugar apple, and tamarind. The stand started in 1960, when seven-year-old Robert sat at this spot selling his father's bumper crop of cucumbers. Today, Robert (still on the scene daily with his wife and kids), ships all over the United States and donates seconds to needy area families. An odd assortment of animals out back—from goats to emus—adds entertainment value for kids. Picnic tables, benches, and a waterfall with a koi pond add some serenity to the experience. The stand, on the way to

Everglades National Park, opens at 8 am and stays open until at least 7. It shuts down between September and October. ⊠ *19200 S.W. 344th St.* ☎ *305/246–1592.*

WHERE TO EAT

$$

ITALIAN

✕ **Capri Restaurant.** Locals have come to this family-owned enterprise for affordable Italian-American classics since 1958. Interior dining areas have redbrick accent walls with plenty of round tables; the sunny court-yard has umbrella-covered tables. Tasty options range from pizza with a light, crunchy crust and ample toppings to broiled steaks and seafood-pasta classics; spaghetti comes 16 ways. Old Time Capri Favorites, at $12.95, include chop steak with mushroom gravy or sausage and pepper, with either soup or salad. Daily early-bird entrées (4:30–6:30 for $12–$14) include soup or salad and potato or spaghetti. The Tuesday family night (after 4 pm, $6.95) comes with all-you-can-eat pasta and salad or soup. Specialty martinis and fruity cocktails supplement the international wine list. ⊠ *935 N. Krome Ave.* ☎ *305/247–1542* ⊕ *www.dinecapri.com* ⊗ *No lunch Sun.*

$$

SEAFOOD

✕ **Captain's Restaurant and Seafood Market.** A comfortable place where the chef prepares seafood with flair, this is among the town's best bets. Locals and visitors alike gather in the cozy dining room or outdoors on the patio. Blackboards describe a varied menu of sandwiches, pasta, seafood, steak, and nightly specials running up to $28.95, plus stone crabs in season. Inventive offerings include a lobster Reuben sandwich, crawfish pasta, and pan-seared tuna topped with balsamic onions and shallots. ⊠ *404 S.E. 1st Ave.* ☎ *305/247–9456.*

$

AMERICAN

★

✕ **Farmers' Market Restaurant.** Although it's in the farmers' market on the edge of town and serves fresh vegetables, seafood figures prominently on the menu. A family of fishermen runs the place, so fish and shellfish are only hours from the sea, and there's a fish fry on Friday nights. Catering to anglers and farmers, it opens at 5:30 am, serving pancakes, jumbo eggs, and fluffy omelets with home fries or grits in a pleasant dining room with checkered tablecloths. Lunch and dinner menus have fried shrimp, seafood pasta, country-fried steak, roast turkey, and fried conch, as well as burgers, salads, and sandwiches. ⊠ *300 N. Krome Ave.* ☎ *305/242–0008.*

$$$

SEAFOOD

☢

✕ **Mutineer Restaurant.** Families and older couples flock to the quirky yet well-dressed setting of this roadside steak-and-seafood outpost with a fish-and-duck pond and a petting zoo for kids. It was built in 1980 to look like a ship, back when Florida City was barely on the map. Etched glass divides the bi-level dining rooms, with velvet-upholstered chairs, an aquarium, and nautical antiques. Topping the menu of about a dozen seafood entrées is the stuffed grouper, Florida lobster tails, and snapper Oscar, plus another half-dozen daily seafood specials, as well as poultry, ribs, and steaks. Burgers and seafood sandwiches are popular for lunch, as is a happy-hour buffet until 7 pm in the lounge for $2.25 and the purchase of a drink. You also can dine in the restaurant's Wharf Lounge. Most Friday and Saturday nights feature live entertainment and dancing. ⊠ *11 S.E. 1st Ave. (U.S. 1), at Palm Dr.* ☎ *305/245–3377* ⊕ *www.mutineer.biz.*

MEXICAN

✗ **Rosita's Restaurante.** With its growing Mexican population this area can boast the authenticity that you just don't get in the Tex-Mex chains. Order à la carte specialties or dinners and combos with beans and rice, and salad. A large variety of breakfast, lunch, and dinner entrées are served all day and range from Mexican eggs, enchiladas, and taco salad to stewed beef, shrimp ranchero-style, and fried pork chop. Food is on the spicy side, and if you like more fire, each table is equipped with fresh-tasting salsa, pickled jalapeños, and bottled habanero sauce. Clean (with lingering whiffs of bleach to prove it) and pleasant, with an open kitchen, take-out counter, and Formica tables, it's a favorite with locals and budget-minded guests at the Everglades International Hostel across the street. ✉ *199 W. Palm Dr.* ☎ *305/246–3114.*

WHERE TO STAY

For expanded hotel reviews, visit Fodors.com.

$$–$$$
HOTEL

🖥 **Best Western Gateway to the Keys.** If you want easy access to Everglades and Biscayne national parks as well as the Florida Keys, you'll be well-placed at this modern, two-story motel two blocks off Florida's Turnpike. **Pros:** convenient to national parks, outlet shopping, and Keys; business services; pretty pool area. **Cons:** traffic noise; generic rooms; fills up fast during high season. **TripAdvisor:** "comfortable clean room," "very pleasant pool and spa area," "good basic hotel nothing more and nothing less." ✉ *411 S. Krome Ave.* ☎ *305/246–5100 or 888/981–5100* ⊕ *www.bestwestern.com/gatewaytothekeys* ⤵ *114 rooms* ⏚ *In-room: a/c Internet. In-hotel: pool, laundry facilities* ❑ *Breakfast.*

$
HOTEL

🖥 **Econo Lodge.** Close to Florida's Turnpike with access to the Keys, this is a good overnight pullover spot. **Pros:** convenient location; business services; microwaves and refrigerators in rooms. **Cons:** urban-ugly location; noisy. **TripAdvisor:** "overpriced yuck," "great places to eat near by," "beds were lumpy." ✉ *553 N.E. 1st Ave.* ☎ *305/248–9300 or 800/553–2666* ⊕ *www.econolodge.com* ⤵ *42 rooms* ⏚ *In-room: a/c, Internet, Wi-Fi. In-hotel: pool, laundry facilities, business center* ❑ *Breakfast.*

¢
HOTEL

🖥 **Everglades International Hostel.** Stay in clean and spacious private or dorm-style rooms (generally six to a room), relax in indoor or outdoor quiet areas, and watch videos or TV on a big screen. **Pros:** affordable; Everglades tours; free services. **Cons:** communal living; no elevator; old structure. **TripAdvisor:** "amazing outdoor area with rope swings hammocks and waterfall," "stay was fantastic," "quirky wonderful." ✉ *20 S.W. 2nd Ave.* ☎ *305/248–1122 or 800/372–3874* ⊕ *www.evergladeshostel.com* ⤵ *46 beds in dorm-style rooms with shared bath, 2 private rooms with shared bath, 2 suites, tent space* ⏚ *In-room: a/c, no TV. In-hotel: water sports, laundry facilities, business center, some pets allowed* ❑ *No meals.*

$
HOTEL

🖥 **Fairway Inn.** Two stories high with a waterfall pool, this motel has some of the area's lowest chain rates, and it's next to the Chamber of Commerce visitor center so you'll never be short of reading and planning material. **Pros:** affordable; convenient to restaurants, parks, and raceway. **Cons:** plain, small rooms; no-pet policy. **TripAdvisor:** "in poor shape," "a great value," "beds were hard as a rock." ✉ *100 S.E. 1st*

5

Ave. ☎ *305/248–4202 or 888/340–4734* ⇥ *160 rooms* ♿ *In-room: a/c, Internet, Wi-Fi. In-hotel: pool, laundry facilities* ❍| *Breakfast.*

$$
HOTEL
★

Ramada Inn. If you're looking for an upgrade from the other chains, this pet-friendly property offers more amenities and comfort, such as 32-inch flat-screen TVs, duvet-covered beds, closed closets, and stylish furnishings. **Pros:** extra room amenities; business clientele perks; convenient location. **Cons:** chain anonymity. **TripAdvisor:** "disgustingly dirty," "rooms are large," "had a good breakfast." ✉ *124 E. Palm Dr.* ☎ *305/247–8833* ⊕ *www.hotelfloridacity.com* ⇥ *123 rooms* ♿ *In-room: a/c, Internet, Wi-Fi. In-hotel: pool* ❍| *Breakfast.*

$–$$$
HOTEL

Travelodge. This bargain motor lodge is close to Florida's Turnpike, Everglades and Biscayne national parks, the Florida Keys, and the Homestead Miami Speedway. **Pros:** pet-friendly for a $10 per night fee; convenience to U.S. 1; complimentary breakfast. **Cons:** small rooms; busy location. **TripAdvisor:** "rooms are spotless and quiet," "attention to customer service," "small but nice clean pool." ✉ *409 S.E. 1st Ave.* ☎ *305/248–9777 or 800/758–0618* ⊕ *www.tlflcity.com* ⇥ *88 rooms* ♿ *In-room: a/c, Internet, Wi-Fi. In-hotel: pool, laundry facilities, business center* ❍| *Breakfast.*

HOMESTEAD

30 mi southwest of Miami.

In recent years Homestead has redefined itself as a destination for tropical agro- and ecotourism. At the juncture between Miami and the Keys as well as Everglades National Park and Biscayne National Park, the area has the added dimension of shopping centers, residential development, hotel chains, and the Homestead-Miami Speedway—when car races are scheduled, hotels hike up their rates and require minimum stays. The historic downtown has become a preservation-driven Main Street. Krome Avenue, where it cuts through the city's heart, is lined with restaurants, an arts complex, antiques shops, and low-budget, sometimes undesirable accommodations. West of north–south Krome Avenue, miles of fields grow fresh fruits and vegetables. Some are harvested commercially, and others beckon with "U-pick" signs. Stands selling farm-fresh produce and nurseries that grow and sell orchids and tropical plants abound. In addition to its agricultural legacy, the town has an eclectic flavor, attributable to its population mix: descendants of pioneer Crackers, Hispanic growers and farm workers, professionals escaping Miami hubbub, and latter-day Northern retirees.

WHAT TO SEE

Coral Castle. Driven by unrequited love, 100-pound Latvian immigrant Ed Leedskalnin (1887–1951) built this castle in the early 1900s out of massive slabs of coral rock, a feat he likened to the building of the pyramids. Visitors can learn how he peopled his fantasy world with his imaginary wife and three children, studied astronomy, and created a simple home and elaborate courtyard with no engineering education and tools he mostly fashioned himself. Highlights of this National Register of Historic Places site include the Polaris telescope built to spot the North Star, a working sundial, a 5,000-pound heart-shape table featured in Ripley's *Believe It or Not,* a banquet table in the shape of Florida, and a playground Ed named "Grotto of the Three Bears." ⊠ *28655 S. Dixie Hwy.* ☎ *305/248–6345* ⊕ *www.coralcastle. com* ☎ *$9.75* ⊙ *Daily 8–6.*

SPORTS AND THE OUTDOORS

AUTO RACING

Homestead-Miami Speedway. Buzzing more than 280 days each year with racing, manufacturer testing, car-club events, driving schools and ride-along programs, this facility with 65,000 grandstand seats, has club seating eight stories above racing action, and two tracks—a 2.21-mi continuous road course and a 1.5-mi oval. A packed schedule includes GRAND-AM and NASCAR events. ⊠ *1 Speedway Blvd.* ☎ *866/409–7223* ⊕ *www.homesteadmiamispeedway.com.*

WATER SPORTS

Homestead Bayfront Park. Boaters, anglers, and beachgoers give high ratings to the facilities at this recreational area adjacent to Biscayne National Park. The 174-slip marina has a ramp, dock, bait-and-tackle shop, fuel station, ice, and dry storage. The facility can handle vessels up to 50 feet long. The park also has a tidal swimming area, a beach with lifeguards, a playground, ramps for people with disabilities (including a ramp that leads into the swimming area), and a picnic pavilion with grills, showers, and restrooms. ⊠ *9698 S.W. 328th St.* ☎ *305/230–3033* ☎ *$6 per passenger vehicle; $12 per vehicle with boat Mon.–Thurs., $15 Fri.–Sun.; $15 per RV or bus* ⊙ *Daily sunrise–sunset.*

WHERE TO EAT

¢ ✕ **Bobbie Jo's Diner.** Head to Bobbie Jo's with the locals for good, old,
SOUTHERN Southern-style home cooking. Burgers, sandwiches, and dinners—including chicken livers, chicken and dumplings, and fried clams—come with fresh-baked corn bread and a daily selection of sides such as okra with tomatoes, turnip greens, pickled beets, or onion rings. The Bobbie Jo burger comes with fries for under five bucks. Don't miss out on the changing selection of homemade soups and desserts. All this goodness comes cheap, but at the expense of anything-but-glamorous dining environs and often slow service. ⊠ *1320 N. Krome Ave.* ☎ *305/246–2990* ⊙ *No dinner Sun.*

¢ ✕ **NicaMex.** Among the local Latin population this 68-seat eatery is a
MEXICAN low-budget favorite for Nicaraguan and Mexican flavors. It helps if you speak Spanish, but usually some staffers on hand speak English, and the menu is bilingual. Although they term it *comidas rapidas* (fast food), the cuisine is not Americanized. You can get authentic huevos rancheros or *chilaquiles* (corn tortillas cooked in red-pepper sauce) for breakfast, and specialties such as *chicharron en salsa verde* (fried pork skin in hot-green-tomato sauce) and shrimp in garlic all day. Hearty seafood and beef soups are best sellers. Choose a domestic or imported beer, pop a coin into the Wurlitzer jukebox, select a Latin tune, and escape south of the border. ⊠ *32 N.W. 1st St., across from Krome Ave. bandstand* ☎ *305/247–0727.*

WHERE TO STAY

For expanded hotel reviews, visit Fodors.com.

$ ⏃ **Grove Inn Country Guesthouse.** Away from downtown but close to
B&B/INN   Homestead's agricultural attractions, Grove Inn offers notably person-
★   alized service and lushly landscaped environs. **Pros:** fresh fruit; privacy; delicious breakfast; rural location. **Cons:** far from downtown
and national parks; no restaurants nearby; not suited to families.
⊠ *22540 S.W. Krome Ave., 6 mi north of downtown* ☎ *305/247–6572
or 877/247–6572* ⊕ *www.groveinn.com* ⤳ *13 rooms, 1 2-bedroom
suite, 1 cottage* ♨ *In-room: a/c, kitchen (some), Wi-Fi. In-hotel: pool,
laundry facilities, some pets allowed* ⎮◯⎮ *Breakfast.*

$–$$ ⏃ **Redland Hotel.** Of downtown Homestead's smattering of mom-and-
HOTEL   pop lodging options, this historic inn is the most desirable with its
★   Victorian-style rooms decorated in pastels and reproduction antique
furniture. **Pros:** historic character; convenient to downtown; well
maintained; smoke free. **Cons:** traffic noise; some small rooms; ugly
street location. **TripAdvisor:** "charming inn," "room was very clean,"
"seemed rundown." ⊠ *5 S. Flagler Ave.* ☎ *305/246–1904 or 800/595–
1904* ⊕ *www.redlandhotel.com* ⤳ *13 rooms* ♨ *In-room: a/c, Internet,
Wi-Fi. In-hotel: bar* ⎮◯⎮ *No meals.*

TAMIAMI TRAIL

An 80-mi stretch of U.S. 41 (known as the Tamiami Trail) traverses the
Everglades, Big Cypress National Preserve, and Fakahatchee Strand
Preserve State Park. The road was conceived in 1915 to link Miami
to Fort Myers and Tampa. When it finally became a reality in 1928, it
cut through the Everglades and altered the natural flow of water and
lives of the Miccosukee Indians, who were trying to eke out a living
fishing, hunting, farming, and frogging here. The landscape is surprisingly varied, changing from hardwood hammocks to pinelands, then
abruptly to tall cypress trees dripping with Spanish moss and back to
saw grass marsh. Slow down to take in the scenery and you'll likely
be rewarded with glimpses of alligators sunning themselves along the
banks of roadside canals or in the shallow waters, and hundreds of
waterbirds, especially in the dry winter season. The man-made landscape has American Indian villages, chickee huts, and airboats parked
at roadside enterprises. Between Miami and Naples the road goes by
several names, including Tamiami Trail, U.S. 41, 9th Street in Naples,
and, at the Miami end, S.W. 8th Street. ■ TIP➔ Businesses along the trail
give their addresses either based on their distance from Krome Avenue,
Florida's Turnpike, and Miami on the east coast or Naples on the west coast.

WHAT TO SEE

☾   **Everglades Gator Park.** Here you can get face-to-face with and even touch
an alligator—albeit a baby one—during the park's exciting Wildlife
Show. You also can squirm in a "reptilium" of venomous and nonpoi-
sonous native snakes or learn about American Indians of the Everglades
through a reproduction of a Miccosukee village. The park also has
35-minute airboat tours and RV campsites ($30 per night), as well as a
gift shop and restaurant serving fare from burgers to gator tail. ⊠ *24050
Tamiami Trail, 12 mi west of Florida's Turnpike, Miami* ☎ *305/559–*

Are baby alligators more to your liking than their daddies? You can pet one at Everglades Gator Park.

2255 or 800/559–2205 ⊕ *www.gatorpark.com* ✉ *Tours, wildlife show, and park $22.95; show and park $10* ⊙ *Daily 9–5.*

Everglades Safari Park. A perennial favorite with tour-bus operators, the park has an arena, seating up to 300, for an alligator show and wrestling demonstration. Before and after the show, get a closer look at both alligators and crocodiles on Gator Island; walk through a small wildlife museum, follow the jungle trail, or climb aboard an airboat for a 40-minute ride on the River of Grass (included in admission). There's also a restaurant, gift shop, and an observation platform looking out over the Glades. Smaller, private airboats are available for an extra charge for tours lasting 40 minutes to 2 hours. ⊠ *26700 Tamiami Trail, 15 mi west of Florida's Turnpike, Miami* ☎ *305/226–6923 or 305/223–3804* ⊕ *www.evsafaripark.com* ✉ *$23* ⊙ *Daily 9–5, last tour departs 3:30.*

© ★ **Miccosukee Indian Village and Gift Shop.** Showcasing the culture, skills, and lifestyle of the Miccosukee Tribe of Florida, this cultural center offers crafts demonstrations and insight into the interactions between alligators and the American Indians. Narrated 30-minute airboat rides take you into the wilderness where these American Indians hid after the Seminole Wars and Indian Removal Act of the mid-1800s. In modern times many of the Miccosukee have relocated to this village along Tamiami Trail, but most still maintain their hammock farming and hunting camps. The village museum shows a film and displays chickee structures and artifacts. Guided tours run throughout the day, and a gift shop stocks dolls, apparel for adults and children, silver jewelry, beadwork, and other handcrafted items. The Miccosukee Everglades

Music and Craft Festival falls on a July weekend, and the 10-day Miccosukee Indian Arts Festival is in late December. ✉ *Just west of Shark Valley entrance on U.S. 41/Tamiami Trail, 25 mi west of Florida's Turnpike at MM 70, Miami* ☎ *305/552–8365* ⊕ *www.miccosukee.com* ✉ *Village $8, airboat rides $10* ⊗ *Daily 9–5.*

SPORTS AND THE OUTDOORS

BOAT TOURS

Many Everglades-area tours operate only in season, roughly November through April.

Coopertown Airboats. Running since 1945, this is the oldest airboat operator in the Everglades. The 35- to 40-minute tour ($21) takes you 9 mi to hammocks and alligator holes. Private charters of up to two hours are also available. ✉ *11 mi west of Florida's Turnpike, on Tamiami Trail* ☎ *305/226–6048* ⊕ *www.coopertownairboats.com.*

Everglades Alligator Farm. Southwest of Florida City near the entrance to Everglades National Park, this outfit runs a 4-mi, 30-minute airboat tour of the River of Grass with departures 20 minutes after the hour. The tour ($23) includes free hourly alligator, snake, and wildlife shows, or see the 2,000-strong gator farm and shows only ($15.50). ✉ *40351 S.W. 192nd Ave.* ☎ *305/247–2628* ⊕ *www.everglades.com.*

Everglades Safari Park. Try a 40-minute eco-adventure airboat ride for $23 or smaller, private airboat tours for an extra charge, lasting from 40 minutes to 2 hours. The price includes the alligator show, natural-museum admission, and walking-trail access. ✉ *26700 S.W. 8th St., 15 mi west of Florida's Turnpike, on Tamiami Trail* ☎ *305/226–6923 or 305/223–3804* ⊕ *www.evsafaripark.com.*

Gator Park Airboat Tours. Forty-five minute narrated airboat tours ($22.95) include a park tour and wildlife show. ✉ *12 mi west of Florida's Turnpike, on Tamiami Trail* ☎ *305/559–2255 or 800/559–2205* ⊕ *www.gatorpark.com.*

Wooten's Everglades Airboat Tour. A classic Florida roadside attraction runs airboat tours through the Everglades and swamp-buggy tours through the Big Cypress Swamp lasting approximately 30 minutes each (swamp buggies are giant tractorlike vehicles with oversize rubber wheels). More personalized airboat tours on smaller boats (seating six to eight) are also available for 45 minutes to one hour and start at $37.10. The on-site animal sanctuary offers the typical Everglades array of alligators, snakes, panthers, and other creatures. Discounts are available online. ✉ *Wooten's Alligator Farm, 1½ mi east of Rte. 29 on Tamiami Trail,*

CROCS OR GATORS?

You can tell you're looking at a crocodile, not an alligator, if you can see its lower teeth protruding when its jaws are shut. Gators are much darker in color—a grayish black—compared with the lighter tan color of crocodiles. Alligator snouts—sort of U-shape—are also much broader than their long, thin A-shape crocodilian counterparts. South Florida is the world's only place where both coexist. Alligators are primarily found in freshwater habitats, while crocodiles (better at expelling salt from water) are typically in coastal estuaries.

Ochopee ☎ *239/695–2781 or 800/282–2781* ⊕ *www.wootensairboats. com* 🗐 *$25 for ½-hr tour, $8 for animal exhibits; $59.36 combo ticket for all attractions* ◑ *Daily 8:30–5; last ride departs at 4:30.*

SHOPPING

Miccosukee Indian Village. Wares include American Indian crafts such as beadwork, moccasins, dolls, pottery, baskets, and patchwork fabric and clothing. ✉ *Just west of Shark Valley entrance, 25 mi west of Florida's Turnpike at MM 70* ☎ *305/223–8380.*

WHERE TO EAT

$

ECLECTIC

✕ **Coopertown Restaurant.** Make this a pit stop for local color and cuisine fished straight from the swamp. Starting a half century ago as a sandwich stand, this small casual eatery inside an airboat concession storefront has attracted the famous and the humbly hungry. House specialties are frogs' legs and alligator tail breaded in cornmeal and deep-fried, casually served on paper ware with a lemon wedge and Tabasco. More conventional options include catfish, shrimp, burgers, hot dogs, or grilled cheese sandwiches. ✉ *22700 S.W. 8th St., 11 mi west of Florida's Turnpike, on Tamiami Trail, Miami* ☎ *305/226–6048* ⊕ *www.coopertownairboats.com.*

$

SOUTHWESTERN

★

✕ **Miccosukee Restaurant.** For a taste of culture at breakfast or lunch (or dinner until 9 November–April), this roadside cafeteria a quarter mile from the Miccosukee Indian Village and overlooking the River of Grass, provides the best variety of food along Tamiami Trail in Everglades territory where you won't find all that much choice. Atmosphere comes from the River of Grass view, servers wearing traditional Miccosukee patchwork vests, and a mural depicting American Indian women cooking and men engaged in a powwow. Catfish and frogs' legs are breaded and deep-fried. Other favorites include Indian fry bread and pumpkin bread, but you'll also find burgers, salads, and dishes from south of the border. The Miccosukee Platter ($24.95) offers a sampling of local favorites, including gator bites. Gator Nuggets (slightly larger than gator bites) are $2.25 each. ✉ *U.S. 41 (Tamiami Trail), 18 mi west of Miccosukee Resort and Gaming; 25 mi west of Florida's Turnpike* ☎ *305/894–2374.*

$

SOUTHERN

☻

✕ **Pit Bar-B-Q.** At the edge of Miami, this old-fashioned roadside eatery along Tamiami Trail near Krome Avenue was launched in 1965 by the late Tommy Little, who wanted anyone heading into or out of the Everglades to have access to cold drinks and rib-sticking fare. His vision remains a holdout from the Everglades' backwoods heritage and a popular, affordable option for families. Order at the counter, pick up your food, and eat at one of the picnic tables on the screened porch or outdoors. Specialties include barbecued chicken and ribs with a tangy sauce, fries, coleslaw, and a fried biscuit, plus burgers and fish sandwiches. The whopping double-decker beef or pork sandwich with slaw requires at least five napkins. Latin specialties include deep-fried pork and fried green plantains. Beer is by the bottle or pitcher. Locals flock here with kids on weekends for pony rides. ✉ *16400 Tamiami Trail, 5 mi west of Florida's Turnpike, Miami* ☎ *305/226–2272* ⊕ *www. thepitbarbq.com.*

5

WHERE TO STAY

For expanded hotel reviews, visit Fodors.com.

$$$
RESORT

🏨 **Miccosukee Resort & Gaming.** Like an oasis on the horizon of endless sawgrass, this nine-story resort at the southeastern edge of the Everglades can't help but attract your attention, even if you're not on the lookout for 24-hour gaming action. **Pros:** casino; most modern resort in these parts; golf. **Cons:** cigarette odor in lobby; parking lot fills with gamblers; feels incompatible with the Everglades. **TripAdvisor:** "buffet was more of the truck stop variety," "food was terrible," "nothing special." ✉ *500 S.W. 177th Ave., 6 mi west of Florida's Turnpike, Miami* ☎ *305/925–2555 or 877/242–6464* ⊕ *www.miccosukee.com* ➘ *256 rooms, 46 suites* ⚐ *In-room: a/c, Wi-Fi. In-hotel: restaurants, bars, golf course, pool, gym, spa, children's programs, business center, parking* ⦿ *No meals.*

The Florida Keys

WORD OF MOUTH

"The Keys are definitely a get out on the water type place instead of a driving up and down U.S. 1 kind of place. Bars and restaurants open early and close early. Get out over the water. That is where the most amazing things in the keys are."

—GoTravel

WELCOME TO THE FLORIDA KEYS

TOP REASONS TO GO

★ **John Pennekamp Coral Reef State Park:** A perfect introduction to the Florida Keys, this nature reserve offers snorkeling, diving, camping, and kayaking. An underwater highlight is the massive Christ of the Deep statue.

★ **Under the Sea:** Whether you scuba, snorkel, or ride a glass-bottom boat, don't miss gazing at the coral reef and its colorful denizens.

★ **Sunset at Mallory Square:** Sure it's touristy, but just once while you're here you've got to witness the circus-like atmosphere of this nightly event.

★ **Duval Crawl:** Shop, eat, drink, repeat. Key West's Duval Street and the nearby streets make a good day's worth of window-shopping and people-watching.

★ **Get on the Water:** From angling for trophy-size fish to zipping out to the Dry Tortugas, a boat trip is in your future. It's really the whole point of the Keys.

1 The Upper Keys. As the doorstep to the islands' coral reefs and blithe spirit, the Upper Keys introduce all that is sporting and sea-oriented about the Keys. They stretch from Key Largo to the Long Key Channel (MM 106–65).

2 The Middle Keys. Centered around the town of Marathon, the Middle Keys hold most of the chain's historic and natural attractions outside of Key West. They go from Conch (pronounced *konk*) Key through Marathon to the south side of the Seven Mile Bridge, including Pigeon Key (MM 65–40).

3 The Lower Keys. Pressure drops another notch in this laid-back part of the region, where wildlife and the fishing lifestyle peak. The Lower Keys go from Little Duck Key south through Big Coppitt Key (MM 40–9).

4 Key West. The ultimate in Florida Keys craziness, the party town Key West isn't the place for those seeking a quiet retreat. The Key West area encompasses MM 9–0.

Gulf of

National Key
Deer Refuge

3
THE LOWER
KEYS

Big Torch Key
Little Torch Key
No Name Key
Cudjoe Key
Mud Keys
Saddlebunch Keys
Big Pine Key
Ramrod Key
Summerland Key
Sugarloaf Key
Bahia Honda Key

Key West
4
Key West
Stock Island
Boca Chica Key
Big Coppitt Key
Key West International Airport

0 ——— 10 mi
0 ——— 10 km

6

GETTING ORIENTED

The Florida Keys are the dribble of islands off the peninsula's southern tip. From Miami International Airport, Key Largo is a 56-mi drive along the Overseas Highway. The rest of the keys—Islamorada, Marathon, Bahia Honda Key, Big Pine Key—fall in succession for the 106 mi between Key Largo and Key West. At their north end, the Florida Keys front Florida Bay, part of Everglades National Park. The Middle and Lower Keys front the Gulf of Mexico; the Atlantic Ocean borders the length of the chain on its eastern shores.

THE FLORIDA KEYS BEACHES

Because the Bahamas steal the Keys' offshore sand, the region has fewer natural beaches than one might expect. But the ones it does have are award-winning, specifically those at Bahia Honda State Park.

Also, just because a beach is not natural, doesn't mean it should be overlooked. Some of the Keys' public man-made beaches provide solid recreation and sunning options for visitors looking to work on their tan. Many resorts provide their own private beachfronts.

The Keys may not have a surplus of beaches, but a surplus of camping makes that one of many ways to enjoy nature while on the beach. Another is keeping an eye out for sea turtles. April through October female sea turtles lay their eggs into the sand for a nearly two-month period of nesting.

■ TIP→ Don't let pests ruin your day at the beach. To avoid the stings of sea lice, remove your swimsuit and shower thoroughly upon exiting the water. Sand fleas (aka no-see-ums) are tiny insects with big teeth that are most likely to attack in the morning and around sunset.

BIRD-WATCHING ON THE BEACH

The Florida Keys beaches can be great places to look to the skies and waters for all varieties of birds. Permanent residents include shorebirds—plovers, ruddy turnstones, willets, and short-billed dowitchers; wading birds—roseate spoonbills, great blue herons, great white egrets, snowy egrets, tri-colored herons, and white ibis; brown pelicans; osprey; and turkey vultures. In the autumn, hawks migrate through the region, while in winter ducks and white pelicans make their debut. In the summer, white-crowned pigeons are commonly seen.

FLORIDA KEYS' BEST BEACHES

BAHIA HONDA STATE PARK

This state park at MM 37 holds three beaches, all of different character. Sandspur Beach is the most removed from crowds with long stretches of powdery sands and a campground. Loggerhead Beach is closer to the park's concession area, where you can rent snorkel equipment and kayaks. Like Sandspur, it faces the Atlantic Ocean, but waves are typically wimpy. Near Loggerhead, Calusa Beach on the gulf side near the marina is popular with families, offering a small and safe swimming venue and picnic facilities, as well as camping.

HIGGS BEACH, KEY WEST

Situated on Atlantic Boulevard, this is as urban as beaches in the Keys get, with lots of amenities, activities, and distractions. Visitors can check out a historic site, eat at a popular beachfront Italian restaurant, rent a kayak, play volleyball, tennis, or at the playground—and all within walking distance of the long sweep of man-made beach and sparkling clear, shallow, and calm water.

LONG KEY STATE PARK

The beach at Long Key State Park at MM 67.5 is typical of Middle Key's beaches, which are more like sand flats where low tide reveals the coral bedrock of the ecosystem. Here you can snorkel or fish (bonefishing is quite popular) during the day and then be lulled to sleep by the sound of gentle sea waves if you spend the night camping. (The beach is accessible only to campers.)

SOMBRERO BEACH

Something of a local hangout—especially on weekends, when it can get crowded—Sombrero Beach in Marathon is worth getting off the beaten Overseas Highway path for (exit at MM 50 onto Sombrero Beach Road). Families will find much to do on the man-made coved beach and its grassy green, manicured lawn, and in its playground area and clear calm waters. Separate sections also accommodate boaters and windsurfers.

ZACHARY TAYLOR HISTORIC STATE PARK

This man-made beach is part of a Civil War–era fort complex at the end of Southard Street and is arguably the best beach in Key West with its typically small waves, swaying Australian pines, water-sports rentals, and shaded picnic grounds. It also hosts, from mid-January through mid-April, an alfresco collection of oversized art called Sculpture Key West, which changes annually and showcases artists from across the country.

Updated by
Chelle Koster
Walton

Being a Conch is a condition of the heart, and foreclosure on the soul. Many throughout the Florida Keys wear that label proudly, yet there's anything but a shared lifestyle here.

To the south, Key West has a Mardi Gras mood with Fantasy Festivals, Hemingway look-alike contests, and the occasional threat to secede from the Union. It's an island whose melting-pot character allows crusty natives to mingle (more or less peacefully) with eccentrics and escape artists who lovingly call this 4-mi sandbar "Paradise." Although life elsewhere in the island chain isn't quite as offbeat, it's nearly as diverse. Flowering jungles, shimmering seas, and mangrove-lined islands are also, conversely, overburdened. Key Largo, nearest the mainland, is becoming more congested as it evolves into a bedroom community and weekend hideaway for residents of Miami and Fort Lauderdale.

A river of tourist traffic gushes along Overseas Highway, the 110-mi artery linking the inhabited islands. Take pleasure, nonetheless, as you cruise down Overseas Highway along the islands. Gaze over the silvery blue-and-green Atlantic and its still-living reef, with Florida Bay, the Gulf of Mexico, and the backcountry on your right (the Keys extend southwest from the mainland). At a few points the ocean and gulf are as much as 10 mi apart; in most places, however, they are from 1 to 4 mi apart, and on the narrowest landfill islands they are separated only by the road. Try to get off the highway. Once you do, rent a boat, anchor, and then fish, swim, or marvel at the sun, sea, and sky. In the Atlantic, dive spectacular coral reefs or pursue grouper, blue marlin, dolphinfish, and other deepwater game fish. Along Florida Bay's coastline, kayak and canoe to secluded islands and bays or seek out the bonefish, snapper, snook, and tarpon that lurk in the grass flats and in the shallow, winding channels of the backcountry.

THE FLORIDA KEYS PLANNER

WHEN TO GO

High season in the Keys falls between Christmas and Easter. November to mid-December crowds are thinner, the weather is wonderful, and hotels and shops drastically reduce their prices. Summer, which is hot and humid, is becoming a second high season, especially among Floridians, families, and European travelers. If you plan to attend the wild Fantasy Fest in October, book your room at least six months in advance. Accommodations are also scarce during the last consecutive Wednesday and Thursday in July (lobster sport season) and starting the first weekend in August, when the commercial lobster season begins.

Winter is typically 10°F warmer than on the mainland; summer is usually a few degrees cooler. The Keys also get substantially less rain, around 40 inches annually, compared with an average 55–60 inches in Miami and the Everglades. Most rainfalls are quick downpours on summer afternoons, except in June through October, when tropical storms can dump rain for two or more days. Winter cold fronts occasionally stall over the Keys, dragging overnight temperatures down to the low 50s.

6

GETTING HERE AND AROUND

About 450,000 passengers use the **Key West International Airport (EYW)** each year. In 2009, the airport completed its four-year renovation, which includes a beach where travelers can catch their last blast of rays after clearing security. Because flights are few, many prefer flying into Miami International Airport (MIA) and driving the 110-mi Overseas Highway (aka U.S. 1).

By car, from Miami International Airport, follow signs to Coral Gables and Key West, which puts you on LeJeune Road, then Route 836 west. Take the Homestead Extension of Florida's Turnpike south (toll road), which ends at Florida City and connects to the Overseas Highway (U.S. 1, currently under construction so expect delays). Tolls from the airport run approximately $3. Payment is collected via **SunPass**, a prepaid toll program, or with **Toll-By-Plate**, a system that photographs each vehicle's license plate and mails a monthly bill for tolls, plus a $2.50 administrative fee, to the vehicle's registered owner. Vacationers traveling in their own cars can obtain a mini-SunPass sticker via mail before their trips for $4.99 and receive the cost back in toll credits and discounts. The pass also is available at many major Florida retailers and turnpike service plazas. It works on all Florida toll roads and many bridges. For details on purchasing a mini-SunPass, call or visit the Web site. For visitors renting cars in Florida, most major rental companies have programs allowing customers to use the Toll-By-Plate system. Tolls, plus varying service fees, are automatically charged to the credit card used to rent the vehicle. For details, including pricing options at participating rental-car agencies, check the program Web site. Under no circumstances should motorists attempt to stop in high-speed electronic tolling lanes. Travelers can contact Florida's Turnpike Enterprise for more information about the all-electronic tolling on Florida's Turnpike.

The alternative from Florida City is Card Sound Road (Route 905A), which has a bridge toll of $1. Continue to the only stop sign and turn right on Route 905, which rejoins Overseas Highway 31 mi south of Florida City. The best Keys road map, published by the Homestead–Florida City Chamber of Commerce, can be obtained for $5.50 from the **Tropical Everglades Visitor Center**.

Those unwilling to tackle the route's 42 bridges and peak-time traffic can take **Greyhound's** Keys Shuttle, which has multiple daily departures from Miami International Airport.

Boaters can travel to and along the Keys either along the Intracoastal Waterway through Card, Barnes, and Blackwater sounds and into Florida Bay or along the deeper Atlantic Ocean route through Hawk Channel. The Keys are full of marinas that welcome transient visitors, but there aren't enough slips for all the boats heading to these waters. Make reservations far in advance and ask about channel and dockage depth—many marinas are quite shallow.

ESSENTIALS

Airport Information Key West International Airport (EYW) (☏ 305/296–5439 ⊕ www.keywestinternationalairport.com).

Bus Information Greyhound (☏ 800/231–2222 ⊕ www.greyhound.com).

Car Information Florida's Turnpike Enterprise (☏ 800/749–7453 ⊕ www.FloridasTurnpike.com/all-electronictolling). **SunPass** (☏ 888/865–5352 ⊕ www.sunpass.com). **TOLL-BY-PLATE** (⊕ www.sunpass.com/rentalcar).

Visitor Information Tropical Everglades Visitor Center (☏ 305/245–9180 or 800/388–9669 ⊕ www.tropicaleverglades.com).

ABOUT THE RESTAURANTS

Seafood rules on the Keys, which is full of chef-owned restaurants with not-too-fancy food. Things get more exotic once you reach Key West. Restaurants serve cuisine that reflects the proximity of the Bahamas and Caribbean. Tropical fruits figure prominently—especially on the beverage side of the menu. Florida spiny lobster should be local and fresh from August to March, and stone crabs from mid-October to mid-May. And don't dare leave the islands without sampling conch, be it in a fritter or in ceviche. Keep an eye out for authentic key lime pie—yellow custard in a graham-cracker crust. If it's green, just say "no." Note: Particularly in Key West and particularly during spring break, the more affordable and casual restaurants can get loud and downright rowdy, with young visitors often more interested in drinking than eating. Live music contributes to the decibel levels. If you're more of the quiet, intimate dining type, avoid such overly exuberant scenes by eating early or choosing a restaurant where the bar is not the main focus.

ABOUT THE HOTELS

Throughout the Keys, the types of accommodations are remarkably varied, from '50s-style motels to cozy inns to luxurious resorts. Most are on or near the ocean, so water sports are popular. Key West's lodging portfolio includes historic cottages, restored Conch houses, and large resorts. Some larger properties throughout the Keys charge a mandatory daily resort fee of $15 or more, which can cover equipment rental, fitness-center use, and other services, plus expect another 12.5% (or more) sales/resort tax. Some guesthouses and inns do not welcome children, and many do not permit smoking.

WHAT IT COSTS					
	¢	$	$$	$$$	$$$$
Restaurants	under $10	$10–$15	$15–$20	$20–$30	over $30
Hotels	under $80	$80–$100	$100–$140	$140–$220	over $220

Restaurant prices are per person for a main course at dinner. Hotel prices are for a standard double room, excluding 12.5% sales tax (or more) in sales and resort taxes.

6

THE MILE MARKER SYSTEM

Getting lost in the Keys is almost impossible once you understand the unique address system. **Many addresses are simply given as a mile marker (MM) number.** The markers are small, green, rectangular signs along the side of the Overseas Highway (U.S. 1). They begin with MM 126, 1 mi south of Florida City, and end with MM 0, in Key West. **Keys residents use the abbreviation BS for the bay side of Overseas Highway and OS for the ocean side.** From Marathon to Key West, residents may refer to the bay side as the gulf side.

THE UPPER KEYS

Diving and snorkeling rule in the Upper Keys, thanks to the tropical coral reef that runs a few miles off the seaward coast. Divers of all skill levels benefit from accessible dive sites and an established tourism infrastructure. Fishing is another huge draw, especially around Islamorada, known for its sportfishing in both deep offshore waters and in the backcountry. Offshore islands accessible only by boat are popular destinations for kayakers. In short, if you don't like the water you might get bored here.

Other nature lovers won't feel shortchanged. Within 1½ mi of the bay coast lie the mangrove trees and sandy shores of Everglades National Park, to where naturalists lead tours of one of the world's few saltwater forests. Here you'll see endangered manatees, curious dolphins, and other underwater creatures. Although the number of birds has dwindled since John James Audubon captured their beauty on canvas, the rare Everglade snail kite, bald eagles, ospreys, and a colorful array of egrets and herons delight bird-watchers. At sunset flocks take to the skies as

GREAT ITINERARIES

3 DAYS

Spend your first morning diving or snorkeling at John Pennekamp Coral Reef State Park in Key Largo. If you aren't certified, sign up for a resort course and you'll be exploring the reefs by the afternoon. Dinner at a bay-side restaurant will give you your first look at a fabulous Keys sunset. On Day 2 get an early start to savor the breathtaking views on the two-hour drive to Key West. Along the way make a stop at the natural-history museum that's part of Crane Point Museum, Nature Center and Historic Site in Marathon. Another worthwhile detour is Bahia Honda Key State Park on Bahia Honda Key, where you can stretch your legs on a forest trail or snorkel on an offshore reef. Once you arrive in Key West, watch the sunset at one of the island's restaurants. The next day, take a trolley tour of Old Town, stroll Duval Street, visit a museum or two, and spend some beach time at Fort Zachary Taylor State Park.

7 DAYS

Spend your first three days as you would in the above itinerary, but spend both the second and third nights in Islamorada. In the morning catch a boat or rent a kayak to paddle to Lignumvitae Key Botanical State Park before making the one-hour drive to Marathon. Visit Crane Point Museum, Nature Center and Historic Site and walk out on the Old Seven Mile Bridge or take the ferry to Pigeon Key. The next stop is just 10 mi away at Bahia Honda State Park on Bahia Honda Key. Take a walk on a wilderness trail, go snorkeling around the offshore reef, or wriggle your toes in the beach's soft sand. Spend the night in a waterfront cabin, letting the waves lull you to sleep. Your sixth day starts with either a half day of fabulous snorkeling or diving at Looe Key Reef or a visit to the National Key Deer Refuge on Big Pine Key. Then continue on to Key West, and get in a little sightseeing before watching the sunset.

they gather to find their night's roost, adding a swirl of activity to an otherwise quiet time of day.

The Upper Keys are full of low-key eateries where the owner is also the chef and the food is tasty and never too fussy. The one exception is Islamorada, where you'll find the more upscale restaurants. Restaurants may close for a two- to four-week vacation during the slow season between mid-September and late October.

In the Upper Keys, the accommodations are as varied as they are plentiful. The majority of lodgings are in small waterfront complexes with efficiencies and one- or two-bedroom units. These places offer dockage and often arrange boating, diving, and fishing excursions. There are also larger resorts with every type of activity imaginable and smaller boutique hotels where the attraction is personalized service.

Depending on which way the wind blows and how close the property is to the highway, there may be some noise from Overseas Highway. If this is an annoyance for you, ask for a room as far from the traffic as possible. Some properties require two- or three-day minimum stays during holiday and high-season weekends. Conversely, discounts apply for midweek, weekly, and monthly stays.

GETTING HERE AND AROUND

Airporter operates scheduled van and bus pick-up service from all Miami International Airport (MIA) baggage areas to wherever you want to go in Key Largo ($50) and Islamorada ($55). Groups of three or more passengers receive discounts. There are three departures daily; reservations are required 48 hours in advance. The SuperShuttle charges about $165 for two passengers for trips from Miami International Airport to the Upper Keys; reservations are required. For a trip to the airport, place your request 24 hours in advance.

ESSENTIALS

Transportation Contacts Airporter (☎ 305/852–3413 or 800/830–3413). **SuperShuttle** (☎ 305/871–2000 ⊕ www.supershuttle.com).

KEY LARGO

The first of the Upper Keys reachable by car, 30-mi-long Key Largo is also the largest island in the chain. Key Largo—named Cayo Largo ("Long Key") by the Spanish—makes a great introduction to the region.

6

The history of Largo is similar to that of the rest of the Keys, with its succession of native people, pirates, wreckers, and developers. The first settlement on Key Largo was named Planter, back in the days of pineapple and later key lime plantations. For a time it was a convenient shipping port, but when the railroad arrived Planter died on the vine. Today three communities—North Key Largo, Key Largo, and Tavernier—make up the whole of Key Largo.

If you've never tried diving, Key Largo is the perfect place to learn. Dozens of companies will be more than happy to show you the ropes. Nobody comes to Key Largo without visiting John Pennekamp Coral Reef State Park, one of the jewels of the state-park system. Also popular is the adjacent Key Largo National Marine Sanctuary, which encompasses about 190 square mi of coral reefs, sea-grass beds, and mangrove estuaries. Both are good for underwater exploration.

Fishing is the other big draw, and world records are broken regularly. There are plenty of charter operations to help you find the big ones and teach you how to hook the elusive bonefish, sometimes known as the ghost fish. On land, restaurants will cook your catch or dish up their own offerings with inimitable style.

Key Largo offers all the conveniences of a major resort town, with most businesses lined up along Overseas Highway (U.S. 1), the four-lane highway that runs down the middle of the island. Cars whiz past at all hours—something to remember when you're booking a room. Most lodgings are on the highway, so you'll want to be as far back as possible.

GETTING HERE AND AROUND

Key Largo is 56 mi south of Miami International Airport, with the mile markers going from 106 to 91. The island runs northeast–southwest, with Overseas Highway running down the center. If the highway is your only glimpse of the island, you're likely to feel barraged by its tacky commercial side. Make a point of driving Route 905 in North Key Largo and down side streets to the marinas to get a better feel for it.

ESSENTIALS

Visitor Information **Key Largo Chamber of Commerce** (✉ *MM 106 BS, Key Largo* ☎ *305/451–4747 or 800/822–1088* ⊕ *www.keylargochamber.org*).

EXPLORING

Dagny Johnson Key Largo Hammock Botanical State Park. American crocodiles, mangrove cuckoos, white-crowned pigeons, Schaus swallowtail butterflies, mahogany mistletoe, wild cotton, and 100 other rare critters and plants inhabit these 2,400 acres, sandwiched between Crocodile Lake National Wildlife Refuge and Pennekamp Coral Reef State Park. The park is also a user-friendly place to explore the largest remaining stand of the vast West Indian tropical hardwood hammock and mangrove wetland that once covered most of the Keys' upland areas. Interpretive signs describe many of the tropical tree species along a wide 1-mi paved road (2-mi round-trip) that invites walking and biking. There are also more than 6 mi of nature trails accessible to bikes and wheelchairs. Pets are welcome if on a leash no longer than 6 feet. You'll also find restrooms, information kiosks, and picnic tables. ✉ *0.5 mi north of Overseas Hwy. on Rte. 905 OS, North Key Largo* ☎ *305/451–1202* ⊕ *www. floridastateparks.org/keylargohammock* ✎ *$2.50* ⊙ *Daily 8–sundown.*

Dolphin Cove. This educational program begins at the facility's lagoon with a get-acquainted session from a platform. After that, you slip into the water for some frolicking with your new dolphin pals. The cost is $135 to $185. Spend the day shadowing a dolphin trainer for $630. Admission for nonparticipants is $10 for adults. ✉ *MM 101.9 BS, 101900 Overseas Hwy., Key Largo* ☎ *305/451–4060 or 877/365–2683* ⊕ *www.dolphinscove.com.*

Dolphins Plus. A sister property to Dolphin Cove, Dolphin Plus offers some of the same programs. Costing $135, the Natural Swim program begins with a one-hour briefing; then you enter the water to become totally immersed in the dolphins' world. In this visual orientation, participants snorkel but are not allowed to touch the dolphins. For tactile interaction (kissing, fin tows, etc.), sign up for the Structured Swim program ($185). The same concept with different critters, the sea lion swim costs $120. ✉ *MM 99, 31 Corrine Pl., Key Largo* ☎ *305/451–1993 or 866/860–7946* ⊕ *www.dolphinsplus.com.*

Jacobs Aquatic Center. Take the plunge at one of three swimming pools: an 8-lane, 25-meter lap pool with a diving well; a 3- to 4-foot-deep pool accessible to people with mobility problems; and an interactive play pool with a waterslide, pirate ship, waterfall, and sloping zero entry instead of steps. ✉ *MM 99.6 OS, 320 Laguana Ave.* ☎ *305/453–7946* ⊕ *www.jacobsaquaticcenter.org* ✎ *$8–$10* ⊙ *Daily 10–6, 10–7 in summer.*

Laura Quinn Wild Bird Center. Have a nose-to-beak encounter with ospreys, hawks, herons, and other unreleasable birds at this bird rehabilitation center, recently renamed for its founder, who passed away in 2010 (formerly the Florida Keys Wild Bird Center). The birds live in spacious screened enclosures along a boardwalk running through some of the best waterfront real estate in the Keys. Rehabilitated birds are set free, whereas these have become permanent residents. Free birds—especially pelicans and egrets—come to visit. The center is popular among photographers, who arrive at 3:30 pm, when hundreds of wild waterbirds fly in and feed within arm's distance as the staff tries to draw in injured animals. A short nature trail runs into the mangrove forest (bring bug spray May to October). ✉ *MM 93.6 BS,93600 Overseas Hwy., Tavernier* ☎ *305/852–4486* ⊕ *www.fkwbc.org* ⬚ *Free, donations accepted* ⊙ *Daily sunrise–sunset.*

BEACHES

John Pennekamp Coral Reef State Park. This state park is on everyone's list for close access to the best diving and snorkeling sites in the Sunshine State. The underwater treasure encompasses 78 square mi of coral reefs, sea-grass beds, and mangrove swamps and lies adjacent to the Florida Keys National Marine Sanctuary, which contains 40 of the 52 species of coral in the Atlantic Reef System and nearly 600 varieties of fish, from the colorful stoplight parrot fish to the demure cocoa damselfish. The park's visitor center has a 30-gallon floor-to-ceiling fish tank surrounded by smaller ones, so you can get a closer look at many of the underwater creatures. When you want to head out to sea, a concessionaire rents kayaks and powerboats, as well as snorkeling and diving equipment. You can also sign up for snorkeling and diving trips ($30 and $60, respectively, equipment extra) and glass-bottom-boat rides to the reef ($24). One of the most popular excursions is the snorkeling trip to see *Christ of the Deep*, the 2-ton underwater statue of Jesus. The park also has short nature trails, two man-made beaches, picnic shelters, a snack bar, and a campground. ✉ *MM 102.5 OS, 102601 Overseas Hwy.* ☎ *305/451–1202 for park, 305/451–6300 for excursions* ⊕ *www.pennekamppark.com, www.floridastateparks.org/pennekamp* ⬚ *$4.50 for 1 person in vehicle, $8 for 2–8 people, $2 for pedestrians and cyclists or extra people* ⊙ *Daily 8–sunset.*

SPORTS AND THE OUTDOORS
BOATING

Everglades Eco-Tours. Captain Sterling operates Everglades and Florida Bay ecology tours ($50 per person) and sunset cruises ($75 per person). ✉ *MM 104 BS, Sundowners Restaurant, 103900 Overseas Hwy., Key Largo* ☎ *305/853–5161 or 888/224–6044* ⊕ *www.captainsterling.com.*

M.V. Key Largo Princess. Two-hour glass-bottom-boat trips and sunset cruises on a luxury 75-foot motor yacht with a 280-square-foot glass viewing area (each $30) depart from the Holiday Inn docks three times a day. ✉ *MM 100 OS, 99701 Overseas Hwy., Key Largo* ☎ *305/451–4655 or 877/648–8129* ⊕ *www.keylargoprincess.com.*

CANOEING AND KAYAKING

Sea kayaking continues to gain popularity in the Keys. You can paddle for a few hours or the whole day, on your own or with a guide. Some outfitters even offer overnight trips. The **Florida Keys Overseas Paddling Trail,** part of a statewide system, runs from Key Largo to Key West. You can paddle the entire distance, 110 mi on the Atlantic side, which takes 9–10 days. The trail also runs the chain's length on the bay side, which is a longer route.

Coral Reef Park Co. At John Pennekamp Coral Reef State Park, this operator has a fleet of canoes and kayaks for gliding around the 2½-mi mangrove trail or along the coast. It also rents powerboats. ⊠ *MM 102.5 OS, 102601 Overseas Hwy.* ☎ *305/451–6300* ⊕ *www.pennekamppark. com.*

Florida Bay Outfitters. Rent canoes or sea kayaks from this company, which sets up self-guided trips on the Florida Keys Overseas Paddling Trail, helps with trip planning, and matches equipment to your skill level. It also runs myriad guided tours around Key Largo. Take a full-moon paddle or a one- to seven-day canoe or kayak tour to the Everglades, Lignumvitae Key, or Indian Key. Trips start at $60 for a half-day. ⊠ *MM 104 BS, 104050 Overseas Hwy.* ☎ *305/451–3018* ⊕ *www.kayakfloridakeys.com.*

FISHING

Private charters and big head boats (so named because they charge "by the head") are great for anglers who don't have their own vessel.

Sailors Choice. Fishing excursions depart twice daily ($40 cash for half-day trips). The 65-foot boat leaves from the Holiday Inn docks. Rods, bait, and license are included. ⊠ *MM 100 OS, Holiday Inn Resort & Marina, 99701 Overseas Hwy.* ☎ *305/451–1802 or 305/451–0041* ⊕ *www.sailorschoicefishingboat.com.*

SCUBA DIVING AND SNORKELING

Much of what makes the Upper Keys a singular dive destination is variety. Places like Molasses Reef, which begins 3 feet below the surface and descends to 55 feet, have something for everyone from novice snorkelers to experienced divers. The *Spiegel Grove*, a 510-foot vessel, lies in 130 feet of water, but its upper regions are only 60 feet below the surface. On rough days, Key Largo Undersea Park's Emerald Lagoon is a popular spot. Expect to pay about $80 for a two-tank, two-site-dive trip with tanks and weights, or $35–$40 for a two-site-snorkel outing. Get big discounts by booking multiple trips.

Amy Slate's Amoray Dive Resort. This outfit makes diving easy. Stroll down to the full-service dive shop (NAUI, PADI, TDI, and BSAC certified), then onto a 45-foot catamaran. The rate for a two-dive trip is $80. ⊠ *MM 104.2 BS, 104250 Overseas Hwy.* ☎ *305/451–3595 or 800/426–6729* ⊕ *www.amoray.com.*

★ **Conch Republic Divers.** Book diving instruction as well as scuba and snorkeling tours of all the wrecks and reefs of the Upper Keys. Two-location dives are $80 with tank and weights or $65 without the equipment. ⊠ *MM 90.8 BS, 90800 Overseas Hwy.* ☎ *305/852–1655 or 800/274–3483* ⊕ *www.conchrepublicdivers.com.*

Coral Reef Park Co. At John Pennekamp Coral Reef State Park, this company gives 3½-hour scuba ($60) and 2½-hour snorkeling ($30) tours of the park. In addition to the great location and the dependability it's also suited for water adventurers of all levels. ⊠ *MM 102.5 OS, 102601 Overseas Hwy.* ☎ *305/451–6300* ⊕ *www.pennekamppark.com.*

Ocean Divers. The PADI five-star Caribbean Drive facility offers day and night dives, a range of courses, and dive-lodging packages. The cost is $80 for a two-tank reef dive with tank and weight rental. Snorkel trips cost $45 without equipment, $50 including snorkel, mask, and fins provided. There are two shops in Key Largo. ⊠ *MM 100 OS, 522 Caribbean Dr.* ⊠ *MM 105.8 BS, 105800 Overseas Hwy.* ☎ *305/451–1113 (Caribbean Dr. location), 305/451–0037 (Overseas Hwy. location) or 800/451–1113* ⊕ *www.oceandivers.com.*

Quiescence Diving Services. This operator sets itself apart in two ways: it limits groups to six to ensure personal attention and offers day and night dives, as well as twilight dives when sea creatures are most active. Two-dive trips start at $66 without equipment. ⊠ *MM 103.5 BS, 103680 Overseas Hwy.* ☎ *305/451–2440* ⊕ *www.quiescence.com.*

SHOPPING

For the most part, shopping is sporadic in Key Largo, with a couple of shopping centers and fewer galleries than you find on the other big islands. If you're looking to buy scuba or snorkel equipment, you'll have plenty of places from which to choose.

NIGHTLIFE

The semiweekly *Keynoter* (Wednesday and Saturday), weekly *Reporter* (Thursday), and Friday through Sunday editions of the *Miami Herald* are the best sources of information on entertainment and nightlife. Daiquiri bars, tiki huts, and seaside shacks pretty well summarize Key Largo's bar scene.

Breezers Tiki Bar & Grille. Mingle with locals over cocktails and sunsets at Marriott's Key Largo Bay Beach Resort. ⊠ *MM 103.8 BS, 103800 Overseas Hwy.* ☎ *305/453–0000.*

★ **Caribbean Club.** Walls plastered with Bogart memorabilia remind customers that the classic 1948 Bogart–Bacall flick *Key Largo* has a connection with this club. It draws boaters, curious visitors, and local barfly types, all of whom happily mingle and shoot pool. Postcard-perfect sunsets and live music draw revelers on weekends. ⊠ *MM 104 BS* ☎ *305/451–4466.*

Coconuts. Live music fills both the indoor and outdoor areas of this Marina Del Mar Resort throughout most of the week. Outside around the resort pool it's a family scene, with food service and a bar. Inside is strictly a thirty- and fortysomething crowd, including a few seasoned townies, playing pool, watching sports TV, and enjoying the music. ⊠ *MM 100 OS, Marina Del Mar Resort, 528 Caribbean Dr.* ☎ *305/453–9794.*

WHERE TO EAT

$ ✕ **Alabama Jack's.** Calories be damned—the conch fritters here are
SEAFOOD heaven on a plate. The crab cakes, made from local blue crabs, earn
★ hallelujahs, too. The conch salad is as good as any you'll find in the Bahamas and a third of the price in trendy Keys restaurants. This weathered, circa-1950 restaurant floats on two roadside barges in an old fishing community. Regulars include weekend cyclists, Miamians on the lam, and boaters, who come to admire tropical birds in the nearby

mangroves, the occasional crocodile in the canal, or the bands that play on weekend afternoons. ■ **TIP→** It's about a half-hour drive from Key Largo, so you may want to plan a visit for your drive in or out. Jack's closes by 7, when the mosquitoes start biting. ⊠ *58000 Card Sound Rd., Key Largo* ☎ *305/248–8741* ⊕ *www.alabamajacks.com* ⚏ *Reservations not accepted.*

$$$ ✕ **The Fish House.** Restaurants not on the water have to produce the
SEAFOOD highest quality food to survive in the Keys. That's how the Fish House
★ has succeeded since the 1980s—so much so that it built the Fish House Encore next door to accommodate fans. The pan-sautéed black grouper will make you moan with pleasure, but it's just one of many headliners in this nautical eatery. On the fin side, the choices include mahimahi, swordfish, tuna, and yellowtail snapper that can be broiled, blackened, baked, or fried. The Matecumbe Catch prepares the day's fresh fish so simply and flavorfully it should be patented—baked with tomatoes, capers, olive oil, and lemon juice. Prefer shellfish? Choose from shrimp, lobster, and (mid-October to mid-May) stone crab. For a sweet ending, try the homemade key lime pie. ⊠ *MM 102.4 OS, 102341 Overseas Hwy.* ☎ *305/451–4665* ⊕ *www.fishhouse.com* ⚏ *Reservations not accepted* ⊗ *Closed Sept.*

¢ ✕ **Harriette's Restaurant.** If you're looking for comfort food—like melt-
AMERICAN in-your-mouth buttermilk biscuits—try this refreshing throwback. The kitchen makes fresh muffins daily, in flavors like mango, chocolate, and key lime. Little has changed over the years in this yellow-and-turquoise eatery. Owner Harriette Mattson often personally greets guests who come for steak and eggs with hash browns or old-fashioned hotcakes with sausage or bacon. Stick to simple dishes; the eggs Benedict are a disappointment. At lunch- and dinnertime, Harriette's shines in the burger department, but there are also hot meals such as chicken-fried steak and steak-and-shrimp combo. ⊠ *MM 95.7 BS, 95710 Overseas Hwy.* ☎ *305/852–8689* ⚏ *Reservations not accepted* ⊗ *No dinner Fri.–Sun.*

$ ✕ **Mrs. Mac's Kitchen.** Townies pack the counters and booths at this tiny
SEAFOOD eatery, where license plates are stuck on the walls and made into chandeliers. Got a hankering for meat loaf or crab cakes? You'll find them here, along with specials like grilled yellowfin tuna. Bring your appetite for the all-you-can-eat fish specials on Tuesday and Thursday. There's also champagne breakfast, an assortment of tasty burgers and sandwiches, and its famous chili and key lime freeze (somewhere between a shake and a float). Ask about the hogfish special du jour. ⊠ *MM 99.4 BS, 99336 Overseas Hwy.* ☎ *305/451–3722* ⊕ *www.mrsmacskitchen. com* ⚏ *Reservations not accepted* ⊗ *Closed Sun.*

$$$ ✕ **Rib Daddy's Chop House.** Two Key Largo sister operations combined
SEAFOOD to create a comfort-food haven open for breakfast, lunch, and din-
☼ ner. Dieters, keep driving. Sunday's brunch buffet has everything the restaurant is famous for with a $14.95 price tag. You'll swoon after tasting the Memphis-style smoked prime rib, bison strip steak, and barbecue chicken flavored with specially formulated rubs and sauces. The menu includes seafood options, too, such as crab cakes and all-you-can-eat lobster and stone crab specials. Try the Hemingway (fried mahimahi, eggs, and grits) for breakfast or either the hand-pulled pork

6

sandwich or blackened chicken wrap for lunch. Save room for the key lime pie, creamy mango pie, or coconut cake. Kids love staring at the reef aquarium, the highlight of this rather plain, open dining room. ✉ *MM 102.2 BS, 102570 Overseas Hwy.* ☎ *305/451–0900* ⊕ *www. ribdaddysrestaurant.com* ⌂ *Reservations not accepted.*

$$$
SEAFOOD
★
✕ **Snapper's.** "You hook 'em, we cook 'em" is the motto here. Alas, "cleanin' 'em" is not part of the bargain. If you bring in your ready-for-the-grill fish, dinner here is $12 for a single, $13.95 per person family style. Otherwise, they'll catch and prepare you a plank-roasted yellowtail snapper, a grilled tuna steak, fish of the day baked with 36 herbs and spices, or a little something from the raw bar. The ceviche of yellowtail, shrimp, and conch (merrily spiced) wins raves, too. Lunch's seafood burrito is a keeper. All this is served up in a lively, mangrove-ringed waterfront setting with live music, an aquarium bar, Sunday brunch (including a Finlandia Bloody Mary bar), killer rum drinks, and seating alongside the fishing dock. Three-course early-bird dinner specials are available 5–6 for $18.50. ✉ *MM 94.5 OS, 139 Seaside Ave.* ☎ *305/852–5956* ⊕ *www.snapperskeylargo.com* ⌂ *Reservations not accepted.*

$$$
AMERICAN
✕ **Sundowners.** The name doesn't lie. If it's a clear night and you can snag a reservation, this restaurant will treat you to a sherbet-hue sunset over Florida Bay. If you're here in mild weather—anytime other than the dog days of summer or the rare winter cold snap—the best seats are on the patio. The food is excellent: try the key lime seafood, a happy combo of sautéed shrimp, lobster, and lump crabmeat swimming in a tangy sauce spiked with Tabasco served over penne or rice. Wednesday and Saturday are all about prime rib, and Friday draws the crowds with an all-you-can-eat fish fry ($16). Sunday brunch features Bloody Marys. ✉ *MM 104 BS, 103900 Overseas Hwy.* ☎ *305/451–4502* ⊕ *sundown-erskeylargo.com* ⌂ *Reservations essential.*

WHERE TO STAY

For expanded hotel reviews, visit Fodors.com.

$$$
HOTEL
★
🛏 **Azul del Mar.** The dock points the way to many beautiful sunsets at this adults-only boutique hotel. **Pros:** great garden; good location; sophisticated design. **Cons:** small beach; close to highway; high-priced. **TripAdvisor:** "relaxing and enjoyable," "very secluded," "private beach with nice sitting areas." ✉ *MM 104.3 BS, 104300 Overseas Hwy.* ☎ *305/451–0337 or 888/253–2985* ⊕ *www.azulhotels.us* ⇱ *2 studios, 3 1-bedroom suites, 1 2-bedroom suite* ⌂ *In-room: a/c, kitchen, Wi-Fi. In-hotel: beach, water sports, some age restrictions* ❢⊙ *No meals.*

$$
RESORT
🛏 **Coconut Bay Resort & Bay Harbor Lodge.** Some 200 feet of waterfront is the main attraction at this property, a combination of two lodging options. **Pros:** bay front; neatly kept gardens; walking distance to restaurants; complimentary kayak and paddleboat use. **Cons:** a bit dated; small sea-walled sand beach. **TripAdvisor:** "convenient," "landscaping was amazing," "great place to escape." ✉ *MM 97.7 BS, 97702 Overseas Hwy.* ☎ *305/852–1625 or 800/385–0986* ⊕ *www.coconutbaykeylargo. com* ⇱ *7 rooms, 5 efficiencies, 2 suites, 1 2-bedroom villa, 6 1-bedroom cottages* ⌂ *In-room: a/c, kitchen (some), Wi-Fi (some). In-hotel: pool, beach, some pets allowed* ❢⊙ *No meals.*

$$$$ Dove Creek Lodge. Old-school anglers will likely be scandalized by
B&B/INN this 2004 fishing camp's sherbet-hue paint and plantation-style furnishings. **Pros:** great for fishing enthusiasts; luxurious rooms; close to
Snapper's restaurant with charging privileges. **Cons:** loud music next
door. **TripAdvisor:** "warmth and intimacy," "room was clean and spacious," "well maintained and attractive." ⊠ *MM 94.5 OS, 147 Seaside
Ave.* ☎ *305/852–6200 or 800/401–0057* ⊕ *www.dovecreeklodge.com*
⤴ *4 room, 10 suites* ⚂ *In-room: a/c, kitchen (some), Internet, Wi-Fi.
In-hotel: pool* ⓄⓁ *Breakfast.*

$$$$ Kona Kai Resort & Gallery. Brilliantly colored bougainvilleas, coco-
RESORT nut palms, guava trees, and a new botanical garden make this 2-acre
Fodor's Choice hideaway one of the prettiest places to stay in the Keys. **Pros:** lush
★ landscaping; free use of sports equipment; knowledgeable staff. **Cons:**
expensive; some rooms are very close together. **TripAdvisor:** "beautiful small grounds," "wonderful experience," "no small detail has been
overlooked." ⊠ *MM 97.8 BS, 97802 Overseas Hwy.* ☎ *305/852–7200
or 800/365–7829* ⊕ *www.konakairesort.com* ⤴ *8 suites, 3 rooms* ⚂ *In-
room: a/c, kitchen (some). In-hotel: tennis court, pool, beach, some age
restrictions* ⓄⓁ *No meals* ⊘ *Closed Sept.*

$$$ Largo Lodge. When you drive under the dense canopy of foliage at the
B&B/INN entrance to Largo Lodge you'll feel like you've escaped Overseas High-
★ way's bustle. **Pros:** lush grounds; great sunset views; affordable rates;
boat docking. **Cons:** no pool; some traffic noise outdoors. **TripAdvisor:**
"friendly quaint lovely," "great place to stay," "like living in a botanical
garden." ⊠ *MM 101.7 BS, 101740 Overseas Hwy.* ☎ *305/451–0424
or 800/468–4378* ⊕ *www.largolodge.com* ⤴ *2 rooms, 6 cottages* ⚂ *In-
room: a/c, kitchen (some), Wi-Fi. In-hotel: beach, some age restrictions*
ⓄⓁ *No meals.*

$$$$ Marriott's Key Largo Bay Beach Resort. Park the car and toss the
RESORT keys in the bottom of your bag; there's no need to go anywhere else
⚲ (except maybe John Pennekamp Coral Reef State Park, just a half
★ mile north). **Pros:** lots of activities; free covered parking; dive shop on
property; free Wi-Fi. **Cons:** rooms facing highway can be noisy; thin
walls; unspectacular beach. **TripAdvisor:** "balconies on each room are
very large," "pool was great," "a good location." ⊠ *MM 103.8 BS,
103800 Overseas Hwy.* ☎ *305/453–0000 or 866/849–3753* ⊕ *www.
marriottkeylargo.com* ⤴ *132 rooms, 20 2-bedroom suites, 1 penthouse
suite* ⚂ *In-room: a/c, kitchen (some), Wi-Fi. In-hotel: restaurants, bars,
pool, gym, spa, beach, water sports, children's programs, laundry facili-
ties* ⓄⓁ *No meals.*

¢   The Pelican. This 1950s throwback is reminiscent of the days when
HOTEL parents packed the kids into the station wagon and headed to no-frills
seaside motels, complete with an old-timer fishing off the dock. **Pros:**
free use of kayaks and paddleboats; well-maintained dock; reasonable
rates. **Cons:** some small rooms; basic accommodations and amenities.
TripAdvisor: "good value," "nice place for a no-frills stay," "right on
the waterfront." ⊠ *MM 99.3, 99340 Overseas Hwy.* ☎ *305/451–3576
or 877/451–3576* ⊕ *www.thepelicankeylargo.com* ⤴ *13 rooms, 4 effi-
ciencies, 4 suites* ⚂ *In-room: a/c, kitchen (some), Wi-Fi. In-hotel: beach,
water sports* ⓄⓁ *No meals.*

$ **Seafarer Resort**. It's budget lodg-
HOTEL ing, but the Seafarer Resort is not
without its charms. **Pros:** sandy
beach; complimentary kayak use.
Cons: some rooms close to road
noise; basic accommodations. **TripAdvisor:** "off the beaten path,"
"clean but very dated," "great
bargain." ⊠ *MM 97.6 BS, 97684
Overseas Hwy.* ☎ *305/852–5349*
⊕ *www.seafarerresort.com* ⤳ *8
rooms, 3 studios, 3 1-bedroom
cottages, 1 2-bedroom cottage, 2
apartments* ♿ *In-room: kitchen
(some), Wi-Fi. In-hotel: beach, water sports, laundry facilities* ⦿ *No
meals.*

WORD OF MOUTH

"Went on the snorkeling trip out
of John Pennekamp State Park.
The total was $44 for snorkel
trip, full rental including wet suit.
Really enjoyed the trip, but wished
I had driven down for the 9 am
trip—there were fewer snorkelers and the website offered a
discount coupon for the morning
tour."   —starrsville

CAMPING

☾ **John Pennekamp Coral Reef State Park**. Divers and snorkelers won't
★ find a better location in the Upper Keys. Pennekamp's campsites are
carved out of hardwood hammock, providing shade and privacy away
from the heavy day-use areas. Activities include boating, fishing, scuba
diving, snorkeling, and hiking. There's no restaurant, but there are
vending machines for late-night snack attacks. ♿ *Flush toilets, partial
hook-ups (electric and water), dump station, drinking water, showers, fire pits, picnic tables, electricity, public telephone, general store,
ranger station, swimming (ocean)* ⤳ *47 partial hook-ups for RVs and
tents* ⊠ *MM 102.5 OS, 102601 Overseas Hwy.* ☎ *305/451–1202 park,
800/326–3521 reservations* ⊕ *www.reserveamerica.com.*

ISLAMORADA

Islamorada is between mile markers 90.5 and 70.

Early settlers named this key after their schooner, *Island Home*, but
to make it sound more romantic they translated it into Spanish: *Isla
Morada*. The chamber of commerce prefers to use its literal transla-
tion "Purple Island," which refers either to a purple-shelled snail that
once inhabited these shores or to the brilliantly colored orchids and
bougainvilleas.

Early maps show Islamorada as encompassing only Upper Matecumbe
Key. But the incorporated "Village of Islands" is made up of a string of
islands that the Overseas Highway crosses, including Plantation Key,
Windley Key, Upper Matecumbe Key, Lower Matecumbe Key, Craig
Key, and Fiesta Key. In addition, two state-park islands accessible only
by boat—Indian Key and Lignumvitae Key—belong to the group.

Islamorada (locals pronounce it "*eye*-la-mor-*ah*-da") is one of the
world's top fishing destinations. For nearly 100 years, seasoned anglers
have fished these clear, warm waters teeming with trophy-worthy fish.
There are numerous options for those in search of the big ones, including chartering a boat with its own crew or heading out on a vessel
rented from one of the plethora of marinas along this 20-mi stretch of

Islamorada's warm waters attract large fish and the anglers, including charters, who want to catch them.

the Overseas Highway. Islamorada is one of the more affluent resort areas of the Keys. Sophisticated resorts and restaurants meet the needs of those in search of luxury, but there's also plenty for those looking for something more casual and affordable. Art galleries and boutiques make Islamorada's shopping scene the best in the Upper Keys, but if you're shopping for groceries, head to Marathon or Key Largo.

ESSENTIALS

Visitor Information Islamorada Chamber of Commerce & Visitors Center (✉ *MM 83.2 BS, 83224 Overseas Hwy, Upper Matecumbe Key, Islamorada* ☎ *305/664–4503 or 800/322–5397* ⊕ *www.islamoradachamber.com*).

EXPLORING

History of Diving Museum. Adding to the region's reputation for world-class diving, this museum plunges into the history of man's thirst for undersea exploration. Among its 13 galleries of interactive and other interesting displays are a submarine and helmet from the film *20,000 Leagues Under the Sea.* Historic equipment, sunken treasures, and photographs are part of the extensive collection donated by a local couple. ✉ *MM 83 BS, 82990 Overseas Hwy., Upper Matecumbe Key* ☎ *305/664–9737* ⊕ *www.divingmuseum.org* 🎫 *$12* ☉ *Daily 10–5.*

Robbie's Marina. Huge, prehistoric-looking denizens of the not-so-deep, silver-sided tarpon congregate around the docks at this marina on Lower Matecumbe Key. Children—and lots of adults—pay $4 to feed them sardines or $1 just to watch. Spend some time hanging out at this authentic Keys community, where you can grab a bite to eat, do a little shopping, or charter a boat. ✉ *MM 77.5 BS, 77522 Overseas Hwy.,*

Lower Matecumbe Key ☎ *305/664–9814 or 877/664–8498* ⊕ *www. robbies.com* ✉ *Dock access $1* ⊙ *Daily 8–5.*

☻ **Theater of the Sea.** The second-oldest marine-mammal center in the world doesn't attempt to compete with more modern, more expensive parks. Even so, it's among the better attractions north of Key West, especially if you have kids in tow. Like the pricier parks, there are dolphin, sea lion, and stingray encounters ($55–$175, which includes general admission; reservations required) where you can get up close and personal with underwater creatures. These are popular, so reserve in advance. Ride a "bottomless" boat to see what's below the waves and take a guided tour of the marine-life exhibits. Entertaining educational shows highlight conservation issues. You can stop for lunch at the grill, shop in the boutique, or sunbathe at a lagoon-side beach. This easily could be an all-day attraction. ✉ *MM 84.5 OS, 84721 Overseas Hwy., Windley Key* ☎ *305/664–2431* ⊕ *www.theaterofthesea.com* ✉ *$26.95* ⊙ *Daily 9:30–5 (last ticket sold at 3:30).*

Upper Matecumbe Key. This was one of the first of the Upper Keys to be permanently settled. Early homesteaders were so successful at growing pineapples in the rocky soil that at one time the island yielded the country's largest annual crop. However, foreign competition and the hurricane of 1935 killed the industry. Today, life centers on fishing and tourism, and the island is filled with bait shops, marinas, and charter-fishing boats. ✉ *MM 84–79.*

OFF THE
BEATEN
PATH

Indian Key Historic State Park. Mystery surrounds 10-acre Indian Key, on the ocean side of the Matecumbe islands. Before it became one of the first European settlements outside of Key West, it was inhabited by American Indians for several thousand years. The islet served as a base for 19th-century shipwreck salvagers until an Indian attack wiped out the settlement in 1840. Dr. Henry Perrine, a noted botanist, was killed in the raid. Today his plants grow in the town's ruins. Most people kayak or canoe here from Indian Key Fill to explore the nature trails and the town ruins or to snorkel. Florida Keys Kayak has an office at Robbie's Marina. There are no restrooms or picnic facilities on the island. ⌂ *Box 1052* ☎ *305/664–2540* ⊕ *www.floridastateparks.org/indiankey* ✉ *Free* ⊙ *Daily sunrise–sunset.*

OFF THE
BEATEN
PATH

Lignumvitae Key Botanical State Park. On the National Register of Historic Places, this 280-acre bay-side island is the site of a virgin hardwood forest and the 1919 home of chemical magnate William Matheson. His caretaker's cottage serves as the park's visitor center. Access is by boat—your own, a rented vessel, or a ferry operated by Robbie's Marina (reservations required). Paddling here from Indian Key Fill, at MM 78.5, is a popular pastime. The only way to do the trails is by a guided ranger walk, offered at 10 am and 2 pm Friday to Sunday. Wear long sleeves and pants, and bring mosquito repellent. On the first weekend in December is the Lignumvitae Christmas Celebration. ⌂ *Box 1052* ☎ *305/664–2540 park, 305/664–9814 ferry* ⊕ *www.floridastateparks. org/lignumvitaekey* ✉ *$1 for tours; ferry prices fluctuate according to season* ⊙ *Park (Matheson yard/picnic grounds) open daily 9–5; house tours Fri.–Sun 10 and 2.*

Windley Key Fossil Reef Geological State Park. The fossilized-coral reef, dating back about 125,000 years, demonstrates that the Florida Keys were once beneath the ocean. Excavation of Windley Key's limestone bed by the Florida East Coast Railway exposed the petrified reef, full of beautifully fossilized brain coral and sea ferns. Visitors can see the fossils along a 300-foot quarry wall when hiking the park's three trails. There are guided (Friday, Saturday, and Sunday only) and self-guided tours along the trails, which lead to the railway's old quarrying equipment and cutting pits, where you can make rubbings of the quarry walls. The **Alison Fahrer Environmental Education Center** holds historic, biological, and geological displays about the area, including videos. The first Saturday in March is Windley Key Day, when the park sells native plants and hosts environmental exhibits. ⊠ *MM 84.9 BS, Windley Key* 🕾 *305/664–2540* ⊕ *www.floridastateparks.org/windleykey* 🄳 *Education center free, $2.50 for park self-tours, $1 for ranger-guided tours* ⊙ *Education center Fri.–Sun. 9–5 (tours at 10 and 2).*

BEACHES

Anne's Beach Park. On Lower Matecumbe Key is a popular village park, named for a local environmental activist. Its "beach" (really a typical Keys-style sand flat) is best enjoyed at low tide. The nicest feature here is a ½-mi, elevated, wooden boardwalk that meanders through a natural wetland hammock. Covered picnic areas along the way give you places to linger and enjoy the view. Restrooms are at the north end. Weekends are packed with Miami day-trippers as it's the only public beach until you reach Marathon. ⊠ *MM 73.5 OS, Lower Matecumbe Key* 🕾 *305/853–1685.*

SPORTS AND THE OUTDOORS
BOATING

Marinas pop up every mile or so in the Islamorada area, so finding a rental or tour is no problem. Robbie's Marina is a prime example of a salty spot where you can find it all—from fishing charters and kayaking rentals to lunch and tarpon feeding.

Bump & Jump. This one-stop shop for windsurfing, sailboat and powerboat rentals, sales, and lessons delivers to your hotel or house, or drops equipment off right at the beach. ⊠ *MM 81.2 OS, 81197 Overseas Hwy., Upper Matecumbe Key* 🕾 *305/664–9404 or 877/453–9463* ⊕ *www.keysboatrental.com.*

Houseboat Vacations of the Florida Keys. See the islands from the comfort of your own boat (captain's cap optional). The company maintains a fleet of 42- to 55-foot boats that accommodate up to 10 people and come outfitted with everything you need besides food. You may provision yourself at a nearby grocery store. The three-day minimum starts at $1,112; one week costs $1,950 and up. Kayaks, canoes, and skiffs suitable for the ocean are also available. ⊠ *MM 85.9 BS, 85944 Overseas Hwy. Plantation Key* 🕾 *305/664–4009* ⊕ *www.floridakeys.com/ houseboats.*

Robbie's Boat Rentals & Charters. This full-service company will even give you a crash course on how not to crash your boat. The rental fleet includes an 18-foot skiff with a 60-horsepower outboard for $150

Renting wave runners is a fun way to catch some surf and sun in Florida Keys. Each fits one to three people.

for four hours and $200 for the day to a 23-foot deck boat with a 130-horsepower engine for $185 for a half day and $235 for eight hours. Robbie's also rents fishing and snorkeling gear (there's good snorkeling nearby) and sells bait, drinks and snacks, and gas. Want to hire a guide who knows the local waters and where the fish lurk? Robbie's offers offshore-fishing trips, patch-reef trips, and party-boat fishing. Backcountry flats trips are a specialty. ⊠ *MM 77.5 BS, 77522 Overseas Hwy., Lower Matecumbe Key* ☎ *305/664–9814 or 877/664– 8498* ⊕ *www.robbies.com.*

Treasure Harbor Marine. Captains Pam and Pete Anderson provide everything you'll need for a sailing vacation at sea. They also give excellent advice on where to find the best anchorages, snorkeling spots, or lobstering sites. Vessels range from a 23.5-foot Hunter to a 41-foot Morgan Out Island. Rates start at $160 a day; $700 a week. Hire a captain for $175–$200 a day. Marina facilities are basic—water, electric, ice machine, laundry, picnic tables, and restrooms with showers. A store sells snacks, beverages, and sundries. ⊠ *MM 86.5 OS, 200 Treasure Harbor Dr., Plantation Key* ☎ *305/852–2458 or 800/352–2628* ⊕ *www.treasureharbor.com.*

FISHING

Here in the self-proclaimed "Sportfishing Capital of the World," sailfish is the prime catch in the winter and dolphinfish in the summer. Buchanan Bank just south of Islamorada is a good spot to try for tarpon in the spring. Blackfin tuna and amberjack are generally plentiful in the area, too. ■TIP→ The Hump at Islamorada ranks highest among anglers' favorite fishing spots in Florida due to the incredible offshore marine life.

Captain Ted Wilson. Go into the backcountry for bonefish, tarpon, redfish, snook, and shark aboard a 17-foot boat that accommodates up to three anglers. For two people, half-day trips run $375, full-day trips $550, two-hour sunset bonefishing $225, and evening excursions $400. There's a $100 charge for an extra person. ✉ *MM 79.9 OS, 79851 Overseas Hwy., Upper Matecumbe Key* ☎ *305/942–5224 or 305/664–9463* ⊕ *www.captaintedwilson.com.*

Florida Keys Fly Fish. Like other top fly-fishing and light-tackle guides, Captain Geoff Colmes helps his clients land trophy fish in the waters around the Keys ($500–$550). ✉ *105 Palm La., Upper Matecumbe Key* ☎ *305/853–0741* ⊕ *www.floridakeysflyfish.com.*

Florida Keys Outfitters. Long before fly-fishing became popular, Sandy Moret was fishing the Keys for bonefish, tarpon, and redfish. Now he attracts anglers from around the world on a quest for the big catch. Weekend fly-fishing classes, which include classroom instruction, equipment, and daily lunch, cost $985. Add $1,070 for two additional days of fishing. Guided fishing trips cost $395 for a half day, $535 for a full day. Packages combining fishing and accommodations at Islander Resort are available. ✉ *Green Turtle, MM 81.2, 81219 Overseas Hwy., Upper Matecumbe Key* ☎ *305/664–5423* ⊕ *www.floridakeysoutfitters.com.*

★ **Hubba Hubba Charters.** Captain Ken Knudsen quietly poles his flatboat through the shallow water, barely making a ripple. Then he points and his clients cast. Five seconds later there's a zing, and the excitement of bringing in a snook, redfish, trout, or tarpon begins. Knudsen has fished Keys waters for more than 40 years. Now a licensed backcountry guide, he's ranked among Florida's top 10 by national fishing magazines. He offers four-hour sunset trips for tarpon ($425) and two-hour sunset trips for bonefish ($200), as well as half- ($375) and full-day ($550) outings. Prices are for one or two anglers, and tackle and bait are included. ✉ *MM 79.8 OS, Upper Matecumbe Key* ☎ *305/664–9281.*

Miss Islamorada. The 65-foot party boat has full-day trips for $60. Bring your lunch or buy one from the dockside deli. ✉ *Bud n' Mary's Marina, MM 79.8 OS, 79851 Overseas Hwy., Upper Matecumbe Key* ☎ *305/664–2461 or 800/742–7945* ⊕ *www.budnmarys.com.*

SCUBA DIVING AND SNORKELING

About 1¼ nautical mi south of Indian Key is the **San Pedro Underwater Archaeological Preserve State Park** (✉ *MM 85.5 OS* ☎ *305/664–2540* ⊕ *www.floridastateparks.org/sanpedro*), which includes the wreck of a Spanish treasure-fleet ship that sank in 1733. The state of Florida protects the site for divers; no spearfishing or souvenir collecting is allowed. Resting in only 18 feet of water, its ruins are visible to snorkelers as well as divers and attract a colorful array of fish.

Florida Keys Dive Center. Dive from John Pennekamp Coral Reef State Park to Alligator Light with this outfitter. The center has two 46-foot Coast Guard–approved dive boats, offers scuba training, and is one of the few Keys dive centers to offer Nitrox and Trimix (mixed gas) diving. Two-tank dives cost $60 with no equipment; two-location snorkeling is $38. ✉ *MM 90.5 OS, 90451 Overseas Hwy. Plantation Key* ☎ *305/852–4599 or 800/433–8946* ⊕ *www.floridakeysdivectr.com.*

Holiday Isle Dive Shop. With a resort, pool, restaurant, lessons, and twice-daily dive and snorkel trips this a one-stop dive shop. Rates start at $50 for a two-tank dive without equipment. ⊠ *MM 84 OS, 84001 Overseas Hwy., Windley Key* ☎ *305/664–3483 or 800/327–7070* ⊕ *www.diveholidayisle.com.*

WATER SPORTS

Florida Keys Kayak. Rent kayaks for trips to Indian and Lignumvitae keys, two favorite destinations for paddlers. Kayak rental half-day rates (and you'll need plenty of time to explore those mangrove canopies) are $40 for a single kayak and $55 for a double. Pedal kayaks are available for $50 single and $65 double. The company also offers guided three-hour tours, including a snorkel trip to Indian Key ($45). It also rents stand-up paddleboards, at $50 for a half-day including lessons, and canoes. ⊠ *Robbie's Marina, MM 77.5 BS, 77522 Overseas Hwy., Lower Matecumbe Key* ☎ *305/664–4878* ⊕ *www.kayakthefloridakeys.com.*

SHOPPING

Art galleries, upscale gift shops, and the mammoth World Wide Sportsman (if you want to look the part of a local fisherman, you must wear a shirt from here) make up the variety and superior style of Islamorada shopping.

Banyan Tree. A sharp-eyed husband-and-wife team successfully combines antiques and contemporary gifts for the home and garden with plants, pots, and trellises in a stylishly sophisticated indoor–outdoor setting. ⊠ *MM 81.2 OS, 81197 Overseas Hwy., Upper Matecumbe Key* ☎ *305/664–3433 or 877/453–9463* ⊕ *www.banyantreegarden.com.*

Gallery Morada. The go-to destination for one-of-a-kind gifts beautifully displays blown-glass objects, original sculptures, paintings, lithographs, and jewelry by top South Florida artists. ⊠ *MM 81.6 OS, 81611 Old Hwy., Upper Matecumbe Key* ☎ *305/664–3650* ⊕ *www.gallerymorada.com.*

Hooked on Books. Among the best buys in town are the used best sellers at this bookstore, which also sells new titles, audiobooks, and CDs. ⊠ *MM 82.6 OS, 82681 Overseas Hwy., Upper Matecumbe Key* ☎ *305/517–2602* ⊕ *www.hookedonbooksfloridakeys.com.*

Island Silver & Spice. The shop stocks tropical-style furnishings, rugs, and home accessories, as well as women's and men's resort wear and a large jewelry selection with high-end watches and marine-theme pieces. ⊠ *MM 82 OS, 81981 Overseas Hwy., Upper Matecumbe Key* ☎ *305/664–2714.*

Rain Barrel. This is a natural and unhurried shopping showplace. Set in a tropical garden of shady trees, native shrubs, and orchids, the crafts village has shops with works by local and national artists and resident artists in studios, including John Hawver, noted for Florida landscapes and seascapes. The Main Gallery up front showcases the craftsmanship of the resident artisans, who create marine-inspired artwork while you watch. ⊠ *MM 86.7 BS, 86700 Overseas Hwy. Plantation Key* ☎ *305/852–3084.*

Redbone Gallery. One of the largest sportfishing–art galleries in Florida stocks hand-stitched clothing and giftware, in addition to work by wood and bronze sculptors such as Kendall van Sant; watercolorists Chet Reneson, Jeanne Dobie, and Kathleen Denis; and painters C.D. Clarke and Tim Borski. Proceeds benefit cystic fibrosis research. ⊠ *MM 81.5 OS, 200 Industrial Dr., Upper Matecumbe Key* ☏ *305/664–2002* ⊕ *www.redbone.org.*

World Wide Sportsman. Former U.S. presidents, celebrities, and record holders beam alongside their catches in black-and-white photos on the walls of this two-level retail center that sells upscale fishing equipment, resort clothing, sportfishing art, and other gifts. When you're tired of shopping, relax at the Zane Grey Long Key Lounge just above World Wide Sportsman. ⊠ *MM 81.5 BS, 81576 Overseas Hwy., Upper Matecumbe Key* ☏ *305/664–4615 or 800/327–2880.*

NIGHTLIFE

Islamorada is not known for its raging nightlife, but for local fun Lorelei's is legendary. Others cater to the town's sophisticated clientele and fishing fervor.

★ **Lorelei Restaurant & Cabana Bar.** Behind a larger-than-life mermaid, this is the kind of place you fantasize about during those long cold winters up north. It's all about good drinks, tasty pub grub, and beautiful sunsets set to live bands playing island tunes and light rock nightly. ⊠ *MM 82 BS, 81924 Overseas Hwy., Upper Matecumbe Key* ☏ *305/664–2692* ⊕ *www.loreleicabanabar.com.*

WHERE TO EAT

$$$ ✕ **Green Turtle Inn.** This circa-1928 landmark inn and its vintage neon
SEAFOOD   sign is a slice of Florida Keys history. Period photographs decorate the wood-paneled walls. Breakfast and lunch options include surprises like coconut French toast made with Cuban bread and yellowfin tuna tartare. Chef Dan Harris relies heavily on Cajun cuisine with Italian touches for the dinner menu; think turtle chowder (don't gasp; it's made from farm-raised freshwater turtles), barbecued shrimp, gumbo, and lobster lasagna. Naturally, there's a Turtle Sundae on the dessert menu. ⊠ *MM 81.2 OS, 81219 Overseas Hwy., Upper Matecumbe Key* ☏ *305/664–2006* ⊕ *www.greenturtlekeys.com* ⌕ *Reservations essential* ⊘ *Closed Mon.*

$$ ✕ **Island Grill.** Don't be fooled by appearances; this shack on the water-
SEAFOOD   front takes island breakfast, lunch, and dinner cuisine up a notch. The
★   eclectic menu tempts you with such dishes as tuna nachos and lobster rolls. Southern-style shrimp and andouille sausage with grits join island-style specialties such as grilled ribs with guava barbecue sauce on the list of entrées. There's an air-conditioned dining room and bar as well as outdoor seating under the trees. The outdoor bar hosts live entertainment Wednesday to Sunday. ⊠ *MM 85.5 OS, 85501 Overseas Hwy., Windley Key* ☏ *305/664–8400* ⊕ *www.keysislandgrill.com* ⌕ *Reservations not accepted.*

$$ ✕ **Kaiyó Grill & Sushi.** Kaiyó's decor—an inviting setting that includes
JAPANESE   colorful abstract mosaics, polished wood floors, and upholstered banquettes—almost steals the show here, but the food is equally interesting.

Continued on page 303

UNDER THE SEA
SNORKELING AND DIVING
IN THE FLORIDA KEYS by Lynne Helm

Up on the shore they work all day...

> While we devotin',
>
> Full time to floatin',
>
> Under the sea...

—"Under the Sea,"
from Disney's Little Mermaid

All Floridians—even those long-accustomed to balmy breezes and swaying palms—turn ecstatic at the mere thought of tripping off to the Florida Keys. Add the prospect of underwater adventure, and hot diggity, it's unparalleled bliss.

Perennially laid back, the Keys annually attract nearly 800,000 snorkeling and scuba diving aficionados, and why not? There's arguably no better destination to learn these sports that put you up close to the wonders of life under the sea.

THE BARRIER REEF

The continental United States' only living coral barrier reef stretches 5 mi offshore of the Keys and is a teeming backbone of marine life, ranging from brilliant corals to neon-colored fish from blue-striped grunts to green moray eels. This is the prime reason why the Keys are where you descend upon intricate natural coral formations and encrusted shipwrecks, some historic, others sunk by design to create artificial reefs that attract divers

and provide protection for marine life. Most diving sites have mooring buoys (nautical floats away from shore, sometimes marking specific sites); these let you tie up your boat so you don't need to drop anchor, which could damage the reef. Most of these sites also are near individual keys, where dozens of dive operators can cater to your needs.

Reef areas thrive in waters as shallow as 5 feet and as deep as 50 feet. Shallow reefs attract snorkelers, while deeper reefs suit divers of varying experience levels. The Keys' shallow diving offers two benefits: longer time safely spent on the bottom exploring, and more vibrant colors because of sunlight penetration. Most divers log maximum depths of 20 to 30 feet.

6

IN FOCUS UNDER THE SEA

(left) Shallow-water coral reef, (top) Nine Foot Stake is a popular site for underwater photography.

WHERE TO SNORKEL AND DIVE

KEY WEST
Mile Marker 0–4

You can soak up a mesmerizing overview of submerged watery wonders at the Florida Keys Eco-Discovery Center, opened in 2007 on Key West's Truman Annex waterfront. Both admission and parking are free at the 6,000 square–foot center (☉ *9–4 Tues.–Sat.* ☎ *305/809–4750)*; interactive exhibits here focus on Keys marine life and habitats. Key West's offshore reefs are best accessed via professional charters, but it's easy to snorkel from shore at Key West Marine Park. Marked by a lighthouse, Sand Key Reef attracts snorkelers and scuba divers. Joe's Tug, at 65-foot depths, sets up encounters with Goliath grouper. Ten-Fathom Ledge, with coral caves and

Nine Foot Stake

dramatic overhangs, shelters lobster. The Cayman Salvor, a buoy tender sunk as an artificial reef in 1985, shelters baitfish. Patch reef Nine Foot Stake, submerged 10 to 25 feet, has soft corals and juvenile marine life. Kedge Ledge features a pair of coral-encrusted anchors from 18th-century sailing vessels. 🚹 *Florida Keys main visitor line at* ☎ *800/FLA-KEYS (352-5397)*.

BIG PINE KEY/LOWER KEYS
Mile Marker 4–47

Many devotees feel a Florida dive adventure would not be complete without heading 5 mi from Big Pine Key to Looe Key National Marine Sanctuary, an underwater preserve named for the HMS Looe running aground in 1744. If you time your visit for July, you might hit the one-day free underwater music festival for snorkelers

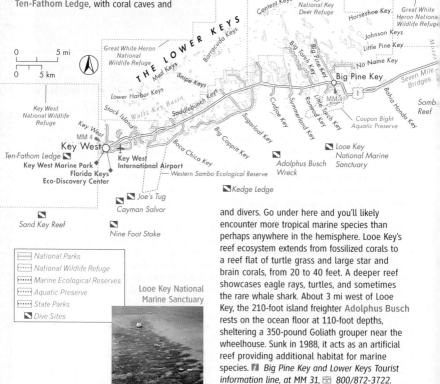

Looe Key National
Marine Sanctuary

and divers. Go under here and you'll likely encounter more tropical marine species than perhaps anywhere in the hemisphere. Looe Key's reef ecosystem extends from fossilized corals to a reef flat of turtle grass and large star and brain corals, from 20 to 40 feet. A deeper reef showcases eagle rays, turtles, and sometimes the rare whale shark. About 3 mi west of Looe Key, the 210-foot island freighter Adolphus Busch rests on the ocean floor at 110-foot depths, sheltering a 350-pound Goliath grouper near the wheelhouse. Sunk in 1988, it acts as an artificial reef providing additional habitat for marine species. 🚹 *Big Pine Key and Lower Keys Tourist information line, at MM 31,* ☎ *800/872-3722.*

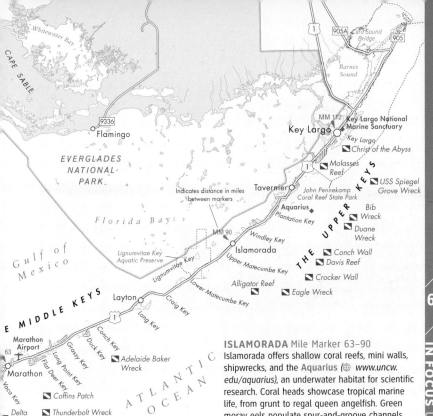

Map labels:

Whitewater Bay

CAPE SABLE

Card Sound Bridge — 905A — 905

1

Barnes Sound

9336

Flamingo

MM 112 — Key Largo National Marine Sanctuary

Key Largo

EVERGLADES NATIONAL PARK

Key Largo — Christ of the Abyss

Molasses Reef

Tavernier — John Pennekamp Coral Reef State Park

USS Spiegel Grove Wreck

Indicates distance in miles between markers

Florida Bay

Aquarius — Plantation Key

Bib Wreck

Duane Wreck

MM 90 — Windley Key

Lignumvitae Key Aquatic Preserve

Lignumvitae Key

Islamorada

Upper Matecumbe Key

THE UPPER KEYS

Conch Wall

Davis Reef

Crocker Wall

Gulf of Mexico

Lower Matecumbe Key

Alligator Reef

Eagle Wreck

Layton — Craig Key

THE MIDDLE KEYS

Long Key

1

Marathon Airport

Conch Key

Duck Key

Grassy Key

Adelaide Baker Wreck

63

Long Point Key

Flat Deer Key

Marathon

Voca Key

Coffins Patch

ATLANTIC OCEAN

Delta Shoal

Thunderbolt Wreck

6

MARATHON/MIDDLE KEYS

Mile Marker 47–63

The Middle Keys yield a marine wilderness of a spur-and-groove coral and patch reefs. The Adelaide Baker historic shipwreck has a pair of stacks in 25 feet of water.

Sombrero Reef

Popular Sombrero Reef, with coral canyons and archways, is marked by a 140-foot lighted tower. Six distinct patch reefs known as Coffin's Patch have shallow elkhorn forests. Delta Shoals, a network of coral canyons fanning seaward from a sandy shoal, attracts divers to its elkhorn, brain, and star coral heads. Marathon's Thunderbolt, a 188-foot ship sunk in 1986, sits upright at 115-foot depths, coated with sponge, coral, and hydroid, and attracting angelfish, jacks, and deep-water pelagic creatures. 🔖 Greater Marathon Chamber and visitors center at MM 53.5, ☎ 800/262-7284.

ISLAMORADA Mile Marker 63–90

Islamorada offers shallow coral reefs, mini walls, shipwrecks, and the Aquarius (🌐 www.uncw. edu/aquarius), an underwater habitat for scientific research. Coral heads showcase tropical marine life, from grunt to regal queen angelfish. Green moray eels populate spur-and-groove channels, and nurse sharks linger around overhangs. Submerged attractions include the Eagle, a 287-foot ship in 110 feet of water; Davis Reef, with gorgonian coral; Alligator Reef, where the USS Alligator sank while fighting pirates; the sloping Conch Wall, with barrel sponges and gorgonian; and Crocker Wall, featuring spur-and-groove and block corals. 🔖 Islamorada Chamber and visitor center at MM 83.2, ☎ 800/322-5397.

KEY LARGO Mile Marker 90–112

Key Largo marine conservation got a big leg up with creation of John Pennekamp Coral Reef State Park in 1960, the nation's first undersea preserve, followed by 1975's designation of the Key Largo National Marine Sanctuary. A popular underwater attraction is the bronze statue of Christ of the Abyss between coral formations. Explorers with a "lust for rust" can dive down to 60 to 90 feet and farther to see the murky cemetery for two twin 327-foot U.S. Coast Guard cutters, Duane and Bibb, used during World War II; USS Spiegel Grove, a 510-foot Navy transport ship sunk in 2002 to create an artificial reef; and Molasses Reef, showcasing coral heads. 🔖 Key Largo Chamber at MM 106, ☎ 800/822-1088.

SCUBA DIVING

A diver explores the coral reef in the Florida Keys National Marine Sanctuary off Key Largo.

Florida offers wonderful opportunities to spend your vacation in the sun and become a certified diver at the same time. In the Keys, count on setting aside three to five days for entry-level or so-called "Open Water" certification offered by many dive shops. Basic certification (covering depths to about 60 feet) involves classroom work and pool training, followed by one or more open-water dives at the reef. After passing a knowledge test and completing the required water training (often starting in a pool), you become a certified recreational scuba diver, eligible to rent dive gear and book dive trips with most operations worldwide. Learning through video or online computer programs can enable you to complete classroom work at home, so you can more efficiently schedule time in the Keys for completing water skills and getting out to the reef for exploration.

Many would-be divers opt to take the classroom instruction and pool training at home at a local dive shop and then spend only two days in the Keys completing four dives. It's not necessarily cheaper, but it can be far more relaxing to commit to only two days of diving.

Questions you should ask: Not all dive shops are created equal, and it may be worthwhile to spend extra money for a better diving experience. Some of the larger dive shops take out large catamarans that can carry as many as 24 to 40 people. Many people prefer the intimacy of a smaller boat.

Good to know: Divers can become certified through PADI *(www.padi.com)*, NAUI *(www.naui.org)*, or SSI *(www.divessi.com)*. The requirements for all three are similar, and if you do the classroom instruction and pool training with a dive shop associated with one organization, the referral for the open water dives will be honored by most dive shops. Note that you are not allowed to fly for at least 24 hours after a dive, because residual nitrogen in the body can pose health risks upon decompression. While there are no rigid rules on diving after flying, make sure you're well-hydrated before hitting the water.

Cost: The four-day cost can range from $300 to $475, but be sure to ask if equipment, instruction manuals, and log books are extra. Some dive shops have relationships with hotels, so check for dive/stay packages. Referral dives (a collaborative effort among training agencies) run from $285 to $300 and discover scuba runs around $175 to $200.

SNUBA

Beyond snorkeling or the requirements of scuba, you also have the option of "Snuba." The word is a trademarked portmanteau or combo of snorkel and scuba. Marketed as easy-to-learn family fun, Snuba lets you breathe underwater via tubes from an air-supplied vessel above, with no prior diving or snorkel experience required.

NOT CERTIFIED?

Not sure if you want to commit the time and money to become certified? Not a problem. Most dive shops and many resorts will offer a discover scuba day-long course. In the morning, the instructor will teach you the basics of scuba diving: how to clear your mask, how to come to the surface in the unlikely event you lose your air supply, etc. In the afternoon, instructors will take you out for a dive in relatively shallow water—less than 30 feet. Be sure to ask where the dive will take place. Jumping into the water off a shallow beach may not be as fun as actually going out to the coral. If you decide that diving is something you want to pursue, the open dive may count toward your certification.

■TIP➔ You can often book the discover dives at the last minute. It may not be worth it to go out on a windy day when the currents are stronger. Also the underwater world looks a whole lot brighter on sunny days.

(top) Scuba divers; (bottom) Diver ascending line.

SNORKELING

Snorklng lets you see the wonders of the sea from a new perspective.

The basics: Sure, you can take a deep breath, hold your nose, squint your eyes, and stick your face in the water in an attempt to view submerged habitats . . . but why not protect your eyes, retain your ability to breathe, and keep your hands free to paddle about when exploring underwater? That's what snorkeling is all about.

Equipment needed: A mask, snorkel (the tube attached to the mask), and fins. In deeper waters (any depth over your head), life jackets are advised.

Steps to success: If you've never snorkeled before, it's natural to feel a bit awkward at first, so don't sweat it. Breathing through a mask and tube, and wearing a pair of fins take getting used to. Like any activity, you build confidence and comfort through practice.

If you're new to snorkeling, begin by submerging your face in shallow water or a swimming pool and breathing calmly through the snorkel while gazing through the mask.

Next you need to learn how to clear water out of your mask and snorkel, an essential skill since splashes can send water into tube openings and masks can leak. Some snorkels have built-in drainage valves, but if a tube clogs, you can force water up and out by exhaling through your mouth. Clearing a mask is similar: lift your head from water while pulling forward on mask to drain. Some masks have built-in purge valves, but those without can be cleared underwater by pressing the top to the forehead and blowing out your nose (charming, isn't it?), allowing air to bubble into the mask, pushing water out the bottom. If it sounds hard, it really isn't. Just try it a few times and you'll soon feel like a pro.

Now your goal is to get friendly with fins—you want them to be snug but not too tight—and learn how to propel yourself with them. Fins won't help you float, but they will give you a leg up, so to speak, on smoothly moving through the water or treading water (even when upright) with less effort.

Flutter stroking is the most efficient underwater kick, and the farther your foot bends forward the more leg power you'll be able to transfer to the water and the farther you'll travel with each stroke. Flutter kicking movements involve alternately separating the legs and then drawing them back together. When your legs separate, the leg surface encounters drag from the water, slowing you down. When your legs are drawn back together, they produce a force pushing you forward. If your kick creates more forward force than it causes drag, you'll move ahead.

Submerge your fins to avoid fatigue rather than having them flailing above the water when you kick, and keep your arms at your side to reduce drag. You are in the water—stretched out, face down, and snorkeling happily away—but that doesn't mean you can't hold your breath and go deeper in the water for a closer look at some fish or whatever catches your attention. Just remember that when you do this, your snorkel will be submerged, too, so you won't be breathing (you'll be holding your breath). You can dive head-first, but going feet-first is easier and less scary for most folks, taking less momentum. Before full immersion, take several long, deep breaths to clear carbon dioxide from your lungs.

If your legs tire, flip onto your back and tread water with inverted fin motions while resting. If your mask fogs, wash condensation from lens and clear water from mask.

TIPS FOR SAFE SNORKELING

- Snorkel with a buddy and stay together.

- Plan your entry and exit points prior to getting in the water.

- Swim into the current on entering and then ride the current back to your exit point.

- Carry your flippers into the water and then put them on, as it's difficult to walk in them.

- Make sure your mask fits properly and is not too loose.

- Pop your head above the water periodically to ensure you aren't drifting too far out, or too close to rocks.

- Think of the water as someone else's home—don't take anything that doesn't belong to you, or leave any trash behind.

- Don't touch any sea creatures; they may sting.

- Wear a T-shirt over your swimsuit to help protect you from being fried by the sun.

- When in doubt, don't go without a snorkeling professional; try a guided tour.

Cayman Salvor

TOP OUTFITTERS

COMPANY	ADDRESS & PHONE	COST	DESCRIPTION
AMY SLATE'S AMO-RAY DIVE CENTER www.amoray.com	104250 Overseas Hwy. (MM 104.2), Key Largo 305/451-3595	Daily Scuba classes for kids ages 8 and up and adults $100-$200.	Sign up for dive/snor-kel trips, scuba instruc-tion and kid programs.
DIVE KEY WEST www.divekeywest.com	3128 N. Roosevelt Blvd., Key West 305/296-3823	Snorkel from $49, dive from $69	Operating nearly 40 years. Has charters, in-struction, and gear.
ECO SCUBA KEY WEST www.ecoscuba.com	5930 Peninsular Ave. (MM 5), Key West 305/851-1899	Daily Snorkel from $35, scuba from $99.	Debuted in 2009. Offers eco-tours, lobstering, snorkeling, and scuba.
FLORIDA KEYS DIVE CENTER www.floridakeys-divectr.com	90451 Old Hwy. (MM 90.5), Tavernier 305/852-4599	Daily Classes from $175.	Charters for snorkerlers and divers go to Pen-nekamp, Key Largo, and Islamorada.
HORIZON DIVERS www.horizondivers.com	100 Ocean Dr. #1, Key Largo 305/453-3535	Daily Snorkel from $50, scuba from $80.	Take customized dive/snorkel trips on a 45-foot catamaran.
ISLAND VENTURES www.islandventure.com	103900 Overseas Hwy. (MM 103.9), Key Largo 305/451-4957	Two trips daily Snorkel $45, scuba from $80.	Go on snorkeling and scuba explorations to the Key Largo reef and shipwrecks.
KEYS DIVER SNORKEL TOURS www.keysdiver.com	99696 Overseas Hwy. (MM 99.6), Key Largo 305/451-1177	Three daily snorkel tours from $28. Includes gear.	Family-oriented snorkel-only tours head to coral reefs such as Pen-nekamp.
LOOE KEY REEF RE-SORT & DIVE CENTER www.diveflakeys.com	27340 Overseas Hwy. (MM 27.5), Ramrod Key 305/872-2215	Daily Snorkel from $44, scuba from $85.	Beginner and advanced scuba instruction, a photographer course, and snorkel gear rental.
RON JON SURF SHOP www.ronjons.com	503 Front St., Key West 305/293-8880	Daily Sells snorkel gear.	Several locations in Florida; its HQ is in Cocoa Beach.
SNUBA OF KEY WEST www.snubakeywest.com	600 Palm Ave., Key West 305/292-4616	Daily $99 per person, $44 for ride-alongs.	Swimmers ages 8 and up can try Snuba.
TILDENS SCUBA CENTER www.tildensscuba-center.com	4650 Overseas Hwy. (MM 49.5), Marathon 305/743-7255	Daily Snorkel from $35.99, scuba from $60.99.	Operating for 25 years. Has lessons, tours, snorkeling, scuba, snuba, gear, and a kids club.

The menu, a fusion of East and West, offers sushi and sashimi and rolls that combine local ingredients with traditional Japanese tastes. A wood grill dimension is used to prepare such dishes as grilled catch-of-the-day with a smoked Scotch bonnet pepper aioli crust and hardwood grilled rack of lamb. ⊠ *MM 81.5 OS, 81701 Overseas Hwy., Upper Matecumbe Key* 🕾 *305/664–5556* ⊕ *www.kaiyogrill.com* ⊘ *No lunch.*

$$$
SEAFOOD
★
✕ **Marker 88.** A few yards from Florida Bay, this seafood restaurant has been popular for more than 40 years. Large picture windows offer great sunset views, but the bay is lovely no matter what time of day you visit. Chef Sal Barrios serves such irresistible entrées as onion-crusted mahimahi, crispy yellowtail snapper, and mangrove-honey-and-chipotle–glazed rib eye. In addition, there are a half-dozen burgers and sandwiches, and you can't miss the restaurant's famous key lime baked Alaska dessert. The extensive wine list is an oenophile's delight. ⊠ *MM 88 BS, 88000 Overseas Hwy., Plantation Key* 🕾 *305/852–9315* ⊕ *www.marker88.info* ⚴ *Reservations essential.*

$$$
ECLECTIC
☾
★
✕ **Morada Bay Beach Café.** This bay-front restaurant wins high marks for its surprisingly stellar cuisine, tables planted in the sand, and tiki torches that bathe the evening in romance. Entrées feature alluring combinations like banana curry lobster, and coconut-crusted yellowtail snapper. Seafood takes center stage, but you can always get grilled chicken pasta or a Wagyu burger. A tapas menu caters to smaller appetites or those who can't decide with offerings like grouper ceviche, conch fritters, and tuna rolls. Lunch adds interesting sandwiches to the mix. Sit in a dining room outfitted with surfboards, or outdoors on a beach, where the sunset puts on a mighty show and kids (and your feet) play in the sand. There's nightly live music and a monthly full-moon party. ⊠ *MM 81 BS, 81600 Overseas Hwy., Upper Matecumbe Key* 🕾 *305/664–0604* ⊕ *www.moradabay-restaurant.com.*

$$$
FRENCH
Fodor's Choice
★
✕ **Pierre's.** One of the Keys' most elegant restaurants, Pierre's marries colonial style with modern food trends. Full of interesting architectural artifacts, the place oozes style, especially the wicker chair–strewn veranda overlooking the bay. Save your best "tropical chic" duds for dinner here, so you don't stand out from your surroundings. The food, drawn from French and Floridian influences, is multilayered and beautifully presented. Among the appetizer choices, few can resist the lamb ravioli or shrimp bisque. A changing list of entrées might include hogfish meunière and steak au poivre. The downstairs bar is a perfect spot for catching sunsets, sipping martinis, and enjoying light eats. ⊠ *MM 81.5 BS, 81600 Overseas Hwy., Upper Matecumbe Key* 🕾 *305/664–3225* ⊕ *www.pierres-restaurant.com* ⚴ *Reservations essential.*

$$$
ITALIAN
✕ **Uncle's Restaurant.** Former fishing guide Joe LePree adds Italian flair to standard seafood dishes. Here you can have your seafood almandine, Milanese (breaded and fried), LePree (with artichokes, mushrooms, and lemon-butter wine sauce), or any of five other different preparations. For starters, feast on mussels or littleneck clams in a marinara or garlic sauce. Specials sometimes combine game (bison, caribou, or elk) with seafood. Portions are huge, so share dishes or take home a doggie bag. Alternatively arrive early (between 5 and 7) for the lighter menu, priced $12.95 to $17.95. Weather permitting, sit outdoors in the

6

garden; poor acoustics make dining indoors unusually noisy. ⊠ *MM 81 OS, 80939 Overseas Hwy., Upper Matecumbe Key* ☎ *305/664–4402* ⊕ *www.unclesrestaurant.com* ⊙ *Closed Mon.*

WHERE TO STAY

For expanded hotel reviews, visit Fodors.com.

$$$$
HOTEL
Fodor'sChoice
★

🏨 **Casa Morada.** This relic from the 1950s was rescued and restyled into a suave, design-forward, all-suites property in 2000. **Pros:** cool design; complimentary snacks and bottled water; complimentary use of bikes, kayaks, and snorkel gear. **Cons:** trailer park across the street; beach is small and inconsequential. **TripAdvisor:** "pool area was very clean and pretty," "rooms were very comfortable," "great place for couples." ⊠ *MM 82 BS, 136 Madeira Rd., Upper Matecumbe Key* ☎ *305/664–0044 or 888/881–3030* ⊕ *www.casamorada.com* ⇱ *16 suites* ⚬ *In-room: a/c, Wi-Fi. In-hotel: restaurant, room service, bar, pool, water sports, some age restrictions* ⧆ *Breakfast.*

$$$$
RESORT
★

🏨 **Cheeca Lodge & Spa.** In the main lodge, West Indian–style rooms boast luxurious touches like elegant balcony tubs that fill from the ceiling. **Pros:** beautifully landscaped grounds; new designer rooms; dive shop on property. **Cons:** expensive rates; $39 resort fee for activities; busy. **TripAdvisor:** "pool and lagoon were ideal for our son," "excellent resort for a great escape," "services were not up to the asking price." ⊠ *MM 82 OS, Box 527, Upper Matecumbe Key* ☎ *305/664–4651 or 800/327–2888* ⊕ *www.cheeca.com* ⇱ *214 rooms, 44 1-bedroom suites, 4 2-bedroom suites* ⚬ *In-room: a/c, kitchen (some) Wi-Fi. In-hotel: restaurants, bars, golf course, tennis courts, pools, gym, spa, beach, water sports, children's programs, business center* ⧆ *No meals.*

$$
RESORT
★

🏨 **Drop Anchor Resort and Marina.** It's easy to find your cottage here, as they are painted in an array of Crayola colors. **Pros:** bright and colorful; attention to detail; laid-back charm. **Cons:** noise from the highway; beach is better for fishing than swimming. **TripAdvisor:** "spotlessly clean and well maintained," "air conditioner was very noisy," "quiet and peaceful." ⊠ *MM 85 OS, 84959 Overseas Hwy., Windley Key* ☎ *305/664–4863 or 888/664–4863* ⊕ *www.dropanchorresort.com* ⇱ *18 suites* ⚬ *In-room: a/c, kitchen (some), Wi-Fi. In-hotel: pool, beach, laundry facilities* ⧆ *No meals.*

$$$$
RESORT

🏨 **The Islander Resort.** Although the vintage sign is straight out of a *Happy Days* rerun, this property has undergone a top-to-bottom transformation while the general layout retained a 1950s feel. **Pros:** spacious rooms; nice kitchens; eye-popping views. **Cons:** pricey for what you get; beach has rough sand; no a/c in the screened gym. **TripAdvisor:** "this property was beautiful," "loved the funky resort vibe," "layout of the hotel was easy to navigate." ⊠ *MM 82.1 OS, 82200 Overseas Hwy., Upper Matecumbe Key* ☎ *305/664–2031 or 800/753–6002* ⊕ *www.islanderfloridakeys.com* ⇱ *114 rooms* ⚬ *In-room: a/c, kitchen, Wi-Fi. In-hotel: restaurant, bar, pools, gym, beach, water sports, laundry facilities, some pets allowed* ⧆ *Breakfast.*

$$$$
HOTEL
Fodor'sChoice
★

🏨 **The Moorings Village.** This tropical retreat is everything you imagine when you think of the Keys—from hammocks swaying between towering trees to sugar-white sand (arguably the Keys' best resort beach) lapped by aqua-green waves. **Pros:** romantic setting; good dining options with room-charging privileges; beautiful beach. **Cons:** no room service; extra fee for housekeeping; daily resort fee for activities. **TripAdvisor:** "secluded peaceful beautiful magical," "has its excellent reviews for a reason," "very lovely place." ⊠ *MM 81.6 OS, 123 Beach Rd., Upper Matecumbe Key* ☎ *305/664–4708* ⊕ *www.themooringsvillage.com* ⤵ *4 cottages, 14 houses* ♿ *In-room: a/c, kitchen, Wi-Fi. In-hotel: tennis court, pool, gym, spa, beach, water sports, laundry facilities* ⏀ *No meals.*

$ 🏨 **Ragged Edge Resort.** Tucked away in a residential area at the ocean's

HOTEL   edge, this hotel is big on value but short on style. **Pros:** oceanfront location; boat docks and ramp; cheap rates. **Cons:** dated decor; guests can be noisy. **TripAdvisor:** "clean and spacious," "close to restaurants," "restful ambiance." ⊠ *MM 86.5 OS, 243 Treasure Harbor Rd., Plantation Key* ☎ *305/852–5389 or 800/436–2023* ⊕ *www.ragged-edge.com* ⤵ *6 studios, 1 efficiency, 3 2-bedroom suites* ♿ *In-room: a/c, kitchen (some), Wi-Fi. In-hotel: pool* ⏀ *No meals.*

LONG KEY

Long Key isn't a tourist hot spot, making it a favorite destination for those looking to avoid the masses and enjoy some ecological history in the process.

6

GETTING HERE AND AROUND

Long Key runs from mile markers 70 to 65.5, with the tiny town of Layton at its heart. Many people get around by bike.

EXPLORING

★ **Long Key State Park.** Come here for solitude, hiking, fishing, and camping. On the ocean side, the Golden Orb Trail leads to a boardwalk that cuts through the mangroves (may require some wading) and alongside a lagoon where waterfowl congregate (as do mosquitoes, so be prepared). A 1¼-mi canoe trail leads through a tidal lagoon, and a broad expanse of shallow grass flats is perfect for bonefishing. Bring a mask and snorkel to observe the marine life in the shallow water. The park is particularly popular with campers who long to stake their tent at the campground on a beach. In summer, no-see-ums (biting sand flies) also love the beach, so again—be prepared. The picnic area is on the water, too, but lacks a beach. Canoes rent for $10 per day, and kayak rentals start at $17 for a single for two hours, $21.50 for a double. Rangers lead tours every Thursday at 10 on birding, boating, or beachcombing. ⊠ *MM 67.5 OS, 67400 Overseas Hwy.* ☎ *305/664–4815* ⊕ *www. floridastateparks.org/longkey* 🎟 *$4.50 for 1 person, $5.50 for 2 people, and 50¢ for each additional person in the group* ⊙ *Daily 8–sunset.*

BEACHES

Long Key State Park. Camping, snorkeling, and bonefishing are the favored activities along this narrow strip of natural, rocky beach. It lines the park's campground, which is open only to registered campers. ⊠ *MM 67.5 OS, 67400 Overseas Hwy.* ☎ *305/664–4815* ⊕ *www. floridastateparks.org/longkey* 🎟 *$4.50 for 1 person, $5.50 for 2 people, and 50¢ for each additional person in the group* ⊙ *Daily 8–sunset.*

WHERE TO EAT AND STAY

For expanded hotel reviews, visit Fodors.com.

$$

RESORT

⊞ Lime Tree Bay Resort. Easy on the eye and the wallet, this 2½-acre resort on Florida Bay is far from the hustle and bustle of the larger islands. **Pros:** great views; friendly staff; close to Long Key State Park. **Cons:** only one restaurant nearby, shared balconies. **TripAdvisor:** "small inexpensive older motel rooms," "hammocks were great for a relaxing evening," "views are amazing." ⊠ *MM 68.5 BS, 68500 Overseas Hwy., Layton* ☎ *305/664–4740 or 800/723–4519* ⊕ *www.limetreebayresort. com* ⇗ *10 rooms, 10 studios, 8 suites, 5 apartments, 4 efficiencies* ৬ *In-room: a/c, kitchen (some), Wi-Fi. In-hotel: tennis court, pool, beach, business center, some pets allowed* ⏐⊙⏐ *No meals.*

EN
ROUTE

Long Key Viaduct. As you cross Long Key Channel, look beside you at the old viaduct. The second-longest bridge on the former rail line, this 2-mi-long structure has 222 reinforced-concrete arches. The old bridge is popular with cyclists and anglers, who fish off the sides day and night.

THE MIDDLE KEYS

Most of the activity in this part of the Florida Keys centers on the town of Marathon—the region's third-largest metropolitan area. On either end of it, smaller keys hold resorts, wildlife research and rehab facilities, a historic village, and a state park. The Middle Keys make a fitting transition from the Upper Keys to the Lower Keys not only geographically but mentally. Crossing Seven Mile Bridge prepares you for the slow pace and don't-give-a-damn attitude you'll find a little farther down the highway. Fishing is one of the main attractions—in fact, the region's commercial-fishing industry was founded here in the early 1800s. Diving is another popular pastime. There are many beaches and natural areas to enjoy in the Middle Keys, where mainland stress becomes an ever more distant memory.

If you get bridge fever—the heebie-jeebies when driving over long stretches of water—you may need a pair of blinders (or a couple of tranquilizers) before tackling the Middle Keys. Stretching from Conch Key to the far side of the Seven Mile Bridge, this zone is home to the region's two longest bridges: Long Key Viaduct and Seven Mile Bridge, both historic landmarks.

Overseas Highway takes you from one end of the region to the other in a direct line that takes in most of the sights, but you'll find some interesting resorts and restaurants off the main drag.

DUCK AND GRASSY KEYS

Grassy Key is between mile markers 60 and 57.

Duck Key holds one of the region's nicest marina resorts, Hawks Cay. To its south, sleepy little Grassy Key, local lore has it, was named not for its vegetation—mostly native trees and shrubs—but for an early settler by the name of Grassy. There's no marked definition between it and Marathon, so it feels sort of like a suburb of its much larger neighbor to the south. Grassy Key's sights-to-see tend toward the natural, including a worthwhile dolphin attraction and a small state park.

EXPLORING

Dolphin Connection. Hawk's Cay Resort's Dolphin Connection offers three programs, including Dockside Dolphins, a 30-minute encounter from the dry training docks ($60); Dolphin Discovery, an in-water program that lasts about 45 minutes and lets you kiss, touch, and feed the dolphins ($155); and Trainer for a Day, a three-hour session with the animal training team ($295). ⊠ *MM 61 OS, 61 Hawks Cay Blvd., Duck Key* ☎ *305/743–7000* ⊕ *www.dolphinconnection.com.*

☾ **Dolphin Research Center.** The 1963 movie *Flipper* popularized the notion
★ of humans interacting with dolphins, and Milton Santini, the film's creator, also opened this center, which is home to a colony of dolphins and sea lions. The nonprofit center has tours, narrated programs, and programs that allow you to greet the dolphins from dry land or play with them in their watery habitat. You can even paint a T-shirt with a dolphin—you pick the paint, the dolphin "designs" your shirt ($55). The center also offers five-day programs for children and adults with disabilities. ⊠ *MM 59 BS, 58901 Overseas Hwy.* ☎ *305/289–1121 or 305/289–0002* ⊕ *www.dolphins.org* 🖂 *$19.50* ☾ *Daily 9–4:30.*

6

OFF THE BEATEN PATH

Curry Hammock State Park. Looking for a slice of the Keys that's far removed from tiki bars? On the ocean and bay sides of Overseas Highway are 260 acres of upland hammock, wetlands, and mangroves. On the bay side, there's a trail through thick hardwoods to a rocky shoreline. The ocean side is more developed, with a sandy beach, a clean bathhouse, picnic tables, a playground, grills, and a 28-site campground open November to May. Locals consider the paddling trails under canopies of arching mangroves one of the best kayaking spots in the Keys. Manatees frequent the area, and it's a great spot for bird-watching. Herons, egrets, ibis, plovers, and sanderlings are commonly spotted. Raptors are often seen in the park, especially during migration periods. ⊠ *MM 57 OS, 56200 Overseas Hwy., Little Crawl Key* ☎ *305/289– 2690* ⊕ *www.floridastateparks.org/curryhammock* 🖂 *$4.50 for 1 person, $6 for 2, 50¢ per additional person* ☾ *Daily 8–sunset.*

WHERE TO EAT AND STAY

For expanded hotel reviews, visit Fodors.com.

$$$
LATIN AMERICAN
★
✕ **Alma.** A refreshing escape from the Middle Keys' same-old menus, Alma serves expertly prepared Florida and Latin-Caribbean dishes in an elegant setting. Nightly changing menus often include yellowtail snapper ceviche with Peruvian popcorn, the divine calabaza-squash-and-lobster risotto, roasted breadfruit gnocchi, curried goat stew with breadfruit tostones, and the grilled bone-in rib eye. Finish your meal with the silky, smooth, passion fruit crème brûlée, which has just the right amount of tartness to balance the delicate caramelized crust. ⊠ *Hawks Cay Resort, 61 Hawks Cay Blvd., Duck Cay* ☎ *305/743– 7000 or 888/432–2242* ⊕ *www.hawkscay.com* ☾ *No lunch.*

$$$
AMERICAN
✕ **Hideaway Café.** The name says it all. Tucked between Grassy Key and Marathon, it's easy to miss if you're barnstorming through the middle islands. When you find it (upstairs at Rainbow Bend Resort), you'll

discover a favorite of locals who appreciate a well-planned menu, lovely ocean view, and quiet evening away from the crowds. For starters, dig into escargots à la Edison (sautéed with vegetables, pepper, cognac, and cream). Then feast on several specialties, such as a rarely found chateaubriand for one, a whole roasted duck, or the seafood medley combining the catch of the day with scallops and shrimp in a savory sauce. ⊠ *MM 58 OS, Rainbow Bend Resort, 57570 Overseas Hwy., Grassy Key* ☎ *305/289–1554* ⊕ *www.hideawaycafe.com* ☉ *No lunch.*

$$
RESORT

☎ **Bonefish Resort.** Set on a skinny lot bedecked with palm trees, banana trees, and hibiscus plantings, this motel-style hideaway is the best choice among the island's back-to-basics properties. **Pros:** ocean-side setting. **Cons:** decks are small; simple decor. **TripAdvisor:** "mildew and mold are winning the war in the bathrooms," "shabby overpriced," "absolute dump." ⊠ *MM 58 OS, 58070 Overseas Hwy.* ☎ *305/743–7107 or 800/274–9949* ⊕ *www.bonefishresort.com* ⌁ *3 rooms, 11 efficiencies* ⚂ *In-room: a/c, kitchen (some), Wi-Fi. In-hotel: beach, pool, laundry facilities, some pets allowed* ⫩*No meals.*

$$$
RESORT
ⓒ
Fodor's Choice
★

☎ **Hawks Cay Resort.** An in-the-water program that lets you get up close and personal with dolphins makes this sprawling resort a family favorite. **Pros:** huge rooms; restful spa; full-service marina and dive shop. **Cons:** no real beach; far from Marathon's attractions. **TripAdvisor:** "room was beautiful and very comfortable," "excellent customer service," "had a wonderful stay." ⊠ *MM 61 OS, 61 Hawks Cay Blvd., Duck Key* ☎ *305/743–7000 or 888/432–2242* ⊕ *www.hawkscay.com* ⌁ *161 rooms, 16 suites, 225 2- to 4-bedroom villas* ⚂ *In-room: a/c, kitchen (some), Wi-Fi. In-hotel: restaurants, bars, tennis courts, pools, gym, spa, water sports, children's programs, laundry facilities* ⫩*No meals.*

MARATHON

Marathon runs from mile markers 53 to 47.5.

Most of what there is to see lies right off the Overseas Highway, with the exception of a couple of hidden restaurants.

Marathon is a bustling town, at least compared to other communities in the Keys. As it leaves something to be desired in the charm department, Marathon will probably not be your first choice of places to stay. But there are a number of good dining options, so you'll definitely want to stop for a bite even if you're just passing through on the way to Key West.

Outside of Key West, Marathon has the most historic attractions, which merit a visit, along with its Sombrero Beach. Fishing, diving, and boating are the main events here. It throws tarpon tournaments in April and May, more fishing tournaments in June and September, a seafood festival in March, and lighted boat parades around the winter holidays.

GETTING HERE AND AROUND

The SuperShuttle charges $102 per passenger for trips from Miami International Airport to the Upper Keys. To go farther into the Keys, you must book an entire 11-person van, which costs about $250 to Marathon. For a trip to the airport, place your request 24 hours in advance.

DID YOU KNOW?

Dolphins come in various forms, from the Atlantic bottlenose dolphin to the killer whale. These playful and smart creatures love to leap out of the water and synchronize their movements with others. By swimming next to ships, dolphins can conserve energy.

Miami Dade Transit provides daily bus service from MM 50 in Marathon to the Florida City Walmart Supercenter on the mainland. The bus stops at major shopping centers as well as on-demand anywhere along the route during daily round trips on the hour from 6 am to 10 pm. The cost is $2 one-way, exact change required. The Lower Keys Shuttle bus runs from Marathon to Key West ($3 one-way), with scheduled stops along the way.

ESSENTIALS

Transportation Contacts Lower Keys Shuttle (☎ *305/809–3910* ⊕ *www. kwtransit.com*). Miami Dade Transit (*formerly the Dade–Monroe Express* ☎ *305/770–3131*). SuperShuttle (☎ *305/871–2000* ⊕ *www.supershuttle.com*).

Visitor Information Greater Marathon Chamber of Commerce and Visitor Center (✉ *MM 53.5 BS, 12222 Overseas Hwy., Marathon* ☎ *305/743–5417 or 800/262–7284* ⊕ *www.floridakeysmarathon.com*).

EXPLORING

☾ ★ **Crane Point Museum, Nature Center, and Historic Site.** Tucked away from the highway behind a stand of trees, Crane Point—part of a 63-acre tract that contains the last-known undisturbed thatch-palm hammock—is delightfully undeveloped. This multiuse facility includes the **Museum of Natural History of the Florida Keys,** which has displays about local wildlife, a seashell exhibit, and a marine-life display that makes you feel you're at the bottom of the sea. Kids love the replica 17th-century galleon and pirate dress-up room where they can play, and the re-created **Cracker House** filled with insects, sea-turtle exhibits, and children's activities. On the 1-mi indigenous loop trail, visit the **Laura Quinn Wild Bird Center** and the remnants of a Bahamian village, site of the restored **George Adderly House.** It is the oldest surviving example of Bahamian tabby (a concretelike material created from sand and seashells) construction outside of Key West. A boardwalk crosses wetlands, rivers, and mangroves before ending at Adderly Village. From November to Easter, docent-led tours are available; bring good walking shoes and bug repellent during warm weather. ✉ *MM 50.5 BS, 5550 Overseas Hwy.* ☎ *305/743–9100* ⊕ *www.cranepoint.net* 🖃 *$12.50* ☉ *Mon.–Sat. 9–5, Sun. noon–5; call to arrange trail tours.*

QUICK BITES **Leigh Ann's (More Than Just A) Coffee House.** If you don't get a buzz just from breathing in the robust aroma order an espresso shot, Cuban or Italian, for a satisfying jolt. Pastries are baked fresh daily, but the biscuits with sausage gravy and the breakfast burrito with homemade salsa are among the big movers. Leigh Ann's also serves lunch—quiche, and hot and cold sandwiches. It's open weekdays 7–5, Saturday 7–3, and Sunday 8–noon. ✉ *MM 50 OS, 7537 Overseas Hwy.* ☎ *305/743–2001* ⊕ *www. leighannscoffeehouse.com.*

Seven Mile Bridge. This is one of the most photographed images in the Keys. Actually measuring slightly less than 7 mi, it connects the Middle and Lower Keys and is believed to be the world's longest segmental bridge. It has 39 expansion joints separating its various concrete sections. Each April runners gather in Marathon for the annual Seven Mile

Bridge Run. The expanse running parallel to Seven Mile Bridge is what remains of the **Old Seven Mile Bridge,** an engineering and architectural marvel in its day that's now on the National Register of Historic Places. Once proclaimed the Eighth Wonder of the World, it rested on a record 546 concrete piers. No cars are allowed on the old bridge today, but a 2-mi segment is open for biking, walking, and fishing.

OFF THE
BEATEN
PATH

Pigeon Key. There's much to like about this 5-acre island under the Old Seven Mile Bridge. You can reach it by walking across a 2-mi section of the bridge or by ferry. Once there, tour the island on your own or join a guided tour to explore the buildings that formed the early-20th-century work camp for the Overseas Railroad that linked the mainland to Key West. Later the island became a fish camp, a state park, and then government-administration headquarters. Exhibits in a small museum recall the history of the Keys, the railroad, and railroad baron Henry M. Flagler. Pick up the ferry outside the gift shop, which occupies an old railroad car on Knight's Key (MM 47 OS), for a two-hour excursion. Visitors can self-tour and catch the ferry back in a half hour. ⊠ *MM 45 OS, 1 Knights Key Blvd., Pigeon Key* ☎ *305/289–0025 general information, 305/743–5999 reservations* ⊕ *www.pigeonkey.net* ⊒ *$11* ☉ *Daily 9:30–4; ferryboat departures at 10, 11:30, 1, 2:30.*

6

☾ **The Turtle Hospital.** More than 100 injured sea turtles check in here every year. The 90-minute guided tours take you into recovery and surgical areas at the world's only state-certified veterinary hospital for sea turtles. If you're lucky, you can visit hatchlings. In the "hospital bed" tanks, you can see recovering patients and others that are permanent residents due to their injuries. If you're lucky, you can visit hatchlings. Call ahead—tours are sometime cancelled due to medical emergencies. ⊠ *MM 48.5 BS, 2396 Overseas Hwy.* ☎ *305/743–2552* ⊕ *www. turtlehospital.org* ⊒ *$15* ☉ *Daily 9–5; tours at 10, 1, and 4.*

SPORTS AND THE OUTDOORS
BEACH

☾
★ **Sombrero Beach.** Here, pleasant, shaded picnic areas overlook a coconut palm–lined grassy stretch and the Atlantic Ocean. Separate areas allow swimmers, boaters, and windsurfers to share the narrow cove. Facilities include barbecue grills, showers, and restrooms, as well as a large playground, a pier, and a volleyball court. Sunday afternoons draw lots of local families toting coolers. The park is accessible for those with disabilities and allows leashed pets. Turn east at the traffic light in Marathon and follow signs to the end. Best for: families. ⊠ *MM 50 OS, Sombrero Beach Rd.* ☎ *305/743–0033 Ext. 6* ⊒ *Free* ☉ *Daily 8–sunset.*

BIKING

Tooling around on two wheels is a good way to see Marathon. There's easy cycling on a 1-mi off-road path that connects to the 2 mi of the Old Seven Mile Bridge leading to Pigeon Key.

Bike Marathon Bike Rentals. "Have bikes, will deliver" could be the motto of this company, which gets beach cruisers to your hotel door for $35 per week, including a helmet and basket. Note that there's no physical location, but services are available Monday through Saturday 9–4 and Sunday 9–2. ☎ *305/743–3204* ⊕ *www.bikemarathonbikerentals.com.*

Bubba's. Book a custom biking tour through the Keys along the heritage trail. A van accompanies tours to carry luggage and tired riders. Operated by former police officer Bubba Barron, Bubba's hosts an annual one-week ride down the length of the Keys every November. Riders can opt for tent camping ($595) or motel-room accommodations (prices vary). Meals are included on the annual ride and bike rentals are extra. ☎ 321/759–3433 ⊕ *www.bubbafestbiketours.com.*

Overseas Outfitters. Aluminum cruisers and hybrid bikes are available for rent for $10 to $15 per day. The company also rents tandem bikes. It's open weekdays 9–6, Saturday 9–3, and Sunday 10–2. ✉ *MM 48 BS, 1700 Overseas Hwy.* ☎ *305/289–1670* ⊕ *www.overseasoutfitters.com.*

BOATING

Sail, motor, or paddle—whatever your choice of modes, boating is what the Keys is all about. Brave the Atlantic waves and reefs or explore the backcountry islands on the gulf side. If you don't have a lot of boating and chart-reading experience, it's a good idea to tap into local knowledge on a charter.

Captain Pip's. This operator rents 19- to 24-foot outboards, $195–$330 per day, as well as tackle and snorkeling gear. You also can charter a small boat with a guide, $500–$550 for a half day and $750–$800 for a full day. ✉ *MM 47.5 OS,1410 Overseas Hwy.* ☎ *305/743–4403 or 800/707–1692* ⊕ *www.captainpips.com.*

Fish 'n Fun. Get out on the water on 19- to 26-foot powerboats starting at $140 for a half day, $190 for a full day. The company offers free delivery in the Middle Keys. You also can rent Jet Skis and kayaks. ✉ *MM 49.5 OS, 4590 Overseas Hwy., at Banana Bay Resort & Marina* ☎ *305/743–2275 or 800/471–3440* ⊕ *www.fishnfunrentals.com.*

FISHING

For recreational anglers, the deepwater fishing is superb in both bay and ocean. Marathon West Hump, one good spot, has depths ranging from 500 to more than 1,000 feet. Locals fish from a half-dozen bridges, including Long Key Bridge, the Old Seven Mile Bridge, and both ends of Tom's Harbor. Barracuda, bonefish, dolphinfish, and tarpon all frequent local waters. Party boats and private charters are available.

★ ***Marathon Lady.*** Morning, afternoon, and night, fish for mahimahi, grouper, and other tasty catch aboard this 73-footer, which departs on half-day ($45) excursions from the Vaca Cut Bridge, north of Marathon. Join the crew for night fishing ($55) from 6:30 to midnight from Memorial Day to Labor Day; it's especially beautiful on a full-moon night. ✉ *MM 53 OS, at 117th St.* ☎ *305/743–5580* ⊕ *fishfloridakeys. com/marathonlady.*

Sea Dog Charters. Captain Jim Purcell, a deep-sea specialist for ESPN's *The American Outdoorsman,* provides one of the best values in Keys fishing. Next to the Seven Mile Grill, his company offers half- and full-day offshore, reef and wreck, and backcountry fishing trips, as well as fishing and snorkeling trips aboard 30- to 37-foot boats. The cost is $60 per person for a half day, regardless of whether your group fills the boat, and includes bait, light tackle, ice, coolers, and fishing licenses. If you prefer an all-day private charter on a 37-foot boat, he offers those, too, for $600 for up to six people. A fuel surcharge may apply. ⊠ *MM 47.5 BS, 1248 Overseas Hwy.* ☏ *305/743–8255* ⊕ *www.seadogcharters.net.*

SCUBA DIVING AND SNORKELING

Local dive operations take you to Sombrero Reef and Lighthouse, the most popular down-under destination in these parts. For a shallow dive and some lobster-nabbing, Coffins Patch, off Key Colony Beach, is a good choice. A number of wrecks such as *Thunderbolt* serve as artificial reefs. Many operations out of this area will also take you to Looe Key Reef.

Hall's Diving Center & Career Institute. The institute has been training divers for more than 40 years. Along with conventional twice-a-day snorkel and two-tank dive trips ($30–$55) to the reefs at Sombrero Lighthouse and wrecks like the *Thunderbolt,* the company has more unusual offerings like digital and video photography. ⊠ *MM 48.5 BS, 1994 Overseas Hwy.* ☏ *305/743–5929 or 800/331–4255* ⊕ *www.hallsdiving.com.*

Spirit Snorkeling. Snorkeling excursions to Sombrero Reef and Lighthouse Reef cost $30 a head. ⊠ *MM 47.5 BS, 1410 Overseas Hwy., Slip No. 1* ☏ *305/289–0614* ⊕ *www.spiritsnorkeling.net.*

WHERE TO EAT

¢ ✕ **Fish Tales Market and Eatery.** This roadside eatery with its own seafood
SEAFOOD market serves signature dishes such as oysters on a roll and snapper on grilled rye with coleslaw and melted Muenster cheese. You also can slurp lobster bisque or red-conch chowder. There are burgers, chicken, and dogs for those who don't do seafood. Plan to dine early; it's only open until 6:30 pm. This is a no-frills kind of place with a loyal local following, a couple of picnic tables, and friendly service. ⊠ *MM 52.5 OS, 11711 Overseas Hwy.* ☏ *305/743–9196 or 888/662–4822* ⊕ *www. floridalobster.com* ⚏ *Reservations not accepted* ⊙ *Closed Sun.*

$$ ✕ **Key Colony Inn.** The inviting aroma of an Italian kitchen pervades this
ITALIAN family-owned favorite with a supper-club atmosphere. As you'd expect, the service is friendly and attentive. For lunch there are fish and steak entrées served with fries, salad, and bread in addition to Italian specialties. At dinner you can't miss with traditional dishes like veal Oscar and New York strip, or such specialties as seafood *Italiano,* a dish of scallops and shrimp sautéed in garlic butter and served with marinara sauce over a bed of linguine. The place is renowned for its Sunday brunch, served from November to April. ⊠ *MM 54 OS, 700 W. Ocean Dr., Key Colony Beach* ☏ *305/743–0100* ⊕ *www.kcinn.com.*

$$ ✕ **Keys Fisheries Market & Marina.** From the parking lot, this commercial
SEAFOOD warehouse flanked by fishing boats and lobster traps barely hints at the
ⓒ restaurant inside. Order at the window outside, pick up your food, then
★ dine at one of the waterfront picnic tables outfitted with rolls of paper towels. The menu is comprised of fresh seafood and a token hamburger and chicken sandwich. A huge lobster Reuben ($15.95) served on thick slices of toasted bread is the signature dish. Other delights include the shrimp burger, very rich whiskey-peppercorn snapper, and the Keys Kombo (broiled or grilled lobster, shrimp, scallops, and mahimahi for $29). There are also sushi and a bar serving beer and wine. Kids like feeding the fish while they wait for their food. ⊠ *MM 49 BS, 3390*

6

Gulfview Ave. (turn west on 35th St.), end of 35th St. ☎ *305/743–4353 or 866/743–4353* ⊕ *www.keysfisheries.com* ⟁ *Reservations not accepted.*

$$$
SEAFOOD
★
✕ **Lazy Days South.** Tucked into Marathon Marina a half-mile north of the Seven Mile Bridge, the restaurant offers views just as spectacular as the highly lauded food. A spin-off of an Islamorada favorite, here you'll find a wide range of daily offerings from garlic-baked clams and a coconut-fried fish du jour sandwich to seafood pastas and beef tips over rice. Choose a table on the outdoor deck, or inside underneath paddle fans and surrounded by local art. ⊠ *MM 47.3 OS, 725 11th St.* ☎ *306/289–0839* ⊕ *www.keysdining.com/lazydays.*

¢
AMERICAN
✕ **The Stuffed Pig.** With only eight tables and a counter inside, this break-fast-and-lunch place is always hopping. When the weather's right, grab a table out back. The kitchen whips up daily lunch specials like burgers, seafood platters, or pulled pork with hand-cut fries, but a quick glance around the room reveals that the all-day breakfast is the main draw. You can get the usual breakfast plates, but most newcomers opt for oddities like the lobster omelet, alligator tail and eggs, or "grits and grunts" (that's fish, to the rest of us). ⊠ *MM 49 BS, 3520 Overseas Hwy.* ☎ *305/743–4059* ⊕ *www.thestuffedpig.com* ⟁ *Reservations not accepted* ▭ *No credit cards* ◷ *No dinner.*

WHERE TO STAY
For expanded hotel reviews, visit Fodors.com.

$$$$
RESORT
☾
★
⛱ **Tranquility Bay.** Ralph Lauren could have designed the rooms at this luxurious beach resort. **Pros:** secluded setting; gorgeous design; lovely crescent beach. **Cons:** a bit sterile; no real Keys atmosphere; cramped building layout. **TripAdvisor:** "family pool is terrific," "great choice for our family," "tiki bar was nice." ⊠ *MM 48.5 BS, 2600 Overseas Hwy.* ☎ *305/289–0888 or 866/643–5397* ⊕ *www.tranquilitybay.com* ⟋ *45 2-bedroom suites, 41 3-bedroom suites* ⚭ *In-room: a/c, kitchen, Wi-Fi. In-hotel: restaurants, bars, pools, gym, beach, water sports* ⑩ *No meals.*

THE LOWER KEYS

Beginning at Bahia Honda Key, the islands of the Florida Keys become smaller, more clustered, and more numerous—a result of ancient tidal water flowing between the Florida Straits and the gulf. Here you're likely to see more birds and mangroves than other tourists, and more refuges, beaches, and campgrounds than museums, restaurants, and hotels. The islands are made up of two types of limestone, both denser than the highly permeable Key Largo limestone of the Upper Keys. As a result, freshwater forms in pools rather than percolating through the rock, creating watering holes that support alligators, snakes, deer, rabbits, raccoons, and migratory ducks. Many of these animals can be seen in the National Key Deer Refuge on Big Pine Key. Nature was generous with her beauty in the Lower Keys, which have both Looe Key Reef, arguably the Keys' most beautiful tract of coral, and Bahia Honda State Park, considered one of the best beaches in the world for its fine-sand dunes, clear warm waters, and panoramic vista of a historic bridge, hammocks, and azure sky and sea. Big Pine Key is fishing headquarters for a laid-back community that swells with retirees in the winter. South of it, the dribble of islands can flash by in a blink of an eye if you don't take the time to stop at a roadside eatery or check out tours and charters at the little marinas. In truth, the Lower Keys include Key West, but since it is as different from the rest of the Lower Keys as peanut butter is from jelly, it is covered in its own section.

GETTING HERE AND AROUND

The Lower Keys in this section include the keys between MM 37 and MM 9. The Seven Mile Bridge drops you into the lap of this homey, quiet part of the Keys.

Heed speed limits in these parts. They may seem incredibly strict given the traffic is lightest of anywhere in the Keys, but the purpose is to protect the resident Key deer population, and officers of the law pay strict attention and will readily issue speeding tickets.

BAHIA HONDA KEY

Bahia Honda Key is between mile markers 38 and 36.

All of Bahia Honda Key is devoted to its eponymous state park, which keeps it in a pristine state. Besides the park's outdoor activities, it offers an up-close look at the original railroad bridge.

EXPLORING

Fodor's Choice ★

Bahia Honda State Park. Most first-time visitors to the region are dismayed by the lack of beaches—but then they discover sun-soaked Bahia Honda Key. The 524-acre park here sprawls across both sides of the highway, giving it 2½ mi of fabulous sandy coastline. The snorkeling isn't bad, either; there's underwater life (soft coral, queen conchs, random little fish) just a few hundred feet offshore. Although swimming, kayaking, fishing, and boating are the main reasons to visit, you shouldn't miss biking along the 2½ mi of flat roads or hiking the Silver Palm Trail, with rare West Indian plants and several species found nowhere else in the nation. Along the way you'll be treated to a variety of butterflies. Seasonal ranger-led nature programs take place at or depart from the Sand and Sea Nature Center. There are rental cabins, a campground, snack bar, gift shop, 19-slip marina, nature center, and facilities for renting kayaks and arranging snorkeling tours. Get a panoramic view of the island from what's left of the railroad—the Bahia Honda Bridge. ⊠ *MM 37 OS, 36850 Overseas Hwy.* ☎ *305/872–2353* ⊕ *www.floridastateparks.org/bahiahonda* 🖼 *$4.50 for 1 person, $9 for 2 people, 50¢ per additional person* ⊙ *Daily 8–sunset.*

BEACHES

Bahia Honda State Park. The park contains three beaches in all—on both the Atlantic Ocean and the Gulf of Mexico. Sandspur Beach, the largest, is regularly declared the best beach in Florida, and you'll be hard-pressed to argue. The sand is baby-powder soft, and the aqua water is warm, clear, and shallow. With their mild currents, the beaches are great for swimming, even with small fry. **Best for:** snorkeling. ⊠ *MM 37 OS,*

36850 Overseas Hwy. ☎ *305/872–2353* ⊕ *www.floridastateparks.org/ bahiahonda* ⊑ *$4.50 for 1 person, $9 for 2 people, 50¢ per additional person* ⊘ *Daily 8–sunset.*

SPORTS AND THE OUTDOORS

SCUBA DIVING AND SNORKELING

Bahia Honda Dive Shop. The concessionaire at Bahia Honda State Park manages a 19-slip marina; rents wet suits, snorkel equipment, and corrective masks; and operates twice-a-day offshore-reef snorkel trips ($30 plus $9 for equipment). Park visitors looking for other fun can rent kayaks ($10 per hour for a single, $18 for a double) and beach chairs. ⊠ *MM 37 OS, 36850 Overseas Hwy.* ☎ *305/872–3210* ⊕ *www. bahiahondapark.com.*

WHERE TO STAY

For expanded hotel reviews, visit Fodors.com.

$$$ ⛺ **Bahia Honda State Park.** Elsewhere you'd pay big bucks for the won-
HOTEL   derful water views available at these cabins on Florida Bay. **Pros:** great
★   bay-front views; beachfront camping; affordable rates. **Cons:** books up
fast; area can be buggy. **TripAdvisor:** "a great base for more explora-
tions," "bathrooms were as you would expect," "beach is very nice."
⊠ *MM 37 OS, 36850 Overseas Hwy.* ☎ *305/872–2353 or 800/326–
3521* ⊕ *www.reserveamerica.com* ↪ *80 partial hook-up campsites, 6
cabin units* ⚭ *In-room: a/c, kitchen, no TV. In-hotel: beach, water sports*
⊕⊘ *No meals.*

BIG PINE KEY

Big Pine Key runs from mile marker 32 to 30.

Welcome to the Keys' most natural holdout, where wildlife refuges pro-
tect rare and endangered animals. Here you have left behind the com-
mercialism of the Upper Keys for an authentic backcountry atmosphere.

ESSENTIALS

Visitor Information Big Pine and the Lower Keys Chamber of Commerce
⊠ *MM 31 OS, 31020 Overseas Hwy., Big Pine Key* ☎ *305/872–2411 or 800/872–
3722* ⊕ *www.lowerkeyschamber.com.*

EXPLORING

★   **National Key Deer Refuge.** This 84,351-acre refuge was established in
1957 to protect the dwindling population of the Key deer, one of more
than 20 animals and plants classified as endangered or threatened in the
Florida Keys. The Key deer, which stands about 30 inches at the shoul-
ders and is a subspecies of the Virginia white-tailed deer, once roamed
throughout the Lower and Middle Keys, but hunting, destruction of
their habitat, and a growing human population caused their numbers
to decline to 27 by 1957. The deer have made a comeback, increasing
their numbers to approximately 750. The best place to see Key deer
in the refuge is at the end of Key Deer Boulevard and on No Name
Key, a sparsely populated island just east of Big Pine Key. Mornings
and evenings are the best time to spot them. Deer may turn up along
the road at any time of day, so drive slowly. They wander into nearby
yards to nibble tender grass and bougainvillea blossom, but locals do

DID YOU KNOW?

An old railroad bridge used to connect Bahia Honda Key with Key West until a hurricane destroyed it in 1935. While it is no longer in operation, the bridge is used by visitors as a place for viewing the island.

not appreciate tourists driving into their neighborhoods after them. Feeding them is against the law and puts them in danger. The refuge also has 21 other listed endangered and threatened species of plants and animals, including five that are found nowhere else.

Blue Hole. A quarry left over from railroad days, the Blue Hole is the largest body of freshwater in the Keys. From the observation platform and nearby walking trail, you might see the resident alligator, turtles, and other wildlife. There are two well-marked trails: the Jack Watson Nature Trail (.6 mi), named after an environmentalist and the refuge's first warden; and the Fred Mannillo Nature Trail, one of the most wheelchair-accessible places to see an unspoiled pine-rockland forest and wetlands. The visitor center has exhibits on Keys biology and ecology. The refuge also provides information on the Key West National Wildlife Refuge and the Great White Heron National Wildlife Refuge. Accessible only by water, both are popular with kayak outfitters. ⊠ *MM 30.5 BS, Visitor Center–Headquarters, Big Pine Shopping Center, 28950 Watson Blvd.* ☎ *305/872–2239* ⊕ *www.fws.gov/nationalkeydeer* ⊡ *Free* ⊙ *Daily sunrise–sunset; headquarters weekdays 8–5.*

SPORTS AND THE OUTDOORS
BIKING
A good 10 mi of paved roads run from MM 30.3 BS, along Wilder Road, across the bridge to No Name Key, and along Key Deer Boulevard into the National Key Deer Refuge. Along the way you might see some Key deer. Stay off the trails that lead into wetlands, where fat tires can do damage to the environment.

Big Pine Bicycle Center. Owner Marty Baird is an avid cyclist and enjoys sharing his knowledge of great places to ride. He's also skilled at selecting the right bike for the journey, and he knows his repairs, too. His old-fashioned single-speed, fat-tire cruisers rent for $8 per half day and $10 for a full day. Helmets, baskets, and locks are included. Although the shop is officially closed on Sunday, Marty leads free off-road fun rides on Sunday mornings at 8 from December to Easter. ⊠ *MM 30.9 BS, 31 County Rd.* ☎ *305/872–0130.*

BOATING
Strike Zone Charters. Glass-bottom-boat excursions venture into the backcountry and Atlantic Ocean. The five-hour Island Excursion ($55 plus fuel surcharge) emphasizes nature and Keys history; besides close encounters with birds, sea life, and vegetation, there's a fish cookout on an island. Snorkel and fishing equipment, food, and drinks are included. This is one of the few nature outings in the Keys with wheelchair access. ⊠ *MM 29.6 BS, 29675 Overseas Hwy., Big Pine Key* ☎ *305/872–9863 or 800/654–9560* ⊕ *www.strikezonecharter.com.*

KAYAKING
★ **Big Pine Kayak Adventures.** There's no excuse to skip a water adventure with this convenient kayak rental service, which delivers them to your lodging or anywhere between Seven Mile Bridge and Stock Island. The company, headed by *The Florida Keys Paddling Guide* author Bill Keogh, will rent you a kayak and then ferry you—called taxi-yakking— to remote islands with clear instructions on how to paddle back on

your own. Rentals are by the half day or full day. Group kayak tours ($50 each for three hours) explore the mangrove forests of Great White Heron and Key Deer National Wildlife Refuges. Custom tours ($125 and up, four hours) transport you to exquisite backcountry areas teeming with wildlife. Kayak fishing charters are also popular. ✉ *MM 30 BS, Old Wooden Bridge Fishing Camp, turn right at traffic light, continue on Wilder Rd. toward No Name Key* ☎ *305/872–7474* ⊕ *www. keyskayaktours.com.*

SCUBA DIVING AND SNORKELING

Strike Zone Charters. Dive excursions head to the wreck of the 110-foot *Adolphus Busch* ($55), and scuba ($45) and snorkel ($35) trips to Looe Key Reef, prime scuba and snorkeling territory, aboard glass-bottom boats. Strike Zone also offers a five-hour island excursion that combines snorkeling, fishing, and an island cookout for $55 per person. A large dive shop is on-site. ✉ *MM 29.5 BS, 29675 Overseas Hwy.* ☎ *305/872–9863 or 800/654–9560* ⊕ *www.strikezonecharter.com.*

WHERE TO EAT

¢ ✕ **Good Food Conspiracy.** Like good wine, this small natural-foods eatery and market surrenders its pleasures a little at a time. Step inside to the aroma of brewing coffee, and then pick up the scent of fresh strawberries or carrots blending into a smoothie, the green aroma of wheatgrass juice, followed by the earthy odor of hummus. Order raw or cooked vegetarian and vegan dishes, organic soups and salads, and organic coffees and teas. Bountiful sandwiches (available halved) include the popular tuna melt or hummus and avocado. If you can't sit down for a bite, stock up on healthful snacks like dried fruits, raw nuts, and carob-covered almonds. Dine early: The shop closes at 7 pm Monday to Saturday, and at 5 pm on Sunday. ✉ *MM 30.2 OS, 30150 Overseas Hwy.* ☎ *305/872–3945* ⊕ *www.goodfoodconspiracy.com* ⬥ *Reservations not accepted.*

VEGETARIAN

$ ✕ **No Name Pub.** This no-frills honky-tonk has been around since 1936, delighting inveterate locals and intrepid vacationers who come for the excellent pizza, cold beer, and *interesting* companionship. The decor, such as it is, amounts to the autographed dollar bills that cover every inch of the place. The full menu printed on place mats includes a tasty conch chowder, a half-pound fried-grouper sandwich, spaghetti and meatballs, and seafood baskets. The lighting is poor, the furnishings are rough, and the music is oldies. This former brothel and bait shop is just before the No Name Key Bridge. It's a bit hard to find, but worth the trouble if you want a singular Keys experience. ✉ *MM 30 BS, turn west on Wilder Rd., left on South St., right on Ave. B, right on Watson Blvd.* ☎ *305/872–9115* ⊕ *www.nonamepub.com* ⬥ *Reservations not accepted.*

AMERICAN

WHERE TO STAY

For expanded hotel reviews, visit Fodors.com.

¢ ▦ **Big Pine Key Fishing Lodge.** There's a congenial atmosphere at this lively family-owned lodge-campground-marina. **Pros:** local fishing crowd; nice pool; great price. **Cons:** RV park is too close to motel; deer will eat your food if you're camping. **TripAdvisor:** "noise and light level in

HOTEL

6

the entire park was kept pleasantly low," "facilities were very clean," "there's a nature trail beach with good snorkeling." ⊠ *MM 33 OS, 33000 Overseas Hwy.* ☎ *305/872–2351* ⤴ *16 rooms; 158 campsites, 97 with full hook-ups, 61 without hook-ups* ⚲ *In-room: kitchen (some), refrigerator. In-hotel: pool, laundry facilities* ¶⊙¶ *No meals.*

$$$$ 🏠 **Deer Run Bed & Breakfast**. Key deer wander the grounds of this beach-
B&B/INN   front bed-and-breakfast, set on a quiet street lined with buttonwoods
  ★   and mangroves. **Pros:** quiet location; healthy breakfasts; complimentary bike and kayak use. **Cons:** price is a bit high; hard to find. **TripAdvisor:** "just gorgeous," "don't be afraid of the vegan thing it was wonderful," "rooms are large very clean." ⊠ *MM 33 OS, 1997 Long Beach Dr.* ☎ *305/872–2015* ⊕ *www.deerrunfloridabb.com* ⤴ *4 rooms* ⚲ *In-room: Wi-Fi. In-hotel: pool, beach, water sports, some age restrictions* ¶⊙¶ *Breakfast.*

LITTLE TORCH KEY

Little Torch Key is between mile markers 29 and 10.

Little Torch Key and its neighbor islands, Ramrod Key and Summerland Key, are good jumping-off points for divers headed for Looe Key Reef. The islands also serve as a refuge for those who want to make forays into Key West but not stay in the thick of things.

The undeveloped backcountry at your door makes Little Torch Key an ideal location for fishing and kayaking. Nearby **Ramrod Key**, which also caters to divers bound for Looe Key, derives its name from a ship that wrecked on nearby reefs in the early 1800s.

**NEED A
BREAK?**   **Baby's Coffee.** The aroma of rich roasting coffee beans arrests you at the door of "the Southernmost Coffee Roaster." Buy it by the pound or by the cup along with fresh baked goods. ⊠ MM 15 OS, 3178 Overseas Hwy., Saddlebunch Keys ☎ 305/744–9866 or 800/523–2326 ⊕ www.babyscoffee.com.

SPORTS AND THE OUTDOORS
SCUBA DIVING AND SNORKELING

★ **Looe Key Reef.** In 1744 the HMS *Looe*, a British warship, ran aground and sank on one of the most beautiful coral reefs in the Keys. Today the key owes its name to the ill-fated ship. The 5.3-square-nautical-mi reef, part of the **Florida Keys National Marine Sanctuary,** has strands of elkhorn coral on its eastern margin, purple sea fans, and abundant sponges and sea urchins. On its seaward side, it drops almost vertically 50 to 90 feet. In its midst, **Shipwreck Trail** plots the location of nine historic wreck sites in 14 to 120 feet of water. Buoys mark the sites, and underwater signs tell the history of each site and what marine life to expect. Snorkelers and divers will find the sanctuary a quiet place to observe reef life—except in July, when the annual Underwater Music Festival pays homage to Looe Key's beauty and promotes reef awareness with six hours of music broadcast via underwater speakers. Dive shops, charters, and private boats transport about 500 divers and snorkelers to hear the spectacle, which includes classical, jazz, new age, and Caribbean music, as well as a little Jimmy Buffett. There are even underwater Elvis impersonators. ⊠ *MM 27.5 OS, 216 Ann St., Key West* ☏ *305/292–0311.*

Looe Key Reef Resort & Dive Center. Rather than the customary morning and afternoon two-tank, two-location trips offered by most dive shops, this center, the closest dive shop to Looe Key Reef, runs a single three-tank, three-location dive ($84 for divers, $44 for snorkelers). The maximum depth is 30 feet, so snorkelers and divers go on the same boat. On Wednesday it runs a trip that visits a wreck and reefs in the area for the same price for either snorkeling or diving. The dive boat, a 45-foot catamaran, is docked at the full-service Looe Key Reef Resort. ⊠ *Looe Key Reef Resort, MM 27.5 OS, 27340 Overseas Hwy., Ramrod Key* ☏ *305/872–221 or 877/816–3483* ⊕ *www.diveflakeys.com.*

WATER SPORTS

Sugarloaf Marina. Rent a paddle-propelled vehicle for exploring local gulf waters. Rates for one-person kayaks start at $25 for one hour to $30 for a full day. Two-person kayaks are also available. Delivery is free for multiple-day rentals. ⊠ *MM 17 BS, 17015 Overseas Hwy., Sugarloaf Key* ☏ *305/745–3135.*

WHERE TO EAT

$$
6
$$

$$
AMERICAN
✕ **Geiger Key Smokehouse Bar & Grill.** There's a strong hint of the Old Keys at this oceanside marina restaurant, which came under new management in 2010. "On the backside of paradise," as the sign says, its tiki structures overlook quiet mangroves at an RV park marina. Locals usually outnumber tourists; they come for the daily dinner specials: pot roast on Tuesday, Italian on Wednesday, prime rib on Friday, and so on. For lunch, try a fish sandwich or pulled pork. The all-day menu spans an ambitious array of sandwiches, tacos, seafood, and steaks. In season, local fishermen stop here for breakfast before heading out in search of the big one. ⊠ *MM 10, Geiger Key at 5 Geiger Key Rd., off Boca Chica Rd.* ☏ *305/296–3553 or 305/294–1230* ⊕ *www.geigerkeymarina.com.*

$$$$
ECLECTIC
★
✕ **Little Palm Island Restaurant.** The oceanfront setting calls to mind St. Barts and the other high-end destinations of the Caribbean. Keep that in mind as you reach for the bill, which can also make you swoon. The restaurant at the exclusive Little Palm Island Resort—its dining room and adjacent outdoor terrace lit by candles and warmed by live music—is one of the most romantic spots in the Keys. The seasonal menu is a melding of French and Caribbean flavors, with exotic little touches. Think shrimp and yellowtail ceviche or coconut lobster bisque as a starter, followed by mahimahi with cilantro and creamy polenta. The Saturday and Sunday brunch buffet, the full-moon dinners with live entertainment, and Chef's Table Dinner are very popular. The dining room is open to nonguests on a reservations-only basis. ⊠ *MM 28.5 OS, 28500 Overseas Hwy.* ☏ *305/872–2551* ⊕ *www.littlepalmisland.com* ⌀ *Reservations essential.*

WHERE TO STAY

For expanded hotel reviews, visit Fodors.com.

$$$$ ☷ **Little Palm Island Resort & Spa.** *Haute tropicale* best describes this lux-
RESORT ury retreat, and "second mortgage" might explain how some can afford
Fodor's Choice the extravagant prices. **Pros:** secluded setting; heavenly spa; easy wild-
★ life viewing. **Cons:** expensive; might be too quiet for some. **TripAdvisor:** "attention to detail is astonishing," "great dinner and breakfast,"
"completely private quiet and relaxing." ⊠ *MM 28.5 OS, 28500 Overseas Hwy.* ☎ *305/872–2524 or 800/343–8567* ⊕ *www.littlepalmisland.
com* ⤴ *30 suites* ⚭ *In-room: a/c, no TV, Wi-Fi. In-hotel: restaurant,
bars, pool, gym, spa, beach, water sports, parking, some age restrictions* ⟊*Some meals.*

$ ☷ **Looe Key Reef Resort & Center.** If your Keys vacation is all about diving,
HOTEL you'll be well served at this scuba-obsessed operation. **Pros:** guests get
discounts on dive and snorkel trips; fun bar. **Cons:** small rooms; unheated
pool; close to road. **TripAdvisor:** "rooms were spartan but satisfactory,"
"nickel and dime for everything," "total dump but I absolutely love it."
⊠ *MM 27.5 OS, 27340 Overseas Hwy. Ramrod Key* ☎ *305/872–2215
Ext. 2 or 877/816–3483* ⊕ *www.diveflakeys.com* ⤴*23 rooms, 1 suite*
⚭ *In-room: a/c, Wi-Fi. In-hotel: bar, pool* ⟊*No meals.*

$$ ☷ **Parmer's Resort.** Almost every room at this budget-friendly option has
HOTEL a view of South Pine Channel, with the lovely curl of Big Pine Key in
the foreground. **Pros:** bright rooms; pretty setting; good value. **Cons:**
a bit out of the way; housekeeping costs extra; little shade around the
pool. **TripAdvisor:** "wonderful hospitality," "grounds are beautiful,"
"view is gorgeous." ⊠ *MM 28.7 BS, 565 Barry Ave.* ☎ *305/872–2157*
⊕ *www.parmersresort.com* ⤴*18 rooms, 12 efficiencies, 15 apartments,
1 penthouse, 1 2-bedroom cottage* ⚭ *In-room: a/c, kitchen (some). In-
hotel: pool, laundry facilities* ⟊*Breakfast.*

**EN
ROUTE** The huge object that looks like a white whale floating over Cudjoe Key
(MM 23–21) is not a figment of your imagination. It's Fat Albert, a
radar balloon that monitors local air and water traffic.

KEY WEST

Situated 150 mi from Miami, 90 mi from Havana, and an immeasurable
distance from sanity, this end-of-the-line community has never been like
anywhere else. Even after it was connected to the rest of the country—
by the railroad in 1912 and by the highway in 1938—it maintained a
strong sense of detachment.

Key West reflects a diverse population: Conchs (natives, many of whom
trace their ancestry to the Bahamas), freshwater Conchs (longtime resi-
dents who migrated from somewhere else years ago), Hispanics (primar-
ily descendants of Cuban immigrants), recent refugees from the urban
sprawl of mainland Florida, military personnel, and an assortment of
vagabonds, drifters, and dropouts in search of refuge. The island was
once a gay vacation hot spot, and it remains a decidedly gay-friendly
destination. Some of the most renowned gay guesthouses, however, no
longer cater to an exclusively gay clientele. Key Westers pride them-
selves on their tolerance of all peoples, all sexual orientations, and even

all animals. Most restaurants allow pets, and it's not surprising to see stray cats, dogs, and even chickens roaming freely through the dining rooms. The chicken issue is one that government officials periodically try to bring to an end, but the colorful iconic fowl continue to strut and crow, particularly in the vicinity of Old Town's Bahamian Village.

Although the rest of the Keys are known for outdoor activities, Key West has something of a city feel. Few open spaces remain, as promoters continue to churn out restaurants, galleries, shops, and museums to interpret the city's intriguing past. As a tourist destination, Key West has a lot to sell—an average temperature of 79°F, 19th-century architecture, and a laid-back lifestyle. Yet much has been lost to those eager for a buck. Duval Street looks like a miniature Las Vegas lined with garish signs for T-shirt shops and tour company offices. Cruise ships dwarf the town's skyline and fill the streets with day-trippers gawking at the hippies with dogs in their bike baskets, gay couples walking down the street holding hands, and the oddball lot of locals, some of whom bark louder than the dogs.

GETTING HERE AND AROUND

Between mile markers 4 and 0, Key West is the one place in the Keys where you could conceivably do without a car, especially if you plan on staying around Old Town. If you've driven the 106 mi down the chain, you're probably ready to abandon your car in the hotel parking lot anyway. Trolleys, buses, bikes, scooters, and feet are more suitable alternatives. To explore the beaches, New Town, and Stock Island, you'll probably need a car.

Greyhound Lines runs a special Keys shuttle two times a day (depending on the day of the week) from Miami International Airport (departing from Concourse E, lower level) and stops throughout the Keys. Fares run about $39 for Key West (3535 S. Roosevelt, Key West International Airport). Keys Shuttle runs scheduled service six times a day in 15-passenger vans between Miami Airport and Key West with stops throughout the Keys for $70 to $90 per person. Key West Express operates air-conditioned ferries between the Key West Terminal (Caroline and Grinnell streets) and Marco Island and Fort Myers Beach. The trip from Fort Myers Beach takes at least four hours each way and costs $85.50 one-way, $145 round-trip. Ferries depart from Fort Myers Beach at 8:30 am and from Key West at 6 pm. The Marco Island ferry costs $85.50 one-way and $119 round-trip, and departs at 8:30 am. A photo ID is required for each passenger. Advance reservations are recommended. The SuperShuttle charges $102 per passenger for trips from Miami International Airport to the Upper Keys. To go farther into the Keys, you must book an entire 11-person van, which costs about $350 to Key West. You need to place your request for transportation back to the airport 24 hours in advance.

The City of Key West Department of Transportation has six color-coded bus routes traversing the island from 6:30 am to 11:30 pm. Stops have signs with the international bus symbol. Schedules are available on buses and at hotels, visitor centers, and shops. The fare is $2 one-way.

KEY WEST'S COLORFUL HISTORY

The United States acquired Key West from Spain in 1821, along with the rest of Florida. The Spanish had named the island Cayo Hueso, or Bone Key, after the American Indians' skeletons they found on its shores. In 1823, President James Monroe sent Commodore David S. Porter to chase pirates away. For three decades the primary industry in Key West was wrecking—rescuing people and salvaging cargo from ships that foundered on the nearby reefs. According to some reports, when pickings were lean the wreckers hung out lights to lure ships aground. Their business declined after 1849 when the federal government began building lighthouses.

In 1845 the army began construction on Fort Taylor, which kept Key West on the Union side during the Civil War, even though most of Florida seceded. After the fighting ended, an influx of Cubans unhappy with Spain's rule brought the cigar industry here. Fishing, shrimping, and sponge-gathering became important industries, as did pineapple canning. Through much of the 19th century and into the 20th, Key West was Florida's wealthiest city in per-capita terms. But in 1929 the local economy began to unravel. Cigar-making moved to Tampa, Hawaii dominated the pineapple industry, and the sponges succumbed to blight. Then the Depression hit, and within a few years half the population was on relief.

Tourism began to revive Key West, but that came to a halt when a hurricane knocked out the railroad bridge in 1935. To help the tourism industry recover from that crushing blow, the government offered incentives for islanders to turn their charming homes—many of them built by shipwrights—into guesthouses and inns. The wise foresight has left the town with more than 100 such lodgings, a hallmark of Key West vacationing today. In the 1950s the discovery of "pink gold" in the Dry Tortugas boosted the economy of the entire region. Harvesting Key West shrimp required a fleet of up to 500 boats and flooded local restaurants with sweet luscious shrimp. The town's artistic community found inspiration in the colorful fishing boats.

The Lower Keys Shuttle bus runs from Marathon to Key West ($3 one-way), with scheduled stops along the way.

Old Town Key West is the only place in the Keys where parking is a problem. There are public parking lots that charge by the hour or day (some hotels and B&Bs provide parking or discounts at municipal lots). If you arrive early, you can sometimes find a spot on side streets off Duval and Whitehead, where you can park for free—just be sure it's not marked for residential parking only. Your best bet is to bike or take the trolley around town if you don't want to walk. You can disembark and reboard the trolley at will.

ESSENTIALS

Transportation Contacts City of Key West Department of Transportation (☎ 305/809–3910). **Greyhound Lines** (☎ 800/410–5397 or 800/231–2222). **Keys Shuttle** (☎ 305/289–9997 or 888/765–9997 ⊕ www.floridakeysshuttle.com). **Key West Express** (✉ 100 Grinnell St. ☎ 888/539–2628 ⊕ www.seakeywestexpress.com

com). **Lower Keys Shuttle** (☎ *305/809–3910* ⊕ *www.monroecounty-fl.gov).*
SuperShuttle (☎ *305/871–2000* ⊕ *www.supershuttle.com).*

Visitor Information Greater Key West Chamber of Commerce (✉ *510
Greene St.* ☎ *305/294–2587 or 800/527–8539* ⊕ *www.keywestchamber.org).*

EXPLORING

OLD TOWN

The heart of Key West, this historic Old Town area runs from White
Street to the waterfront. Beginning in 1822, wharves, warehouses, chan-
dleries, ship-repair facilities, and eventually in 1891 the U.S. Custom
House sprang up around the deep harbor to accommodate the navy's
large ships and other sailing vessels. Wreckers, merchants, and sea captains built lavish houses near the bustling waterfront. A remarkable
number of these fine Victorian and pre-Victorian structures have been
restored to their original grandeur and now serve as homes, guesthouses, shops, restaurants, and museums. These, along with the dwellings of famous writers, artists, and politicians who've come to Key West
over the past 175 years, are among the area's approximately 3,000
historic structures. Old Town also has the city's finest restaurants and
hotels, lively street life, and popular nightspots.

6

TOP ATTRACTIONS

Audubon House and Tropical Gardens. If you've ever seen an engraving by
ornithologist John James Audubon, you'll understand why his name is
synonymous with birds. See his works in this three-story house, which
was built in the 1840s for Captain John Geiger and filled with period
furniture. It now commemorates Audubon's 1832 stop in Key West
while he was traveling through Florida to study birds. Docents lead a
guided tour ($7.50) that points out the rare indigenous plants and trees
in the garden. An art gallery sells lithographs of the artist's famed portraits. ✉ *205 Whitehead St.* ☎ *305/294–2116 or 877/294–2470* ⊕ *www.
audubonhouse.com* 🎫 *$12; additional $7.50 for tours* ⊙ *Daily 9:30–5,
last tour starts at 4:30.*

★ **Ernest Hemingway Home and Museum.** Amusing anecdotes spice up the
guided tours of Ernest Hemingway's home, built in 1801 by the town's
most successful wrecker. While living here between 1931 and 1942,
Hemingway wrote about 70% of his life's work, including classics like
For Whom the Bell Tolls. Few of his belongings remain aside from some
books, and there's little about his actual work, but photographs help
you visualize his day-to-day life. The supposed six-toed descendants
of Hemingway's cats—many named for actors, artists, authors, and
even a hurricane—have free rein of the property. Tours begin every 10
minutes and take 30 minutes; then you're free to explore on your own.
✉ *907 Whitehead St.* ☎ *305/294–1136* ⊕ *www.hemingwayhome.com*
🎫 *$12* ⊙ *Daily 9–5.*

★ **Fort Zachary Taylor Historic State Park.** Construction of the fort began in
1845 but was halted during the Civil War. Even though Florida seceded
from the Union, Yankee forces used the fort as a base to block Confederate shipping. More than 1,500 Confederate vessels were detained in

Key West

DREDGERS KEY

WISTERIA ISLAND

SUNSET KEY

FLEMING KEY

See inset at left

Key West International Airport

Key West Municipal Beach

ATLANTIC OCEAN

Garrison Bight

Key West Bight

1 mile

1 km

Audubon House
and Tropical Gardens **4**

C.B. Harvey Rest
Beach **21**

City Cemetery **14**

Dog Beach **18**

Eco-Discovery Center **13**

Ernest Hemingway
Home and Museum **1**

Fort East Martello
Museum & Gardens **23**

Fort Zachary Taylor
Historic State Park **12**

Harry S. Truman
Little White
House Museum **6**

Higgs Beach—Astro
City Playground **19**

Historic Seaport
at Key West Bight **11**

Key West Aquarium **8**

Key West Butterfly &
Nature Conservatory **15**

Key West Lighthouse
Museum and Keeper's
Quarters Museum **2**

Key West Museum of
Art & History in the
Custom House **7**

Key West Shipwreck
Treasures Museum **9**

Mallory Square and Pier .. **10**

Mel Fisher Maritime
Museum **5**

Nancy Forrester's
Secret Garden **3**

Smathers Beach **22**

South Beach **17**

Southernmost Point **16**

West Martello Tower **20**

KEY WEST: A GOOD TOUR

To cover many sights, take the Old Town Trolley, which lets you get off and reboard a later trolley, or the Conch Train, which is a set guided tour. Old Town is also manageable by foot, bicycle, moped, or electric car. The area is expansive, so you'll want either to pick and choose from the stops on this tour or break it into two or more days. Start on Whitehead Street at the Ernest Hemingway Home and Museum, and then cross the street and climb to the top of the Key West Lighthouse Museum & Keeper's Quarters Museum for a spectacular view. Return to Whitehead Street and follow it north to Angela Street, where you'll turn right. At Margaret Street, the City Cemetery is worth a look for its aboveground vaults and unusual headstone inscriptions. Head north on Margaret Street, turn left onto Southard Street, then right onto Simonton Street. Halfway up the block, Nancy Forrester's Secret Garden occupies Free School Lane. Follow Southard Street south through Truman Annex to Fort Zachary Taylor Historic State Park.

Walk west into Truman Annex to see the Harry S. Truman Little White House Museum, President Truman's vacation residence. Return east on Caroline and turn left on Whitehead to visit the Audubon House and Tropical Gardens, honoring the famed artist and naturalist. Follow Whitehead north to Greene Street and turn left to see the salvaged sea treasures of the Mel Fisher Maritime Museum. At Whitehead's northern end are the Key West Aquarium and the Key West Museum of Art & History, in the historic former U.S. Custom House. By late afternoon you should be ready to cool off with a dip or catch a few rays at the beach. From the aquarium, head east about a mile, where you'll find South Beach, located at Southernmost Hotel at the Beach and named for its location at the southern end of Duval Street. If you've brought your pet, stroll a few blocks east to Dog Beach, at the corner of Vernon and Waddell streets. A little farther east is Higgs Beach–Astro City Playground, on Atlantic Boulevard between White and Reynolds streets. As the sun starts to sink, return to the west side of Old Town and follow the crowds to Mallory Square, behind the aquarium, to watch Key West's nightly sunset spectacle. Those lucky enough may see a green flash—the brilliant splash of green or blue that sometimes appears as the sun sinks into the ocean on a clear night. For dinner, head east on Caroline Street to Historic Seaport at Key West Bight, a renovated area where there are numerous restaurants and bars.

TIMING

Allow two full days to see all the Old Town museums and homes, especially with a little shopping thrown in. For a narrated trip on the Conch Train or trolley, budget 1½ hours to ride the loop without getting off, or an entire day if you plan to get off and on the trolley at sights and restaurants.

Sailboats big and small make their way into Key West Harbor; photo by John Franzis, Fodors.com member.

Key West's harbor. The fort, finally completed in 1866, was also used in the Spanish-American War. Take a 30-minute guided walking tour of the redbrick fort, a National Historic Landmark, at noon and 2, or self-tour anytime between 8 and 5. In February a celebration called Civil War Heritage Days includes costumed reenactments and demonstrations. From mid-January to mid-April the park serves as an open-air gallery for pieces created for Sculpture Key West. One of its most popular features is its man-made beach, a rest stop for migrating birds in the spring and fall; there are also hiking and biking trails and a kayak launch. ⊠ *Box 6565; end of Southard St., through Truman Annex* ☎ *305/292–6713* ⊕ *www.floridastateparks.org/forttaylor* ⊐ *$4.50 for 1 person, $7 for 2 people, 50¢ per additional person* ☉ *Daily 8–sunset, tours noon and 2.*

NEED A BREAK?

Key West Library. Check out the pretty palm garden next to the Key West Library at 700 Fleming Street, just off Duval. This leafy, outdoor reading area, with shaded benches, is the perfect place to escape the frenzy and crowds of downtown Key West. There's free Internet access in the library, too. ⊠ *700 Fleming St.*

Harry S. Truman Little White House Museum. Recent renovations to this circa-1890 landmark have restored the home and gardens to the Truman era, down to the wallpaper pattern. A free photographic review of visiting dignitaries and presidents—John F. Kennedy, Jimmy Carter, and Bill Clinton are among the chief executives who passed through here—is on display in the back of the gift shop. Engaging 45-minute tours begin every 15 minutes until 4:30. They start with an excellent 10-minute video on the history of the property and Truman's visits. On the grounds of **Truman Annex,** a 103-acre former military parade grounds and barracks, the home served as a winter White House for presidents Truman, Eisenhower, and Kennedy. Note: The tour does require climbing steps. Visitors can do a self-guided botanical tour of the grounds with a free brochure from the museum store. ⊠ *111 Front St.* ☎ *305/294–9911* ⊕ *www.trumanlittlewhitehouse.com* ⊠ *$15* ⊗ *Daily 9–5, grounds 7–6; last tour at 4:30.*

Historic Seaport at Key West Bight. What used to be a funky—in some places even seedy—part of town is now an 8½-acre historic restoration of 100 businesses, including waterfront restaurants, open-air bars, museums, clothing stores, bait shops, dive shops, docks, a marina, and water-sports concessions. It's all linked by the 2-mi waterfront **Harborwalk,** which runs between Front and Grinnell streets, passing big ships, schooners, sunset cruises, fishing charters, and glass-bottom boats. ⊠ *100 Grinnell St.* ☎ *305/293–8309.*

NEED A BREAK?

Coffee Plantation. Get your morning (or afternoon) buzz, and hook up to the Internet in the comfort of a homelike setting in a circa-1890 Conch house. Munch on sandwiches, wraps, and pastries, and sip a hot or cold espresso beverage. ⊠ *713 Caroline St.* ☎ *305/295–9808* ⊕ *www. coffeeplantationkeywest.com.*

6

Key West Butterfly & Nature Conservatory. This air-conditioned refuge for butterflies, birds, and the human spirit gladdens the soul with hundreds of colorful wings—more than 45 species of butterflies alone—in a lovely glass-encased bubble. Waterfalls, artistic benches, paved pathways, birds, and lush, flowering vegetation elevate this above most butterfly attractions. The gift shop and gallery are worth a visit on their own. ⊠ *1316 Duval St.* ☎ *305/296–2988 or 800/839–4647* ⊕ *www. keywestbutterfly.com* ⊠ *$12* ⊗ *Daily 9–5 (last admission 4:30); gallery and shop open until 5:30.*

Key West Lighthouse Museum & Keeper's Quarters Museum. For the best view in town, climb the 88 steps to the top of this 1847 lighthouse. The 92-foot structure has a Fresnel lens, which was installed in the 1860s at a cost of $1 million. The keeper lived in the adjacent 1887 clapboard house, which now exhibits vintage photographs, ship models, nautical charts, and lighthouse artifacts from all along the Key reefs. A kids' room is stocked with books and toys. ⊠ *938 Whitehead St.* ☎ *305/295–6616* ⊕ *www.kwahs.com* ⊠ *$10* ⊗ *Daily 9:30–5; last admission at 4:30.*

Fodor's Choice ★ **Key West Museum of Art & History in the Custom House.** When Key West was designated a U.S. port of entry in the early 1820s, a customhouse was established. Salvaged cargoes from ships wrecked on the reefs were brought here, setting the stage for Key West to become—for a time—the richest city in Florida. The imposing redbrick-and-terra-cotta Richardsonian Romanesque–style building reopened as a museum and art gallery in 1999. Smaller galleries have long-term and changing exhibits about the history of Key West, including a Hemingway room and a fine collection of folk artist Mario Sanchez's wood paintings. In 2011, to

See the typewriter Hemingway used at his home office in Key West. He lived here from 1931 to 1942.

commemorate the 100th anniversary of the railroad's arrival to Key West in 1912, a new permanent Flagler exhibit opened. ⊠ *281 Front St.* ☎ *305/295–6616* ⊕ *www.kwahs.com* ✉ *$7* ☉ *Daily 9:30–5.*

Mallory Square and Pier. For cruise-ship passengers, this is the disembarkation point for an attack on Key West. For practically every visitor, it's the requisite venue for a nightly sunset celebration that includes street performers—human statues, sword swallowers, tightrope walkers, musicians, and more—plus craft vendors, conch fritter fryers, and other regulars who defy classification. (Wanna picture with my pet iguana?) With all the activity, don't forget to watch the main show: a dazzling tropical sunset. ⊠ *Mallory Sq.* ☎ *No phone.*

The Southernmost Point. Possibly the most photographed site in Key West (even though the actual geographic southernmost point in the continental United States lies across the bay on a naval base, where you see a satellite dish), this is a must-see. Who wouldn't want his picture taken next to the big striped buoy that marks the southernmost point in the continental United States? A plaque next to it honors Cubans who lost their lives trying to escape to America and other signs tell Key West history. ⊠ *Whitehead and South Sts.* ☎ *No phone.*

WORTH NOTING

City Cemetery. You can learn almost as much about a town's history through its cemetery as through its historic houses. Key West's celebrated 20-acre burial place may leave you wanting more, with headstone epitaphs such as "I told you I was sick," and, for a wayward husband, "Now I know where he's sleeping at night." Among the interesting plots are a memorial to the sailors killed in the sinking of

CLOSE UP

Hemingway Was Here

In a town where Pulitzer Prize–winning writers are almost as common as coconuts, Ernest Hemingway stands out. Bars and restaurants around the island claim that he ate or drank there (except Bagatelle, where the sign reads "Hemingway never liked this place").

Hemingway came to Key West in 1928 at the urging of writer John dos Passos and rented a house with wife number two, Pauline Pfeiffer. They spent winters in the Keys and summers in Europe and Wyoming, occasionally taking African safaris. Along the way they had two sons, Patrick and Gregory. In 1931, Pauline's wealthy uncle Gus gave the couple the house at 907 Whitehead Street. Now known as the Ernest Hemingway Home & Museum, it's Key West's number-one tourist attraction. Renovations included the addition of a pool and a tropical garden.

In 1935, when the visitor bureau included the house in a tourist brochure, Hemingway promptly built the brick wall that surrounds it today. He wrote of the visitor bureau's offense in a 1935 essay for *Esquire,* saying, "The house at present occupied by your correspondent is listed as number eighteen in a compilation of the forty-eight things for a tourist to see in Key West. So there will be no difficulty in a tourist finding it or any other of the sights of the city, a map has been prepared by the local F.E.R.A. authorities to be presented to each arriving visitor. This is all very flattering to the easily bloated ego of your correspondent but very hard on production."

During his time in Key West, Hemingway penned some of his most important works, including *A Farewell to Arms, To Have and Have Not, Green Hills of Africa,* and *Death in the Afternoon.* His rigorous schedule consisted of writing almost every morning in his second-story studio above the pool, then promptly descending the stairs at midday. By afternoon and evening he was ready for drinking, fishing, swimming, boxing, and hanging around with the boys.

One close friend was Joe Russell, a craggy fisherman and owner of the rugged bar Sloppy Joe's, originally at 428 Greene Street but now at 201 Duval Street. Russell was the only one in town who would cash Hemingway's $1,000 royalty check. Russell and Charles Thompson introduced Hemingway to deep-sea fishing, which became fodder for his writing. Another of Hemingway's loves was boxing. He set up a ring in his yard and paid local fighters to box with him, and he refereed matches at Blue Heaven, then a saloon at 729 Thomas Street.

Hemingway honed his macho image, dressed in cutoffs and old shirts, and took on the name Papa. In turn, he gave his friends new names and used them as characters in his stories. Joe Russell became Freddy, captain of the *Queen Conch* charter boat in *To Have and Have Not.*

Hemingway stayed in Key West for 11 years before leaving Pauline for wife number three. Pauline and the boys stayed on in the house, which sold in 1951 for $80,000, 10 times its original cost.

—Jim and Cynthia Tunstall

6

the battleship USS *Maine,* carved angels and lambs marking graves of children, and grand aboveground crypts that put to shame many of the town's dwellings for the living. There are separate plots for Catholics, Jews, and refugees from Cuba. You're free to walk around the cemetery on your own, but the best way to see it is on a 90-minute tour given by the staff and volunteers of the Historic Florida Keys Foundation. Tours leave from the main gate, and reservations are required. ✉ *Margaret and Angela Sts.* ☎ *305/292–6718* 🎟 *Tours $15* ☉ *Daily sunrise–6 pm, tours Tues. and Thurs. at 9:30 year-round; call for additional times.*

Dog Beach. Next to Louie's Backyard, this tiny beach—the only one in Key West where dogs are allowed unleashed—has a shore that's a mix of sand and rocks. **Best for:** dog owners. ✉ *Vernon and Waddell Sts.* ☎ *No phone* 🎟 *Free* ☉ *Daily sunrise–sunset.*

↻ **Eco-Discovery Center.** While visiting Fort Zachary Taylor Historic State Park, stop in at this 6,400-square-foot interactive attraction, which encourages visitors to venture through a variety of Florida Keys habitats from pinelands, beach dunes, and mangroves to the deep sea. Walk through a model of NOAA's (National Oceanic and Atmospheric Administration) Aquarius, a unique underwater ocean laboratory 9 mi off Key Largo, to virtually discover what lurks beneath the sea. Touch-screen computer displays, a dramatic movie, a 2,450-gallon aquarium, and live underwater cameras show off North America's only contiguous barrier coral reef. ✉ *35 E. Quay Rd., at end of Southard St. in Truman Annex* ☎ *305/809–4750* ⊕ *floridakeys.noaa.gov* 🎟 *Free, donations accepted* ☉ *Tues.–Sat. 9–4.*

↻ **Key West Aquarium.** Pet a nurse shark and explore the fascinating underwater realm of the Keys without getting wet at this historic aquarium. Hundreds of tropical fish and enormous sea creatures live here. A touch tank enables you to handle starfish, sea cucumbers, horseshoe and hermit crabs, even horse and queen conchs—living totems of the Conch Republic. Built in 1934 by the Works Progress Administration as the world's first open-air aquarium, most of the building has been enclosed for all-weather viewing. Guided tours, included in the admission price, feature shark feedings. ✉ *1 Whitehead St.* ☎ *305/296–2051* ⊕ *www.keywestaquarium.com* 🎟 *$12* ☉ *Daily 10–6; tours at 11, 1, 3, and 4:30.*

↻ **Key West Shipwreck Treasures Museum.** Much of Key West's history, early prosperity, and interesting architecture come from ships that ran aground on its coral reef. Artifacts from the circa-1856 *Isaac Allerton,* which yielded $150,000 worth of wreckage, comprise the museum portion of this multifaceted attraction. Actors and films add a bit of Disneyesque drama. The final highlight is climbing to the top of the 65-foot lookout tower, a reproduction of the 20 or so towers used by Key West wreckers during the town's salvaging heydays. ✉ *1 Whitehead St.* ☎ *305/292–8990* ⊕ *www.shipwreckhistoreum.com* 🎟 *$12* ☉ *Daily 9:40–5.*

Mel Fisher Maritime Museum. In 1622 two Spanish galleons laden with riches from South America foundered in a hurricane 40 mi west of the Keys. In 1985 diver Mel Fisher recovered the treasures from the lost ships, the *Nuestra Señora de Atocha* and the *Santa Margarita*. Fisher's incredible adventure tracking these fabled hoards and battling the state of Florida for rights is as amazing as the loot you'll see, touch, and learn about in this museum. Artifacts include a gold bar (that you can lift to get an idea of what $15,000 feels like) and a 77.76-carat natural emerald crystal worth almost $250,000. Exhibits on the second floor rotate and might cover slave ships, including the excavated 17th-century *Henrietta Marie*, or the evolution of Florida maritime history. ⊠ *200 Greene St.* ☎ *305/294–2633* ⊕ *www.melfisher.org* 🖃 *$12* ⊙ *Weekdays 8:30–6, weekends 9:30–6 (last tickets sold at 5:15)*.

Nancy Forrester's Secret Garden. It's hard to believe that this green escape still exists in the middle of Old Town Key West. Despite damage by hurricanes and pressures from developers, Nancy Forrester has maintained her naturalized garden for more than 40 years. Growing in harmony are rare palms and cycads, ferns, bromeliads, bright gingers and heliconias, gumbo-limbo trees strewn with orchids and vines, and a colorful crew of birds, reptiles, cats, and a few surprises. An art gallery has botanical prints and environmental art. One-hour private tours cost $35 per person, four-person minimum. ⊠ *1 Free School La. (off 500 block of Simonton)* ☎ *305/294–0015* ⊕ *www.nancyforrester.com* 🖃 *$10* ⊙ *Daily 10–5.*

NEW TOWN

The Overseas Highway splits as it enters Key West, the two forks rejoining to encircle New Town, the area east of White Street to Cow Key Channel. The southern fork runs along the shore as South Roosevelt Boulevard (Route A1A) skirting Key West International Airport. Along the north shore, North Roosevelt Boulevard (U.S. 1) leads to Old Town. Part of New Town was created with dredged fill. The island would have continued growing this way had the Army Corps of Engineers not determined in the early 1970s that it was detrimental to the nearby reef.

★ **Fort East Martello Museum & Gardens.** This redbrick Civil War fort never saw a lick of action during the war. Today it serves as a museum, with historical exhibits about the 19th and 20th centuries. Among the latter are relics of the USS *Maine*, cigar factory and shipwrecking exhibits, and the citadel tower you can climb to the top. The museum, operated by the Key West Art and Historical Society, also has a collection of Stanley Papio's "junk art" sculptures inside and out, and a gallery of Cuban folk artist Mario Sanchez's chiseled and painted wooden carvings of historic Key West street scenes. ⊠ *3501 S. Roosevelt Blvd.* ☎ *305/296–3913* ⊕ *www.kwahs.com* 🖃 *$6* ⊙ *Daily 9:30–4:30.*

West Martello Tower. Among the arches and ruins of this redbrick Civil War–era fort, the Key West Garden Club maintains lovely gardens of native and tropical plants, fountains, and sculptures. It also holds art, orchid, and flower shows February through April and leads private garden tours one weekend in March. ⊠ *Atlantic Blvd. and White St.*

☎ *305/294–3210* ⊕ *www.keywestgardenclub.com* ✉ *Donation welcome* ☉ *Tues.–Sat. 9:30–5.*

OFF THE BEATEN PATH

History buffs might remember long-deactivated Fort Jefferson as the prison that held Dr. Samuel Mudd for his role in the Lincoln assassination. But today's "guests" are much more captivated by this sanctuary's thousands of birds and marine life.

Dry Tortugas National Park. This park, 70 mi off the shores of Key West, consists of seven small islands. Tour the fort; then lay out your blanket on the sunny beach for a picnic before you head out to snorkel on the protected reef. Many people like to camp here ($3 per person per night, eight sites plus group site and overflow area; first come, first served), but note that there's no freshwater supply and you must carry off whatever you bring onto the island. ⊡ *Box 6208, Key West33040* ☎ *305/242–7700* ⊕ *www.nps.gov/drto* ✉ *$5.*

Dry Tortugas National Park Ferry. The fast, sleek, 100-foot catamaran *Yankee Freedom II* cuts the travel time to the Dry Tortugas to 2¼ hours. The time passes quickly on the roomy vessel equipped with three restrooms, two freshwater showers, and two bars. Stretch out on two decks: one an air-conditioned salon with cushioned seating, the other an open sundeck with sunny and shaded seating. Continental breakfast and lunch are included. On arrival, a naturalist leads a 40-minute guided tour, which is followed by lunch and a free afternoon for swimming, snorkeling (gear included), and exploring. The vessel is ADA–certified for visitors using wheelchairs. ■TIP→ The Dry Tortugas lies in the central time zone. ✉ *Lands End Marina, 240 Margaret St., Key West* ☎ *305/294–7009 or 800/634–0939* ⊕ *www.yankeefreedom. com* ✉ *$160, plus $5 park fee* ☉ *Trips daily at 8 am; check in 7:15.*

BEACHES

C. B. Harvey Rest Beach. This beach and park were named after Cornelius Bradford Harvey, former Key West mayor and commissioner. It has half a dozen picnic areas, dunes, and a wheelchair and bike path. **Best for:** quiet. ✉ *Atlantic Blvd., east side of White St. Pier* ☎ *No phone* ✉ *Free* ☉ *Daily 7 am–11 pm.*

☺
★ **Fort Zachary Taylor Historic State Park.** The park's beach is the best and safest place to swim in Key West. There's an adjoining picnic area with barbecue grills and shade trees, a snack bar, and rental equipment, including snorkeling gear. A café serves sandwiches and other munchies. **Best for:** history-lovers and families. ✉ *Box 6565; end of Southard St., through Truman Annex* ☎ *305/292–6713* ⊕ *www.floridastateparks. org/forttaylor* ✉ *$4.50 for 1 person, $7 for 2 people, 50¢ per additional person* ☉ *Daily 8–sunset, tours noon and 2.*

☺ **Higgs Beach–Astro City Playground.** This Monroe County park with its groomed pebbly sand is a popular sunbathing spot. A nearby grove of Australian pines provides shade, and the West Martello Tower provides shelter should a storm suddenly sweep in. Kayak and beach-chair rentals are available, as is a volleyball net. The beach also has a marker and cultural exhibit commemorating the gravesite of 295 enslaved Africans who died after being rescued from three South America–bound slave ships in 1860. Across the street, **Astro City Playground** is popular with

Island Belle

KEY WEST TOURS

BICYCLE TOURS

Lloyd's Original Tropical Bike Tour. Explore the natural, noncommercial side of Key West at a leisurely pace, stopping on backstreets and in backyards of private homes to sample native fruits and view indigenous plants and trees with a 30-year Key West veteran. The behind-the-scenes tours run two hours and cost $37, including bike rental. ✉ *Truman Ave. and Simonton St., Key West* ☎ *305/304–4700 or 305/294–1882* ⊕ *www.lloydstropicalbiketour.com.*

BOAT TOURS

Dancing Dolphin Spirit Charters. Victoria Impallomeni, a 34-year wilderness guide and marine scientist, invites up to six nature lovers—especially children—aboard the *Imp II*, a 25-foot Aquasport, for four-hour ($500) and seven-hour ($700) ecotours that frequently include encounters with wild dolphins. While island-hopping, you visit underwater gardens, natural shoreline, and mangrove habitats. For her Dolphin Day for Humans tour, Impallomeni pulls you through the water, equipped with mask and snorkel, on a specially designed "dolphin water massage board" that simulates dolphin swimming motions. Sometimes dolphins follow the boat and swim among participants. All equipment is supplied. ✉ *MM 5 OS, Murray's Marina, 5710 Overseas Hwy., Key West* ☎ *305/304–7562 or 888/822–7366* ⊕ *www.captainvictoria.com.*

White Knuckle Thrill Boat Ride. For something with an adrenaline boost, book with this speedboat. It holds up to 10 people and does 360s, fishtails, and other water stunts in the gulf. Cost is $59 each, and includes pickup shuttle. ✉ *Sunset Marina, 555 College Rd., Key West* ☎ *305/797-0459* ⊕ *www.whiteknucklethrillboatride.com.*

KAYAK TOURS

Lazy Dog Kayak Guides. Take a four-hour guided sea kayak–snorkel tour around the mangrove islands just east of Key West. The $60 charge covers transportation, bottled water, a snack, and supplies, including snorkeling gear. A $35 two-hour guided kayak tour is also available. ✉ *5114 Overseas Hwy., Key West* ☎ *305/295–9898* ⊕ *www.lazydog.com.*

WALKING TOURS

Historic Florida Keys Foundation. In addition to publishing several good guides on Key West, the foundation conducts tours of the City Cemetery Tuesday and Thursday at 9:30. ✉ *510 Greene St., Old City Hall, Key West* ☎ *305/292-6718.*

young children. **Best for:** families. ✉ *Atlantic Blvd. between White and Reynolds Sts.* ☎ *No phone* 🔁 *Free* ⏱ *Daily 6 am–11 pm.*

Smathers Beach. This wide beach has nearly 2 mi of sand, plus restrooms, picnic areas, and volleyball courts, all of which make it popular with the spring-break crowd. Trucks along the road rent rafts, windsurfers, and other beach "toys." Metered parking is on the street. **Best for:** partying. ✉ *S. Roosevelt Blvd.* ☎ *No phone* 🔁 *Free* ⏱ *Daily 7 am–11 pm.*

South Beach. On the Atlantic, this stretch of sand, also known as City Beach, is popular with travelers staying at nearby motels. It is now part of the new Southernmost Hotel on the Beach resort, but is open to the public with a fun beach bar and grill. There's no parking however, so visitors must walk or bike to the beach. ⊠ *Foot of Duval St.* ☎ *No phone* 🖥 *Free* ⊗ *Daily 7 am–11 pm.*

SPORTS AND THE OUTDOORS

Unlike the rest of the region, Key West isn't known primarily for outdoor pursuits. But everyone should devote at least half a day to relaxing on a boat tour, heading out on a fishing expedition, or pursuing some other adventure at sea. The ultimate excursion is a boat trip to Dry Tortugas National Park for snorkeling and exploring Fort Jefferson. Other excursions cater to nature lovers, scuba divers and snorkelers, fishing anglers, and those who would just like to get out in the water and enjoy the scenery and sunset. For those who prefer their recreation land based, biking is the way to go. Hiking is limited, but walking the streets of Old Town provides plenty of exercise.

BIKING

Key West was practically made for bicycles, but don't let that lull you into a false sense of security. Narrow and one-way streets along with car traffic result in several bike accidents a year. Some hotels rent or lend bikes to guests; others will refer you to a nearby shop and reserve a bike for you. Rentals usually start at about $10 a day, but some places also rent by the half day. ■TIP➔ Lock up! Bikes—and porch chairs!—are favorite targets for local thieves.

A&M Rentals. Rent beach cruisers with large baskets for $10 a day. Rates for scooters start at $30 for four hours. Look for the huge American flag on the roof. ⊠ *523 Truman Ave.* ☎ *305/294–0399* ⊕ *www. amscooterskeywest.com.*

Eaton Bikes. Tandem, three-wheel, and children's bikes are available in addition to the standard beach cruisers ($18 for first day) and seven-speed cruisers ($18). It delivers free to all Key West rentals. ⊠ *830 Eaton St.* ☎ *305/295–0057* ⊕ *www.eatonbikes.com.*

Moped Hospital. This outfit supplies balloon-tire bikes with yellow safety baskets for adults and kids ($12 for the first day, $8 for extra days), as well as scooters ($35) and double-seater scooters ($55). ⊠ *601 Truman Ave.* ☎ *305/296–3344 or 866/296–1625* ⊕ *www.mopedhospital.com.*

FISHING

Key West Bait & Tackle. Prepare to catch a big one with the live bait, frozen bait, and fishing equipment provided here. It also has the Live Bait Lounge, where you can sip ice-cold beer while telling fish tales. ⊠ *241 Margaret St.* ☎ *305/292–1961* ⊕ *www.keywestbaitandtackle.com.*

Key West Pro Guides. Trips include flats and backcountry fishing ($400–$425 for a half day) and reef and offshore fishing (starting at $550 for a half day). ⊠ *G-31 Miriam St.* ☎ *866/259–4205* ⊕ *www. keywestproguides.com.*

THE CONCH REPUBLIC

Beginning in the 1970s, pot smuggling became a source of income for islanders who knew how to dodge detection in the maze of waterways in the Keys. In 1982, the U.S. Border Patrol threw a roadblock across the Overseas Highway just south of Florida City to catch drug runners and undocumented aliens. Traffic backed up for miles as Border Patrol agents searched vehicles and demanded that the occupants prove U.S. citizenship. Officials in Key West, outraged at being treated like foreigners by the federal government, staged a protest and formed their own "nation," the so-called Conch Republic. They hoisted a flag and distributed mock border passes, visas, and Conch currency. The embarrassed Border Patrol dismantled its roadblock, and now an annual festival recalls the city's victory.

GOLF

Key West Resort Golf Course. Key West isn't a major golf destination, but there is one course on Stock Island. This 18-hole, par 70 course has $70–$95 greens fees. Book your tee time early in the season. ✉ *6450 E. College Rd.* ☎ *305/294–5232* ⊕ *www.keywestgolf.com.*

KAYAKING

Key West Eco-Tours. Key West is surrounded by marinas, so it's easy to find what you're looking for, whether it's sailing with dolphins or paddling in the mangroves. These sail-kayak-snorkel excursions take you into backcountry flats and mangrove forests. The 4½-hour trip costs $95 per person and includes lunch. Sunset sails ($295) and private charters ($495) are also available. ✉ *Historic Seaport, 100 Grinnell St.* ☎ *305/294–7245* ⊕ *www.javacatcharters.com.*

SCUBA DIVING AND SNORKELING

Captain's Corner. This PADI–certified dive shop has classes in several languages and twice-daily snorkel and dive trips ($40–$65) to reefs and wrecks aboard the 60-foot dive boat *Sea Eagle.* Use of weights, belts, masks, and fins is included. ✉ *125 Ann St.* ☎ *305/296–8865* ⊕ *www. captainscorner.com.*

Snuba of Key West. Safely dive the coral reefs without getting a scuba certification. Ride out to the reef on a catamaran, then follow your guide underwater for a one-hour tour of the coral reefs. You wear a regulator with a breathing hose that is attached to a floating air tank on the surface. No prior diving or snorkeling experience is necessary, but you must know how to swim. The $99 price includes beverages. ✉ *Garrison Bight Marina, Palm Ave. between Eaton St. and N. Roosevelt Blvd.* ☎ *305/292–4616* ⊕ *www.snubakeywest.com.*

SHOPPING

On these streets you'll find colorful local art of widely varying quality, key limes made into everything imaginable, and the raunchiest T-shirts in the civilized world. Browsing the boutiques—with frequent pub stops along the way—makes for an entertaining stroll down Duval Street.

MALLS AND SHOPPING CENTERS

Bahama Village. Where to start your shopping adventure? This cluster of spruced-up shops, restaurants, and vendors is responsible for the restoration of the colorful historic district where Bahamians settled in the 19th century. The village lies roughly between Whitehead and Fort streets and Angela and Catherine streets. Hemingway frequented the bars, restaurants, and boxing rings in this part of town.

ARTS AND CRAFTS

Key West is filled with art galleries, and the variety is truly amazing. Much is locally produced by the town's large artist community, but many galleries carry international artists from as close as Haiti and as far away as France. Local artists do a great job of preserving the island's architecture and spirit.

Alan S. Maltz Gallery. The owner, declared the state's official wildlife photographer by the Wildlife Foundation of Florida, captures the state's nature and character in stunning portraits. Spend four figures for large-format images on canvas or save on small prints and closeouts. ⊠ *1210 Duval St.* ☎ *305/294–0005* ⊕ *www.alanmaltz.com.*

Cuba, Cuba! Check out the stock of paintings, sculptures, and photos by Cuban artists. ⊠ *814 Duval St.* ☎ *305/295–9442 or 800/621–3596* ⊕ *cubacubastore.com.*

Gallery on Greene. Showcasing politically incorrect art by Jeff MacNelly and three-dimensional paintings by Mario Sanchez, this is the largest gallery–exhibition space in Key West. ⊠ *606 Greene St.* ☎ *305/294–1669* ⊕ *www.galleryongreene.com.*

Gingerbread Square Gallery. The oldest private art gallery in Key West represents local and internationally acclaimed artists on an annually changing basis, in mediums ranging from graphics to art glass. ⊠ *1207 Duval St.* ☎ *305/296–8900* ⊕ *www.gingerbreadsquaregallery.com.*

Glass Reunions. Find a collection of wild and impressive fine-art glass here. It's worth a stop in just to see the imaginative and over-the-top glass chandeliers, jewelry, dishes, and platters. ⊠ *825 Duval St.* ☎ *305/294–1720* ⊕ *www.glassreunions.com.*

KW Light Gallery. Historian, photographer, and painter Sharon Wells opened this gallery to showcase her own fine-art photography and painted tiles and canvases, as well as the works of other national artists. You can find historic photos here as well. ⊠ *1203 Duval St.* ☎ *305/294–0566* ⊕ *www.kwlightgallery.com.*

Lucky Street Gallery. High-end contemporary paintings are the focus. There are also a few pieces of jewelry by internationally recognized Key West–based artists. Changing exhibits, artist receptions, and special events make this a lively venue. ⊠ *1130 Duval St.* ☎ *305/294–3973* ⊕ *luckystreetgallery.com.*

Pelican Poop Shoppe. Caribbean art sells in a historic building (with Hemingway connections, of course). For a $2 admission or a $10 purchase, you can stroll the tropical courtyard garden. The owners buy directly from the artisans every year, so the prices are very attractive. ⊠ *314 Simonton St.* ☎ *305/292–9955* ⊕ *www.pelicanpoopshoppe.com.*

Nightlife, shops, and some interesting street art can all be found on Key West's Duval Street.

Whitehead St. Pottery. Potters Charles Pearson and Timothy display their porcelain stoneware and raku-fired vessels. The setting, around two koi ponds with a burbling fountain, is as sublime as the art. ✉ *322 Julia St.* ☎ *305/294–5067* ⊕ *www.whiteheadstreetpottery.com.*

BOOKS

Key West Island Bookstore. This home away from home for the large Key West writers' community carries new, used, and rare titles. It specializes in Hemingway, Tennessee Williams, and South Florida mystery writers. ✉ *513 Fleming St.* ☎ *305/294–2904.*

CLOTHING AND FABRICS

Fairvilla Megastore. Don't leave town without a browse through the legendary shop, where you'll find an astonishing array of fantasy wear, outlandish costumes (check out the pirate section), and other interesting souvenirs. ✉ *520 Front St.* ☎ *305/292–0448* ⊕ *www.fairvilla.com.*

Seam Shoppe. Take home a shopping bag full of scarlet hibiscus, fuchsia heliconias, blue parrot fish, and even pink flamingo fabric, selected from the city's widest selection of tropical-print fabrics. ✉ *1114 Truman Ave.* ☎ *305/296–9830* ⊕ *www.tropicalfabricsonline.com.*

FOOD AND DRINK

Fausto's Food Palace. Since 1926 Fausto's has been the spot to catch up on the week's gossip and to chill out in summer—it has groceries, organic foods, marvelous wines, a sushi chef on duty 8 am–6 pm, and box lunches to go. ✉ *522 Fleming St.* ☎ *305/296–5663* ✉ *1105 White St.* ☎ *305/294–5221* ⊕ *www.faustos.com.*

★ **Kermit's Key West Lime Shoppe.** You'll see Kermit himself standing on the corner every time a trolley passes, pie in hand. Besides pie, his shop carries a multitude of key lime products from barbecue sauce to jellybeans. His prefrozen pies, dressed with a special long-lasting whipped cream instead of meringue, travels well. ✉ *200 Elizabeth St., Historic Seaport* ☎ *305/296–0806 or 800/376–0806* ⊕ *www.keylimeshop.com.*

Key West Winery. You'll be pleasantly surprised with the fruit wines sold here. Display crates hold bottles of wines made from blueberries, blackberries, pineapples, cherries, mangoes, watermelons, tomatoes, and, of course, key limes. Stop in for a free tasting. ✉ *103 Simonton St.* ☎ *305/292–1717 or 866/880–1717* ⊕ *www.thekeywestwinery.com.*

Peppers of Key West. If you like it hot, you'll love this collection of hundreds of sauces, salsas, and sweets guaranteed to light your fire. ✉ *602 Greene St.* ☎ *305/295–9333 or 800/597–2823* ⊕ *www.peppersofkeywest.com.*

GIFTS AND SOUVENIRS

Cayo Hueso y Habana. Part museum, part shopping center, this circa-1879 warehouse includes a hand-rolled cigar shop, one-of-a-kind souvenirs, a Cuban restaurant, and exhibits that tell of the island's Cuban heritage. Outside, a memorial garden pays homage to the island's Cuban ancestors. ✉ *410 Wall St., Mallory Sq.* ☎ *305/293–7260.*

★ **Fast Buck Freddie's.** Find a classy, hip selection of gifts, including every flamingo item imaginable here. It also has a whole department called "Tropical Trash," and carries such imaginative items as an electric fan in the shape of a rooster. ✉ *500 Duval St.* ☎ *305/294–2007* ⊕ *www.fastbuckfreddies.com.*

★ **Montage.** For that unique (but slightly overpriced) souvenir of your trip to Key West head here, where you'll discover hundreds of handcrafted signs of popular Key West guesthouses, inns, hotels, restaurants, bars, and streets. If you can't find what you're looking for, they'll make it for you. ✉ *512 Duval St.* ☎ *305/395–9101 or 877/396–4278* ⊕ *montage-keywest.com.*

NIGHTLIFE

Rest up: Much of what happens in Key West does so after dark. Open your mind and have a stroll. Scruffy street performers strum next to dogs in sunglasses. Brawls tumble out the doors of Sloppy Joe's. Drag queens strut across stages in Joan Rivers garb. Tattooed men lick whipped cream off of women's body parts. And margaritas flow like a Jimmy Buffett tune.

BARS AND LOUNGES

Capt. Tony's Saloon. When it was the original Sloppy Joe's in the mid-1930s Hemingway was a regular. Later, a young Jimmy Buffett sang here and made this watering hole famous in his song "Last Mango in Paris." Bands play nightly. ✉ *428 Greene St.* ☎ *305/294–1838* ⊕ *www.capttonyssaloon.com.*

Durty Harry's. The megasize entertainment complex has live music in a variety of indoor-outdoor bars including Rick's Dance Club Wine

& Martini Bar and the tiny Red Garter strip club. ⊠ *208 Duval St.* ☎ *305/296–5513* ⊕ *www.ricksanddurtyharrys.com.*

Green Parrot Bar. Pause for a libation in the open-air. Built in 1890, the bar is said to be Key West's oldest. The sometimes-rowdy saloon has locals outnumbering out-of-towners, especially on weekends when bands play. ⊠ *601 Whitehead St., at Southard St.* ☎ *305/294–6133* ⊕ *www.greenparrot.com.*

Hog's Breath Saloon. Belly up to the bar for a cold mug of the signature Hog's Breath Lager at this infamous joint, a must-stop on the Key West bar crawl. Live bands play daily 1 pm–2 am. ⊠ *400 Front St.* ☎ *305/296–4222* ⊕ *www.hogsbreath.com.*

Margaritaville Café. A youngish, touristy crowd mixes with aging Parrot Heads. It's owned by former Key West resident and recording star Jimmy Buffett, who has been known to perform here. The drink of choice is, of course, a margarita, made with Jimmy's own brand of Margaritaville tequila. There's live music nightly, as well as lunch and dinner. ⊠ *500 Duval St.* ☎ *305/292–1435* ⊕ *www.margaritaville.com.*

Pier House. The party begins with a steel-drum band to celebrate the sunset on the beach (on select Thursdays and Fridays), then moves indoors to the Wine Galley piano bar for live jazz. ⊠ *1 Duval St.* ☎ *305/296–4600 or 800/327–8340* ⊕ *www.pierhouse.com.*

Schooner Wharf Bar. An open-air waterfront bar and grill in the historic seaport district retains its funky Key West charm and hosts live entertainment daily. Its margarita ranks among Key West's best. ⊠ *202 William St.* ☎ *305/292–3302* ⊕ *www.schoonerwharf.com.*

Sloppy Joe's. There's history and good times at the successor to a famous 1937 speakeasy named for its founder, Captain Joe Russell. Decorated with Hemingway memorabilia and marine flags, the bar is popular with travelers and is full and noisy all the time. A Sloppy Joe's T-shirt is a de rigueur Key West souvenir, and the gift shop sells them like crazy. ⊠ *201 Duval St.* ☎ *305/294–5717* ⊕ *www.sloppyjoes.com.*

The Top. On the seventh floor of the La Concha Crowne Plaza, this is one of the best places in town to view the sunset and enjoy live entertainment. ⊠ *430 Duval St.* ☎ *305/296–2991* ⊕ *www.laconchakeywest.com.*

Virgilio's. In the best traditions of a 1950s cocktail lounge, this bar serves chilled martinis to the soothing tempo of live jazz and blues nightly. ⊠ *524 Duval St.* ☎ *305/296–8118* ⊕ *www.virgilioskeywest.com.*

WHERE TO EAT

$$–$$$

JAPANESE

✕ **Ambrosia.** Ask any savvy local where to get the best sushi on the island and you'll undoubtedly be pointed to this tiny wood-and-tatami-paneled dining room with indoor waterfall tucked away into a resort near the beach. Grab a seat at the sushi bar and watch owner and head sushi chef Masa prepare an impressive array of superfresh sashimi delicacies. Sushi lovers can't go wrong with the Ambrosia special ($35), a sampler of five kinds of sashimi, seven pieces of sushi, and sushi rolls. There's an assortment of lightly fried tempura and teriyaki dishes and a killer bento box at lunch. Enjoy it all with a glass of premium sake or

Sloppy Joe's is one must-stop on most Key West visitors' barhop stroll, also known as the Duval Crawl.

a cold glass of Sapporo beer. ⊠ *Santa Maria Resort, 1401 Simonton St.* ☎ *305/293–0304* ⊕ *www.keywestambrosia.com* ⊗ *No lunch weekends. Closed 2 weeks after Labor Day.*

$$$
CARIBBEAN
★
✕**Blue Heaven.** The outdoor dining area here is often referred to as "the quintessential Keys experience," and it's hard to argue. There's much to like about this historic restaurant where Hemingway refereed boxing matches and customers cheered for cockfights. Although these events are no more, the free-roaming chickens and cats add that "what-a-hoot" factor. Nightly specials include black bean soup, Provençal sea scallops, jerk chicken, and sautéed yellowtail snapper in citrus beurre blanc sauce. Desserts and breads are baked on the premises; the banana bread and lobster Benedict with key lime hollandaise are hits during "breakfast with the roosters." Breakfast is the signature meal here. ⊠ *729 Thomas St.* ☎ *305/296–8666* ⊕ *www.blueheavenkw.com* ⚑ *Reservations not accepted* ⊗ *Closed after Labor Day for 6 weeks.*

¢
SEAFOOD
✕**B.O.'s Fish Wagon.** What started out as a fish house on wheels appears to have broken down on the corner of Caroline and William streets and is today the cornerstone for one of Key West's junkyard-chic dining institutions. Step up to the wood-plank counter window and order the specialty: a grouper sandwich fried or grilled and topped with key lime sauce. Other choices include fish nuts (don't be scared, they're just fried nuggets), hot dogs, and shrimp or soft-shell-crab sandwich. Talk sass with your host and find a picnic table or take a seat at the plank. Grab some paper towels off one of the rolls hanging around and busy yourself reading graffiti, license plates, and irreverent signs. It's a must-do Key West experience. ⊠ *801 Caroline St.* ☎ *305/294–9272* ⊕ *www. bosfishwagon.com* ⚑ *Reservations not accepted* ▬ *No credit cards.*

EVERYTHING'S FISHY IN THE KEYS

Fish. It's what's for dinner in the Florida Keys. The Keys's runway between the Gulf of Mexico or Florida Bay and Atlantic warm waters means fish of many fin. Restaurants take full advantage by serving it fresh, whether you caught it or a local fisherman did.

Menus at a number of colorful waterfront shacks such as **Snapper's** (⊠ *139 Seaside Ave., Key Largo* ☎ *305/852–5956*) in Key Largo and **Half Shell Raw Bar** (⊠ *231 Margaret St., Key West* ☎ *305/294–7496*) range from basic raw, steamed, broiled, grilled, or blackened fish to some Bahamian and New Orleans–style interpretations. Other seafood houses dress up their fish in creative haute-cuisine styles, such as **Pierre's** (⊠ *MM 81.5 BS, Islamorada* ☎ *305/664–3225*) hogfish *meunière* or yellowtail snapper with pear, ricotta pasta purses with caponata, and red pepper coulis at **Café Marquesa** (⊠ *600 Fleming St., Key West* ☎ *305/292–1244* ⊕ *www.marquesa.com*). Try a Keys–style breakfast of "grits and grunts"—fried fish and grits—at the **Stuffed Pig** (⊠ *3520 Overseas Hwy., Marathon* ☎ *305/743–4059*).

BUILT-IN FISH

You know it's fresh when you see a fish market as soon as you open the door to the restaurant where you're dining. It happens all the time in the Keys. You can even peruse the seafood showcases and pick the fish fillet or lobster tail you want.

Many of the Keys' best restaurants are found in marina complexes, where the commercial fishermen bring their catches straight from the sea. Those in **Stock Island** (one island north of Key West) and at **Keys Fisheries Market & Marina** (⊠ *MM 49 BS, end of 35th St., Marathon* ☎ *305/743–4353 or 866/743–4353*) take some finding.

CONCH

One of the tastiest legacies of the Keys' Bahamian heritage, conch shows up on nearly every restaurant menu. It's so prevalent in local diets that natives refer to themselves as Conchs. Conch fritter is the most popular culinary manifestation, followed by cracked (pounded, breaded, and fried) conch, and conch salad, a ceviche-style refresher. Since the harvesting of queen conch is now illegal, most of the islands' conch comes from the Bahamas.

FLORIDA LOBSTER

What happened to the claws? Stop looking for them: Florida spiny lobsters don't have 'em, never did. The sweet tail meat, however, makes up for the loss. Commercial and sports divers harvest these glorious crustaceans from late July through March. Check with local dive shops on restrictions, then get ready for a fresh feast. Restaurants serve them broiled with drawn butter or in creative dishes such as lobster Benedict, lobster sushi rolls, lobster Reuben, and lobster tacos.

GROUPER

Once central to Florida's trademark seafood dish—fried grouper sandwich—its populations have been overfished in recent years, meaning that the state has exerted more control over bag regulations and occasionally closes grouper fishing on a temporary basis during the

winter season. Some restaurants have gone antigrouper to try to bring back the abundance, but most grab it when they can. Black grouper is the most highly prized of the several varieties.

STONE CRAB

In season October 15 through May 15, it gets its name from its rock-hard shell. Fishermen take only the claws, which can regenerate in a sustainable manner. Connoisseurs prefer them chilled with tangy mustard sauce. Some restaurants give you a choice of hot claws and drawn butter, but this means the meat will be cooked twice, because it's usually boiled or steamed quickly after taken from its crab trap.

YELLOWTAIL SNAPPER

The preferred species of snappers, it is more plentiful in the Keys than any other Florida waters. As pretty as it is tasty, it's a favorite of divers and snorkelers. Mild, sweet, and delicate, its meat lends itself to any number of preparations. It is available pretty much year-round, and many restaurants will give you a choice of broiled, baked, fried, or blackened. Chefs top it with everything from key lime beurre blanc to mango chutney. **Ballyhoo's** in Key Largo (⊠ MM 97.8, *in the median* ☎ *305/852–0822*) serves it 10 different ways.

6

$

VEGETARIAN

✕ **The Café, A Mostly Vegetarian Place.** You don't have to be a vegetarian to love this new-age café decorated with bright artwork and a corrugated tin–fronted counter. Local favorites include homemade soup, veggie burgers (order them with a side of sweet potato fries), grilled portobello mushroom salad, seafood, vegan specialties, and grilled Gorgonzola pizza. For bigger appetites there are offerings like the Szechuan-style vegetable stir-fry. ⊠ *509 Southard St.* ☎ *305/296–5515* ⌦ *Reservations not accepted.*

$$$

CONTINENTAL

Fodor's Choice

★

✕ **Café Marquesa.** Chef Susan Ferry presents seven or more inspired entrées on her changing menu each night; delicious dishes can include yellowtail snapper with pear, ricotta pasta purses with caponata, and red pepper coulis; and Australian rack of lamb crusted with goat cheese and a port-fig sauce. End your meal on a sweet note with key lime napoleon with tropical fruits and berries. There's also a fine selection of wines and custom martinis such as the key limetini and the Irish martini. Adjoining the intimate Marquesa Hotel, the dining room is equally relaxed and elegant. ⊠ *600 Fleming St.* ☎ *305/292–1244* ⊕ *www.marquesa.com* ⌦ *Reservations essential* ⊘ *No lunch.*

$$$

FRENCH

✕ **Café Solé.** Welcome to the "home of the hog snapper," a deliciously roasted local fish seasoned with a red-pepper-custard sauce. This little piece of France is concealed behind a high wall and a gate in a residential neighborhood. Inside, chef John Correa marries his French training with local ingredients, creating delicious takes on classics, including portobello mushroom soup, snapper with mango salsa, and some of the best bouillabaisse that you'll find outside of Marseilles. From the land, there is filet mignon with a wild-mushroom demi-glaze. The restaurant serves lunch and Sunday brunch in the winter and spring. ⊠ *1029 Southard St.* ☎ *305/294–0230* ⊕ *www.cafesole.com* ⌦ *Reservations essential.*

$$

CARIBBEAN

✕ **El Meson de Pepe.** If you want to get a taste of the island's Cuban heritage, this is the place. Perfect for after watching a Mallory Square sunset, you can dine alfresco or in the dining room on refined versions of Cuban classics. Begin with a megasized mojito while you enjoy the basket of bread and savory sauces. The expansive menu offers *tostones rellenos* (green plantains with different traditional fillings), ceviche (raw fish "cooked" in lemon juice), and more. Choose from Cuban specialties such as roasted pork in a cumin mojo sauce and *ropa vieja* (shredded beef stew). At lunch, the local Cuban population and cruise-ship passengers enjoy Cuban sandwiches and smaller versions of dinner's most popular entrées. A salsa band performs outside at the bar during sunset celebration. ⊠ *Mallory Sq., 410 Wall St.* ☎ *305/295–2620* ⊕ *www. elmesondepepe.com.*

$

CARIBBEAN

✕ **El Siboney.** Dining at this family-style restaurant is like going to Mom's for Sunday dinner—if your mother is Cuban. The dining room is noisy, and the food is traditional *cubano*. There are well-seasoned black beans, a memorable paella, traditional ropa vieja (shredded beef and roast pork), and local seafood served grilled, stuffed, and breaded. Dishes come with Cuban bread, salad or plantains, and rice or fries. To make a good thing even better, the prices are very reasonable. ⊠ *900 Catherine*

St. ☎ *305/296–4184* ⊕ *www.elsiboneyrestaurant.com* ⬥ *Reservations not accepted.*

$ ✗**Finnegan's Wake Irish Pub and Eatery.** "Come for the beer. Stay for the
IRISH food. Leave with the staff," is the slogan of this popular pub. The pictures of Beckett, Shaw, Yeats, and Wilde on the walls and the creaky
wood floors underfoot exude Irish country warmth. The certified Angus
beef is priciest; most of the other dishes are bargains. Traditional fare
includes bangers and mash, chicken potpie, and colcannon—rich
mashed potatoes with scallions, sauerkraut, and melted white cheddar
cheese. Bread pudding soaked with a honey-whiskey sauce is a true
treat. Live music on weekends and daily happy hours from 4 to 7 and
midnight to 2 featuring nearly 30 beers on tap make it popular with
the spring break and sometimes-noisy drinking crowd. ⬥ *320 Grinnell
St.* ☎ *305/293–0222* ⊕ *www.keywestirish.com.*

$$ ✗**Half Shell Raw Bar.** Smack-dab on the docks, this legendary institution
SEAFOOD gets its name from the oysters, clams, and peel-and-eat shrimp that are
🕐 a departure point for its seafood-based diet. It's not clever recipes or
fine dining (or even air-conditioning) that packs 'em in; it's fried fish,
po'boy sandwiches, and seafood combos. For a break from the deep
fryer, try the fresh and light conch ceviche "cooked" with lime juice.
The potato salad is flavored with dill, and the "Pama Rita" is a new
twist in Margaritaville. ⬥ *Lands End Village at Historic Seaport, 231
Margaret St.* ☎ *305/294–7496* ⊕ *www.halfshellrawbar.com* ⬥ *Reser-
vations not accepted.*

¢ ✗**Lobo's Mixed Grill.** Famous for its selection of wrap sandwiches, Lobo
AMERICAN has a reputation among locals for its 8-ounce, charcoal-grilled ground
🕐 chuck burger—thick and juicy and served with lettuce, tomato, and
pickle on a toasted bun. Mix it up with toppings like Brie, blue cheese,
or portobello mushroom. The menu of 30 wraps includes rib eye, oys-
ter, grouper, Cuban, and chicken Caesar. The menu includes salads
and quesadillas, as well as a fried-shrimp-and-oyster combo. Beer and
wine are served. This courtyard food stand closes at 6, so eat early.
Most of Lobo's business is takeout (it has a half-dozen outdoor picnic
tables), and it offers free delivery within Old Town. ⬥ *5 Key Lime
Sq., east of intersection of Southard and Duval Sts.* ☎ *305/296–5303*
⊕ *www.loboskeywest.com* ⬥ *Reservations not accepted* ⬥ *No credit
cards* ☽ *Closed Sun. Apr.–early Dec.*

$$$$ ✗**Louie's Backyard.** Feast your eyes on a steal-your-breath-away view
ECLECTIC and beautifully presented dishes prepared by executive chef Doug
★ Shook. Once you get over sticker shock on the seasonally chang-
ing menu (appetizers cost around $9–$18; entrées can hover around
the $36 mark), settle in on the outside deck and enjoy dishes like
grilled scallops with shrimp cream, sautéed veal sweetbreads with
crabmeat, and greens-stuffed chicken breast. A more affordable option
upstairs is the Upper Deck, which serves tapas such as flaming ouzo
shrimp, roasted olives with onion and feta, and Gruyère and duck
confit pizza. If you come for lunch, the menu is less expensive but
the view is just as fantastic. For night owls, the tin-roofed Afterdeck
Bar serves cocktails on the water until the wee hours. ⬥ *700 Waddell
Ave.* ☎ *305/294–1061* ⊕ *www.louiesbackyard.com* ⬥ *Reservations*

6

essential ✆ *Closed Labor Day to mid-Sept, Upper Deck closed Sun. and Mon.*

$–$$ ✕**Mangia Mangia.** This longtime
ITALIAN favorite serves large portions of homemade pastas that can be matched with any of the homemade sauces. Tables are arranged in a brick garden hung with twinkling lights and in a cozy, casual dining room in an old house. Everything out of the open kitchen is outstanding, including the *bollito misto di mare* (fresh seafood sautéed with garlic, shallots, white wine, and pasta) or the memorable spaghettini "schmappellini," homemade pasta with asparagus, tomatoes, pine nuts, and Parmesan. The wine list—with more than 350 offerings—includes old and rare vintages, and also has a good by-the-glass selection. ⊠ *900 Southard St.* ☎ *305/294–2469* ⊕ *www.mangia-mangia.com* ⚒ *Reservations not accepted* ✆ *No lunch.*

$$$ ✕**Michaels Restaurant.** White tablecloths, subdued lighting, and roman-
AMERICAN tic music give Michaels the feel of an urban eatery. Garden seating reminds you that you are in the Keys. Chef–owner Michael Wilson flies in prime rib, cowboy steaks, and rib eyes from Allen Brothers in Chicago, which has supplied top-ranked steak houses for more than a century. Also on the menu is a melt-in-your-mouth grouper stuffed with jumbo lump crab, Kobe and tenderloin meat loaf, veal saltimbocca, and a variety of made-to-order fondue dishes (try the pesto pot, spiked with hot pepper and basil). To lighten up, smaller portions of many of the favorites are available until 7:30 Sunday through Thursday. The Hemingway (mojito-style) and the Third Degree (raspberry vodka and white crème de cacao) top the cocktail menu. ⊠ *532 Margaret St.* ☎ *305/295–1300* ⊕ *www.michaelskeywest.com* ⚒ *Reservations essential* ✆ *No lunch.*

$$$ ✕**Nine One Five.** Twinkling lights draped along the lower- and upper-
ECLECTIC level outdoor porches of a 100-year-old Victorian mansion set an elegant—though unstuffy—stage at this very cool tapas-style eatery. If you like to sample and sip, you'll appreciate the variety of smaller plate selections and wines by the glass. Taster-portioned tapas include olives, cheese, shrimp, and pâté, or try a combination with the tapas platter or the signature "tuna dome" with fresh crab, lemon-miso dressing, and an ahi tuna–sashimi wrapping. There are also larger plates if you're craving something like seafood soup or steak au poivre frites. Dine outdoors and people-watch along upper Duval, or sit at a table inside while listening to light jazz. ⊠ *915 Duval St.* ☎ *305/296–0669* ⊕ *www.915duval.com* ✆ *No lunch.*

$$$$ ✕**Pisces.** In a circa-1892 former store and home, chef William Arnel
CONTINENTAL and staff create a contemporary setting with a stylish granite bar,
★ Andy Warhol originals, and glass oil lamps. Favorites include "lobster tango mango," flambéed in cognac and served with saffron butter sauce and sliced mangoes; Pisces Aphrodite (seafood in puff pastry);

veal tenderloin with wild mushrooms; and black grouper bouillabaise. ✉ *1007 Simonton St.* ☎ *305/294–7100* ⊕ *www.pisceskeywest.com* ⌂ *Reservations essential* ⊘ *No lunch.*

$$ ✗**Salute Ristorante at the Beach.** This colorful restaurant sits on Higgs
ITALIAN Beach, giving it one of the island's best lunch views—and a bit of sand
★ and salt spray on a windy day. Owners of the popular Blue Heaven restaurant took it over and have designed an intriguing dinner menu that includes linguine with mussels, vegetable or three-meat lasagna, and white bean soup. At lunch the gazpacho refreshes with great flavor and texture, and the calamari marinara, antipasti sandwich, pasta primavera, and yellowtail sandwich do not disappoint. ✉ *1000 Atlantic Blvd., Higgs Beach* ☎ *305/292–1117* ⊕ *saluteonthebeach.com* ⌂ *Reservations not accepted.*

$$ ✗**Seven Fish.** A local hot spot, this intimate, off-the-beaten-track eatery
SEAFOOD is good for an eclectic mix of dishes like tropical shrimp salsa, wild-
★ mushroom quesadilla, seafood marinara, and old-fashioned meat loaf with real mashed potatoes. For dessert, the sweet potato pie provides an added measure of down-home comfort. Those in the know arrive for dinner early to snag one of the 12 or so tables clustered in the bare-bones dining room. ✉ *632 Olivia St.* ☎ *305/296–2777* ⊕ *www.7fish.com* ⊘ *Closed Tues. No lunch.*

$$ ✗**Turtle Kraals.** Named for the kraals, or corrals, where sea turtles were
SEAFOOD once kept until they went to the cannery, this place calls to mind the
♺ island's history. The lunch–dinner menu offers an assortment of marine cuisine that includes seafood enchiladas, mesquite-grilled fish of the day, and mango crab cakes. The slow-cook wood smoker results in wonderfully tender ribs, brisket, mesquite-grilled oysters with Parmesan and cilantro, and mesquite grilled chicken sandwich. Breakfast offers some interesting and quite tasty options like barbecued hash and eggs or huevos rancheros. The open restaurant overlooks the marina at the Historic Seaport. Turtle races entertain during happy hour on Monday and Friday at 6 pm. ✉ *231 Margaret St.* ☎ *305/294–2640* ⊕ *www.turtlekraals.com* ⌂ *Reservations not accepted.*

WHERE TO STAY

Historic cottages, restored century-old Conch houses, and large resorts are among the offerings in Key West, the majority charging from $100 to $300 a night. In high season, December through March, you'll be hard-pressed to find a decent room for less than $200, and most places raise prices considerably during holidays. Many guesthouses and inns do not welcome children under 16, and most do not permit smoking indoors; rates often include an expanded continental breakfast and afternoon wine or snack.

For expanded hotel reviews, visit Fodors.com.

$$$$ ⌂**Ambrosia Key West.** If you desire personal attention, a casual atmo-
B&B/INN sphere, and a dollop of style, stay at these twin inns spread out on
★ nearly 2 acres. **Pros:** spacious rooms; poolside breakfast; friendly staff. **Cons:** on-street parking can be tough to come by; a little too spread out. **TripAdvisor:** "exterior areas are beautiful," "walking distance to

everything," "magnificent." ✉ *615, 618, 622 Fleming St.* ☎ *305/296–9838 or 800/535–9838* ⊕ *www.ambrosiakeywest.com* ↪ *6 rooms, 3 town houses, 1 cottage, 10 suites* ⟡ *In-room: a/c, kitchen (some), Wi-Fi. In-hotel: pools, parking, some pets allowed* ⭘❘ *Breakfast.*

$$
B&B/INN
🛏 **Angelina Guest House.** The high rollers and ladies of the night were chased away long ago, but this charming guesthouse revels in its past as a gambling hall and bordello. **Pros:** good value; nice garden; friendly staff. **Cons:** thin walls; basic rooms; shared balcony. **TripAdvisor:** "attractive and comfortable," "price is worth it," "in the fairly quiet end of Key West." ✉ *302 Angela St.* ☎ *305/294–4480 or 888/303–4480* ⊕ *www.angelinaguesthouse.com* ↪ *13 rooms* ⟡ *In-room: a/c, no TV, Wi-Fi. In-hotel: pool, some age restrictions* ⭘❘ *Breakfast.*

$$$
HOTEL
🛏 **Azul Key West.** The ultramodern—nearly minimalistic—redo of this classic circa-1903 Queen Anne mansion is a break from the sensory overload of Key West's other abundant Victorian guesthouses. **Pros:** lovely building; marble-floored baths; luxurious linens. **Cons:** on a busy street. **TripAdvisor:** "small but well-appointed rooms," "inn is charming," "lovely place to relax." ✉ *907 Truman Ave.* ☎ *305/296–5152 or 888/253–2985* ⊕ *www.azulhotels.us* ↪ *10 rooms, 1 suite* ⟡ *In-room: Wi-Fi. In-hotel: pool, some age restrictions* ⭘❘ *Breakfast.*

$$$$
RESORT
☺
★
🛏 **Casa Marina Resort & Beach Club.** At any moment, you expect the landed gentry to walk across the oceanfront lawn, just as they did when this 13-acre resort was built back in the 1920s. **Pros:** nice beach; historic setting; away from the crowds. **Cons:** long walk to Old Town; $25 resort fee. **TripAdvisor:** "money we spent was well worth it," "killer health club available to guests," "top notch service." ✉ *1500 Reynolds St.* ☎ *305/296–3535 or 866/203–6392* ⊕ *www.casamarinaresort.com* ↪ *241 rooms, 70 suites* ⟡ *In-room: a/c, Internet, Wi-Fi. In-hotel: restaurant, bars, tennis courts, pools, gym, spa, beach, water sports, business center, some pets allowed* ⭘❘ *No meals.*

$$$
B&B/INN
🛏 **Courtney's Place.** If you like kids, cats, and dogs, you'll feel right at home in this collection of accommodations ranging from cigar-maker cottages to shotgun houses. **Pros:** near Duval Street; fairly priced. **Cons:** small parking lot; small pool. **TripAdvisor:** "not fancy but clean as a whistle," "walking distance to Duval and surrounding areas," "good value." ✉ *720 Whitemarsh La., off Petronia St.* ☎ *305/294–3480 or 800/869–4639* ⊕ *www.courtneysplacekeywest.com* ↪ *6 rooms, 2 suites, 2 efficiencies, 8 cottages* ⟡ *In-room: a/c, kitchen (some), Internet. In-hotel: pool, laundry facilities, parking, some pets allowed* ⭘❘ *Breakfast.*

$$$$
HOTEL
★
🛏 **Eden House.** From the vintage metal rockers on the street-side porch to the old neon hotel sign in the lobby, this 1920s rambling Key West mainstay hotel is high on character, low on gloss. **Pros:** sunny garden; hot tub is actually hot; daily happy hour around the pool. **Cons:** pricey. **TripAdvisor:** "were super impressed with the front desk staff," "rooms are very basic but clean," "rooms are small but very nice." ✉ *1015 Fleming St.* ☎ *305/296–6868 or 800/533–5397* ⊕ *www.edenhouse.com* ↪ *36 rooms, 8 suites* ⟡ *In-room: a/c, kitchen (some). In-hotel: restaurant, pool, parking* ⭘❘ *No meals.*

$$$$
HOTEL
Fodor's Choice
★

🏨 **The Gardens Hotel.** Built in 1875, this gloriously shaded property covers a third of a city block in Old Town, among orchids, ponytail palms, black bamboo, walks, fountains, and earthen pots imported from Cuba. **Pros:** luxurious bathrooms; secluded garden seating; free phone calls. **Cons:** hard to get reservations; expensive. **TripAdvisor:** "room was beautiful quiet and romantic," "bed was very comfortable," "wine bar is great." ⊠ *526 Angela St.* ☎ *305/294–2661 or 800/526–2664* ⊕ *www.gardenshotel.com* ↪ *17 rooms* ⚙ *In-room: a/c, Wi-Fi. In-hotel: bar, pool, parking, some age restriction* ⏐◎⏐ *Breakfast.*

$$$$
RESORT
🌀

🏨 **Hyatt Key West Resort and Spa.** With its own man-made beach, the Hyatt Key West is one of few resorts where you can dig your toes in the sand, then walk a short distance away to the streets of Old Town. **Pros:** a little bit away from the bustle of Old Town; plenty of activities. **Cons:** beach is small; cramped-feeling property; chain-hotel feel. **TripAdvisor:** "has a small private beach," "great layout," "a great location." ⊠ *601 Front St.* ☎ *305/809–1234* ⊕ *www.keywest.hyatt.com* ↪ *118 rooms* ⚙ *In-room: a/c, Internet, Wi-Fi. In-hotel: restaurants, bars, pool, gym, spa, beach, water sports, business center, parking* ⏐◎⏐ *No meals.*

$$$
B&B/INN

🏨 **Key Lime Inn.** This 1854 Grand Bahama–style house on the National Register of Historic Places succeeds by offering amiable service, a great location, and simple rooms with natural-wood furnishings. **Pros:** free parking; some rooms have private outdoor spaces. **Cons:** standard rooms are pricey; pool faces a busy street; mulch-covered paths. **TripAdvisor:** "inclusive breakfasts by the pool," "within easy walking distance of all the main sights," "excellent air conditioning." ⊠ *725 Truman Ave.* ☎ *305/294–5229 or 800/549–4430* ⊕ *www.keylimeinn.com* ↪ *37 rooms* ⚙ *In-room: a/c, Internet, Wi-Fi. In-hotel: pool, parking* ⏐◎⏐ *Breakfast.*

$$
B&B/INN
★

🏨 **Key West Bed and Breakfast/The Popular House.** Local art—large, splashy canvases and a Gauguinesque mural—decorates the walls, while hand-made textiles (owner Jody Carlson is a talented weaver) drape chairs, couches, and beds at this historic home. **Pros:** lots of art; tiled outdoor shower; hot tub and sauna area is a welcome hangout. **Cons:** some rooms are small. **TripAdvisor:** "balcony is private and nice," "wonderful getaway home," "haven away from the bustle." ⊠ *415 William St.* ☎ *305/296–7274 or 800/438–6155* ⊕ *www.keywestbandb.com* ↪ *8 rooms, 6 with bath* ⚙ *In-room: a/c, no TV, Wi-Fi (some). In-hotel: pool, some age restrictions* ⏐◎⏐ *Breakfast.*

$$$$
HOTEL

🏨 **Key West Marriott Beachside Hotel.** This new hotel vies for convention business with the biggest ballroom in Key West. **Pros:** private beach; poolside cabanas. **Cons:** small beach; can't walk to Old Town; cookie-cutter facade. **TripAdvisor:** "there is very little beach access," "kitchen is first class," "ocean views are beautiful." ⊠ *3841 N. Roosevelt Blvd., New Town* ☎ *305/296–8100 or 800/546–0885* ⊕ *www.keywestmarriottbeachside.com* ↪ *93 rooms, 93 1-bedroom suites, 10 2-bedroom suites, 26 3-bedroom suites* ⚙ *In-room: a/c, kitchen (some), Internet. In-hotel: restaurants, bars, pool, gym, business center, parking* ⏐◎⏐ *No meals.*

6

$$$$
HOTEL
Fodor's Choice
★

⌂ **Marquesa Hotel.** In a town that prides itself on its laid-back luxury, this complex of four restored 1884 houses stands out. **Pros:** elegant setting; romantic atmosphere; turndown service. **Cons:** street-facing rooms can be noisy; expensive rates. **TripAdvisor:** "food is amazing," "rooms are very well maintained," "beautiful and clean." ✉ *600 Fleming St.* ☎ *305/292–1919 or 800/869–4631* ⊕ *www.marquesa.com* ➣ *27 rooms* ⌂ *In-room: a/c, Wi-Fi. In-hotel: restaurant, pools, business center, parking, some age restrictions* ⌽ *No meals.*

$$$
B&B/INN
★

⌂ **Merlin Guesthouse.** Key West guesthouses don't usually welcome families, but this laid-back jumble of rooms and suites is an exception. **Pros:** good location near Duval Street; good rates. **Cons:** neighbor noise; common areas are dated; street parking. **TripAdvisor:** "cramped shower," "pleasant garden sitting areas," "good breakfast." ✉ *811 Simonton St.* ☎ *305/296–3336 or 800/642–4753* ⊕ *www.merlinguesthouse.com* ➣ *10 rooms, 6 suites, 4 cottages* ⌂ *In-room: a/c, kitchen (some), Wi-Fi. In-hotel: pool* ⌽ *Breakfast.*

$$$
B&B/INN
★

⌂ **Mermaid & the Alligator.** An enchanting combination of flora and fauna makes this 1904 Victorian house a welcoming retreat. **Pros:** hot plunge pool; massage pavilion; island-getaway feel. **Cons:** minimum stay required (length depends on season); dark public areas; plastic lawn chairs. **TripAdvisor:** "romantic getaway," "best place to stay," "own lush gardens." ✉ *729 Truman Ave.* ☎ *305/294–1894 or 800/773–1894* ⊕ *www.kwmermaid.com* ➣ *9 rooms* ⌂ *In-room: a/c, no TV, Wi-Fi. In-hotel: pool, some age restrictions* ⌽ *Breakfast.*

$$$$
RESORT
★

⌂ **Ocean Key Resort & Spa.** A pool and lively open-air bar and restaurant sit on Sunset Pier, a popular place to watch the sun sink into the horizon. **Pros:** well-trained staff; lively pool scene; best spa on the island. **Cons:** confusing layout; too bustling for some. **TripAdvisor:** "good and not too overpriced," "fantastic sunsets," "right on the pier." ✉ *Zero Duval St.* ☎ *305/296–7701 or 800/328–9815* ⊕ *www.oceankey.com* ➣ *64 rooms, 36 suites* ⌂ *In-room: a/c, kitchen (some), Wi-Fi In-hotel: restaurants, bars, pool, spa, water sports, laundry facilities, parking* ⌽ *No meals.*

$$$$
HOTEL
★

⌂ **Parrot Key Resort.** The same people who created Tranquility Bay in Marathon opened this high-end Key West resort in 2008. **Pros:** four pools; finely appointed units; access to marina and other facilities at three sister properties in Marathon. **Cons:** outside of walking distance to Old Town and no transportation provided; expensive; hefty resort fee. **TripAdvisor:** "pool was warm room was comfortable," "well maintained landscaping," "stainless steel appliances." ✉ *2801 N. Roosevelt Blvd., New Town* ☎ *305/809-2200* ⊕ *www.parrotkeyresort.com* ➣ *44 2-bedroom town houses, 30 3-bedroom town houses* ⌂ *In-room: a/c, kitchen, Wi-Fi. In-hotel: restaurant, bar, pools, beach* ⌽ *No meals.*

$$$$
RESORT
★

⌂ **Pier House Resort and Caribbean Spa.** The location—on a quiet stretch of beach at the foot of Duval—is ideal as a buffer from and gateway to the action. **Pros:** beautiful beach; good location; nice spa. **Cons:** lots of conventions; cookie-cutter feel; poolside rooms are small; minimum stays during busy times. **TripAdvisor:** "fast and accurate service with a smile," "very comfortable king size bed," "private beach and covered patio." ✉ *1 Duval St.* ☎ *305/296–4600 or 800/327–8340* ⊕ *www.*

Sunset Key cottages are right on the water's edge, far away from the action of Old Town.

pierhouse.com ↴ *113 rooms, 29 suites* ♿ *In-room: a/c, Wi-Fi. In-hotel: restaurants, bars, pool, gym, spa, beach* ❦ *No meals.*

$$$$
RESORT
★

⌂ **The Reach Resort.** Embracing Key West's only natural beach, this recently reinvented and reopened full-service resort has its roots in the 1980s when locals rallied against the loss of the topless beach it displaced. **Pros:** removed from Duval hubbub; great sunrise views; pullout sofas in most rooms. **Cons:** $20 per day per room resort fee; expensive. **TripAdvisor:** "stay was OK but not great," "private beach and pool were perfect," "bit of a walk to anything in Key West." ✉ *1435 Simonton St.* ☎ *305/296–5000 or 888/318–4316* ⊕ *www.reachresort. com* ↴ *72 rooms, 78 suites* ♿ *In-room: a/c, Wi-Fi. In-hotel: restaurant, room service, bars, pools, gym, beach, water sports, business center, parking, some pets allowed* ❦ *No meals.*

$$$$
B&B/INN
★

⌂ **Simonton Court.** A small world all of its own, this lodging makes you feel deliciously sequestered from Key West's crasser side, but close enough to get there on foot. **Pros:** lots of privacy; well-appointed accommodations; friendly staff. **Cons:** minimum stays required in high season. **TripAdvisor:** "beautiful place," "comfortable bed," "charming." ✉ *320 Simonton St.* ☎ *305/294–6386 or 800/944–2687* ⊕ *www.simontoncourt.com* ↴ *17 rooms, 6 suites, 6 cottages* ♿ *In-room: a/c, kitchen (some), Wi-Fi. In-hotel: pools, some age restrictions* ❦ *Breakfast.*

$$$$
HOTEL

⌂ **Southernmost Hotel.** This hotel's location on the quiet end of Duval means you don't have to deal with the hustle and bustle of downtown unless you want to—it's within a 20-minute walk (but around sunset, this end of town gets its share of car and foot traffic). **Pros:** pool attracts a lively crowd; access to nearby properties; free parking. **Cons:** public beach is small; can get crowded around the pool and public areas. **TripAdvisor:** "real jewel," "good value for money," "has a private beach." ⊠ *1319 Duval St.* ☎ *305/296–6577 or 800/354–4455* ⊕ *www. southernmostresorts.com* ⟿ *126 rooms* ⚐ *In-room: a/c, Wi-Fi. In-hotel: pool, laundry facilities* ⎮◎⎮ *No meals.*

$$$
B&B/INN

⊞ **Speakeasy Inn.** During Prohibition, Raul Vasquez made this place popular by smuggling in liquor from Cuba. **Pros:** good location; reasonable rates; kitchenettes. **Cons:** no pool; basic decor. **TripAdvisor:** "very good deal for the price," "ask for Room 1A if you can," "don't miss the Rum bar downstairs." ⊠ *1117 Duval St.* ☎ *305/296–2680* ⊕ *www.speakeasyinn.com* ⟿ *2 rooms* ⚐ *In-room: a/c, Wi-Fi. In-hotel: bar* ⎮◎⎮ *Breakfast.*

$$$$
RESORT
Fodor's Choice
★

⊞ **Sunset Key.** This private island retreat feels completely cut off from the world, yet you're just minutes away from the action. **Pros:** peace and quiet; roomy verandas; free 24-hour shuttle. **Cons:** luxury doesn't come cheap. **TripAdvisor:** "pricey but worth it," "beautiful and well maintained," "nice but not great." ⊠ *245 Front St.* ☎ *305/292–5300 or 888/477–7786* ⊕ *westinsunsetkeycottages.com* ⟿ *40 cottages* ⚐ *In-room: a/c, kitchen, Internet, Wi-Fi. In-hotel: restaurant, bars, tennis courts, pool, gym, spa, beach, parking* ⎮◎⎮ *Breakfast.*

Travel Smart
Florida

WORD OF MOUTH

". . . The vast majority of U.S. colleges have spring break in [early to mid March]. There are a handful of schools that might be in late February or the first week of April but not many. . . ."

—cheryllj

". . . The way to avoid spring breakers [isn't to avoid one area of the Florida coast or another but rather] to stay at very expensive resorts and properties. . . ."

—garyt22

www.fodors.com/community

GETTING HERE AND AROUND

▌ AIR TRAVEL

Average flying times to South Florida are 3 hours from New York, 4 hours from Chicago, 2¾ hours from Dallas, 4½–5½ hours from Los Angeles, and 8–8½ hours from London.

AIRPORTS

Most visitors begin and end their trip to South Florida at Miami International (MIA), which is neck-and-neck with Orlando for the title of the state's busiest airport. If you're destined for the north side of Miami-Dade, try flying instead into Fort Lauderdale–Hollywood International (FLL), a 30- to 40-minute drive away. Its smaller size usually means easier access and shorter security lines.

■TIP→ Flying to secondary airports can save you money—sometimes even when there are additional ground transportation costs—so shop around.

Airport Information **Fort Lauderdale–Hollywood International Airport (FLL)** (☎ 866/435–9355 ⊕ www.broward.org/airport). **Key West International Airport (EYW)** (☎ 305/296–5439 ⊕ www.keywestinternational airport. com). **Miami International Airport (MIA)** (☎ 305/876–7000 ⊕ www.miami-airport. com). **Orlando International Airport (MCO)** (☎ 407/825–2001 ⊕ www.orlandoairports. net). **Palm Beach International Airport (PBI)** (☎ 561/471–7420 ⊕ www.pbia.org).

GROUND TRANSPORTATION

There's SuperShuttle service to and from Miami International Airport. The trip between the airport and South or Mid Beach takes 30- to 45-minutes and typically costs $31 per person each way. Although buying a round-trip ticket and reserving for the return trip doesn't save you any money, it does make departure that much easier. Otherwise it's a good idea to book a shuttle from your hotel to the airport at least 24 hours in advance. Expect to be picked up 2½ before your scheduled departure.

Although SuperShuttle doesn't pick up from Palm Beach or Fort Lauderdale-Hollywood international airports, it does drop off at both. The 90-minute trip from Miami to PBI costs $94 per person and takes about 90 minutes; to FLL it's $31 per person and 30–40 minutes.

The flat rate cab fares from Miami International into town vary by zone but run between $19 and $53. The rates to South and Mid Beach are $32 and $37, respectively.

Shuttle Service **SuperShuttle** (☎ 800/258–3826 ⊕ www.supershuttle.com).

▌ CAR TRAVEL

If you're driving in Florida, you'll likely become acquainted with the three main highways that run into, then through Florida: I–95, I–75, and I–10. The first two (originating in Maine and Michigan, respectively) extend south; the last (starting in California) extends west.

SAMPLE SOUTH FLORIDA DRIVING TIMES		
FROM–TO	MILES	HOURS +/-
Miami–Palm Beach	75 mi	1:30
Miami–Ft. Lauderdale	30	0:30
Miami–Naples	125	2:15
Miami–Key Largo	65	1
Miami–Orlando	250	4:30
Ft. Lauder-dale–Orlando	210	3:15
Ft. Lauder-dale–Palm Beach	45	1
Key Largo–Key West	100	2

PARKING

On-street parking in Miami averages $1 an hour; in some places it goes as high as $1.50. Garages also charge, on average, $1 an hour, with discounted flat-fees for a full-day or night. In Fort Lauderdale, meters run between 50 cents and $1 an hour; garages are generally about $3 for the first hour and $1 per hour thereafter.

RENTAL CARS

Unless you plan to plant yourself at a beach or theme-park resort, you really need a car to get around. In-season rental rates average $35 a day/$160 a week, plus tax ($2 per day). In Florida you must be 21 to rent a car, and rates are higher if you're under 25.

ROAD CONDITIONS

Downtown areas of Miami and other South Florida cities can be extremely congested during rush hours, usually 7–9 am and 3:30–6:30 pm on weekdays. When you drive the interstate system in Florida, try to plan your trip so that you are not entering, leaving, or passing through a large city during rush hour when traffic can slow to 10 mph for 10 mi or more.

■**TIP→** Florida has a Web site (⊕ www. fl511.com) with real-time traffic information—including details on congestion owing to construction or accidents.

ROADSIDE EMERGENCIES

If you need emergency assistance while traveling on roads in Florida, dial 911 or the Florida Highway Patrol at *FHP (*347) from your cell phone.

RULES OF THE ROAD

Speed limits are 60 mph on state highways, 30 mph within city limits and residential areas, and 70 mph on interstates and Florida's Turnpike. Be alert for signs announcing exceptions.

Children younger than four years old must be strapped in a separate carrier or child seat; children four through five can be secured in a separate carrier, integrated child seat, or by a seat belt. The driver will be held responsible for passengers under the age of 18 who are not wearing seat belts, and all front-seat passengers are required to wear seat belts.

Florida's Alcohol/Controlled Substance DUI Law is one of the toughest in the United States. A blood-alcohol level of .08 or higher can have serious repercussions even for the first-time offender.

CAR RENTAL RESOURCES

Local Agencies

Continental (Fort Lauderdale, Miami, Orlando)	800/221-4085 or 954/332-1125	www.continentalcar.com
Sunshine Rent A Car (Fort Lauderdale)	888/786-7446 or 954/467-8100	www.sunshinerentacar.com

Major Agencies

Alamo	877/222-9075	www.alamo.com
Avis	800/230-4898	www.avis.com
Budget	800/527-0700	www.budget.com
Hertz	800/654-3131	www.hertz.com
National Car Rental	800/227-7368	www.nationalcar.com

■ CRUISE TRAVEL

The port of Miami has the world's largest year-round fleet. It also handles more megaships—vessels capable of transporting more than 2,000 people at a time—than any other port in the world.

Port Everglades, 30 mi north of Miami in the greater Fort Lauderdale area, is also a cruise-ship mecca, and it's been vying to eclipse its neighbor. In 2010 it got a step closer to this goal when it welcomed the second of Royal Caribbean's 5,400-passenger ships with a sparkling new terminal to handle the increased traffic.

ESSENTIALS

▮ ACCOMMODATIONS

In the busy seasons, reserve ahead for the top properties. In general, the peak seasons are over Christmas and from late January through Easter in the southern half of the state and all over state during holiday weekends at any point during the year but especially in summer.

Fall is the slowest season, with only a few exceptions (Key West is jam-packed for Fantasy Fest at Halloween). Rates are low and availability is high, but this is also the prime time for hurricanes.

Children are welcome generally everywhere in Florida. Pets are another matter, so inquire ahead of time if you're bringing an animal with you.

APARTMENT AND HOUSE RENTALS

Contacts Florida Keys Rental Store/Marr Properties (🖀 800/585–0584 or 305/451–3879 ⊕ www.floridakeysrentalstore.com). Freewheeler Vacations (🖀 866/664–2075 or 305/664–2075 ⊕ www.freewheeler-realty. com). Interhome (🖀 954/791–8282 or 800/882–6864 ⊕ www.interhomeusa.com). Villas International (🖀 415/499–9490 or 800/221–2260 ⊕ www.villasintl.com). Wyndham Vacation Resorts (🖀 800/251–8736 ⊕ www.wyndhamvacationresorts.com).

BED-AND-BREAKFASTS

Small inns and guesthouses in Florida range from modest, cozy places with home-style breakfasts and owners who treat you like family, to elegantly furnished Victorian houses with four-course breakfasts and rates to match. The associations listed below offer descriptions and suggestions for B&Bs throughout the state.

Reservation Services BedandBreakfast.com (🖀 512/322–2710 or 800/462–2632 ⊕ www.bedandbreakfast.com). Bed & Breakfast Inns Online (🖀 800/215–7365 ⊕ www.bbonline.com). BnBFinder.com (🖀 888/547–8226 ⊕ www.bnbfinder.com). Florida Bed & Breakfast Inns (🖀 877/303–3224 ⊕ www.florida-inns.com).

HOME EXCHANGES

With a direct home exchange you stay in someone else's home while they stay in yours. Some outfits also deal with vacation homes, so you're not actually staying in someone's full-time residence, just their weekend place.

Exchange Clubs Home Exchange.com (🖀 800/877–8723 ⊕ www.homeexchange.com); $119.40 for a 1-year membership. HomeLink International (🖀 800/638–3841 ⊕ www.homelink.org); $119 for a 1-year membership. Intervac USA Home Exchange (🖀 800/756–4663 ⊕ www.intervacus.com); $99.99 for 1-year membership.

HOTELS

Wherever you look in Florida you'll find lots of plain, inexpensive motels and luxurious resorts, independents alongside national chains, and an ever-growing number of modern properties as well as quite a few classics. In fact, since Florida has been a favored travel destination for some time, vintage hotels are everywhere, though some of the most famous are in South Florida. There are grand edifices like the Breakers in Palm Beach, Boca Raton Resort & Club in Boca Raton, the Biltmore in Coral Gables, and Casa Marina in Key West.

All hotels listed have private bath unless otherwise noted.

▮ EATING OUT

Smoking is banned statewide in most enclosed indoor workplaces, including restaurants. Exemptions are permitted for stand-alone bars where food takes a backseat to the libations.

One caution: raw oysters are a potential problem for people with chronic illness of the liver, stomach, or blood, or who have immune disorders. All Florida restaurants that serve raw oysters must post a notice in plain view warning of the risks associated with consuming them.

CUBAN FOOD

A trip to South Florida is not complete without a taste of Cuban food. The cuisine is heavy, with pork dishes like *lechon asado*, served in garlic-based sauces. The two most typical dishes are *arroz con frijoles* (the staple side dish of rice and black beans) and *arroz con pollo* (chicken in sticky yellow rice).

Key West is famous for its key lime pie (the best is found here) and conch fritters. Stone-crab claws, a South Florida delicacy, can be savored from October through May.

MEALS AND MEALTIMES

Unless otherwise noted, the restaurants listed in this guide are open daily for lunch and dinner.

RESERVATIONS AND DRESS

We discuss reservations only when they're essential (there's no other way you'll ever get a table) or when they are not accepted. It's always smart to make reservations when you can, particularly if your party is large. It's critical to do so at popular restaurants (book as far ahead as possible, often 30 days, and reconfirm on arrival).

We mention dress only when men are required to wear a jacket or a jacket and tie. Expect places with dress codes to truly adhere to them.

Contacts **OpenTable** (⊕ www.opentable.com). **DinnerBroker** (⊕ www.dinnerbroker.com).

Sunburn and heat prostration are concerns, even in winter. So hit the beach or play tennis, golf, or another outdoor sport before 10 am or after 3 pm. If you must be out at midday, limit exercise, drink plenty of non-alchoholic liquids, and wear a hat. If you feel faint, get out of the sun and sip water slowly.

Even on overcast days, ultraviolet rays shine through the haze, so use a sunscreen with an SPF of at least 15, and

have children wear a waterproof SPF 30 or higher.

While you're frolicking on the beach, steer clear of what look like blue bubbles on the sand. These are Portuguese men-of-war, and their tentacles can cause an allergic reaction. Also be careful of other large jellyfish, some of which can sting.

If you walk across a grassy area on the way to the beach, you'll probably encounter the tiny, light-brown, incredibly prickly sand spurs. If you get stuck with one, just pull it out.

∎ HOURS OF OPERATION

Many museums are closed Monday but have late hours on another weekday and are usually open on weekends. Some museums have a day when admission is free. Popular attractions are usually open every day but Thanksgiving and Christmas Day.

∎ MONEY

Prices throughout this guide are given for adults. Substantially reduced fees are almost always available for children, students, and senior citizens.

CREDIT CARDS

We cite information about credits only if they aren't accepted at a restaurant or a hotel. Otherwise, assume that most major credit cards are acceptable.

It's good to inform your credit-card company before you travel to prevent it from putting a hold on your card owing to unusual activity—not a good thing halfway through your trip. Record all your credit-card numbers—as well as the phone numbers to call if your cards are lost or stolen—in a safe place, so you're prepared should something go wrong.

Both MasterCard and Visa have general numbers you can call if your card is lost, but you're better off calling the number of your issuing bank, since MasterCard and Visa usually just transfer you to your bank; your bank's number is usually printed on your card.

Reporting Lost Cards American Express (☎ 800/992–3404 ⊕ www.americanexpress. com). **Diners Club** (☎ 800/234–6377 ⊕ www. dinersclub.com). **Discover** (☎ 800/347–2683 ⊕ www.discovercard.com). **MasterCard** (☎ 800/622–7747 ⊕ www.mastercard.com). **Visa** (☎ 800/847–2911 ⊕ www.visa.com).

▌PACKING

Even in summer, ocean breezes can be cool, so it's good to have a lightweight sweater or jacket.

Aside from an occasional winter cold spell (when the mercury drops to, say, 50), Miami and the Naples–Fort Myers areas are warm year-round and extremely humid in summer. Be prepared for sudden storms in summer, and note that plastic raincoats are uncomfortable in the high humidity. Often storms are quick and the sun comes back in no time.

Dress is casual throughout South Florida—sundresses, jeans, or walking shorts are appropriate during the days. Dressy or dressy-casual (read: trendy) attire is a good idea for Miami's nightclubs. A few restaurants request that men wear jackets and ties, but most do not. Where there are dress codes, they tend to be fully adhered to. Be prepared for air-conditioning working in overdrive.

You can generally swim year-round in peninsular Florida from about New Smyrna Beach south on the Atlantic coast and from Tarpon Springs south on the Gulf coast. Bring a sun hat and sunscreen.

▌SAFETY

Stepped-up policing of thieves who prey on tourists in rental cars has helped address what was a serious issue in the early 1990s. Still, visitors should be especially wary when driving in strange neighborhoods and leaving the airport, especially in the Miami area. Don't assume that valuables are safe in your hotel room; use in-room safes or the hotel's safety-deposit boxes. Try to use ATMs only during the day or in brightly lighted, well-traveled locales. Don't leave valuables unattended while you walk the beach or go for a dip.

If you are visiting South Florida during the June through November hurricane season and a hurricane is imminent, be sure to follow directions from local authorities.

▌TAXES

Florida's sales tax is 6% or higher depending on the county, and local sales and tourist taxes can raise what you pay considerably. Miami Beach hoteliers, for example, collect 13% for city and resort taxes. It's best to ask about additional costs up front, to avoid a rude awakening.

▌TIME

South Florida is in the Eastern time zone.

▌TIPPING

Whether they carry bags, open doors, deliver food, or clean rooms, hospitality employees work to receive a portion of your travel budget. In deciding how much to give, base your tip on what the service is and how well it's performed.

SOUTH FLORIDA TIPPING GUIDELINES	
Airport Valet or Hotel Bellhop	$1–$3 per bag
Chambermaid	$1–$2 a night per guest
Hotel Room-Service Waiter	15% (unless a service charge was added)
Helpful door-man or a parking valet	$1–$3
Taxi Driver	15%–20%
Waiter/ Bartender	15%–20% before tax
Golf Caddies	15% of the greens fee
Spa Therapist	15%–20% of the treatment before tax

▌ VISITOR INFORMATION

Florida has a terrific visitors Web site with information about the state as a whole as well as that for individual cities and regions. Many South Florida cities and towns have their own visitor information offices and/or booths. What's more, some tourism offices are pumping out helpful (and smart) apps—Miami's just added one to instantly locate the hottest, latest dining spots.

Contacts **Visit Florida** (☎ *850/488–5607or 866/972–5280 toll-free ⊕ www.visitflorida. com).*

INDEX

PHOTO CREDITS

1, Visit Florida. 2-3, Tim Souter, Fodors.com member. 5, PBorowka/Shutterstock. Chapter 1: Experience South Florida: 8-9, S.Borisov/Shutterstock. 10(top), Rick Gomez/age fotostock. 10 (bottom), borabora98, Fodors.com member. 11 (left), Visit Florida. 11 (right), Pacific Stock/SuperStock. 12, GlyndaK, fodors.com member. 13, funinthetub, Fodors.com member. 14 and 15, Jeff Greenberg/age fotostock. 16 (left), Visit Florida. 16 (right), Jeff Greenberg/Alamy. 17 (left), Sarah and Jason/Flickr. 17 (top right), RIEGER Bertrand/age fotostock. 17 (bottom right), Danita Delimont/Alamy. 19 (left), Ken Canning/Shutterstock. 19 (right), j loveland/Shutterstock. 20 and 21, Visit Florida. 22 (top), Ernest Hemingway Photograph Collection, John F. Kennedy Presidential Library and Museum, Boston. 22 (bottom), Visit Florida. 23 (top), Linda Brinck, Fodors.com member. 23 (bottom), George Peters/iStockphoto. 24, Michael Zegers/imagebroker.net/photolibrary.com. 27, Andrew Woodley/Alamy. Chapter 2: Palm Beach and the Treasure Coast: 29, RIEGER Bertrand/age fotostock. 31 (top), Perry Correll/Shutterstock. 31 (bottom), Bill Bachmann/Alamy. 32, Masa Ushioda/Alamy. 33 (top), Stephen Frink Collection/Alamy. 33 (bottom), Denny Medley/Random Photography/iStockphoto. 34, FloridaStock/Shutterstock. 39, Jon Arnold Images Ltd/Alamy. 43, Andre Jenny/Alamy. 48, mrk_photo/Flickr. 55, FloridaStock/Shutterstock. 60, wikipedia.org. 67, Paddy Eckersley/age fotostock. 68, Tap10/Shutterstock. 71 and 81, Visit Florida. Chapter 3: Fort Lauderdale and Broward County: 85, Visit Florida. 86, Rick Gomez/age fotostock. 87 (top), Dean Bergmann/iStockphoto. 87 (bottom), Jeff Greenberg/Alamy. 88, Nicholas Pitt/Alamy. 89 (top), Medioimages/Photodisc/Thinkstock. 89 (bottom), Claudette, Fodors.com member. 90, Qole Pejorian/Flickr. 96, rockindom, Fodors.com member. 101, Nicholas Pitt/Alamy. 105, Eric Gevaert/Shutterstock. 113, Lago Mar Resort & Club - Fort Lauderdale. 119, Pat Cahill/iStockphoto. Chapter 4: Miami and Miami Beach: 129, iStockphoto. 130, Stuart Westmorland/age fotostock. 131 (top), Jeff Greenberg/age fotostock. 131 (bottom), VISUM Foto GmbH/Alamy. 132, Jeff Greenberg/age fotostock. 133 (top), Picasa 2.7/Flickr. 133 (bottom), murray cohen/iStockphoto. 134, Ivan Cholakov/Shutterstock. 144, Chuck Mason/Alamy. 145 (top), Jeff Greenberg/Alamy. 145 (bottom), David R. Frazier Photolibrary, Inc./Alamy. 146 and 148, Jeff Greenberg/Alamy. 149, Jeff Greenberg/age fotostock. 150, Gregory Wrona/Alamy. 154, Robert Harding Picture Library Ltd/Alamy. 163, Visit Florida. 169 (left), dk/Alamy. 169 (right), Nicholas Pitt/Alamy. 171 (top), M. Timothy O'Keefe/Alamy. 171 (bottom), Miami Design Preservation League. 172 (top), Nicholas Pitt/Alamy. 172 (2nd from top), Park Central Hotel. 172 (3rd from top), Ian Patrick Alamy. 172 (4th from top), Laura Paresky. 172 (bottom), ICIMAGE/Alamy. 173 (top), INTERFOTO Pressebildagentur/Alamy. 173 (bottom left), Ian Patrick/Alamy. 173 (bottom right), culliganphoto/Alamy. 174, iStockphoto. 181, alexdecarvalho/Flickr. 190, Claudia Uribe. 197, Jeff Greenberg/Alamy. 198, Roxana Gonzalez/Shutterstock. 199 (top), JUPITERIMAGES/Brand X/Alamy. 199 (bottom), iStockphoto. 214 (top), Acqualina Resort & Spa on the Beach. 214 (bottom left), Nile Young. 214 (center right), Circa 39. 214 (bottom right), Morgans Hotel Group. 215 (top), Mark Wieland. 215 (center left), Kevin Syms/Four Seasons Hotels and Resorts. 215 (bottom left), Kor Hotel Group. 215 (bottom right), Mandarin Oriental Hotel Group. Chapter 5: The Everglades: 221, David Lyons/Alamy. 222 (top), Visit Florida. 222 (bottom), Jeff Greenberg/age fotostock. 223 (top), FloridaStock/Shutterstock. 223 (bottom), Walter Bibikow/age fotostock. 224-25, tbkmedia.de/Alamy. 228 (left), inga spence/Alamy. 228 (top center), FloridaStock/Shutterstock. 228 (bottom center), Andrewtappert/wikipedia.org. 228 (top right), wikipedia.org. 228 (bottom right), David R. Frazier Photolibrary, Inc./Alamy. 229 (top left), Larsek/Shutterstock. 229 (bottom left), Caleb Foster/Shutterstock. 229 (bottom center), mlorenz/Shutterstock. 229 (top right), umar faruq/Shutterstock. 229 (bottom right), Peter Arnold, Inc./Alamy. 230 (left), John A. Anderson/Shutterstock. 230 (top right), FloridaStock/Shutterstock. 230 (top center), Norman Bateman/Shutterstock. 230 (bottom right), FloridaStock/Shutterstock. 231 (top left), David Drake & Deborah Jaffe. 231 (bottom left), Krzysztof Slusarczyk/Shutterstock. 231 (bottom center), Norman Bateman/Shutterstock. 231 (right), Jerry Zitterman/Shutterstock. 232, Patricia Schmidt/iStockphoto. 233 (top left), Brett Charlton/iStockphoto. 233 (bottom left, bottom center, and right), David Drake & Deborah Jaffe. 234 (left), Walter Bibikow/age fotostock. 234 (right), Stephen Frink Collection/Alamy. 235, Leatha J. Robinson/Shutterstock. 237, Larsek/Shutterstock. 244, Steven Widoff/Alamy. 250, Marc Muench/Alamy. 254, Sarah and Jason/Flickr. 263, Visit Florida. Chapter 6: The Florida Keys: 267, Stephen Frink/Aurora Photos. 268 (top), Pawel Lipiec/iStockphoto. 268 (bottom), David L Amsler/iStockphoto. 269 (top), Pacific Stock/SuperStock. 269 (bottom), Visit Florida. 270, Nick Greaves/Alamy. 271 (top), Ingolf Pompe 77/Alamy. 271 (bottom), Visit Florida. 272, iStockphoto. 281, Stephen Frink/Florida Keys News Bureau. 287, flasporty/Flickr. 290, Visit Florida. 294, PBorowka/Shutterstock. 295 and 296 (top), Douglas Rudolph. 296 (bottom), ANDY NEWMAN/Visit Florida. 297, M. Timothy O'Keefe/Alamy. 298 (top), Bob Care/Florida Keys News Bureau. 298 (bottom), Julie de Leseleuc/iStockphoto. 299 (left), Visit Florida. 299

NOTES

ABOUT OUR WRITERS

After being hired sight unseen by a South Florida newspaper, Fort Lauderdale–based freelance travel writer and editor Lynne Helm arrived from the Midwest anticipating a few years of palm-fringed fun. More than a quarter century later (after covering the state for several newspapers, consumer magazines, and trade publications), she's still enamored of Florida's sun-drenched charms. Lynne updated the Everglades chapters.

Dorothea Hunter Sönne, who updated Experience South Florida and Travel Smart, is a freelance writer who has been enchanted by Florida since her youth—so much so that after dozens of vacations, she relocated to its sunny shores in 2010. Prior to that she was a magazine editor, spending nearly five years at O, The Oprah Magazine. She also co-edited the book, Words That Matter, and her work has appeared in publications including The Knot and Chicago.

From her home of more than 25 years on Sanibel Island, Chelle Koster Walton—author of the Keys and Lower Gulf Coast chapters—has written and contributed to a dozen guidebooks (among them Fodor's Bahamas), two of which have won Lowell Thomas Awards. She has penned thousands of articles about Florida and the Caribbean for Miami Herald, USA Today, Concierge.com, FoxNews.com, and other print and digital media.

Paul Rubio's insatiable quest to discover and learn has taken him to the far corners of the world—81 countries and counting. A Harvard-trained economist with a double masters degree, he took on his passion for travel writing full-time in 2008 and hasn't looked back. Paul, who updated the Fort Lauderdale and Miami chapters, currently contributes to Ocean Home Magazine, Palm Beach Illustrated, and Weddings Illustrated as well as other Fodor's guides, jetsetter.com, and various outlets of Modern Luxury Media.

Palm Beach and the Treasure Coast writer Mary Thurwachter, a Florida resident since 1979, writes travel stories for The Palm Beach Post, Miami Herald and INNsideFlorida.com, a travel site she launched in 2008.